SOFTWARE ENGINEERING
A Practitioner's Approach

McGraw-Hill Series in Software Engineering and Technology

Consulting Editor

Peter Freeman, *University of California, Irvine*

Pressman: *Software Engineering: A Practitioner's Approach*

SOFTWARE ENGINEERING
A Practitioner's Approach

Roger S. Pressman, Ph.D.

Adjunct Professor of Computer Engineering
University of Bridgeport
and
President, R. S. Pressman & Associates, Inc.

McGraw-Hill Book Company

New York   St. Louis   San Francisco   Auckland   Bogotá   Hamburg
Johannesburg   London   Madrid   Mexico   Montreal   New Delhi
Panama   Paris   São Paulo   Singapore   Sydney   Tokyo   Toronto

This book was set in Times Roman by World Composition Services, Inc.
The editors were Charles E. Stewart and Gail Gavert;
the production supervisor was Dominick Petrellese.
New drawings were done by Fine Line Illustrations, Inc.
R. R. Donnelley & Sons Company was printer and binder.

SOFTWARE ENGINEERING
A Practitioner's Approach

34567890 DODO 89876543

ISBN 0-07-050781-3

Library of Congress Cataloging in Publication Data

Pressman, Roger S.
    Software engineering.

    (McGraw-Hill software engineering and technology
series)
    Includes bibliographies and index.
    1. Electronic digital computers—Programming.
I. Title. II. Series.
QA76.6.P73   001.64′2   81-20718
ISBN 0-07-050781-3   AACR2

CONTENTS

PREFACE

In the brief history of the electronic digital computer, the 1950s and 1960s were decades of hardware. The 1970s were a period of transition and a time of recognition of software. The decade of software is now upon us. In fact, advances in computing may become limited by our inability to produce quality software that can tap the enormous capacity of 1980-era processors.

During the past decade we have grown to recognize circumstances that are collectively called the *software crisis.* Software costs escalated dramatically, becoming the largest dollar item in many computer-based systems. Schedules and completion dates were set but rarely kept. As software systems grew larger, quality became suspect. Individuals responsible for software development projects had limited historical data to use as guides and less control over the course of a project.

A set of techniques, collectively called *software engineering,* has evolved as a response to the software crisis. These techniques deal with software as an engineered product that requires planning, analysis, design, implementation, testing, and maintenance. The goal of this text is to provide a concise presentation of each step in the software engineering process.

The contents of this book closely parallel the software life cycle. Early chapters present the planning phase, emphasizing system definition (computer systems engineering), software planning, and software requirements analysis. Specific techniques for software costs and schedule estimation should be of particular interest to project managers as well as to technical practitioners and students.

In subsequent chapters emphasis shifts to the software development phase. The fundamental principles of software design are introduced. In addition, descriptions of two important classes of software design methodology are presented in detail. A variety of software tools are discussed. Comparisons among techniques and among tools are provided to assist the practitioner and student alike. Coding style is also stressed in the context of the software engineering process.

The concluding chapters deal with software testing techniques, reliability, and software maintenance. Software engineering steps associated with testing are described and specific techniques for software testing are presented. The current status of software reliability prediction is discussed and an overview of reliability models and program correctness approaches is presented. The concluding chapter considers both management and technical aspects of software maintenance.

This book is an outgrowth of a senior-level/first-year-graduate course in software engineering offered at the University of Bridgeport. The course and this text cover both management and technical aspects of the software development process. The chapters of the text correspond roughly to major lecture topics. In fact, the text is derived in part from edited versions of transcribed notes of these lectures. Writing style is therefore purposely casual and figures are derived from viewgraphs used during the course.

Software Engineering: A Practitioner's Approach may be used in a number of ways for various audiences. The text can serve as a concise guide to software engineering for the practicing manager, analyst, or programmer. It can also serve as the basic text for an upper-level undergraduate or graduate course in software engineering. Lastly, the text can be used as a supplementary guide for software development early in computer science or computer engineering undergraduate curricula.

The software engineering literature has expanded rapidly during the past decade. I gratefully acknowledge the many authors who have helped this new discipline evolve. Their work has had an important influence on this book and my method of presentation. I also wish to acknowledge Pat Duran, Leo Lambert, Kyu Lee, John Musa, Claude Walston, Anthony Wasserman, Marvin Zelkowitz, and Nicholas Zvegintzov, the reviewers of this book, and Peter Freeman, the series editor. Their thoughtful insights and suggestions have been invaluable during the final stages of preparation. Special thanks go to Leo Lambert and his colleagues from the Computer Management Operation, General Electric Company, who have allowed me to tap their broad collective experience during my long association with them. In addition, to the students at the University of Bridgeport and the hundreds of software professionals and their managers who have attended short courses that I have taught, my thanks for the arguments, the ideas, and the challenges that are essential in a field such as ours.

Finally, to Barbara, Mathew, and Michael, my love and thanks for tolerating the genesis of book number two.

Roger S. Pressman

ONE

COMPUTER SYSTEM ENGINEERING

Four hundred and fifty years ago Machiavelli said:

> There is nothing more difficult to take in hand, more perilous to conduct or more uncertain in its success, than to take the lead in the introduction of a new order of things. . . .

In the decade of the 1980s computer-based systems will introduce a new order. Although technology has made great strides since Machiavelli spoke, his words continue to ring true.

Software engineering—the topic to which this book is dedicated—and hardware engineering are activities within the broader category that we shall call *computer system engineering.* Each of these disciplines represents an attempt to bring order to the development of computer-based systems.

Engineering techniques for computer hardware developed from electronic design and have reached a state of relative maturity in little more than three decades. Hardware design techniques are well established, manufacturing methods are continually improved, and reliability is a realistic expectation, rather than a modest hope.

Unfortunately, computer software still suffers from the Machiavellian description stated above. In computer-based systems software has replaced hardware as the system element that is most difficult to plan, least likely to succeed (on time and within cost), and most dangerous to manage. Yet the demand for software continues unabated as computer-based systems grow in number, complexity, and application.

Engineering techniques for computer software have only recently gained widespread acceptance. During the 1950s and 1960s computer programming was viewed as an art. No engineering precedent existed, and no engineering approach was applied.

Times are changing!

1.1 COMPUTER SYSTEM EVOLUTION

The context in which software has been developed is closely coupled to three decades of computer system evolution. Better hardware performance, smaller size, and lower cost have precipitated more sophisticated systems. In three and one-half machine generations we've moved from vacuum tube processors to microelectronic devices. In recent popular books on "the computer revolution," Osborne [1] has characterized the 1980s as a "new industrial revolution" and Toffler [2] calls the advent of microelectronics part of "the third wave of change" in human history.

Figure 1.1 depicts the evolution of computer-based systems in terms of application area, rather than hardware characteristics. During the early years of computer system development, hardware underwent continual change while software was viewed by many as an afterthought. Computer programming was a "seat-of-the-pants" art for which few systematic methods existed. Software development was virtually unmanaged—until schedules slipped or costs began to escalate. During this period a batch orientation was used for most systems. Notable exceptions were interactive systems such as the early American Airlines reservation system and real-time defense-oriented systems such as SAGE. For the most part, however, hardware was dedicated to the execution of a single program that in turn was dedicated to a specific application.

During the early years general-purpose hardware became commonplace. Software, on the other hand, was custom designed for each application and had a relatively limited distribution.

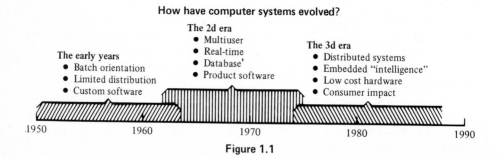

Figure 1.1

Product software (i.e., programs developed to be sold to one or more customers) was in its infancy. Most software was developed and ultimately used by the same person or organization. You wrote it, you got it running, and if it failed, you fixed it. Because job mobility was low, managers could rest assured that you'd be there when bugs were encountered. Because of this personalized software environment, design was an implicit process performed in one's head and documentation was often nonexistent.

During the early years we learned much about the implementation of computer-based systems, but relatively little about computer system engineering. In fairness, however, we must acknowledge the many outstanding computer-based systems that were developed during this era. Some of these systems remain in use today and provide landmark achievements that continue to justify admiration.

The second era of computer system evolution (Figure 1.1) spanned the decade from the mid-1960s to the mid-1970s. Multiprogramming, multiuser systems introduced new concepts of human-machine interaction. Interactive techniques opened a new world of applications and new levels of hardware and software sophistication. Real-time systems could collect, analyze, and transform data from multiple sources, thereby controlling processes and producing output in milliseconds rather than minutes. Advances in on-line secondary memory devices lead to the first generation of database management systems.

The second era was also characterized by the use of product software and the advent of "software houses." Software was developed for widespread distribution in a multidisciplinary market. Entrepreneurs from industry, government, and academia broke away to "develop the ultimate software package" and earn a bundle of money.

As the number of computer-based systems grew, libraries of computer software began to expand. In-house-developed projects produced tens of thousands of program source statements. Software products purchased from the outside added hundreds of thousands of new statements. A dark cloud appeared on the horizon. All of these programs—all of these source statements—had to be maintained when faults were detected, modified as user requirements changed, or adapted to new hardware that was purchased. Effort spent on software maintenance began to absorb resources at an alarming rate. Worse yet, the personalized nature of many programs made them virtually unmaintainable. A "software crisis" had begun.

The third era of computer system evolution began in the early 1970s and continues through the early 1980s. The distributed system—multiple computers, each performing functions concurrently and communicating with one another—greatly increased the complexity of computer-based systems. As microprocessors and related components became more powerful and less expensive, products with "embedded intelligence" replaced larger computers as the most common computer application area.

In addition, the advent of microprocessors has resulted in the availability of complex logical functions at exceptionally low cost. This technology is being integrated into products by technical staff who understand hardware but are frequently novices where software is considered.

Rapid advances in hardware have already begun to outpace our ability to provide supporting software. During the third era, the software crisis intensified. Software maintenance absorbed over 50 percent of data processing budgets, and software development productivity could not keep pace with demands for new systems. In response to a growing crisis, software engineering was taken seriously for the first time.

A transition to a fourth era of computer system evolution has already begun. Sixteen- and 32-bit microprocessors with one megabyte of primary memory will open as yet unforeseen application areas for computer-based systems. The transition from a technical to a consumer marketplace demands professionalism that can be accomplished only through computer system engineering.

1.2 COMPUTER SYSTEM ENGINEERING

Computer system engineering is a problem-solving activity. Desired system functions are uncovered, analyzed, and allocated to individual system elements. An overview of the computer system engineering process is illustrated in Figure 1.2. Techniques for system analysis and definition are discussed in detail in Chapter 3.

The genesis of most new systems begins with a rather nebulous concept of desired function. The objective of system analysis and definition is to uncover the scope of the project that lies ahead. This is accomplished by a systematic refinement of information to be processed, required functions, desired performance, design constraints, and validation criteria.

After scope has been established, the computer system engineer must consider a number of alternative configurations that could potentially satisfy scope. The following trade-off criteria govern the selection of a system configuration:

1. *Business considerations.* Does the configuration represent the most profitable solution? Can it be marketed successfully? Will ultimate payoff justify development risk?

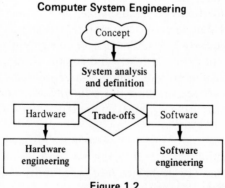

Figure 1.2

2. *Technical analysis.* Does the technology exist to develop all elements of the system? Are function and performance assured? Can the configuration be adequately mantained? Do technical resources exist? What is the risk associated with the technology?
3. *Manufacturing evaluation.* Are manufacturing facilities and equipment available? Is there a shortage of necessary components? Can quality assurance be adequately performed?
4. *Human problems.* Are trained personnel available for development and manufacture? Do political problems exist? Does the requester understand what the system is to accomplish?
5. *Environmental interfaces.* Does the proposed configuration properly interface with the system's external environment? Are machine-machine and human-machine communication handled in an intelligent manner?
6. *Legal considerations.* Does this configuration introduce undue liability risk? Can proprietary aspects be adequately protected? Is there potential infringement?

The weight of the above criteria vary with each system.

After trade-offs have been considered, a configuration is selected and functions allocated among potential system elements. For a computer-based system, hardware, firmware, and software are the elements most likely to be selected.

1.3 HARDWARE CONSIDERATIONS

Computer system engineering always allocates one or more system functions to computer hardware. In the following paragraphs basic hardware components and applications are discussed. In addition, an overview of hardware engineering is presented.

1.3.1 Hardware Components

The computer system engineer selects some combination of hardware components that comprise one element of the computer-based system. Hardware selection, although by no means simple, is aided by a number of characteristics: (1) components are packaged as individual building blocks; (2) interfaces among components are standardized; (3) numerous "off-the-shelf" alternatives are available; and (4) performance, cost, and availability are relatively easy to determine.

The hardware configuration evolves from the "building blocks" shown in Figure 1.3. Discrete components (i.e., integrated circuits and electronic components such as resistors and capacitors) are assembled as a printed circuit board that performs a specific set of operations. Boards are interconnected to form system components (e.g., processor and memory) that in turn are integrated to become the hardware subsystem or the hardware system element.

A complete discussion of the hardware configuration is beyond the scope of

The Hardware Configuration

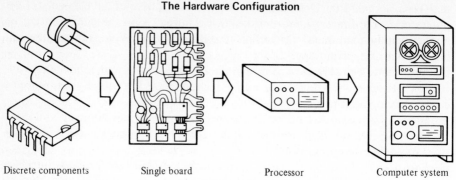

Discrete components   Single board   Processor   Computer system

Figure 1.3

this book and may be found in any one of many references [e.g., 3–5]. For those readers who are unfamiliar with the subject, we shall briefly examine some of the more important elements of a hardware configuration.

The basic elements of a hardware configuration are found in all computer systems. The architecture of these elements, such as the manner in which the elements are organized and the communication paths among them, varies greatly. Figure 1.4 illustrates a typical hardware architecture. The *central processing unit* (CPU) performs arithmetic, logical, and control functions, interacting with all other hardware components. The processing power of the CPU, measured in millions of instructions executed per second (MIPS), is closely tied to system performance. Elements of the architecture are interconnected by *buses,* communication paths that transmit instructions, data, and control information.

Memory provides a storage medium for instructions and data and is accessed (directly or indirectly) through instructions executed by the CPU. *Primary memory* can be defined as a storage medium that is directly addressable by the CPU. *Random-access* (also called read-write) *memory* (RAM) is essential for all applications in which data are transformed and stored. Microprocessor-based systems

Typical Hardware Architecture

Input/output bus

Data bus

| Central processing unit (CPU) | ROM | RAM | Input/ output control | | Peripheral devices |
| | | | | | Secondary memory |

Address bus

Control lines

Figure 1.4

may require only a few hundred bytes of RAM memory, while large-scale computers often require millions of bytes. *Read-only memory* (ROM), as its name implies, can be read only by the CPU. Read-only memory is manufactured with instructions and/or data permanently (and unalterably) inscribed and maintains this information in the absence of electrical power. Other forms of ROM (e.g., PROM and EPROM) can be programmed by using a relatively low cost microprocessor development system. Read-only memory is used extensively in consumer products, home computers, and other microprocessor applications.

Secondary memory is a storage medium that has slower access time and greater capacity than primary memory. The most common secondary memory device can be characterized as a rotating magnetic medium called a *disk*. Information access times for disks are typically in the millesecond range and capacity spans 256,000 bytes to more than 600 million bytes. A *bubble memory* is a solid state secondary memory device that promises to greatly reduce both cost and complexity of large-scale data storage. Magnetic tape, the oldest form of secondary information storage, continues to be used as a relatively slow but inexpensive archival storage medium.

Selection of the memory component for a computer-based system can make or break both function and performance. Computer system engineers frequently err by specifying too little primary and/or secondary memory. The penalty for insufficient memory is often reduced functionality, poor performance, and very costly software. Because memory costs are decreasing rapidly, there is no legitimate excuse for underspecifying memory capacity for computer-based systems produced in small numbers. Issues associated with high-volume products are discussed in Chapter 3.

Communications between the CPU and the outside world are handled by input-output (I/O) or interface hardware. Among its many functions, interface hardware accommodates specific communication protocols between I/O devices (peripherals) and the CPU, controls information transfer rates that may range from tens to hundreds of thousands of characters (bytes) per second, satisfies interface standards (e.g., RS-232C and IEEE-488) for multivendor configurations, and communicates directly with other system components.

Proper definition of interfaces is a key to successful computer system engineering. Selection of appropriate interface hardware has a direct impact on ease of system integration, simplicity of I/O software, and efficiency of communication between the processor and the outside world.

1.3.2 Hardware Applications

Applications for computer hardware may be divided into three broad categories: information processing; process control and real-time applications; and embedded intelligence. The evolution of these applications corresponds roughly to the three computer system eras discussed in Section 1.1.

Today the vast majority of computer-based systems apply hardware as a stand-alone information processor. Information is fed to the computer system, analysis or transformation occurs, other information may be acquired, and results are produced. Primary input is almost always originated by people, and output is formatted for people. Specific applications include commercial data processing, engineering analysis, and database management.

A process control/real-time application integrates hardware as a mechanism for decision making and control. The hardware monitors process parameters, and using heuristics that are normally implemented in software, invokes analysis, control, or reporting. Monitoring is characterized by machine or transducer input. The hardware continuously monitors a process (tranducer input), and produces control commands for the process (feedback control), while at the same time accepting data from human operators and supplying information to them. Typical process control/real-time applications are often characterized as automated manufacturing (e.g., steel mills, petroleum refineries, and chemical processing), system and instrumentation control, real-time data analysis, and reporting. It should be noted that computer hardware can be geographically separated from other system components in process control/real-time applications.

A system has "embedded intelligence" when computer hardware is packaged within a larger product. Nearly all products that contain microprocessor hardware have embedded intelligence. Other applications include on-board flight control systems for aircraft, various weapons systems, "smart" computer terminals, and automotive applications. Unlike more conventional computer hardware applications, the computer does not sit behind glass walls in an air-conditioned room; rather, it is fully integrated with the rest of the product (system), going where the product goes and enduring the same environmental conditions (e.g., heat, humidity, and vibration).

1.3.3 Hardware Engineering

Hardware engineering for digital computers developed from precedents established by decades of electronic design. The hardware engineering process can be viewed in three phases: planning and specification; design and prototype implementation; and manufacturing, distribution, and field service. The phases are illustrated in Figure 1.5a, b, c.

Once system analysis and definition has been conducted, functions are allocated to hardware. The first phase of hardware engineering (Figure 1.5a) includes *development planning* and *hardware requirements analysis*. Development planning is conducted to establish the scope of the hardware effort. That is, we ask the following questions:

- What classes of hardware best address the specified functions?
- What hardware is available for purchase? What are the sources, the availability, and the cost?
- What kind of interfacing is required?
- What do we have to design and build? What are the potential problems and the required resources?

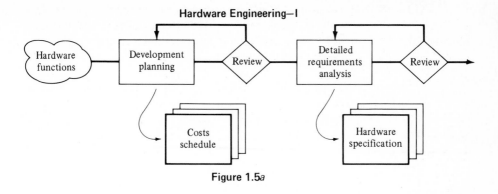

Figure 1.5a

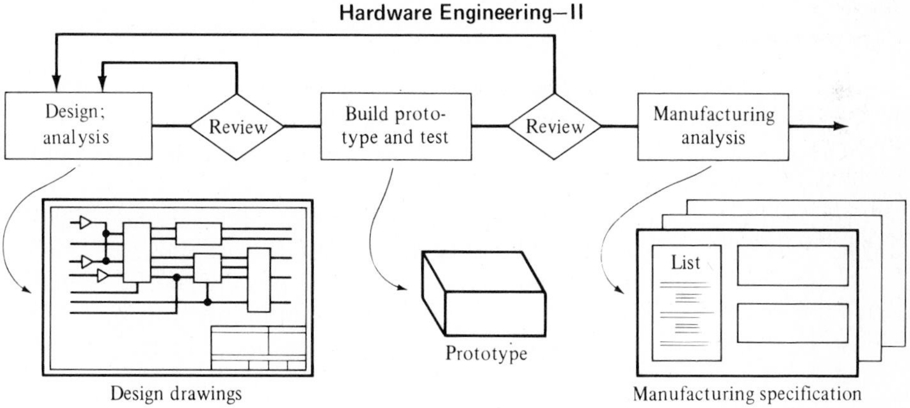

Figure 1.5b

From these questions and others, preliminary cost and schedule estimates for the hardware system element are established. These estimates are reviewed by appropriate managers and technical staff and modified if necessary.

Next, we must establish a "roadmap" for hardware design and implementation. Hardware requirements analysis is conducted to specify precise functional, performance, and interface requirements for all components of the hardware element. In addition, design constraints (e.g., size and environment) and test criteria are established. A *Hardware Specification* is often produced. Review and modification are to be encouraged at this stage.

The popular image of "shirt-sleeve" engineering is characterized by the second phase (Figure 1.5b). Requirements are analyzed, and a preliminary hardware configuration is designed. Technical reviews are conducted as the design evolves toward detailed engineering drawings (a *design specification*). Off-the-shelf components are acquired, custom components are built, and a prototype is assembled. The prototype is tested to assure that it meets all requirements.

The prototype often bears little resemblance to the manufactured product.

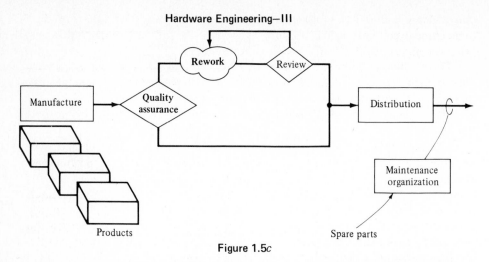

Figure 1.5c

Therefore, *manufacturing specifications* are derived. Breadboards become printed circuit boards, EPROM or PROM become ROM, new packaging is designed, and tooling and equipment are defined. Emphasis shifts from function and performance to ease of manufacture.

The third phase of hardware engineering makes few direct demands on the design engineer but taxes the abilities of the manufacturing engineer. Before production begins, quality assurance methods must be established and a product distribution mechanism defined. Spare parts are placed in inventory and a field service organization is established for product maintenance and repair. The manufacturing phase of hardware engineering is illustrated in Figure 1.5c.

1.4 SOFTWARE CONSIDERATIONS

Computer software is a *logical* rather than a *physical* system element. Therefore, software has characteristics that are considerably different from those of hardware:

- There is no significant manufacturing phase for software; all costs are concentrated in planning and development.
- Software does not *wear out;* there are few spare parts in the software world!
- Software maintenance often includes design modification and enhancement.

In the following paragraphs we consider software components and language classes. We also introduce the phases of software engineering.

1.4.1 Software Components

Computer software is information that exists in two basic forms: non-machine-executable components and machine-executable components. For the purpose of our discussions in this chapter, only those software components that directly lead to machine-executable instructions are presented. The software components comprise a *configuration* that is discussed in later chapters.

Three software components that are closest to machine-executable form are illustrated in Figure 1.6. The software is ultimately translated into a language form that specifies software data structure and procedural attributes. The language form is processed by a translator that converts it into machine-executable instructions.

Ideally, humans would communicate with computers by use of a *natural language* (e.g., English, Spanish, and Russian). Unfortunately, large vocabularies, sophisticated grammars, and our use of context for understanding hamper human-computer communication through natural language. During the 1970s research [6] in semantic information processing and pattern recognition laid the groundwork for the use of natural language as a communication medium with the computer. However, for the next few years, at least, language forms for the specification of programs are limited to *artificial languages.*

All programming languages are artificial languages. Each has a limited vocabulary, an explicitly defined grammar, and well-formed rules of syntax and semantics. These attributes are essential for machine translation. The language forms that are one component of software are characterized as machine-level languages and high-level languages.

Machine-level language, illustrated by the microprocessor assembler language excerpt in Figure 1.7, is a symbolic representation of the CPU instruction set. When a good software developer produces a maintainable, well-documented program, machine-level language can make extremely efficient use of memory and optimize program execution speed. When a program is poorly designed and has little documentation, machine-level language tends to exacerbate the problems that will occur.

Even when machine-level language does provide attractive execution speed and memory characteristics, it has a number of serious disadvantages: (1) implementation time is protracted; (2) the resultant program is difficult to read; (3) testing is difficult; (4) maintenance is extremely difficult; and (5) portability between different processors is not possible. As we shall see in Chapter 4, software

Software Components

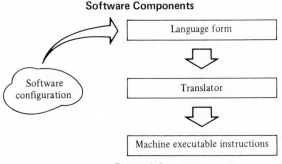

Figure 1.6

```
--------------- 8080/85 ASSEMBLER V01 ----------------------

                        ; PROGRAM TO TEST 337 LAB SETUP
                        ;
0000                             ORG      0000
                        ;
0000 F3                          DI
                        ;
0001 3E00               START:   MVI      A,0
0003 47                          MOV      B,A
0004 D301               LOP1:    OUT      1
0006 3D                          DCR      A
0007 C20400                      JNZ      LOP1
000A 78                          MOV      A,B
000B 3D                          DCR      A
000C CA1500                      JZ       CONT
000F 47                          MOV      B,A
0010 3E00                        MVI      A,0
0012 C30400                      JMP      LOP1
                        ;
0015 3E00               CONT:    MVI      A,0
0017 D303               LOP2:    OUT      3
0019 3D                          DCR      A
001A C21700                      JNZ      LOP2
001D 78                          MOV      A,B
001E 3D                          DCR      A
001F CA2800                      JZ       NEXT
0022 47                          MOV      B,A
0023 3E00                        MVI      A,0
0025 C31700                      JMP      LOP2
                        ;
0028 C30100             NEXT:    JMP      START
002B                             END
```

Figure 1.7

productivity is seriously impaired when machine-level language is used. Because of the disadvantages associated with its use, this language form may very likely disappear during the next decade.

High-level languages allow the software developer and the program to be machine-independent. When a more sophisticated translator is used, the vocabulary, grammar, syntax, and semantics of a high-level language can be much more sophisticated than machine-level (Figure 1.8). In fact, compilers and interpreters (high-level language translators) produce machine-level code as output.

Although over 200 high-level programming languages are in use today, fewer than 10 languages are widely used in the industry. These languages can be divided into three categories:

Foundation languages. Developed in the late 1950s and 1960s, these languages formed the foundation for general-purpose scientific and commercial language forms. FORTRAN and COBOL are representative of this category. ALGOL

```
function nextx(k:integer):real;        (* Solve row k for new x[k]       *)
var
    i: integer;
    new,change: real;
begin
    new:=0;
    for i:=1 to k-1 do     new:=new+a[k,i]*x[i];   (* Accumulate all but   *)
    for i:=k+1 to size do  new:=new+a[k,i]*x[i];   (* kth term in new      *)
    new:=(b[k]-new)/a[k,k];                         (* Solve for x[k]       *)
    if k=1 then norm:=0;                            (* Init norm, 1st call  *)
    change:=abs(x[k]-new);                          (* Save maximum change  *)
    if change>norm then norm:=change;               (* Return result        *)
    nextx:=new
end;

procedure GaussJacobi;
var
    xnew:      array [1..5] of real;     (* Separate storage of new x's   *)
begin
    clearx;
    repeat
        for i:=1 to size do xnew[i]:=nextx(i);  (* Calculate new x's 1st,  *)
        for i:=1 to size do
            begin
                x[i]:=xnew[i];                      (* then replace old ones. *)
                write(x[i]:10:6)
            end;
        writeln(norm:10:6)
    until abs(norm)<0.0000005 (* Continue until result good to 6 digits *)
end;

procedure GaussSeidel;
begin
    clearx;
    repeat
        for i:=1 to size do
            begin
                x[i]:=nextx(i);              (* New x's immediately replace old    *)
                write(x[i]:10:6);
            end;
        writeln(norm:10:6)
    until abs(norm)<0.0000005 (* Continue until result good to 6 digits *)
end;
```

Figure 1.8

can also be considered a foundation language for the structured language category.

Structured languages. These languages emerged as failings in foundation languages were recognized and extensions of good features were desired. Sophisticated data structuring, subprogram definition, statement groupings (block structuring), and logical constructs can be accommodated by these languages. Ada, ALGOL, PL/1, PL/M, PASCAL, and C are representative of this category.

Specialized languages. These languages provide special features for a specific software application or are special by virtue of an unusual or unconventional language form. APL, BLISS, LISP, RPG, and SNOBOL are representative of this category.

We have already alluded to the function of the translator component, that is, to transform a language form to machine-executable instructions. An *assembler* is the translator for machine-level code, performing the relatively simple task of converting symbolic machine instructions to machine-executable instructions. An *interpreter* is a translator that is used to transform high-level languages on a statement-by-statement basis. As each language statement is encountered, it is converted to machine-executable code and executed. APL and BASIC are among the languages that usually are executed with an interpreter. The most common high-level language translator is the *compiler*. By evaluating a program globally, a compiler is capable of optimizing memory size and/or execution speed of the machine-executable instructions that it produces.

Machine-executable instructions are the "bottom line" of the software configuration. An octal, hexadecimal, or specialized code is used to represent the binary pattern of bits that invoke specific CPU processing steps. Referring again to Figure 1.7, the machine-executable instructions ("machine code") corresponding to Intel 8080 machine-level language ("assembler code") are shown.

1.4.2 Software Applications

Software may be applied in any situation for which a prespecified set of procedural steps (i.e., an algorithm) has been defined. Information content and determinacy are important factors in determining the nature of a software application. The term "content" refers to the meaning and form of incoming and outgoing information. For example, many business applications make use of highly structured input data (i.e., a database) and produce formatted "reports." Software that controls an automated machine (e.g., numerical control) accepts discrete data items with limited structure and produces individual machine "commands" in rapid succession.

The term "information determinacy" refers to the predictability of the order and timing of information. An engineering analysis program accepts data that have a predefined order, executes the analysis algorithm(s) without interruption, and produces resultant data in report or graphical format. Such applications are determinate. A multiuser operating system, on the other hand, accepts inputs that have varied content and arbitrary timing, executes algorithms that can be interrupted by external conditions, and produces output that varies as a function of environment and time. Applications with these characteristics are indeterminate.

It is somewhat difficult to develop meaningful generic categories for software applications. As software complexity grows, neat compartmentalization disappears. The following software areas indicate the breadth of potential applications.

System software. System software is a collection of programs written to service other programs. Some system software (e.g., compilers, editors, and file management utilities) process complex, but determinate, information structures. Other system applications (e.g., operating system components, drivers, and telecommunications processors) process largely indeterminate data. In either case the system software area is characterized by heavy interaction with computer hardware; heavy usage by multiple users; concurrent operation that requires scheduling, resource sharing, and sophisticated process management; complex data structures; and multiple external interfaces.

Real-time software. Software that measures, analyzes, and controls real world events as they occur is called *real-time*. Elements of real-time software include a data gathering component that collects and formats information from an external environment, an analysis component that transforms information as required by the application, a control-output component that responds to the external environment, and a monitoring component that coordinates all other components so that real-time response (typically ranging from 1 millisecond to 1 minute) can be maintained. Note that the term "real-time" differs from the term "interactive" or "time-shared." A real-time system must respond within strict time constraints. The response time of an interactive (or time-sharing) system can normally be exceeded without disastrous results.

Business software. Business information processing is the largest single software application area. Discrete "systems" (e.g., payroll, accounts receivable/payable, and inventory) have evolved into management information system (MIS) software that accesses one or more large databases containing business information. Applications in this area restructure existing data in a way that facilitates business operations or management decision making.

Engineering and scientific software. Engineering and scientific software is characterized by "number-crunching" algorithms. Applications range from astronomy to nuclear physics, from automotive stress calculations to spacecraft orbital dynamics, and from molecular biology to automated manufacturing. However, new applications within the engineering and scientific area are moving away from conventional numerical algorithms. Computer aided design, system simulation, and other interactive applications have begun to take on real-time and even system software characteristics.

Combinatorial software. Combinatorial software makes use of nonnumerical algorithms to solve complex problems that require an artificial intelligence approach. Pattern recognition (image and voice), theorem proving, game playing, and software correctness testing represent some of the problems that are addressed by combinatorial techniques.

1.4.3 Software Engineering

The software application areas discussed in Section 1.4.2 demand diverse skills and approaches for problem recognition and solution. The software implementation of a problem solution, however, can be approached by using a set of techniques that are application-independent. These techniques form the basis of a *software engineering* methodology.

Software engineering is modeled on the time-proven techniques, methods, and controls associated with hardware development. Although fundamental differences do exist between hardware and software, the concepts associated with planning, development, review, and management control are similar for both system elements. The key objectives of software engineering are (1) a well-defined methodology that addresses a software life cycle of planning, development, and maintenance, (2) an established set of software components that documents each step in the life cycle and shows traceability from step to step, and (3) a set of predictable milestones that can be reviewed at regular intervals throughout the software life cycle.

The following paragraphs present an overview of the software engineering methodology. We shall briefly discuss each step in the methodology, the deliverables that are produced, and the reviews that occur. In later chapters each of these topics is presented in detail. Each phase described below corresponds to one phase of a *software life cycle*. The life cycle is a long-term view of software—a view that encompasses the activities that occur before development begins and after the software goes into active use.

Planning phase. As we have already noted, software is always part of a larger computer-based system. Therefore, system analysis and definition must occur prior to (or in conjunction with) software planning. System functions must be allocated to software.

The software engineering planning phase (Figure 1.9) begins with the *software planning* step. During this step a bounded description of the scope of software effort is developed, resources required to develop the software are predicted, and cost and schedule estimates are established. The purpose of the software planning step is to provide a preliminary indication of project viability in relationship to cost and schedule constraints that may have already been established. A *Software Plan* is produced and reviewed by project management.

The next step in the planning phase is *software requirements analysis and definition.* During this step the system element allocated to software is defined in detail. Information flow and structure provide the key to system element interface definition and software functional characteristics. Performance requirements or resource limitations are translated into software design characteristics. Global analysis of the software element defines validation criteria that will be used to demonstrate that requirements have been met.

Software requirements analysis and definition is a joint effort conducted by the software developer and the *requester,* that is, the person or organization requesting the software element of a system. A *Software Requirements Specification* is the configuration deliverable produced as a result of this step.

The software planning phase culminates with a technical review of the *Software Requirements Specification,* conducted by the developer and the requester. Once an acceptable requirements definition has been established, the scope, resources, cost, and schedule identified in the *Software Plan* are reevaluated for correctness. Information uncovered during the second planning step may impact estimates made during the first step. Deliverables developed during the software engineering planning phase serve as the foundation for the second phase in the process—software development.

Development phase. The development phase (Figure 1.10) translates a set of requirements into an operational system element that we call *software.* At early

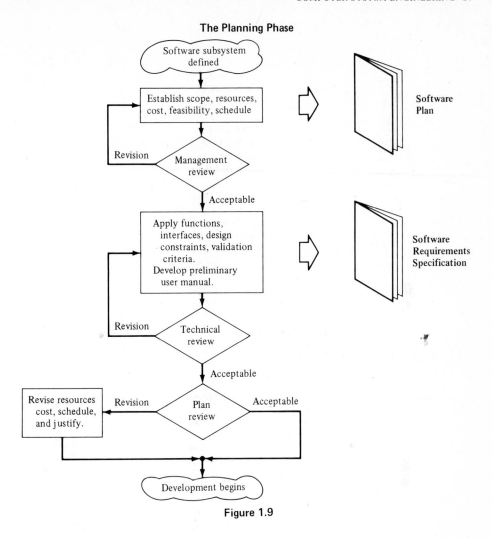

The Planning Phase

Figure 1.9

stages of development a hardware engineer does not reach for a soldering iron. The software engineer should not reach for a coding pad. *Design* must be accomplished first!

The first step of the development phase concentrates on a holistic approach to software. That is, a modular structure is developed, interfaces are defined, and data structure is established. Design heuristics (guidelines) are used for a qualitative evaluation of design quality. This *preliminary design* step is reviewed for completeness and traceability to software requirements. A first-draft *Design Document* is delivered and becomes part of the software configuration.

Procedural aspects of each modular element of the software are considered during the next development step. Design tools are applied to provide a *detailed*

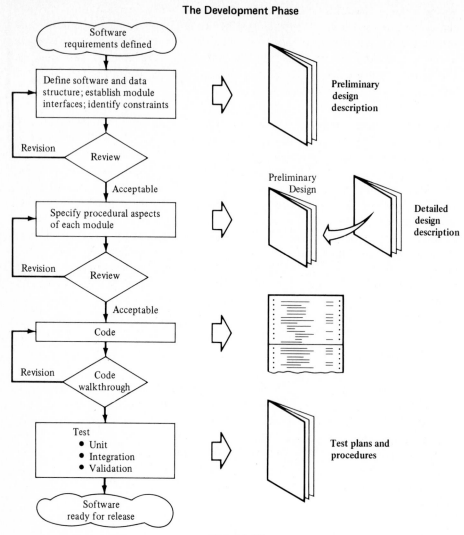

Figure 1.10

design description of the software element. Each detailed procedural description is added to the *Design Document* after review.

Finally, after two development (design) steps, we come to *coding,* that is, the generation of a program with the use of an appropriate programming language. The software engineering methodology views coding as a consequence of good design. Code is reviewed for style and clarity, but should otherwise be directly traceable to a detailed design description. A source language listing for each modular element of software is the deliverable for the coding step.

The final three steps of development are associated with software testing. *Unit testing* attempts to validate the functional performance of an individual modular component of software. *Integration testing* provides a means for assembly of the software modular structure while testing functions and interfaces. *Validation testing* verifies that all software requirements have been met. A *Test Plan and Procedure* may be developed for each of the testing steps. Review of test documentation, test cases, and results is always conducted.

Maintenance phase. Software will be maintained. Recognition of this fact is the first step toward lessening the impact of a task that devours 40 to 70 percent of the budget for many large software organizations.

The software engineering maintenance phase, illustrated in Figure 1.11 and described in Chapter 13, begins prior to release of the software. Review of the software configuration is conducted to assure that all documentation is available and adequate for the maintenance tasks that follow. Maintenance responsibility is established and a reporting scheme for error and system modification defined.

The tasks associated with software maintenance depend on the type of maitenance to be performed. In all cases modification of the software includes the entire configuration (i.e., all documents developed in the planning and development phases), not just code.

1.5 SUMMARY

Computer system engineering has evolved during three decades of enormous change in the computing field. The past emphasis on hardware engineering is now matched by concern for software engineering. The objectives of both methodologies are the same, namely, to apply a systematic methodology to system development, approach system development with a set of reviewable tasks, improve system quality and maintainability, and enhance management control. As demands for computer-based systems continue to grow, we must strive to satisfy all of these objectives.

REFERENCES

1. Osborne, A., *Running Wild—The Next Industrial Revolution,* Osborne/McGraw-Hill, 1979.
2. Toffler, A., *The Third Wave,* Morrow Publishers, 1980.
3. Bell, C., J. Mudge, and J. McNamara, *Computer Engineering,* Digital Press, Digital Equipment Company, 1978.
4. Bartee, T., *Digital Computer Fundamentals,* 4th ed., McGraw-Hill, 1977.
5. Wakerly, J., *Microcomputer Architecture and Programming,* Wiley, 1981.
6. Kaplan, G., R. Reddy, and Y. Kato, "Words into Action," *IEEE Spectrum,* vol. 17, no. 6, June 1980, pp. 22–29.

The Maintenance Phase

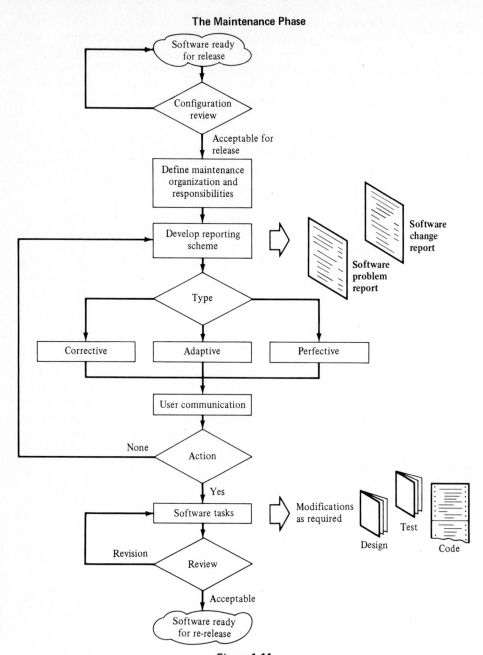

Figure 1.11

PROBLEMS AND POINTS TO PONDER

1-1 In Section 1.1 there is the implication that early (circa 1950s) work in computer programming was an art form learned in an apprenticelike environment. How have the "early days" affected the development of computer software in the 1980s?

1-2 References such as [1] and [2] discuss changes that will occur as a result of computerization in many aspects of our lives. Survey the popular literature and reassess the impact of the software crisis on society in general.

1-3 Select a current hardware configuration (e.g., IBM 3081, VAX 11/780, or Intel IAPX-432) and describe the major elements of the system architecture. Investigate the use of solid state software ("firmware") in the system you select.

1-4 Research the early history and goals of the foundation languages FORTRAN, COBOL, and ALGOL. Has each achieved its potential? What impact has each of these made on more modern languages?

1-5 Research the early history of software engineering, starting with the "structured programming" philosophy and continuing with early attempts at a broader methodology.

1-6 Software is only one element of a larger system. Therefore, the phases of the software life cycle are a subset of the phases of a larger system life cycle. Propose a set of phases for a system life cycle.

FURTHER READINGS

An excellent source of information on the trade-offs, technical considerations, and business decisions associated with computer system engineering can be found in *Computer Engineering* [3]. This text traces the evolution of the Digital Equipment Company through the generations of computers that the company has produced. *The Soul of a New Machine* (T. Kidder, Atlantic–Little, Brown 1981), a nonfiction best seller, offers a more literary view of the "making of a super-computer."

The current state of the art in software engineering can best be determined from conference proceedings such as the International Conference on Software Engineering, sponsored by IEEE/ACM and held every 18 months, or bimonthly publications such as *IEEE Transactions on Software Engineering.*

A recent book by Jensen and Tonies (*Software Engineering,* Prentice-Hall, 1979) complements many of the topics that are presented in this book. An historical perspective of software engineering is contained in Edward Yourdon's anthology, *Classics in Software Engineering* (Yourdon Press, New York, 1979). This book contains reprints of 24 landmark papers in the field.

TWO

THE SOFTWARE CRISIS

The current state of software in the evolution of computers is well summarized in the following quote [1]:

> The problem of the 1970s was to reduce the cost of the electronic functions needed to store and process data. . . .
>
> The problem of the 1980s is different. Now we must reduce the cost of electronic solutions; that is, reducing the cost you incur in using our devices to build a product. Solving this problem will require a shift from the component integration of the 1970s to concentration of system level integration in the 1980s.
>
> We can now talk about putting the power of a mainframe CPU on a single chip. This buys you nothing as a customer, however, unless you can use that power. Hardware is computing potential; it must be harnessed and driven by software to be useful.

The above statement was made by the president of one of the world's largest manufacturers of microelectronic hardware! It represents a growing awareness of the importance of software and a subliminal concern for our ability to adequately produce it.

2.1 THE PROBLEMS

The *software crisis* alludes to a set of problems that are encountered in the development of computer software. The problems are not limited to software that "doesn't function properly." Rather, the software crisis encompasses problems associated with how we develop software, how we maintain a growing volume of existing software, and how we can expect to keep pace with a growing demand for more software. Although reference to a "software crisis" can be criticized for being melodramatic, the phrase does serve a useful purpose by encompassing real problems that are encountered in all areas of software development.

The software crisis is characterized by many problems, but managers responsible for software development concentrate on the "bottom-line" problem: schedule and cost estimates are often grossly inaccurate. Cost overruns of an order of magnitude have been experienced. Schedules slip by months or years. These problems are the most visible manifestation of other software difficulties:

- We haven't taken the time to collect data on the software development process. With no historical data as a guide, estimation has been "seat of the pants" with predictably poor results. With no solid indication of productivity, we can't accurately evaluate the efficacy of new tools, techniques, or standards.
- Customer dissatisfaction with the "completed" system is encountered too frequently. Software development projects are frequently undertaken with only a vague indication of customer requirements. Communication between customer and software developer is often poor.
- Software quality is often suspect. We have only recently begun to understand the importance of systematic, technically complete software testing. Solid quantitative concepts of software reliability and quality assurance are only beginning to emerge [e.g., 2–4].
- Existing software can be very difficult to maintain. The software maintenance task devours the majority of all software dollars. Software maintainability has not been emphasized as an important criterion for software acceptance.

We have presented the bad news first. Now for the good news. Each of the problems described above can be corrected. An engineering approach to the development of software, coupled with continuing improvement of techniques associated with each phase of the software life cycle, provides the key.

One problem (we could call it a fact of life) will remain. Software will absorb an increasing percentage of the overall development cost for computer-based systems. By 1985 it is estimated that 90 percent of system development cost will be associated with software. We had better take the problems associated with software development seriously.

2.2 THE CAUSES

Problems associated with the software crisis have been caused by the character of software itself and by the failings of the people charged with software development responsibility. It is possible, however, that we have expected too much in too short a period of time. After all, our experience spans little more than 30 years.

The character of computer software was discussed briefly in Chapter 1. To review, software is a logical rather than a physical system element; therefore, success is measured by the quality of a single entity, rather than the quality of many manufactured entities. Software does not *wear out*. If faults are encountered, there is a high probability that each was inadvertently introduced during development and went undetected during testing. We replace defective parts during software maintenance, but we have few, if any, spare parts; in other words, maintenance often includes correction or modification of design. Finally, it's much harder to "see" progress during software development. A mock-up or prototype is rarely used.

The logical nature of software provides a challenge to the people who develop it. For the first time we have accepted the task of communicating with an alien intelligence—a machine. The intellectual challenge of software development is certainly one cause of the software crisis, but the problems discussed above have been caused by more mundane human failings.

Middle- and upper-level managers with no background in software are often given responsibility for software development. There is an old management axiom that states: "A good manager can manage any project." We should add: "if he or she is willing to apply effective methods of control, disregard mythology, and become conversant in a rapidly changing technology." The manager must communicate with all constituencies associated with software development—system requester, software developers, users, and others. Communication can break down because the special nature of software and the problems associated with its development are misunderstood. When this occurs, the problems associated with the software crisis are exacerbated.

Technical staff (the current generation has been called *programmers;* hopefully a new generation will earn the title *software engineer*) has had little formal training in new techniques for software development. In many organizations a mild form of anarchy reigns. Each individual approaches the task of "writing programs" with experience derived from past efforts. Some people develop an orderly and efficient approach to software development by trial and error, but many others develop bad habits that result in poor software quality and maintainability.

We all resist change. It is truly ironic, however, that while computing potential (hardware) experiences enormous change, the software people responsible for tapping that potential often oppose change when it is discussed and resist change when it is introduced. Maybe that's the real cause of the software crisis.

2.3 MYTHS

Many causes of a software crisis can be traced to a mythology that arose during the early history of software development. Unlike ancient myths that often provide human lessons that are well worth heeding, software myths propagated misinformation and confusion. Software myths had a number of attributes that made them insidious; for instance, they appeared to be reasonable statements of fact (sometimes containing elements of truth), had an intuitive feel, and were often promulgated by experienced practitioners who "knew the score."

Today, most knowledgeable professionals recognize myths for what they are—misleading attitudes that have caused serious problems for managers and technical people alike. However, old attitudes and habits are difficult to modify, and remnants of software myths are still believed as we move into the fourth decade of software.

The following paragraphs examine some of the more common software myths and present a statement of reality:

Myth: A general statement of objectives is sufficent to begin writing programs—we can fill in the details later.

Reality: Poor up-front definition is the major cause of failed software efforts. A formal and detailed statement of function, performance, interfaces, design constraints, and validation criteria is essential. These characteristics can be determined only after thorough communication between requester (customer) and developer.

Myth: Once we write the program and get it to work, our job is done.

Reality: A software life cycle exists. Initial work concentrates on planning (not "writing programs"); subsequent work focuses on development (design, coding, and testing), and finally, on-going work is required to maintain the software once it is "complete."

Myth: Project requirements continually change, but change can be easily accommodated because software is flexible.

Reality: It is true that software requirements do change, but the impact of change varies with the time at which it is introduced. Figure 2.1 illustrates the impact

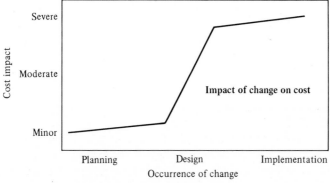

Figure 2.1

of change. If serious attention is given to up-front definition, change can be accommodated easily. The customer can review requirements and recommend modifications with relatively little impact on cost. When changes are requested during software design, cost impact grows rapidly. Resources have been committed and a preliminary design framework has been established. Change can cause upheaval that requires additional resources and major design modification, that is, additional cost. Changes in function, performance, interfaces, or other characteristics during implementation (code and test) have a severe impact on cost. Change, when requested late in a project, can be more than an order of magnitude more expensive than the same change requested early.

Myth: Reviews are superfluous, too time-consuming, or impossible to initiate.

Reality: Reviews are the only known mechanism for management and technical control. During early stages of a software development effort, there is no other means of evaluation. As many as six distinct reviews may be required during the software life cycle.

Myth: If we get behind schedule, we can add more programmers and catch up (sometimes called the "Mongolian horde concept").

Reality: Software development is not a mechanistic process like manufacturing. In the words of Brooks [6]: "Adding people to a late software project makes it later." At first, this statement may seem counterintuitive. However, as new people are added, the need for learning and communication among staff can and does reduce the amount of time spent on productive development effort. People can be added, but only in a planned and well-coordinated manner.

Myth: The only deliverable for a successful project is the working program.

Reality: A working program is only one part of a configuration that includes all elements illustrated in Figure 2.2. Documentation forms the foundation for successful development and, more importantly, provides guidance for the software maintenance task.

Myth: Once software is "working," maintenance is minimal and can be handled on a catch-as-catch-can basis.

Reality: Figure 2.3 illustrates the reality of software maintenance. A relatively small percent of the budget is allocated to maintenance, but to the dismay of many managers, over 50 percent of the budget is actually expended on maintenance [5]. Therefore, software maintenance should be organized, planned, and controlled as if it were the largest project within an organization. It often is!

Myth: Give a good technical person a programming book, and you've got yourself a programmer.

Reality: We have demonstrated the similarity between hardware and software engineering. If we are to accept the need for formal training of hardware engineers, we should recognize that software engineering competence can be achieved only through formal education and worthwhile experience.

Myth: The only deliverable for a successful project is a working program.
Reality:

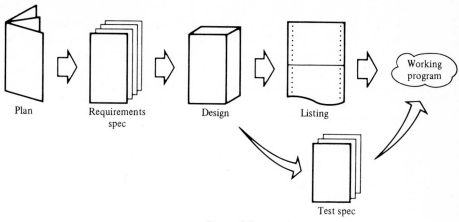

Figure 2.2

Myth: Once software is "working," maintenance is minimal and can be handled on a catch-as-catch-can basis.
Reality:

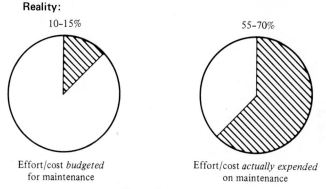

Figure 2.3

Many software professionals have begun to recognize the fallacy of the myths described above. Regrettably, habitual attitudes and methods foster poor management and technical practices even when reality dictates a better approach. Recognition of software realities is the first step toward formulation of practical solutions for software development.

2.4 A SOLUTION

The software crisis will not disappear overnight. Recognizing problems and their causes and debunking software myths are the first steps toward solutions. But solutions themselves must provide practical assistance to the software developer; improve software quality; and finally, allow the "software world" to keep pace with the "hardware world."

There is no single solution to the software crisis. We need a series of solutions that can be applied in combination; better tools for all phases of software development; more powerful building blocks for software implementation; automated techniques for software quality assurance; and an overriding philosophy for coordination, control, and management—software engineering.

Software tools must be available for each phase of the software life cycle. During planning automated costing and scheduling tools should assist the manager and technical staff in project estimation, and special tools should be provided for requirements definition and analysis; during the entire phase tools should provide access to a database of historical software development data. During the development phase design tools should provide assistance to the designer and a mechanism for the evaluation of "design goodness," coding tools should assist (and eventually eliminate) the coder during translation from design to high-level programming language, and test tools should assure software "correctness." Finally, the maintenance phase must have a complement of tools that improve maintenance responsiveness, uncover potential problem areas before errors occur in the field, and assist in the management of software maintenance.

Although a comprehensive, practical set of tools does not yet exist, many individual tools are available and many more are in various stages of development. Those tools that are available should be evaluated, selected, and used as one part of a solution to the software crisis.

The design of modern digital electronic hardware would be impossible without a broad selection of building blocks that perform standard functions accessible through standard interfaces. The hardware designer selects from a set of off-the-shelf integrated circuits (ICs), combinations of integrated circuits such as single-board microcomputers, or packaged systems of hardware components. Catalogs of specifications exist for each building block. Function, performance, limitations, interfaces, and technical detail are available to the designer.

The design of computer software would be greatly enhanced if a broad selection of software building blocks were available. In concept, software building blocks would be analogous to their hardware counterparts, providing standard functions accessed through standard interfaces. Early attempts at building block development, such as the FORTRAN scientific subroutine package (SSP), have saved countless hours of program development effort.

The use of standardized software building blocks may be a first step toward automatic code generation. Automated techniques for the specification of software requirements (to be discussed in Chapter 5) may ultimately lead to generation of code directly from a well-bounded problem definition!

We have seen that software quality is a primary concern to user and developer alike. Techniques that enhance testing through automatic test case generation are already available. Procedures for automated proofs of program correctness are in various stages of development. If a true program correctness prover is achieved,[1] the software crisis will begin to disappear.

The last element of a solution to the software crisis provides a harness for the tools, building blocks, and techniques discussed above. Software engineering combines methods for management control and review with techniques for analysis, design, code, test, and maintenance. Without a solid development methodology, even the most advanced tools and techniques may fail to mitigate the software crisis.

2.5 SUMMARY

Computer software may ultimately become the limiting factor in the evolution of computer-based systems. A software crisis is manifested by management and technical problems with software development. Management problems persist because of an overabundance of misinformation about software and the methods required to develop it. Technical problems can be solved with a new generation of tools and techniques. However, an engineering approach must be applied to the development of computer software—an approach that integrates proven management techniques for control with the best technical methods available, an approach that we shall discuss throughout the remainder of this book—*software engineering*.

REFERENCES

1. Grove, A. S., *Microsystem 80—Advance Information,* Intel Corporation, 1980, preface.
2. Littlewood, B., "Theories of Software Reliability, How Good Are They and How Can They Be Improved," *IEEE Transactions on Software Engineering,* September 1980, pp.489–500.
3. Walters, G., "Software Quality Metrics, Concepts, Application and Tools," in *Software Productivity and Quality Measurement,* GOSAM, General Electric Company, 1981.
4. DeMillo, R. and F. Sayward, in *Statistical Measures of Software Reliability,* A. J. Perlis, (ed.), Report No. 182/80, Yale University, June 1980.
5. Lientz, B., and E. Swanson, *Software Maintenance Management,* Addison-Wesley, 1980.
6. Brooks, F., *The Mythical Man-Month,* Addison-Wesley, 1975.

PROBLEMS AND POINTS TO PONDER

2-1 Write a brief description of a software "horror story" with which you are familiar. Being as objective as you can, delineate the true causes for the calamity.

---

[1] Small LISP programs (100 to 500 source lines) have been proven correct, but larger programs and other languages present roadblocks.

2-2 The discussion of myths in Section 2.2 is by no means all-inclusive. Define three or four additional "myths" and carefully state and support the "reality."

2-3 Section 2.4 describes a set of "solutions" for the software crisis. Which do you feel will provide the greatest benefit in the short term? In the long term?

2-4 Is it possible to develop a truly comprehensive set of software building blocks? What characteristics would such building blocks have to exhibit? What are the practical limitations?

FURTHER READINGS

A voluminous survey of the current state of software technology can be found in *Research Directions in Software Technology*, (Peter Wegner (ed.), MIT Press, 1979). A number of excellent discussions of "the software problem" and methodologies to solve it are presented.

Frederick Brooks's classic book, *The Mythical Man-Month* (Addison-Wesley, 1975) should be *required reading* for all managers with software responsibility. Brooks describes many of the problems that can be associated with the software crisis.

Another worthwhile survey of the software domain is contained in *Dawn of the Software Decade* (*Computerworld Extra,* September 17, 1980). Articles discuss eleven important software related topics ranging from applications software to distributed processing systems. Of particular interest in this issue is Daniel McCracken's "Software in the 80s: Peril and Promises."

THREE

SYSTEM PLANNING

Throughout human history the success of projects large and small can be traced to the clarity with which goals were defined. Today we recognize the importance of planning but understand surprisingly little about the planning process itself. Sometimes we "overplan," spending too much time studying a problem and too little time and/or resources implementing a solution. The following excerpt of a poem (author unknown) is a commentary on our tendency to overplan:

Nay, lad! Deciding's not your ploy,
For that's a risky game.
It's *making* a decision
That's your surest road to fame.

Decide means to take action,
And actions rock the boat,
And if you act and don't succeed
Small chance you'll stay afloat.

But . . . making a decision,
Ah! that's the way to swing.
It keeps the masses happy
And doesn't change a thing.

So get yourself a task force
Well skilled in all the arts
And call them all together
And watch them flip their charts.

Overplanning can destroy the timeliness of a system and adds little to the chances for ultimate success. It is, however, less dangerous than "underplanning."

Underplanning can best be characterized by the following comment: "If you don't know where you're going, it's exceedingly difficult to get there and nearly as difficult to determine that where you are is where you want to be." The major cause of large project failure (i.e., grossly inaccurate cost or schedule estimates, significant problems during implementation, or poor compliance with desired function or performance) is underplanning.

In this chapter we consider the steps that comprise the planning phase of the software engineering process. Each step acts to refine a mental image of the system to be developed, transforming a cloudy concept into an attainable set of elements.

3.1 THE PLANNING PHASE

The planning phase of the software life cycle is a process of definition, analysis, specification, estimation, and review. The flow of the planning phase is illustrated in Figure 3.1.

System definition is the first step of the planning phase and an element of the computer system engineering process described in Chapter 1. At this point in the planning phase, attention is focused on the system as a whole. Functions are allocated to hardware, software, and other system elements based on a preliminary understanding of requirements.

Actually, the system definition step precedes both hardware and software engineering. The major objectives are to (1) evaluate the *system concept* for feasibility, cost benefit, and business need, (2) describe system interfaces, functions, and performance, (3) perform preliminary system analysis and design, (4) allocate functions to hardware, software, and supplementary system elements, and (5) establish cost and schedule constraints. A system definition forms the foundation for all subsequent engineering work. Both hardware and software expertise are required to successfully attain the objectives listed above.

The Planning Phase

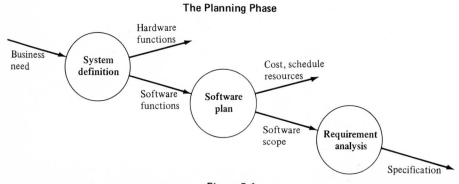

Figure 3.1

The software engineering steps that occur after system definition are also shown in Figure 3.1. *Software planning* and *software requirements analysis* are driven by function and performance developed during the system definition step. Analogous steps occur as part of the hardware engineering process.

The primary objective of software planning is to estimate the cost and development schedule for the software element of a system. In order to accomplish this objective, the scope of the software effort must be completely understood and resources required to satisfy the scope must be carefully defined. Of all steps in software engineering, the software planning step has suffered from the most neglect. Belief in the myth that "software planning is a black art" has perpetuated seat-of-the-pants estimates and acute underplanning.

The last step in the planning phase is software requirements analysis. A detailed specification of software requirements forms a foundation for the software engineering development phase. Working within the scope established during software planning, requirements analysis refines software interface details, functional attributes, performance characteristics, design constraints, and validation criteria.

The value of adequate planning is recognized by the vast majority of people involved in system development. However, three questions arise:

- *How much effort should be expended on planning?* Definitive guidelines for planning effort are difficult to establish. For the planning steps associated with software engineering, 10 to 20 percent of overall project effort should be expended on software planning and requirements analysis. Software size and complexity, application area, end use, and contractual obligations are only a few of many variables that affect overall planning effort.
- *Who does it?* An experienced, well-trained *analyst* should conduct most of the tasks associated with the planning phase. The analyst works in conjunction with management and technical staff of the system requester and system developer. For very large projects, an analysis team may be formed to conduct each planning step.
- *Why is it so difficult?* A nebulous concept must be transformed into a concrete set of tangible elements. Because communication content is exceptionally high during the planning phase, opportunity for misunderstanding, omission, inconsistency, and error abounds. Finally, the perception of the system may change as planning progresses, thereby invalidating earlier work.

The three steps associated with the planning phase—system definition, software planning, and software requirements specification—require a combination of intuition, experience, and tenacity. These traits, however, must be coupled with a set of systematic tasks that allow planning to be conducted in a controlled manner.

In the remainder of this chapter we consider the first step in the planning phase—system definition. Chapter 4 is dedicated to the second step—software planning, and Chapter 5 presents software requirements analysis.

3.2 SYSTEM DEFINITION

System definition does not fall exclusively within the steps associated with software engineering. Definition tasks provide a complete view of a system, allocating functions to each system element.

3.2.1 The Term "System"

Regrettably, the term "system" is much overused in today's jargon. *Webster's Dictionary* provides no fewer than eight definitions of the word, yet *Roget's Thesaurus* provides few suitable synonyms. Nearly anything can be called a "system."

For our purposes in this book, a *system* is defined as a collection of elements related in a way that allows the accomplishment of some tangible objective. Figure 3.2 illustrates a fundamental model of a system. People, procedures, hardware, software, and information—the system elements—are integrated in a manner that transforms input into output. In typical computer-based systems, input and output are represented by information in various forms. The computer-based system elements are combined to accomplish functions that effect the desired transformation. Computer-based system applications are as varied as they are numerous:

- A "payroll system" integrates a reporting and collecting function (human and procedural elements) with analysis, reporting, and file functions (hardware and software elements) to transform work-related data (an input) to paychecks, master file updates, and so on (the output).

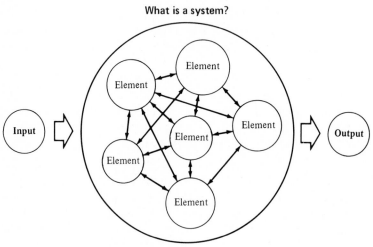

What is a system?

. . . a collection of elements related in a way that allows
the accomplishment of some tangible objective . . .

Figure 3.2

- An "industrial robotics system" integrates a tactile sensing function (hardware) with analysis, control, and recognition functions (hardware and software) to transform analog force data (an input) into servomechanism control commands (an output).
- A "word processing system" integrates text entry and edit functions with a document production function (hardware and software elements) applied by a user (a human element) to transform rough text copy (an input) into a finished letter or document (the output).

Formal classifications of systems have been proposed in the literature. Figure 3.3, adapted from Wetherbe [1], depicts fundamental models for *mechanistic* and *adaptive* systems. These systems represent opposite ends of a spectrum. The computer-based system falls somewhere in between. To illustrate, we shall reconsider the software applications discussed in Section 1.4.2.

Business or engineering-scientific systems use well-defined transforms to process well-defined (although variable) information and produce predictable output. The explicit content of input and output cannot always be predicted beforehand, but the general characteristics of such data are known. Such systems, although not purely mechanistic, reside at the mechanistic end of the classification spectrum. Real-time systems, on the other hand, can be designed to process predictable data arriving at indeterminate time intervals. Algorithms are well defined, and output characteristics, although varied, are predictable. Real-time systems are more adaptive than are business and scientific applications but still reside at the mechanistic end of the spectrum.

Classification of Systems

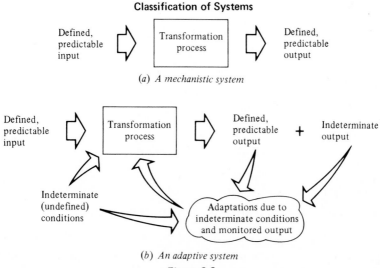

(a) *A mechanistic system*

(b) *An adaptive system*

Figure 3.3

3.2.2 System Definition Tasks

System definition is characterized by three tasks: *analysis, allocation,* and *specification.* The first task focuses on an understanding of the problem and a justification of proposed solution. The second task evaluates alternative implementations of a solution based on predefined criteria. The third task presents a proposed solution in a form that is reviewable.

In the sections that follow, each of the tasks associated with system definition is discussed. For further information on system analysis of computer-based systems, see Wetherbe [1], Atwood [2], Orr [3], or DeMarco [4]. For an excellent treatment of "general systems thinking," two texts by Weinberg [5,6] "demystify areas of systems study." The analysis task for software, a subset of system analysis, is discussed in detail in Chapter 5.

3.3 SYSTEM ANALYSIS

All human experience indicates that new things must be carefully analyzed before they can be properly built. A system is a collection of "things," making the need for thorough analysis even more important.

System analysis is comprised of a number of tasks that define what must be accomplished, whether accomplishment is feasible, and what the cost-benefit of accomplishment will be. Each task requires analysis, followed by evaluation and documentation. In the sections that follow, each system analysis task is described.

3.3.1 A System Analysis Checklist

The process that we call system analysis is actually a problem-solving activity that requires intensive communication between the system requester and the system developer. Because system analysis is problem solving, it can best be understood by considering the topics that are addressed as the problem is analyzed and the deliverables that are produced as a result of problem solving. The following system analysis checklist provides insight into the attributes of the analysis task.

A SYSTEM ANALYSIS CHECKLIST[1]

Analysis Planning

Questions

1. Are the reasons for the analysis project clearly defined in writing?

[1] Adapted from Wenig, R., "Systems Analysis Checklist," Portfolio 32-01-03, in *System Development Management,* Auerbach Publishers, Inc., 1981. With permission.

2. Are the project limits defined (e.g., resources, time, and funds)?
3. Is the completion of the system scheduled?
4. Who will perform the analysis work? Does that person have any previous experience in this application area?
5. Who are the user participants? (The term "user" refers to the requester of the system as well as the people who will actually use it.)
6. Are objectives set for the new or modified system? If so, what are they, and who set them?
7. What priority has the organization set for the project?
8. What previous systems analysis work has been performed in this application area?
9. What is the status of current systems serving the application?
10. What (if any) special legal, security, or audit considerations must be observed in this system?

Deliverables

1. A narrative definition of the project boundaries
2. A tentative work plan for the analysis work
3. A user contact list
4. A tentative resource staffing list
5. A list of existing application systems
6. A priority impact statement concerning the relative importance of the system

User Contacts

Questions

1. Are all user participants and organizational relationships identified?
2. Do users clearly understand the current system and its operation?
3. Are legitimate user complaints about the current system documented? Is the impact of the complaints fully documented?
4. How much time and effort are the users willing to put into the initial analysis work?
5. Are users identified as to who are supporters of, resistant to, and indifferent to the system?
6. Do users expect any specific benefits from the resulting system?
7. Is there clearly defined top-level support for the project? If so, who constitutes this support? How much power do they wield?
8. Who are the key decision makers in the user environment?
9. How many user locations are there? How many people will use the system at various levels? What is their level of computer system experience?

Deliverables

1. An organizational chart of all participating user areas, including their hierarchical relationships
2. A narrative describing the user's background and prior experience
3. Documentation of user problems with the existing system and the impact of these problems
4. A work plan of expected user participation in the analysis
5. A tentative statement of user expectations
6. A narrative on the political relationships and system support expectations of the major user participants
7. A brief history of previous data systems and procedures used in the application area
8. Identification of any other organizational systems or applications that interrelate with the proposed system

System Objectives

Questions

1. Are system objectives formally defined? Or are they loosely stated and subject to interpretation and/or later definition?
2. Will the new system have a major impact on the basic operations of the organization?
3. Will the new system replace an existing one? If so, how old is the current system? How many others preceded it?
4. Is the new system expected to cause relocation or removal of any work functions? If so, how sensitive is the issue? Who will help to combat any resistance?
5. Is an interim system required to satisfy immediate goals or to eliminate intolerable problems with the existing system?
6. Is a phased development and implementation approach feasible? Or is a one-time mass conversion required?
7. What cost can be justified? What resources can be allocated for this project?
8. How close to the state of the art is the new system expected to be?
9. How much time can users allocate for training and start-up? During what period of time?

Deliverables

1. A comprehensive statement of system objectives
2. A statement of general scope and level of project effort required, including tentative cost and resource estimates
3. A statement concerning the current system and procedures considered for change, elimination, and/or replacement

4. A general statement covering the expected project phasing and the overall team approach to the project
5. A tentative statement covering the levels and impact of anticipated organizational changes that will result from the system
6. A commentary on the roles and responsibilities of each participating user department and major user group in the desired system

Current System

Questions

1. What are the problems with the current system as evaluated by the users and the technical team? Do these evaluations agree?
2. How do other organizations perform similar functions? What is the current state of the art in the application area?
3. What other methods and procedures have been tried and/or used to service the application?
4. What is the detailed chronology of the current system's life?
5. What is the organization's history during the current system's life?
6. What development, maintenence, and operational costs are associated with the current system (including user efforts)?
7. Identify the name, rank, and organizational position of those who supported, built, and use the current system.
8. Identify one or more major situational failures that resulted from the current system.

Deliverables

1. A comprehensive narrative on the current system and its operation, history, and users
2. A ranked list of the current system's major faults and problems
3. A full cost analysis of the current system
4. A general statement on how the new system is related to those in other organizations or the state of the art
5. A complete collection of the documents, procedures, and other available details concerning the operation/content of the current system

Data Elements and Structures

Questions

1. Are the current data elements, files, forms, procedures, and so on thoroughly documented?

2. Are the current data elements and structures logical, consistent, and utilized?
3. How clean is the database?
4. Do users have a list of new data elements they would like to see in the new system? Is it feasible to add these data elements?
5. How much redundancy exists between the current system's database and that of other applications in the organization? Are any of the other applications a more logical repository for any elements of the database?
6. Is there enough flexibility in the current data structure to perform to meet the new system's needs?
7. How difficult will it be to convert the current database to a new one? How much error testing will be necessary to achieve a clean conversion?
8. How much maintenence is normally done on the existing database?
9. Can or should extensive data archives from this database be converted?
10. How much of the current database is actively used? By whom?
11. What significant faults or failures were encountered with the data files? How were they dealt with?
12. How many times and in what ways has the database been modified?

Deliverables

1. A comprehensive set of format and content definitions of all data elements, files, and supporting data structures
2. An evaluation of current database content, with emphasis on cleanliness, errors, unused areas, redundancy, conversion, and future use
3. A list of expected changes, additions, deletions, and other modifications to data elements and structures that are anticipated for the new system
4. A summary of the major uses of the data file and its elements
5. A list of faults and failures of the existing data files

User Interviews

Questions

1. Are all users identified?
2. Is there a formal interview plan for each user level covered?
3. Are lists of questions and objectives developed for the interviews at each user level?
4. Is top management supporting and publicizing the interviews, the interview team, and the overall expectations? Is top management making a strong pitch for interviewee cooperation?
5. Are all interviews scheduled during acceptable time periods?
6. Are the interviewers trained in effective interview techniques?
7. Are all scheduled interviews completed? Have canceled, interrupted, or forgotten interviews been rescheduled and conducted?

8. Have the interviewers taken adequate notes and written evaluations of each interview?
9. Have the interviewers compared notes, impressions, and other observations? Are these details documented?
10. Are interviewees given adequate feedback, such as summary reports, notes, and so on?
11. Have follow-up interviews been conducted when special problems or conditions are uncovered during initial interviews?
12. Has management been kept informed about the interview process, any problems uncovered, and uncooperative users?

Deliverables

1. A formal interview plan
2. Documentation of interview results
3. A report summarizing the interviews that includes both consensus answers and significant variances
4. An internal analysis of user attitudes and positions vis-à-vis the system
5. A management report covering interview findings and cooperation of the participants
6. Results of test interviews along with changes in questions, emphasis, and other interviewing guidelines
7. Explanation of any incomplete interviews

Research on Other Systems

Questions

1. What other organizations can be surveyed regarding their approach to the subject application?
2. What (if any) proprietary packages are available that might suit the application area?
3. What (if any) trade and industry associations study or catalog the systems work of others in the same field?
4. What (if any) formal literature is available on the subject application area?
5. How much time and effort should be spent in reviewing other systems?
6. Were the reviews of other systems productive? Should more time be spent on this activity?
7. Are field interviewers of other users and organizations necessary?

Deliverables

1. A list of organizations and sources to review for base knowledge on alternative approaches to the application

2. A narrative report detailing the ways other organizations are solving the application
3. A technical evaluation covering the current state-of-the-art application area
4. A summary report on contacts to other users and organizations
5. A follow-up plan for reviewing or tracking major developments in the industry

Alternative Propositions

Questions

1. How many application alternatives should be considered?
2. How much time and effort should be spent in evaluation of alternatives?
3. How detailed and complete should the considerations of each alternative be?
4. How will the alternatives be developed and documented?
5. Are formal requirements and evaluation criteria established for the alternatives?
6. Who will evaluate the alternatives? Will the users review the alternatives?
7. Are all logical alternatives being considered?
8. Are outside expert opinions being sought on the alternatives?
9. Are the alternatives considered consistent with those evaluated by other organizations?

Deliverables

1. Alternative design definitions
2. Positive and negative factors of each alternative
3. Evaluation reports from each group that studies the alternatives
4. Formal user presentation of the alternatives
5. Preliminary cost predictions for each alternative
6. A technology impact assessment for each alternative
7. A user impact assessment for each alternative

Selecting a Design Alternative

Questions

1. Are all alternatives fully reviewed and evaluated?
2. Are the alternatives ranked in terms of their ability to meet the system requirements criteria?
3. Is there a technical-management team with authority to select the most appropriate alternative?
4. Does one alternative clearly outrank the others?
5. Which alternative(s) do the users support?
6. Which alternative is best to implement in terms of time, cost, resources, and technical risk?

7. Which alternative uses the most advanced concepts?
8. Which alternative is likely to last the longest?

Deliverables

1. A detailed comparison of alternatives
2. A ranking of alternatives
3. A specific recommendation as to the alternative that is best to pursue
4. A report to the users on the alternative selected
5. A summary of reasons for rejecting other alternatives

Structural Analysis

Questions

1. Are all data elements, flows, and expected processing steps defined for the selected alternative?
2. Are procedural and organizational changes that the new system will generate defined and evaluated?
3. Are the content and uses of input files and outputs defined in a general way?
4. Are the equipment requirements for the new system estimated?
5. Is there a list of expected system modules?
6. Is there a tentative data conversion plan?
7. Is there an overall system flow being generated?
8. Are associated clerical procedures outlined?
9. What is the estimated volume of data and transactions?
10. Are the security and accuracy requirements of the data being considered?
11. Are testing procedures for the new approach thoroughly defined?
12. Is a preliminary system implementation plan available?

Deliverables

1. A report of the proposed system approach
2. A system flowchart
3. A user operations and responsibility flowchart
4. A detailed report on the analysis findings
5. A cost-benefit analysis report
6. A preliminary testing plan
7. A tentative implementation plan

Plans for the Next Phase

Questions

1. Are there work tasks and resource estimates for the general design work?

2. Is there a resource loading plan that shows requirements by work task?
3. Are user support tasks identified and planned? Are the users aware of them?
4. Are target dates set to obtain authorization to proceed with the next phase?
5. What is the expected completion date of the proposed work?

Deliverables

1. The work plan and the resource estimates
2. The user support plan
3. A narrative on the approach to managing the next phase.

Management Presentations and Reviews

Questions

1. Are all levels of management in the technical and user areas briefed on the analysis results and recommendations?
2. Are the presentations clearly and logically formulated?
3. Are management's concerns and questions documented and answered?
4. Has the proposed alternative survived management's scrutiny?
5. Does the analysis team have any doubts about the project approach?
6. Have minority opinions and negative comments been properly addressed?

Deliverables

1. Presentation critiques and internal reviews
2. Presentation reports and visual aids
3. Authorization to proceed

The system analysis checklist contains a comprehensive set of questions with a distinct emphasis on activities associated with analysis of business data processing systems. It should be noted, however, that many of these same questions should be addressed during the analysis and definition of engineering and scientific systems, real-time systems, and microprocessor-based systems.

Among the many additional issues that could be included in the checklist are:

1. Hardware and software trade-offs that are encountered in the definition of microprocessor-based systems;
2. Hardware and software design issues (e.g., Is the design of the system to be driven by hardware characteristics or software requirements?);
3. Algorithm design and analysis considerations;
4. Performance, accuracy, and reliability;
5. The interrelation of all system elements and the communication among various development groups (e.g., hardware and software engineering);

6. The impact of a hardware technology that may change before the project development is complete.

These issues and many others become part of the analysis checklist for technical systems. Review of the system analysis task is essential, and the checklist format provides a means for guiding the review process and helping to assure the success of the analysis task.

3.3.2 Feasibility Study

All projects are feasible—given unlimited resources and infinite time! Unfortunately, the development of a computer-based system is more likely plagued by a scarcity of resources and difficult (if not downright unrealistic) delivery dates. It is both necessary and prudent to evaluate the feasibility of a project at the earliest possible time. Months or years of effort, thousands or millions of dollars, and untold professional embarrassment can be averted if an ill-conceived system is recognized early in the planning phase.

The *feasibility study* concentrates on four primary areas of interest:

Economic feasibility. An evaluation of development cost weighed against the ultimate income or benefit derived from the developed system.
Technical feasibility. A study of function, performance, and constraints that may affect the ability to achieve an acceptable system.
Legal feasibility. A determination of any infringement, violation, or liability that could result from development of the system.
Alternatives. An evaluation of alternative approaches to the development of the system.

A feasibility study is not warranted for systems in which economic justification is obvious, technical risk is low, few legal problems are expected, and no reasonable alternative exists. However, if any of the preceding conditions fail, a study of that area should be conducted.

Economic justification is generally the "bottom-line" consideration for most systems (notable exceptions include national defense systems, systems mandated by law, and high-technology applications such as the space program). Economic justification includes a broad range of concerns that include cost-benefit analysis (discussed in the next section), long-term corporate income strategies, impact on other profit centers or products, cost of resources needed for development, and potential market growth.

Technical feasibility is frequently the most difficult area to assess at this stage of the system development process. Because objectives, functions, and performance are somehow hazy, everything seems possible if the "right" assumptions are made. It is essential that the process of analysis and definition be conducted in parallel with an assessment of technical feasibility. In this way, concrete specifications may be judged as they are determined.

The considerations that are normally associated with technical feasibility include:

Development risk. Can the system element be designed so that necessary function and performance are achieved within the constraints uncovered during analysis?

Resource availability. Are skilled staff available who are competent to develop the system element in question? Are other necessary resources (hardware and software) available to build the system?

Technology. Has the relevant technology progressed to a state that will support the system?

Developers of computer-based systems are optimists by nature. (Who else would be foolhardy enough to attempt what we frequently undertake?) However, during an evaluation of technical feasibility, a cynical, if not pessimistic, attitude should prevail. Misjudgment at this stage can be disastrous.

Legal feasibility encompasses a broad range of concerns that include contracts, liability, infringement, and myriad other traps that are frequently unknown to technical staff. An excellent book [8] by Michael Gemignani, a lawyer and a computer scientist, is *must* reading for software engineers who assist in this area of feasibility study.

Issues associated with system alternatives have been addressed in Section 3.3.1 (see "Alternative Propositions" and "Selecting a Design Alternative"). The degree to which alternatives are considered is often limited by cost and time constraints; however, a legitimate but "unsponsored" variation should not be buried.

The feasibility study may be documented as a separate report to upper management and included as an appendix to the *System Specification* (Section 3.5). Although the format of a feasibility report may vary, the following outline covers most important topics.

FEASIBILITY STUDY

1.0. Introduction

A brief statement of the problem, the environment in which the system is to be implemented, and constraints that affect the project.

2.0. Management Summary and Recommendations

A summary of important findings and recommendations for further system development.

3.0. Alternatives

A presentation of alternative system configurations; criteria that were used in selecting the final approach.

4.0. System Description

An abbreviated version of information contained in the *System Specification* or reference to the specification.

5.0. Cost-Benefit Analysis
     An economic justification for the system.
6.0. Evaluation of Technical Risk
     A presentation of technical feasibility.
7.0. Legal Ramifications
8.0. Other Project-Specific Topics

The feasibility study is reviewed first by project management (to assess content reliability) and by upper management (to assess project status). The study should result in a "go/no-go" decision. It should be noted that other go/no-go decisions will be made during the planning, specification, and development steps of both hardware and software engineering.

3.3.3 Cost-Benefit Analysis

Among the most important information contained in a feasibility study is *cost-benefit analysis*—an assessment of the economic justification for a computer-based system project. Cost-benefit analysis delineates costs for project development and weighs them against tangible (i.e., measurable directly in dollars) and intangible benefits of a system.

   Cost-benefit analysis is complicated by criteria that vary with the characteristics of the system to be developed, the relative size of the project, and the expected return on investment that is desired as part of a company's strategic plan. In addition, many benefits derived from computer-based systems are intangible (e.g., better design quality through iterative optimization, increased customer satisfaction through programmable control; and better business decisions through reformatted and preanalyzed sales data). Direct quantitative comparisons may be difficult to achieve.

   As we noted above, analysis of benefits will differ depending on system characteristics. To illustrate, consider the benefits for management information systems [9] shown in Table 3.1 Most data processing systems are developed with "better information quantity, quality, timeliness, or organization" as a primary objective. Therefore, the benefits noted in Table 3.1 concentrate on information access and its impact on the user environment. The benefits that might be associated with an engineering-scientific analysis program or a microprocessor-based product could differ substantially.

   Benefits of a new system are always determined relative to the existing mode of operation. As an example, we consider a computer-aided design (CAD) system that will replace elements of a manual engineering design process. The system analyst must define measurable characteristics for the existing system (manual design) and the proposed system (CAD). Choosing time to produce a finished detailed drawing *(t-draw)* as one of many measurable quantities, the analyst finds that a 4-to-1 reduction in *t-draw* will accrue from the CAD system. To further quantify this benefit, the following data are determined:

Table 3.1 Possible information system benefits*

Benefits from contributions of calculating and printing tasks
   Reduction in per unit costs of calculating and printing (CR)
   Improved accuracy in calculating tasks (ER)
   Ability to quickly change variables and values in calculation programs (IF)
   Greatly increased speed in calculating and printing (IS)
Benefits from contributions to record-keeping tasks
   Ability to "automatically" collect and store data for records (CR, IS, ER)
   More complete and systematic keeping of records (CR, ER)
   Increased capacity for record keeping in terms of space and cost (CR)
   Standardization of record keeping (CR, IS)
   Increase in amount of data that can be stored per record (CR, IS)
   Improved security in records storage (ER, CR, MC)
   Improved portability of records (IF, CR, IS)
Benefits from contributions to record-searching tasks
   Faster retrieval of records (IS)
   Improved ability to access records from large databases (IF)
   Improved ability to change records in databases (IF, CR)
   Ability to link sites that need search capability through telecommunications (IF, IS)
   Improved ability to create records of records accessed and by whom (ER, MC)
   Ability to audit and analyze record-searching activity (MC, ER)
Benefits from contributions to system restructuring capability
   Ability to simultaneously change entire classes of records (IS, IF, CR)
   Ability to move large files of data about (IS, IF)
   Ability to create new files by merging aspects of other files (IS, IF)
Benefits from contributions of analysis and simulation capability
   Ability to perform complex, simultaneous calculations quickly (IS, IF, ER)
   Ability to create simulations of complex phenomena in order to answer "what if?" questions
      (MC, IF)
   Ability to aggregate large amounts of data in various ways useful for planning and decision
      making (MC, IF)
Benefits from contributions to process and resource control
   Reduction of need for work force in process and resource control (CR)
   Improved ability to "fine tune" processes such as assembly lines (CR, MC, IS, ER)
   Improved ability to maintain continuous monitoring of processes and available resources (MC,
      ER, IF)

   *Abbreviations: CR = cost reduction or avoidance; ER = error reduction; IF = increased flexibility; IS = increased speed of activity; MC = improvement in management planning or control.
   Source: King and Schrems [9], p. 23. Reprinted with permission.

t-*draw*, average drawing time = 4 hours
c, cost per drawing-hour = \$20.00
n, number of drawings per year = 8000
p, percentage of drawing to be done on CAD system = 60%

With the above data known, an estimate of yearly cost savings—the benefit—can be ascertained:

   Drawing time cost savings = reduction $*$ t-*draw* $* n * c * p$ = \$96,000 per year

Other tangible benefits for the CAD system would be treated in a similar fashion. Benefits that are intangible (e.g., better design quality and increased employee morale) can be assigned dollar values or used to support a "go" recommendation, if indicated.

Costs associated with the development of a computer-based system [9] are listed in Table 3.2. The analyst can estimate each cost and then use development and on-going costs to determine a *return on investment, a break-even point,* and a *payback period.* The graph shown in Figure 3.4 illustrates these characteristics for the CAD system example noted above. We assume that total cost savings per year have been estimated to be $96,000, total development (or purchase) cost is estimated to be $204,000, and annual costs are estimated to be $32,000.

From the graph shown in Figure 3.4, the payback period requires 3.1 years. In actuality, return on investment is determined with a more detailed analysis that considers the time value of money, tax consequences, and other potential uses for the investment. Taking intangible benefits into account, upper management then decides if such economic results justify the system.

Another aspect of cost benefit analysis considers incremental cost associated

Table 3.2 Possible information system costs

Procurement costs
    Consulting costs
    Actual equipment purchase or lease costs
    Equipment installation costs
    Costs for modifying the equipment site (air conditioning, security, etc.)
    Cost of capital
    Cost of management and staff dealing with procurement
Start-up costs
    Cost of operating system software
    Cost of communications equipment installation (telephone lines, data lines, etc.)
    Cost of start-up personnel
    Cost of personnel searches and hiring activities
    Cost of disruption to the rest of the organization
    Cost of management required to direct start-up activity
Project-related costs
    Cost of applications software purchased
    Cost of software modifications to fit local systems
    Cost of personnel, overhead, etc., from in-house application development
    Cost for training user personnel in application use
    Cost of data collection and installing data collection procedures
    Cost of preparing documentation
    Cost of development management
Ongoing costs
    System maintenance costs (hardware, software, and facilities)
    Rental costs (electricity, telephones, etc.)
    Depreciation costs on hardware
    Cost of staff involved in information systems management, operation, and planning activities

Source: King and Schrems [9], p. 24. Reprinted with permission.

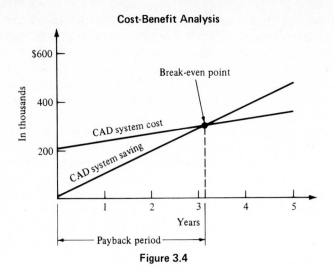

Figure 3.4

with added benefit (more or better function and performance). For computer-based systems, the incremental cost-benefit relationship can be represented as shown in Figure 3.5.

In some cases (curve AA') cost increases proportionally with benefits until some point A. After this point each additional benefit is exceedingly expensive. For example, consider a real-time polling function that has 500 milliseconds of idle time. New tasks can be added with relatively low cost; however, if total task execution approaches 500 milliseconds, the cost to implement increases dramatically because overall performance must be improved.

In other cases (curve $ABCC'$), cost increases proportionally until A and then levels for added benefits (through B) before increasing dramatically (at C) for

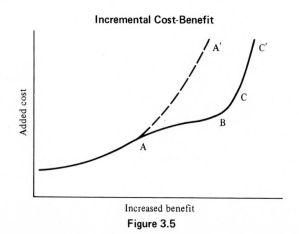

Figure 3.5

subsequent benefits. As an example, consider a single-user operating system that is enhanced incrementally to ultimately support multiple users. Once multiuser support is available, the rate of increase in cost for added multiuser functions may lessen somewhat. However, once processor capacity is reached, added features will require a more powerful processor and a large increment in cost.

The following excerpt [10] may best characterize cost-benefit analysis:

> Like political rhetoric after the election, the cost-benefit analysis may be forgotten after the project implementation begins. However, it is extremely important because it has been the vehicle by which management approval has been obtained.

Only by spending the time to evaluate feasibility do we reduce the chances for extreme embarrassment (or worse) at later stages of a system project. Effort spent on a feasibility analysis that results in cancellation of a proposed project is not effort that has been wasted.

3.4 FUNCTION ALLOCATION AND TRADE-OFFS

Once the questions associated with the analysis task have been answered, alternative solutions are considered. Each system function with requisite performance and interface characteristics is allocated to one or more system elements.

For example, analysis of a new computer graphics system indicates that a major function is three-dimensional transformation of graphics images. Investigation of alternative solutions for the transformation function uncovers the following options:

1. All three-dimensional transformations are performed with the use of software.
2. "Simple" transformations (e.g., scaling and translation) are performed in hardware, while "complex" transformations (e.g., rotation and perspective) are performed in software.
3. All transformations are performed with the use of a geometry processor implemented in hardware.

Each of the above options represents a different *functional allocation* for the same graphics system function. One allocation is selected from among the alternatives. Criteria for selection are established and trade-offs evaluated.

Trade-offs performed during the allocation task rely on established management and technical criteria. In nearly all cases the bottom-line criterion is cost, but the following considerations are also noteworthy: number of systems to be produced (*volume*); performance; degree of human decision making and interaction; standardization of interfaces and/or subsystems; and adaptability to product enhancement. It should be noted that none of these criteria can be considered in a vacuum. The countervailing influences of each make trade-off evaluation a difficult task.

When a computer-based system is a product, the number of systems to be produced (volume) will have a significant impact on allocation. All functions allocated to hardware represent a recurring incremental cost for each system that is manufactured. The addition of a $3000 hardware component will have little cost impact if the system product is a process control system for a steel mill (volume 3 to 5 systems per year) priced at $3,000,000. A $3.00 IC added to an "intelligent" microwave oven (volume 1 to 2 million products per year) can result in significant profit degradation. Software, as we have seen, is not manufactured and thus represents a one-time cost regardless of the number of systems to be produced. For large-volume products, software development cost, no matter how large, can be amortized.

In the context of the allocation task, *performance* alludes to processing speed or system response, RAM and ROM storage requirements, and system reliability. Speed critical functions are always allocated to a hardware element if (1) software cannot meet performance requirements and (2) hardware is available or can be designed within cost bounds. However, the development of a custom IC is still a relatively expensive process. At moderate volumes it is sometimes simpler and cost-effective to use a general-purpose microprocessor with supporting software in ROM.

Memory limitation has been an artificial and often unnecessary impediment to the development of computer-based systems. When system volume is relatively low, additional memory can often decrease software development cost substantially. However, when software is contained in a system (product) that is to be produced in large quantities, a constraint that dictates minimal memory may be justified. Fewer memory chips can result in substantial cost savings when large quantities are considered.

Reliability is the most costly performance characteristic to assess and the most difficult to guarantee. Hardware reliability theory is well established; data collected from prototype testing provide a good foundation for reliability estimates. Software reliability theory is in its formative stages. To help assure reliability in human critical systems (i.e., human life may be lost if the system fails) redundant hardware and software elements may be allocated to work in parallel.

The degree of *human decision making and interaction* depends on the environment in which the system will reside. Functions best performed by humans should be allocated to humans! This seemingly obvious guideline is often unheeded in a rush to automate. Techniques for human-machine interaction will undergo significant change during the next decade. Voice recognition systems will allow spoken input, and computer graphics already provides a visually pleasing mode of output. The human interface must be tuned to accommodate the higher communication bandwidth supported by these techniques.

Interface standardization and *adaptability* to product enhancement are representative of a second tier of trade-off criteria. These factors may serve as the arbiter when the trade-offs discussed above do not lead to a clear choice of allocation alternatives.

3.5 THE *SYSTEM SPECIFICATION*

The third task of the system definition step documents the findings of the preceding tasks. The *System Specification* is the first deliverable in the computer system engineering process. Each major section of the specification is described below.

SYSTEM SPECIFICATION

1.0. Introduction

    The introductory section describes objectives of the system and the environment in which the system will operate. This section also contains an executive summary that specifies the scope of the system development process; feasibility and justification; resources required, and an overview of cost and schedule.

2.0. Functional Description

    A description of each system function is provided in this section. The description includes a functional narrative that describes input information, tasks to be performed, resultant information, and additional interface data.

3.0. Allocation

    Each function described in Section 2.0 of the specification is allocated to the appropriate system element. Hardware and software elements are described separately. Information, particularly existing databases or files, is also described.

4.0. Constraints

    Management and technical constraints that affect development of the system are described in this section. Typical categories include external environment, interfaces, design and implementation, resources, and cost or schedule. Constraints imply limitation. This section must be carefully reviewed to assure that successful implementation of the system is possible within limits specified.

5.0. Cost

    Precise cost estimates may be impossible to determine at this stage of the computer system engineering process. Software planning and its hardware counterpart must be conducted to ascertain detailed cost estimates. However, cost bounds can, and normally are, established and noted in this section.

6.0. Schedule

    A system development schedule may be predicated on an end date determined by customer (requester) demand, market impact, or external forces. Like cost, a detailed development schedule cannot be established without detailed software and hardware planning. Known chronological information (e.g., as specified in contract) is defined in this section.

3.6 SYSTEM DEFINITION REVIEW

Throughout the planning phase there is a natural tendency to short-circuit review and move quickly into development. Managers tend to become increasingly nervous when components are not being soldered and source code is not being written. Technical people want to move into the "creative engineering tasks" as soon as possible. Don't fall prey to these attitudes! As shown in Figure 3.6, the planning phase can be viewed symbolically as a weight that holds down the development balloon; review constitutes the scissors that ultimately releases a system for development.

The *system definition review* evaluates the correctness of the definition contained in the *System Specification*. The review is conducted by both developer and requester to assure that (1) the scope of the project has been correctly delineated, (2) functions, performance, and interfaces have been properly defined, (3) analysis of environment and development risk justify the system, and (4) the developer and the requester have the same perception of system objectives. The system definition review is conducted into two segments. Initially, a management viewpoint is applied. Second, a technical evaluation of system elements and functions is conducted.

Key management considerations generate the following questions:

- Has a firm business need been established; does system justification make sense?
- Does the specified environment (or market) need the system that has been described?
- What alternatives have been considered?
- What is the development risk for each system element?
- Are resources available to perform development?
- Do cost and schedule bounds make sense?

Actually, the above questions should be raised and answered during the analysis task for system definition. Each should be reexamined at this stage.

The level of detail considered during the technical stage of the system review

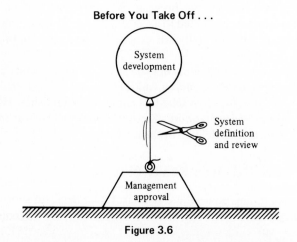

Before You Take Off . . .

Figure 3.6

varies with level of detail considered during the allocation task. The review should include the following issues:

- Does the functional complexity of the system agree with assessments of development risk, cost, and schedule?
- Is the allocation of functions defined in sufficient detail?
- Have interfaces among system elements and with the environment been defined in sufficient detail?
- Are performance, reliability, and maintainability issues addressed in the specification?
- Does the *System Specification* provide sufficient foundation for the hardware and software engineering steps that follow?

Two parallel engineering paths begin once the system review has been completed. Hardware elements of a system are addressed as part of the hardware engineering process. For the remainder of this book we shall trace the other path— software engineering.

3.7 SUMMARY

System definition is the first step in the planning phase for computer-based projects. During the definition step the system is analyzed; functions are allocated to hardware, software, and other elements; characteristics (e.g., performance and interfaces) are described; and a *System Specification* is written.

A system definition is generated through communication between developer and requester. The requester must understand what is required. The developer must know what questions to ask. If communication breaks down, the success of a project is in jeopardy.

REFERENCES

1. Wetherbe, J. C., *Systems Analysis for Computer Based Information Systems,* West Publishing, 1979.
2. Atwood, J. W., *The Systems Analyst,* Hayden, 1977.
3. Orr, K. T., *Structured Systems Development,* Yourdon Press, 1977.
4. DeMarco, T., *Structured Analysis and System Specification,* Prentice-Hall, 1979.
5. Weinberg, G., *An Introduction to General Systems Thinking,* Wiley-Interscience, 1975.
6. Weinberg, G., and D. Weinberg, *On the Design of Stable Systems,* Wiley-Interscience, 1979.
7. Wenig, R., "Systems Analysis Checklist," Portfolio 32-01-03, in *System Development Management,* Auerbach Publishers, Pennsauken, N.J., 1981.
8. Gemignani, M., *Law and the Computer,* CBI Publishing Company, Boston, 1981.
9. King, J., and E. Schrems, "Cost Benefit Analysis in Information Systems Development and Operation," *ACM Computing Surveys,* vol. 10, no. 1, March 1978, pp. 19–34.

10. Fried, L., "Performing Cost Benefit Analysis," portfolio, 32-03-04, *System Development Management,* Auerbach Publishers, Pennsauken, N.J., 1977.

PROBLEMS AND POINTS TO PONDER

3-1 Develop a checklist for attributes to be considered when feasibility of a system is to be evaluated. Discuss the interplay among attributes and attempt to provide a method for grading each so that a quantitative *feasibility number* may be developed.

3-2 A system analyst can come from one of three sources; the system developer; the system requester; or some outside organization. Discuss the pros and cons that apply to each source. Describe an "ideal" analyst.

3-3 Find as many single word synonyms for the word system as you can. Good luck!

3-4 Attempt to draw the equivalent of Figure 3.2 for a system (preferably computer-based) with which you are familiar. Show major input and output, each system element, and the interconnectivity among elements.

3-5 Common system elements are hardware, software, and people. What other elements are frequently encountered in computer-based systems?

3-6 Research the accounting techniques that are used for a detailed cost-benefit analysis of a computer-based system that will require some hardware manufacturing and assembly. Attempt to write a "cookbook" set of guidelines that a technical manager could apply.

3-7 Develop the equivalent of Table 3.1 for engineering and scientific systems. Expand the system to encompass real-time and embedded microprocessor applications.

3-8 Based on documents provided by your instructor, develop an abbreviated *System Specification* for one of the following computer-based systems:
(*a*) A low-cost word processing system
(*b*) A real-time data acquisition system
(*c*) An electronic mail system
(*d*) A university registration system
(*e*) An engineering analysis system
(*f*) An interactive reservation system
(*g*) A system of local interest

3-9 Are there characteristics of a system that cannot be established at system definition? Describe the characteristics, if any, and explain why a consideration of them must be delayed until later in the planning phase.

3-10 Are there situations in which formal system definition can be abbreviated or eliminated entirely? Explain.

FURTHER READINGS

Books by Wetherbe [1] and Leeson (*Systems Analysis and Design,* SRA, 1981) provide worthwhile discussions of the system definition task. Both books contain case study supplements that illustrate the problems, approaches, and solutions that may be applied during system analysis.

Many other textbooks have been published in the general area of system planning. The more recent additions to the literature include the following:

Fitzgerald, J., *Fundamentals of Systems Analysis,* 2d ed., Wiley, 1981.
Kindred, A., *Data Systems and Management,* Prentice-Hall, 1980.
Squire, E., *Introducing Systems Design,* Addison-Wesley, 1980.

These texts are somewhat elementary and directed exclusively to data processing applications.

For those readers actively involved in system definition or interested in a more sophisticated treatment of the topic, Weinberg's books [5,6] provide an excellent discussion of "general systems thinking." Unlike many other texts with a distinct DP orientation, Weinberg describes important and intellectually stimulating characteristics of systems and implicitly proposes a general approach to system analysis and design.

The Auerbach series, *System Development Management* (Auerbach Publishers, Pennsauken, N.J., updated yearly), provides an excellent treatment of system planning and definition for large-scale information systems. Auerbach's pragmatic approach will be especially useful to industry professionals. Another text in this category is *Managing the Systems Development Process* by Charles Biggs et al. of Touche Ross and Company (Prentice-Hall, 1980).

FOUR

SOFTWARE PLANNING

In order to conduct a successful software development project, we must understand the scope of work to be done, the resources to be required, the effort and cost to be expended, and the schedule to be followed. *Software planning,* the first step in the software engineering process, provides that understanding.

Software planning combines two tasks: research and estimation. Research allows us to define the scope of a software element in a computer-based system. Using the *System Specification* as a guide, each major software function can be described in a bounded fashion. A bounded functional description, coupled with other data to be discussed later in this chapter, provides a target for estimation.

Whenever estimates are made, we look into the future and accept some degree of uncertainty as a matter of course. The second facet of software planning is estimation; therefore, a characteristic of planning is uncertainty. To quote Frederick Brooks [1]:

> Our techniques of estimating are poorly developed. More seriously, they reflect an unvoiced assumption that is quite untrue, i.e., that all will go well.
>
> Because we are uncertain of our estimates, software managers often lack the courteous stubbornness to make people wait for a good product.

Although estimating is as much art as it is science, software planning need not be conducted in a haphazard manner. Useful techniques for cost and schedule estimation do exist. Useful approaches to software project planning are available.

Planning provides a roadmap for software development. We would be ill-advised to embark on any software engineering project without it.

4.1 OBSERVATIONS ON ESTIMATING

Asked what single characteristic was most important in a project manager, a leading executive responded, "The ability to know what will go wrong before it actually does." We might add, " . . . and the courage to estimate when the future is cloudy."

Estimation of resources, cost, and schedule for a software development effort requires experience, good information, and the courage for commitment to quantitative measures when qualitative data are all that exist. Estimation carries inherent risk. Factors that increase risk are illustrated in Figure 4.1. The axes shown in the figure represent characteristics of the project to be estimated.

Project *complexity* has a strong effect on uncertainty that is inherent in planning. Complexity, however, is a relative measure that is affected by familiarity with past effort. A real-time application might be perceived as "exceedingly complex" to a software group that has previously developed only batch applications. The same real-time application might be perceived as "run of the mill" for a software group that has been heavily involved in high-speed process control. A number of quantitative software complexity measures have been proposed [e.g., 2]. Such measures are applied at the design or code level and are therefore difficult to use during software planning (before a design and code exist).

Project *size* is another important factor that can affect the accuracy and efficacy of estimates. As size increases, the interdependency among various elements of the software grows rapidly. Problem decomposition, an important approach to estimating, becomes more difficult because decomposed elements may still be formidable. To paraphrase Murphy's law: "what can go wrong will go wrong"—and if there are more things that can fail, more things will fail.

The degree of *project structure* also has an effect on estimation risk. In this

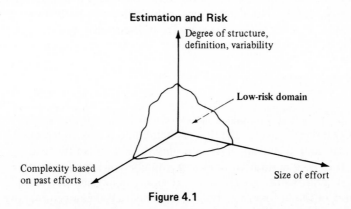

Figure 4.1

context the term "structure" refers to the ease with which functions can be compartmentalized and the hierarchical nature of information that must be processed. Figure 4.1 uses the reciprocal measure of structure; that is, as the degree of structure increases, the ability to accurately estimate is improved and risk decreases.

Risk is measured by the degree of uncertainty in the quantitative estimates established for resources, cost, and schedule. If project scope is poorly understood or project requirements are subject to change, uncertainty and risk become dangerously high. The software planner should demand completeness of function, performance and interface definitions (contained in the *System Specification*). The planner, and more importantly, the requester should recognize that variability in software requirements means instability in cost and schedule.

As a final observation on estimating, let us consider the words of Aristotle (330 B.C.):

> . . . It is the mark of an instructed mind to rest satisfied with the degree of precision which the nature of a subject admits, and not to seek exactness when only an approximation of the truth is possible. . . .

4.2 PLANNING OBJECTIVES

The software project manager is confronted with a dilemma at the very beginning of a development effort. Quantitative estimates are required, but solid information is unavailable. A detailed analysis of software requirements would provide necessary information for estimates, but analysis often takes weeks or months to complete. Estimates are needed *now*!

The objective of software planning is to provide a framework that enables the manager to make reasonable estimates of resources, cost, and schedule. These estimates are made within a limited time frame at the beginning of a software project.

As noted above, the planning objective is achieved through a process of information discovery that leads to reasonable estimates. In the following sections each task associated with software planning is discussed.

4.3 SOFTWARE SCOPE

The first software planning task is a determination of *software scope.* The planner must describe scope in language that is unambiguous and understandable at both management and technical levels. A description of software scope must be *bounded;* that is, quantitative data (e.g., number of simultaneous users, size of mailing list, and maximum allowable response time) are stated explicitly, constraints and/or limitations (e.g., product cost restricts memory size) are noted, and mitigating factors (e.g., desired algorithms are well understood and available in PASCAL) are described.

The topics that are presented as part of software scope are illustrated in Figure 4.2. Software functions are evaluated and in some cases refined to provide more detail. Because both cost and schedule estimates are functionally oriented, some degree of decomposition is often useful. Performance considerations encompass processing time constraints, memory limitations for software, and special machine-dependent features.

Function and performance must be evaluated together. The same function can precipitate an order of magnitude difference in development effort when considered in the context of different performance bounds.

Software interacts with other elements of a computer-based system. The planner considers the nature and complexity of each interface to determine any effect on development resources, cost, and schedule. The concept of an *interface* is interpreted to mean (1) hardware (e.g., processor and peripherals) that executes the software and devices (e.g., machines and displays) that are indirectly controlled by the software, (2) software that already exists (e.g., database access routines, subroutine packages, and operating system) and must be linked to the "new" software, (3) people who make use of the software through terminals or other I/O devices, and (4) procedures that precede or succeed the software as a sequential series of operations. In each case the information transfer across the interface must be clearly understood.

The least precise aspect of software scope is a discussion of reliability. Software reliability measures have been proposed but are still considered to be in the formative stage of development (see Chapter 12). Classic hardware reliability characteristics such as *mean time between failure* (MTBF) are difficult to translate to the software domain. However, the general nature of the software may dictate special considerations to ensure reliability. For example, software for an air traffic control system or the space shuttle (both human-rated systems) must not fail, or human life may be lost. An inventory control system or word processor software should not fail, but the impact of failure is considerably less dramatic. Although we may not be able to quantify software reliability, we can use the nature of the project to aid in formulating estimates of and cost to ensure reliability.

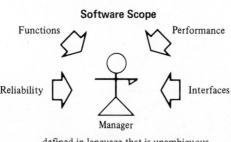

... defined in language that is <u>unambiguous</u>
and <u>understood</u> by all ...

Figure 4.2

If a *System Specification* has been properly developed, nearly all information required for a description of software scope is available and documented before software planning begins. In cases where a specification has not been developed, the planner must take on the role of system analyst to determine attributes and bounds that will influence estimation tasks.

4.4 RESOURCES

The second task of software planning is estimation of resources required to accomplish the software development effort. Figure 4.3 illustrates development resources as a pyramid. At the foundation, *tools*—hardware and software—must exist to support the development effort. At a higher level, the primary resource—*people*—is always required. Each resource is specified with three characteristics: description of the resource; chronological time that the resource will be required; and duration of time that the resource will be applied. The last two characteristics can be viewed as a *time window*. Availability of the resource for a specified window must be established at the earliest practical time.

4.4.1 Human Resources

Among the many problems posed by the software crisis, none is more ominous than the relative scarcity of capable human resources for software development. People are the primary software development resource.

The planner begins by evaluating scope and selecting the skills required to complete development. Both organizational position (manager, senior software engineer, etc.) and specialty (telecommunications, database, microprocessor, etc.) are specified. For relatively small projects (one person-year or less) a single individual may perform all software steps, consulting with specialists as required. For large projects, participation varies throughout the life cycle. Figure 4.4

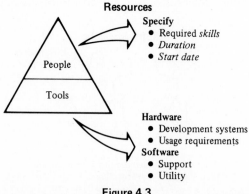

Figure 4.3

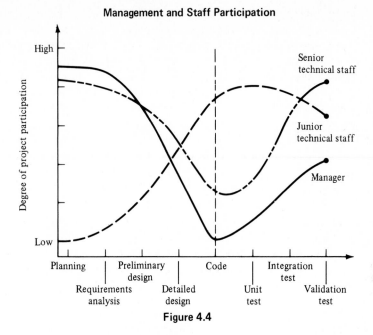

Management and Staff Participation

Figure 4.4

illustrates typical project participation for various staff as the development effort proceeds through each software engineering step.

Referring to Figure 4.4, management participation (noted by the solid curve) occurs early in the life cycle, tapers off to lower levels during the central steps of the development phase, and grows as project completion nears. Senior technical staff (the double dashed curve) also participates actively during planning, requirements analysis, preliminary design, and final testing steps. Junior staff (the dashed curve) is most involved during detailed design, coding, and early testing steps.

The number of people required for a software project can be determined only after an estimate of development effort (e.g., person-months or person-years) is made. Techniques for estimating effort are discussed in Sections 4.6 and 4.7.

4.4.2 Hardware

Earlier in this book we referred to hardware as *computing potential.* Within the resource context, hardware is also a tool for software development.

Three hardware categories should be considered during software planning: the development system; the target machine; and other hardware elements of the new system. The *development system* is a computer and related peripherals that will be used during the software development phase. For example, a 32-bit computer (e.g., VAX 11/780, PRIME 850) may serve as the development system for an 8-bit microporcessor—the *target machine*—on which the software will eventually be executed. The development system is used because it can accommodate multiple users, maintain large volumes of information, and support a rich assortment of software tools (to be discussed in the next section).

Except for very large projects, the development system is not specially acquired. Therefore, the *hardware resource* may be viewed as access to an existing computer, rather than purchase of a new computer. Because most development organizations have multiple constituencies that require development system access, the planner must carefully prescribe the time window required for a resource and verify that the resource will be available.

If software development steps are to be performed through a commercial time-sharing network, extreme care should be taken in making estimates of required processor time, storage, and connect time. Time-sharing access costs can become excessive. Worst case estimates are recommended during planning.

As noted above, the target machine is a processor that executes software as part of the computer-based system. In most mainframe and minicomputer applications the target machine and the development system are identical. Many microcomputer applications require a separate *microprocessor development system* (MDS) that provides facilities for high-level language support, in-circuit emulation, and PROM programming.

Other hardware elements of the computer-based system may be specified as resources for software development. For example, software for a numerical control (NC) used on a class of machines may require a machine tool as part of the validation test step; a software project for automated typesetting may need a phototypesetter at some point during development. Each hardware element must be specified by the planner.

4.4.3 Software

Just as we use hardware as a tool to build new hardware, we use software to aid in the development of new software. The earliest application of software in software development was *bootstrapping*. A primitive assembly language translator was written in machine language and used to develop a more sophisticated assembler. Building on the capabilities of the previous version, software developers eventually bootstrapped high-level language compilers and other tools. Today a vast array of software tools are available: compilers, editors, debuggers, test tools, design aids, and pre- and postprocessors are only a few of the resources that can be tapped by software developers.

Two broad categories of software should be considered by the planner. The first category, *support software,* is used to assist in the development phase. The second category, *utility software,* is acquired from a library and actually becomes part of the new program.

Support software spans a wide spectrum of tools. The most common support tools, programming language compilers, have become sine qua non to the developer. Support software exists for each step in the software engineering process. Automated requirements specification tools are available for the requirements analysis step; design language processors, flowchart/box diagram generators, and simulators are applied during design; dynamic debuggers, cross-assemblers/compilers and macroprocessors are used during coding and unit test; and test drivers and analyzers may be used during testing.

Development productivity can be improved substantially with the proper application of support software. The planner should recognize, however, that substantial effort and cost may have to be expended to "get the software up" on a development system. Cost-benefit is an important issue in the consideration of all support software.

In a world that has solved the software crisis, utility software would abound. Software building blocks would be available to allow construction of large packages with minimum "from scratch" development. Unfortunately, we have not as yet achieved this ideal. Libraries of utility software do exist for commercial applications, systems, and real-time work and for engineering and scientific problems. However, few systematic techniques exist for making additions to a library, standard interfaces for utility software are difficult to enforce, quality and maintainability issues remain unresolved, and the developer is often unaware that appropriate utility software even exists!

Two "rules" should be considered by the software planner when utility software is specified as a resource:

1. If existing utility software meets requirements, acquire it. The cost for acquisition of existing software will almost always be less than the cost of developing equivalent software.
2. If existing utility software requires "some modification" before it can be properly integrated with the system, proceed carefully. The cost of modifying existing software can sometimes be greater than the cost of developing equivalent software.

Ironically, software resources are often neglected during planning, only to become a paramount concern during the development phase of the life cycle. It is far better to specify software resource requirements early. In this way technical evaluation of alternatives can be conducted and timely acquisiton can occur.

4.5 SOFTWARE COSTING

In the early days of computing, software costs comprised a small percentage of overall computer-based system costs. An order of magnitude of error in estimates of software cost had relatively little impact. Today, software is the most expensive element in many computer-based systems. Large cost estimation errors can make the difference between profit and loss. Cost overruns can be disastrous for the developer.

Software costing will never be an exact science. Too many variables—human, technical, environmental, and political—can effect the ultimate cost of software.

However, software costing can be transformed from a black art to a series of systematic steps that estimate dollar costs with acceptable risk.

4.5.1 The Costing Approach

In an earlier section we noted that estimation cannot be undertaken without risk. Because costing is the crucial estimation task of software planning, a costing approach should strive to provide the highest degree of reliability, that is, the lowest risk of major estimation error.

To achieve reliable costing estimates, a number of potential options arise:

1. Delay software costing until late in the project. (Obviously, we can achieve 100% accurate estimates after the project is complete!)
2. Develop a parametric model of software cost.
3. Use relatively simple "decomposition techniques" to generate project cost in two different ways.
4. Acquire an automated costing system.

Unfortunately, the first option, however attractive, is not practical. Cost estimates must be provided "up front." *Cost modeling,* the second option, has been proposed in the literature of [2–4] and offers a potentially valuable cost estimation approach. A model is based on experience (historical data) and takes the form

$$c = f(v_i)$$

where c is software cost and v_i are selected independent parameters affecting cost. The third option, *decomposition techniques,* takes a "divide-and-conquer" approach to software cost. By decomposing a project into major functions and related software engineering tasks, costing (and scheduling) can be performed in a stepwise fashion. *Automated costing systems* provide an attractive option for estimating. In such systems the characteristics of the development organization (e.g., experience) and the software to be developed are described. Cost estimates are derived from these data.

Each viable software cost estimation option is only as good as the historical data used to seed the estimate. If no historical data exist, costing rests on a very shaky foundation. In the next section we examine the characteristics of *software productivity data* and how they are used as a historical basis for cost estimation.

4.5.2 Software Productivity Data

Software productivity is an elusive quantity to measure because software is not manufactured in a classical sense. Hardware productivity measures quantity of components produced in some predefined time interval. The early steps in hardware engineering (e.g., planning, analysis, and design) are not included in productivity measurement because each represents a one-time cost that can be amortized during manufacture. Because software development is a one-time event, software productivity must reflect all steps in the process.

We are therefore left with a dilemma. How do we measure software planning, analysis, or design productivity? How do we represent testing productivity? Hard numbers are needed to provide a historical basis for cost and schedule estimation, but how do we develop these numbers? Unfortunately, a set of satisfactory answers to these questions does not exist. Rather, software productivity data are gathered by measuring quantities that can be measured in a practical way and taking a macroscopic view of the software engineering process, that is, considering end-to-end productivity instead of productivity for a particular step in the process.

Many characteristics of software can be measured but few provide an adequate indicator for macroscopic productivity. The simplest (and most controversial) measure of productivity is the number of validated source lines produced per person-month. This measure can be computed only after a software development project has been completed. It gives us an indication of human effort expended during planning and development to produce a single line of validated source code.

As an example, consider the following data for a hypothetical software development effort:

Task	Effort, person-months
Requirements	1.5
Design	3.0
Code	1.0
Test	3.5

For the above effort, 2900 lines of source code were developed and 2400 were delivered in the completed system (the remaining 500 source lines were used for simulation and testing but are not part of the operational software). The productivity for this project is

$$\text{Productivity} = \text{validated (delivered) source lines per person-month}$$
$$= 2400 \text{ lines of code per 9 person-months}$$
$$= 267 \text{ LOC/PM}$$

If data similar to those indicated in this example are collected for many software projects, an average software productivity measure may be derived.

Many factors influence software productivity. Basili and Zelkowitz [3] define five importance categories:

People factors. The size and expertise of the development organization.
Problem factors. The complexity of the problem to be solved and the number of changes in design constraints or requirements.
Process factors. Analysis and design techniques that are used, languages available, and review procedures.

Product factors. Reliability and performance of the computer-based system.

Resource factors. Availability of development tools, hardware, and software resources.

The effect of these and other factors are best illustrated by the results of a landmark study conducted by Walston and Felix [4]. The authors isolate 29 factors that affect productivity and attempt to show how productivity varies with each factor. Referring to Figure 4.5, reproduced from the study [4], factors are listed in the leftmost column; productivity [delivered source lines per man-month (DSL/MM)] is indicated in the central three columns, with factors varying from favorable to unfavorable; the rightmost column indicates the productivity variance for a particular factor. Referring to Figure 4.5, it can be seen that productivity variance can be significant as factors change from favorable to unfavorable.

It should be noted that the factors listed in Figure 4.5 have complex interrelationships that are disregarded to simplify the data. The Walston and Felix data do provide a worthwhile qualitative feel for the relative impact of a particular factor on lines of code (LOC) productivity.

Collection of software engineering effort and lines of source code is not sufficient for software cost estimation. More detailed historical data are desirable to help quantify LOC/PM results and allow comparison of similar projects. Figure 4.6 provides a brief outline of historical data that is relatively easy to collect and provides useful information for the software planner.

Information shown in Figure 4.6 is an easily collectible subset of factors that may affect productivity. A description of major functions provides a more precise measure of productivity than the project average discussed in the previous example. If similar functions are required on a new project, expected productivity can be estimated with greater assurance. Cost data for major functions provides an important cost estimation multiplier $/LOC, which is extremely useful in the LOC costing technique (to be discussed in Section 4.7). Other information (e.g., documentation and tools used) may be used to temper estimates if extenuating circumstances are indicated. Historical software development data can be extremely useful if it is (1) collected in a consistent manner, (2) recorded in a way that facilitates access, and (3) applied with common sense.

4.6 ESTIMATION MODELS

An estimation model for computer software uses empirically derived formulas to predict data that are required as part of the software planning step. Unfortunately, no estimation model is appropriate for all classes of software and in all development environments. The empirical data that support most models are derived from relatively limited samples of projects. Therefore, estimation models must be used judiciously.

Models of the software development process can be derived to predict many different characteristics, such as people required as a function of time, cost as a

Productivity Variance

Variables that Correlate Significantly with Programming Productivity

Question or variable	Response group mean productivity (DSL/MM)*			Productivity change (DSL/MM)*
Customer interface complexity	<Normal 500	Normal 295	>Normal 124	376
User participation in the definition of requirements	None 491	Some 267	Much 205	286
Customer originated program design changes	Few 297		Many 196	101
Customer experience with the application area of the project	None 318	Some 340	Much 206	112
Overall personnel experience and qualifications	Low 132	Average 257	High 410	278
Percentage of programmers doing development who participated in design of functional specifications	<25% 153	25-50% 242	>50% 391	238
Previous experience with operational computer	Minimal 146	Average 270	Extensive 312	166
Previous experience with programming languages	Minimal 122	Average 225	Extensive 385	263
Previous experience with application of similar or greater size and complexity	Minimal 146	Average 221	Extensive 410	264
Ratio of average staff size to duration (people/month)	<0.5 305	0.5-0.9 310	>0.9 173	132
Hardware under concurrent development	No 297		Yes 177	120
Development computer access, open under special request	0% 226	1-25% 274	>25% 357	131
Development computer access, closed	0-10% 303	11-85% 251	>85% 170	133
Classified security environment for computer and 25% of programs and data	No 289		Yes 156	133
Structured programming	0-33% 169	34-66% —	>66% 301	132

Question or variable	Response group mean productivity (DSL/MM)*			Productivity change (DSL/MM)*
Design and code inspections	0-33% 220	34-66% 300	>66% 339	119
Top-down development	0-33% 196	34-66% 237	>66% 321	125
Chief programmer team usage	0-33% 219	34-66% —	>66% 408	189
Overall complexity of code developed	<Average 314		>Average 185	129
Complexity of application processing	<Average 349	Average 345	>Average 168	181
Complexity of program flow	<Average 289	Average 299	>Average 209	80
Overall constraints on program design	Minimal 293	Average 286	Severe 166	107
Program design constraints on main storage	Minimal 391	Average 277	Severe 193	198
Program design constraints on timing	Minimal 303	Average 317	Severe 171	132
Code for real-time or interactive operation, or executing under severe timing constraint	<10% 279	10-40% 337	>40% 203	76
Percentage of code for delivery	0-90% 159	91-99% 327	100% 265	106
Code classified as nonmathematical application and I/O formatting programs	0-33% 188	33-66% 311	67-100% 267	79
Number of classes of items in the data base per 1000 lines of code	0-15 334	16-80 243	>80 193	141
Number of pages of delivered documentation per 1000 lines of delivered code	0-32 320	33-88 252	>88 195	125

*DSL/MM = delivered source lines/man-month

(Source: Walston and Felix, A method for programming measurement and estimation, IBM Systems Journal, 1977, courtesy of the IBM Corporation.)

Figure 4.5

Historical Data—What to Collect

- Project name
  Description of major functions
  Lines of code
  Relative complexity on scale of 1 to 10
  Effort (man-months)
  Development time (months)
  Number of people
- Project cost
- Totals for major functions
- Documentation (number of pages)
- Total staff
- Tools used
- Maintenance record to date

Figure 4.6

function of software characteristics (e.g., measures of complexity, size, and staff experience), project duration as a function of number of people and programming environment, effort as a function of software characteristics, and software quality as a function of software characteristics. During the software planning step, cost and schedule are the primary project characteristics to be estimated. Therefore, models that relate dollars or effort (in person-months) to estimated software parameters are most desirable.

4.6.1 Resource Models

Resource models consist of a series of empirically derived equations that predict effort (in person-months), project duration (in chronological months), or other pertinent project data. Basili [5] describes four classes of resource models: static single-variable models; static multivariable models; dynamic multivariable models; and theoretical models.

The *static single-variable model* takes the form:

$$\text{Resource} = c_1 \times (\text{estimated characteristic})^{c_2}$$

where the resource could be effort E, project duration D, staff size S, or requisite lines of software documentation DOC. The constants c_1 and c_2 are derived from data collected from past projects. The estimated characteristic is lines of source code, effort (if estimated), or other software characteristics.

As an example of a set of static single-variable models, we again consider the study by Walston and Felix [4]. Based on data collected from 60 software development projects ranging in size from 4000 to 467,000 source lines and 12 to 11,758 person-months, the following models were derived:

$$E = 5.2 \times L^{0.91}$$

$$D = 4.1 \times L^{0.36}$$

$$D = 2.47 \times E^{0.35}$$

$$S = 0.54 \times E^{0.6}$$

$$DOC = 49 \times L^{1.01}$$

Effort (in person-months) E, project duration (in calendar months) D, and pages of documentation DOC, are modeled as a function of estimated number of source lines L. Alternatively, project duration and staffing requirements (people) S may be computed from derived or estimated effort.

The above equations are environment- and application-specific and may not be applied generally. However, simple models such as those above can be derived for a local environment if sufficient historical data are available.

Static multivariable models, like their single-variable counterpart, make use of historical data to derive empirical relationships. A typical model in this category takes the form

$$\text{Resource} = c_{11} \times e_1{}^{c_{12}} + c_{21} \times e_2{}^{c_{22}} + \cdots +$$

where e_i is the ith software characteristic and c_{i1} and c_{i2} are empirically derived constants for the ith characteristic.

A *dynamic multivariable model* projects resource requirements as a function of time. If the model is derived empirically, resources are defined in a series of time steps that allocate some percentage of effort (or other resource) to each step in the software engineering process. Each step may be further subdivided into tasks. A theoretical approach to dynamic multivariable modeling hypothesizes a continuous "resource expenditure curve" [5] and from it derives equations that model the behavior of the resource. The Putnam model, a dynamic multivariable model, is discussed in the next section.

Each of the models discussed above addresses macroscopic issues in software project development. The last resource model category examines software from the microscopic viewpoint; that is, the characteristics of the source code (e.g., number of operators and operands). A number of theoretical models are discussed in Chapter 7.

4.6.2 Putnam Estimation Model

The Putnam estimation model [6] is a dynamic multivariable model that assumes a specific distribution of effort over the life of a software development project. The model has been derived from work force distributions encountered on large projects (total effort of 30 person-years or more). However, extrapolation to smaller software projects may be possible [e.g., 3].

The distribution of effort for large software projects can be characterized as shown in Figure 4.7. The curves in the figure take on a classic shape that was first described analytically by Lord Rayleigh. Empirical data on system development, collected by Norden [7], has been used to substantiate the curves. Hence the distribution of effort shown in Figure 4.7 is generally called the *Rayleigh-Norden curve.*

The Rayleigh-Norden curve may be used to derive [6] a "software equation" that relates the number of delivered lines of code (source statements) to effort and development time:

$$L = C_k K^{1/3} t_d{}^{4/3} \qquad (4\text{-}1)$$

Effort Distribution—Large Projects

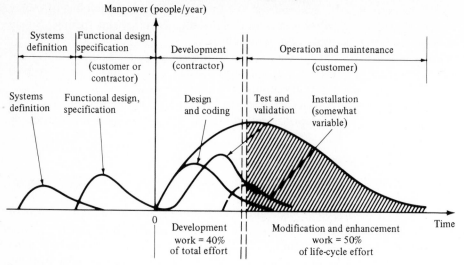

(Source: L. Putnam, Software Cost Estimating and Life Cycle Control, IEEE Computer Society Press, 1980, p. 15. Reproduced with permission.)

Figure 4.7

where C_k is a *state-of-technology constant* and reflects "throughput constraints that impede the progress of the programmer" [6]. Typical values might be: C_k = 6500 for a "poor" software development environment (e.g., no methodology, poor documentation and reviews, or a batch execution mode); C_k = 10,000 for a "good" software development (e.g., methodology in place, adequate documentation and reviews, and interactive execution mode); and C_k = 12,500 for an "excellent" environment (e.g., automated tools and techniques). The constant C_k can be derived for local conditions by using historical data collected from past development efforts. Rearranging equation (4-1), we arrive at an expression for development effort K:

$$K = \frac{L^3}{C_k^3 \, t_d^4} \qquad (4\text{-}2)$$

where t_d is the development time in years and L is the number of delivered lines of code (LOC).

The equation for development effort can be related to development cost by the inclusion of a burdened labor rate factor ($/person-year). Because of the cubed and fourth-power terms in the model, a small change in lines of code L can significantly reduce cost. For example, if software requirements are reduced such that a 10 percent reduction in estimated lines of code results, overall development cost will be reduced by 27 percent (according to the Putnam model). Similar trade-offs can be examined for changes in project completion date (t_d changes) or projected change in technology constant (C_k changes).

4.6.3 Esterling Estimation Model

Esterling [8] has proposed a productivity model that accounts for the *microscopic* characteristics of the work environment. At an individual level the process of software development is affected by the number n of people interacting on a project and the characteristics of the environment in which these people interact. Esterling contends that meetings and other "nonproductive" activities occur during an 8-hour workday and that the most productive period occurs during overtime (time worked beyond the standard work week).

The parameters associated with Esterling's model include the following elements:

a—average fraction of workday spent on administrative or other nondirect work
t—average duration of work interruptions, minutes
r—average recovery time after interruption, minutes
k—number of interruptions per workday from people working directly on the project
p—number of interruptions per workday from other causes
i—indirect (overhead) cost per person expressed as a fraction of base pay
d—differential pay for overtime expressed as a fraction of base pay

Table 4.1, reproduced from Esterling [8], provides typical data for these parameters.

The productivity model consists of five equations. If g is the average number of overtime hours per workday and n is the number of people working on a project, Esterling develops [8] an empirical relationship for the fraction w of useful working time (per workday per person):

Table 4.1 Values for Esterling Model Parameters

Parameter	Range	Factory workers	Programmers		
			Optimistic	Typical	Pessimistic
a	0–0.5	0.0	0.05	0.10	0.15
t	1–20	3	3	5	10
r	5–10	0.5	0.5	2.0	8.0
k	1–10	1	2	3	4
p	1–10	1	1	4	10
i	1–3	0.2	0.2	0.5	1.0
d	1–2	1.5	1.0	1.0	1.5

Source: Esterling, R., "Software Manpower Costs: A Model," *Datamation,* March 1980, p. 166. Copyright by Technical Publishing Company, 1980, all rights reserved. Reprinted with permission.

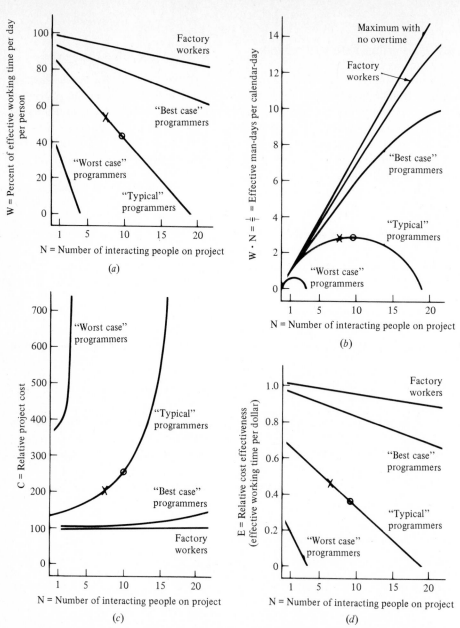

Figure 4.8. (a) The percent of effective working time per day per person, (b) the effective number of man-days per calendar-day, (c) the relative project costs, and (d) the effective working time per dollar. In each case the horizontal axis is the number of interacting people on a project. The different curves are for the four sets of parameters given in Table 4.1. The X represents the point at which the project time-cost product, CT, is at a minimum; the O is the point at which the project completion time is minimized. The maxima in the curves indicates that there is some n for which the addition of more people can increase the project completion time (and cost) even ignoring learning curves for new people.

(Source: Reprinted with permission of DATAMATION Magazine, copyright by Technical Publishing Company, 1980, all rights reserved.)

Figure 4.8

$$w = 0.125 \times \left(8 - 8a + g - \frac{4r}{60} - \frac{p(t + r)}{60} + \frac{k(n - 1)(t + r)}{60} \right)$$

Using w the following equations are developed:

$$T = \frac{7}{5nw}$$

$$c = ns(gd + 8(1 + i))$$

$$e = \frac{nw}{c}$$

$$C = \frac{c}{nw}$$

where T = ratio of calendar time to person-days to complete project
$\quad\ c$ = labor cost per workday for an average base salary s
$\quad\ e$ = cost efficiency
$\quad\ C$ = project cost per person-day

Figure 4.8*a, b, c, d* are reproduced from Esterling and illustrate the effect of number of people on the project variables described in the above equations. Project characteristics can be selected so that the *cost time product CT* is minimized.

The *time study* nature of the required parameters make data difficult to collect and would hinder application of the Esterling model. In addition, the model does not consider software characteristics explicitly. However, the Esterling model is a unique approach to software project estimation and can provide a useful indication of the efficacy of a local programming environment.

4.7 LINES-OF-CODE COSTING TECHNIQUE

When a software development manager is asked to estimate the cost of a new project, he or she must attempt to attach dollars to some measurable characteristic of the software. The *lines-of-code (LOC) costing technique* attaches dollar cost to an estimate of the number of lines of programming language source code that will ultimately be delivered.

4.7.1 Costing Steps

The software scope, determined as part of the software planning step, provides a description of major functions. The first step in the LOC technique specifies all functions that will be implemented in source code. Functions are *decomposed* (i.e., subdivided into smaller functional elements) until a reliable estimate of the number of source lines required to implement the function can be made.

The LOC estimate is provided as a range of values for each decomposed function. Using historical data or (when all else fails) intuition, the planner estimates an optimistic, most likely, and pessimistic LOC value for each function. An implicit indication of the degree of uncertainty is provided when a range of values is specified.

The *expected* (or average) number of LOC and the *deviation* from expected value are computed in the next step of the costing technique. The expected number of LOC L_e, can be computed as a weighted average of the optimistic a, most likely m, and pessimistic b LOC estimates. For example,

$$L_e = \frac{a + 4m + b}{6} \tag{4-3}$$

gives heaviest credence to the "most likely" estimate and follows a *beta* probability distribution.

We assume that there is a very small probability that the actual LOC result will fall outside the optimistic or pessimistic values. Therefore, the deviation in LOC estimates L_d (a measure of the variance in actual result that can be expected) takes the standard form

$$L_d = \sqrt{\sum_{i=1}^{n} \left(\frac{b - a}{6}\right)^2_i} \tag{4-4}$$

where a and b estimates for n software functions are included in the summation. It should be noted that a deviation based on uncertain (estimated) data must be used judiciously.

The last step of the LOC technique makes use of productivity data discussed in Section 4.5.2. Using historical information, the planner selects cost per LOC that characterizes each software function. If such data are not available, an average value (computed for projects recently completed by the organization) for $/LOC may be applied. The average $/LOC may be corrected to reflect inflationary effects, increased project complexity, new people, or other development characteristics. In a similar manner, effort (expressed in person-months per LOC) may be applied to the LOC estimates. Cost and effort are then computed for each function, and total estimated cost and effort are determined for the software project.

Are our estimates correct? The only reasonable answer to this question is: "We can't be sure." It is for this reason that a second costing technique must be applied as a cross-check to the LOC approach. A second technique—*effort per task costing*—is presented in Section 4.8.

4.7.2 An Example

As an example of LOC costing, let us consider a software package to be developed for computer-aided design (CAD) applications. Project scope indicates a microcomputer-based system interfaced with various computer graphics peripherals (e.g., display terminal, digitizer, and plotter).

Cost Table

Function	Optimistic	Most likely	Pessimistic	Expected	Deviation	$/line	Line/month	Cost	Months
User interface control	1800	2400	2650						
2-D geometric analysis	4100	5200	7400						
3-D geometric analysis	4600	6900	8600						
Data structure management	2950	3400	3600						
Computer graphics display	4050	4900	6200						
Peripheral control	2000	2100	2450						
Design analysis	6600	8500	9800						

Figure 4.9

Evaluation of scope indicates that the following major functions are required for the CAD software:

- User interface and control facilities
- Two-dimensional geometric analysis
- Three-dimensional geometric analysis
- Data structure management
- Computer graphics display facilities
- Peripheral control
- Design analysis modules

Following the first step of the LOC technique, a cost table, shown in Figure 4.9, is developed. A range of LOC estimates is developed. Viewing the first three numeric columns of the table in Figure 4.9, it can be seen that the estimator is fairly certain of LOC required for the peripheral control function (only 450 LOC separate optimistic and pessimistic estimates). On the other hand, the three-dimensional geometric analysis function is a relative unknown, as indicated by the 4000-LOC difference between optimistic and pessimistic values.

Calculations for expected value [equation (4-3)] and deviation [equation (4-4)] are performed for each function and placed in the fourth and fifth columns of the table (Figure 4.10). By summing vertically in the expected value column, an estimate of 33,360 LOC is established for the CAD system.[1] Equation (4-4) is applied to the deviation column, resulting in a computed deviation of 1100 LOC.

The optimistic and pessimistic estimates are assumed to be 99 percent probable LOC bounds for each software function. Considering the meaning of standard deviation, it can be assumed that there is a 0.68 statistical probability that the CAD

---

[1] It should be noted that the precision implied by the three low order significant digits (i.e., 360) is not attainable. Round off to the nearest 1000 LOC would be far more realistic. We have chosen to maintain precision to illustrate calculations only.

Cost Table

Function	Optimistic	Most likely	Pessimistic	Expected	Deviation	$/line	Line/month	Cost	Months
User interface control	1800	2400	2650	2340	140				
2-D geometric analysis	4100	5200	7400	5380	550				
3-D geometric analysis	4600	6900	8600	6800	670				
Data structure management	2950	3400	3600	3350	110				
Computer graphics display	4050	4900	6200	4950	360				
Peripheral control	2000	2100	2450	2140	75				
Design analysis	6600	8500	9800	8400	540				
Total				33360	1100				

Figure 4.10

Cost Table

Function	Optimistic	Most likely	Pessimistic	Expected	Deviation	$/line	Line/month	Cost	Months
User interface control	1800	2400	2650	2340	140	14	315	32,760	7.4
2-D geometric analysis	4100	5200	7400	5380	550	20	220	107,600	24.4
3-D geometric analysis	4600	6900	8600	6800	670	20	220	136,000	30.9
Data structure management	2950	3400	3600	3350	110	18	240	60,300	13.9
Computer graphics display	4050	4900	6200	4950	360	22	200	108,900	24.7
Peripheral control	2000	2100	2450	2140	75	28	140	59,920	15.2
Design analysis	6600	8500	9800	8400	540	18	300	151,200	28.
				33360	1100			$656,680	144.5

Estimated LOC and deviation — Estimated project cost ($) — Estimated effort required (PM)

Figure 4.11

software will require 32,000 to 34,500 LOC and a 0.99 probability that 26,000 to 41,000 LOC will be required. These data may be applied to establish a range of cost and effort or to indicate the estimation risk. Again, we should note that the accuracy of statistical inference in this situation can be questioned.

The third, fourth, and fifth steps of the LOC technique are illustrated in Figure 4.11. Productivity data are acquired for $/LOC and LOC/person-month. In this case the estimator uses different values for each function. Average or adjusted average values may also be used. Values contained in the *cost* and *months* columns of the table are determined by taking the product of expected LOC and $/LOC and LOC/person-month, respectively.

From the cost table, the total estimated project cost is $657,000 and the estimated effort is 145 person-months. With an eye toward scheduling, we may use equation (4-1) to provide a rough estimate of the chronological time required to complete the project. Rearranging the equation and recalling that software development effort $E = 0.4\,K$, we can derive an expression for development time:

$$t_d = \left(\frac{L^3}{C_k^3 K} \right)^{1/4} \tag{4-1'}$$

Using data derived from the cost table, we obtain

$$L \sim 33{,}000$$

$$E \sim 145 \text{ person-months} = 12 \text{ person-years}$$

and assuming a standard development environment, $C_k = 10{,}000$. Therefore, from equation (4-1), we derive

$$t_d = \left(\frac{33{,}000^3}{10^{12} \cdot 12} \right)^{1/4} \qquad T \sim 1.3 \text{ years, the development time}$$

Before using the above result, we should recall that (1) the estimation model from which equation (4-1) is derived represents "large" software development efforts, and we cannot be certain that the CAD system fits this category, (2) equation (4-1) is nothing more than a model and must be used with extreme care, and (3) common sense should always prevail.

Recalling that a 1100-LOC standard deviation exists for the CAD software estimate, we can develop a table of cost and effort that indicates the risk associated with variance from expected LOC value. Referring to Figure 4.12, we see that the number of LOC may vary from 26,000 to 41,000 (to remain within a 98 percent probability of accuracy). Cost may vary from $512,000 to $808,000. Applying equation (4-1), we see that development time may vary from 1.1 to 1.5 years— assuming that effort (person-years) is constant. This span of values provides a software manager with one indication of the degree of risk associated with the project. However, it is always better to recognize risk early and establish contingency planning. Playing the ostrich who disregards potential variance will not make actual variance go away.

We have derived what appear to be reasonable estimates of time and effort for the CAD software project. However, these estimates must be validated independently by a second costing approach.

Deviation of Cost and Time

Assuming that results within three L_d (standard deviation) of expected value provide 99% likelihood of accuracy:

	LOC	Cost*($)	Dev. time
$-3 \cdot L_d$	26000	$512,200	1.1 years
expected	33000	$650,100	1.3 years
$+3 \cdot L_d$	41000	$807,700	1.5 years

*assumes $/LOC = $19.70

Figure 4.12

4.8 EFFORT PER TASK COSTING TECHNIQUE

Effort per task costing is the most common technique for costing any engineering development project. A number of person-days, -months, or -years is applied to the solution of each project task. A dollar cost is associated with each unit of effort and an estimated cost is derived.

4.8.1 Costing Steps

Like the LOC technique, effort per task costing begins with a delineation of software functions obtained from the project scope. A series of software engineering tasks—requirements analysis, design, code, and test—must be performed for each function. Functions and related software engineering tasks may be represented as part of a table illustrated in Figure 4.13.

The second step of effort per task costing establishes the effort (e.g., person-months) that will be required to accomplish each software engineering task for each software function. These data comprise the central matrix of the table in Figure 4.13.

The third step of the technique attaches labor rates (i.e., cost per unit effort) to each of the software engineering tasks. It is very likely that the labor rate will vary for each task. Senior staff are heavily involved in requirements analysis and early design tasks; junior staff (who are inherently less costly) are involved in later design tasks, code, and early testing.

Costs and effort for each function and software engineering task are computed as the last step. If effort per task costing is performed independently of lines of

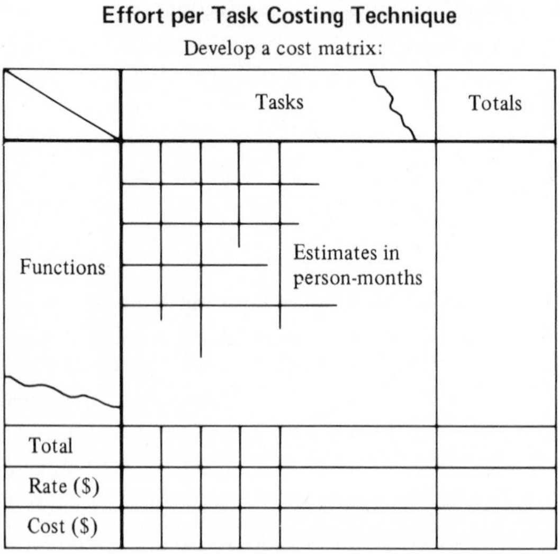

Effort per Task Costing Technique

Develop a cost matrix:

Figure 4.13

code costing, we now have two estimates for cost and effort that may be compared and reconciled. If both sets of estimates show reasonable agreement, there is good reason to believe that the estimates are reliable. If, on the other hand, the results of the costing techniques show little agreement, further investigation and analysis must be conducted.

4.8.2 An Example

To illustrate the use of effort per task costing, we again consider the CAD software introduced in Section 4.7.2. The system configuration and all software functions remain unchanged and are indicated by project scope.

Referring to the completed effort per task cost table shown in Figure 4.14, estimates of effort (in person-months) for each software engineering task are provided for each CAD software function (abbreviated for brevity). Horizontal and vertical totals provide an indication of effort required. It should be noted that 75 person-months are expended on "front-end" development tasks (requirements analysis and design), indicating the relative importance of this work.

Labor rates are associated with each software engineering task and entered in the RATE($) row of the table. These data reflect *burdened* labor costs, that is, labor costs that include company overhead. In this example it is assumed that labor costs for requirements analysis ($5200/person-month) will be 22 percent greater than costs for code and unit test. Unlike software productivity data, average labor rates can be accurately predicted in a software development organization.

Effort per Task Costing — CAD Example

Tasks / Functions	Requirement analysis	Design	Code	Test	Totals*	
UIC	1.0	2.0	0.5	3.5	7	
2DGA	2.0	10.0	4.5	9.5	26	
3DGA	2.5	12.0	6.0	11.0	31.5	
DSM	2.0	6.0	3.0	4.0	15	
CGD	1.5	11.0	4.0	10.5	27	
PC	1.5	6	3.5	5	16	
DA	4	14	5	7	30	Estimated effort for all tasks
Total*	14.5	61	26.5	50.5	152.5	
Rate($)	5200	4800	4250	4500		Estimated cost for all tasks
Cost($)	75,400	292,800	112,625	227,250	708,075	

*All estimates are in person-months except where otherwise noted.

Figure 4.14

Total cost and effort for the CAD software are $708,000 and 153 person-months, respectively. Comparing these values to data derived using the LOC technique, a cost variance of 7 percent and effort variance of 5 percent are found. We have achieved extremely close agreement!

What happens when agreement between estimates is poor? The answer to this question requires a reevaluation of information used to make the estimates. Widely divergent estimates can often be traced to one of two causes:

1. The scope of the project is not adequately understood or has been misinterpreted by the estimator.
2. Productivity data used in the LOC technique is inappropriate for the application, is obsolete (in that it no longer accurately reflects the software development organization), or has been misapplied.

The planner must determine the cause of divergence and reconcile the estimates.

4.9 AUTOMATED COSTING

A growing number of software organizations have developed or acquired an automated costing system for computer software. The configuration of a typical costing system is illustrated in Figure 4.15. A cost model accepts information about the project and the developer and produces an estimate of software cost.

Initially, the characteristics of the development organization are described in quantitative fashion. Development resources, experience of software staff, number of concurrent responsibilities, organizational structure, and other characteristics are used to produce a developer profile. To further calibrate the local development environment, the cost model may be run "in reverse," using data collected from a completed project. Such data can be used to tune model coefficients to better reflect the local organization. After the developer profile has been established,

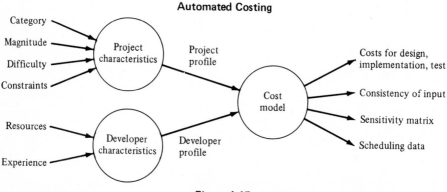

Figure 4.15

project characteristics are specified. Software application area, project magnitude and complexity, design and schedule constraints, performance characteristics, hardware limitations, and other data comprise a project profile.

Developer and project profiles provide primary input for a cost model. The model provides costs for software design, implementation, and test. In addition to basic cost information, an automated costing system may also provide a project schedule, a series of variance reports that indicate estimation risk, and an evaluation of input consistency. If data provided to establish developer and project profiles are accurate, an automated costing system can produce excellent results.

Automated cost and scheduling systems are not a substitute for thorough work breakdown and system definition. However, automated tools can provide insight and cross-checking capability that would be difficult or impossible to achieve manually.

SLIM [9] is an automated costing system that is based on the Rayleigh-Norden curve for the software life cycle and the Putnam estimation model (described in Section 4.6.2). SLIM applies the Putnam software model, linear programming, statistical simulation, and PERT (a scheduling method) techniques to derive software project estimates. The system enables a software planner to perform the following functions in an interactive terminal-oriented session: (1) *calibrate* the local software development environment by interpreting historical data supplied by the planner; (2) create an *information model* of the software to be developed by eliciting basic software characteristics, personnel attributes, and environmental considerations; and (3) conduct software *sizing*—the approach used in SLIM is a more sophisticated, automated version of the LOC costing technique described in Section 4.7.

Once software size (i.e., LOC for each software function) has been established, SLIM computes size deviation—an indication of estimation uncertainty, a *sensitivity profile* that indicates potential deviation of cost and effort, and a *consistency check* with data collected for software systems of similar size.

The planner can invoke a linear programming analysis that considers development constraints on both cost and effort. Using the Rayleigh-Norden curve as a model, SLIM also provides a month-by-month distribution of effort and cost so that staffing and cash flow requirements can be projected.

4.10 SCHEDULING

Scheduling for software development projects can be viewed from two rather different perspectives. In the first an end date for release of a computer-based system has already (and irrevocably!) been established. The software organization is constrained to distribute effort within the prescribed time frame. The second view of software scheduling assumes that rough chronological bounds have been discussed but that the end date is set by the software organization. Effort is distributed to make best use of resources, and an end date is defined after careful analysis of the software element. Unfortunately, the first situation is encountered far more frequently than the second.

Accuracy in scheduling can sometimes be more important than accuracy in costing. In a product-oriented environment added cost can be absorbed by repricing or amortization over large numbers of sales. A missed schedule, however, can reduce market impact, create dissatisfied customers, and raise internal costs by creating additional problems during system integration.

When we approach software scheduling, a number of questions must be asked. How do we correlate people with effort? How is effort distributed throughout the planning and development phases of the software life cycle? What milestones can be used to show progress? How do we physically represent a schedule? Each of these questions is addressed in the following sections.

4.10.1 People-Work Relationships

In a small software development project a single person can analyze requirements, perform design, generate code, and conduct tests. As the size of a project increases, more people must become involved. (We can rarely afford the luxury of approaching a 10 person-year effort with one person working for 10 years!)

There is a common myth that is still believed by many managers who are responsible for software development effort: *"If we fall behind schedule, we can always add more programmers and catch up later in the project. . . ."* Unfortunately, Brook's law [1] is probably closer to the truth: "Adding people to a late project will make it later!"

From a quantitative standpoint, the reason for this seeming anomaly lies in the complex communication paths that must be established among software development staff. Although communication is absolutely essential to successful software development, every new communication path requires additional effort and hence additional time.

As an example, consider four software engineers, each capable of producing 5000 LOC/year when working on an individual project. When these four engineers are placed on a team project, six potential communication paths are possible. Each communication path requires time that could otherwise be spent developing code; therefore, assume that team productivity (when measured in LOC) will be reduced by 250 LOC/year for each communication path. Team productivity is $20,000 - 250 \times 6 = 18,500$ LOC/year.

The 1-year project on which the above team is working falls behind schedule, and with 2 months remaining, two additional people are added to the team. The number of communications paths escalates to 14. The productivity input of the new staff is the equivalent of $840 \times 2 = 1680$ LOC for the two months remaining before delivery. Team productivity now is $20,000 + 1680 - 250 \times 14 = 18,180$ LOC/year! The 250-LOC/year reduction for all paths was taken to reflect the learning curve required of new staff.

Although the above example is a gross oversimplification of real-world circumstances, it does serve to validate Brooks's [1] contention that the relationship between the number of people working on a software project and overall productivity is not a direct linear proportion.

Based on the people-work relationship, are teams counterproductive? The answer is an emphatic "no" if communication serves to improve software quality and maintainability. In fact, peer review conducted by software development teams can lead to better software design and, more importantly, can reduce the number of errors that go undetected until testing (thereby reducing test effort). Hence productivity, when measured by time to project completion, can actually improve.

The Rayleigh-Norden curve model for large projects predicts a highly nonlinear relationship [equation (4-1′)] between chronological time to complete a project and effort. This leads to some interesting results. Recalling the CAD software example (Sections 4.7 and 4.8), an estimated 33,000-LOC, 12-person-year effort could be accomplished with eight people working for 1.3 years. If, however, we extend the end date to 1.75 years, from equation (4-2), we obtain

$$K = \frac{L^3}{C_k^3 t_d^4} \sim 3.8 \text{ person years}$$

This implies that by extending the end date 6 months, we can reduce the number of people from eight to four! The validity of such results is suspect, but the implication is clear: benefit can be gained by using fewer people over a somewhat longer time span to accomplish the same objective.

4.10.2 The 40-20-40 Rule

In both the LOC and effort per task costing techniques, we developed estimates of person-months (or -years) required to complete software development. Figure 4.16 illustrates a classical scheduling chart. But what is the recommended distribution of effort across the planning and development phases? A good distribution of effort, sometimes called the *40-20-40 rule,* emphasizes front-end planning and design tasks and back-end testing. The reader can correctly infer that coding (20 percent of effort) is deemphasized.

The 40-20-40 rule should be used as a guideline only. The characteristics of each project must dictate the actual distribution of effort. Effort expended on planning (preliminary cost and schedule estimation) rarely accounts for more than 5 percent of effort, unless the plan commits an organization to large expenditures with high risk. Requirements analysis may comprise 10 to 20 percent of project effort. Effort expended on requirements specification should increase in direct proportion with project size and complexity. A range of 20 to 30 percent of effort is normally applied to software design. Time expended for design review and subsequent iteration must be considered.

Because of the effort applied to software design, code should follow with relatively little difficulty. A range of 10 to 20 percent of overall effort can be achieved. Testing can account for 30 to 50 percent of software development effort. The criticality of the software system element often dictates the amount of testing that is required. If software is human-rated (i.e., software failure can result in loss of life), even higher percentages may be considered.

4.10.3 Schedule Representation

Scheduling is the most difficult task of the software planning step. The planner attempts to coordinate available resources with projected effort; to consider interdependency among tasks and schedule work in parallel whenever possible; to foresee potential problems or bottlenecks and provide contingency operations; and to specify milestones, reviews, and deliverables that will accurately reflect the progress of a development effort.

Modes of schedule representation are normally dictated by organizational policy. A typical scheduling chart is illustrated in Figure 4.16. *Work units* (days, weeks, months, or years) are indicated across the top row. Project tasks, milestones and deliverables are noted in the left-hand column. The planner indicates task duration by a horizontal bar that spans a requisite number of work units. When effort on different tasks is conducted in parallel, bars will span the same work unit. Applied effort may be summed vertically.

The schedule must explicitly represent tangible milestones and indicate deliverables associated with each milestone. "Problem analysis complete" is not a good milestone but "*Software Requirements Specification* available for review" is. The reason for this subtle distinction is that the development manager expects a tangible document when the latter milestone is reached, while no tangible item exists for the former.

As we have already noted, reviews are a critical part of the software engineering process. The schedule must explicitly represent each review as a task to be conducted. Completion of the review is a milestone to be achieved.

Scheduling Chart

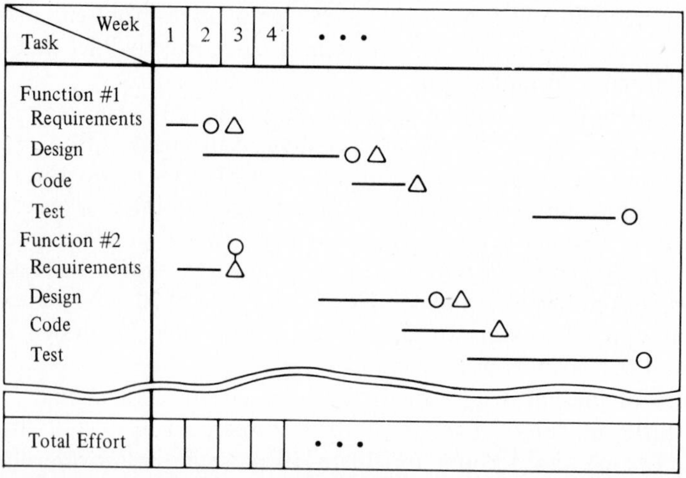

Figure 4.16

Resource availability windows should also be represented during scheduling. The impact of "unavailability" of a resource at the time it is expected should be traced through the schedule, and, if possible, contingency plans (and schedule) should be established.

4.10.4 Scheduling Methods

Scheduling of a software project does not differ greatly from scheduling of any multitask development effort. Therefore, generalized project scheduling tools and techniques can be applied to software with little modification.

The program evaluation and review technique (PERT) and the critical-path method (CPM) are two project scheduling methods [10] that can be applied to software development. Both techniques develop a *network* description of a project, that is, a pictorial or tabular representation of tasks that must be accomplished from beginning to end of a project. The network is defined by developing a list of all tasks associated with a specific project and a list of orderings (sometimes called a *restriction list*) that indicates in what order tasks must be accomplished.

Both PERT and CPM provide quantitative tools that allow the software planner to (1) determine the *critical path*—the chain of tasks that determines the duration of the project, (2) establish *most likely* time estimates for individual tasks by applying statistical models, and (3) calculate *boundary times* that define a time window for a particular task.

Boundary time calculations can be very useful in software project scheduling. Slippage in the design of one function, for example, can retard further development of other functions. Riggs [11] describes important boundary times that may be discerned from a PERT or CPM network: (1) the *earliest time* that a task can begin when all preceding tasks are completed in the shortest possible time; (2) the *latest time* for task initiation before the minimum project completion time is delayed; (3) the *earliest finish*—the sum of the earliest start and the task duration; (4) the *latest finish*—the latest start time added to task duration; and (5) the *total float*—the amount of surplus time or leeway allowed in scheduling tasks to ensure that the network critical path is maintained on schedule. Boundary time calculations lead to a determination of critical path and provide the manager with a quantitative method for evaluating progress as tasks are completed.

As a final comment on scheduling, we recall the Rayleigh-Norden curve representation of effort expended during the software life cycle (Figure 4.7). The planner must recognize that effort expended on software does not terminate at the end of development. Maintenance effort, although not easy to schedule at this stage, will ultimately become the largest cost factor over the entire software life cycle. A primary goal of software engineering is to help reduce this cost.

4.11 ORGANIZATIONAL PLANNING

There are almost as many human organizational structures for software development as there are organizations that develop software. For better or worse, organizational structure cannot be easily modified. Concern with the practical and political consequences of organizational change are not within the software planner's scope of responsibilities. However, organization of the people directly involved in a new software project can be considered during the planning step.

The following options are available for applying human resources to a project that will require n people working for k years:

1. n individuals are assigned to m different functional tasks, relatively little combined work occurs, and coordination is the responsibility of a software manager who may have six other projects to be concerned with;
2. n individuals are assigned to m different functional tasks ($m \leqslant n$) so that informal "teams" are established, an *ad hoc* team leader may be appointed; and coordination among teams is the responsibility of a software manager; and
3. n individuals are organized into k teams; each team is assigned one or more functional tasks and has a specific organization; coordination is controlled by both the team and a software manager.

Although it is possible to voice *pro* and *con* arguments for each of these approaches, there is a growing body of evidence [e.g., 12] that indicates that a formal team organization (option 3) is most productive.

The software development team approach has its origins in the "chief programmer team" concept first proposed by Harlan Mills and described by Baker [13]. The organization of the software development team is illustrated in Figure 4.17. The nucleus of the team is comprised of a *senior engineer* ("the chief programmer") who plans, coordinates, and reviews all technical activities of the team; *technical staff* (normally two to five people) who conduct analysis and development activities, and a *backup engineer* who supports the senior engineer in his or her activities and can replace the senior engineer with minimum loss in project continuity.

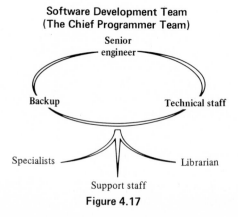

Software Development Team
(The Chief Programmer Team)

Figure 4.17

The software development team may be served by one or more specialists (e.g., telecommunications expert or database designer), support staff (e.g., technical writers and clerical personnel) and a *software librarian.* The librarian serves many teams and performs the following functions: maintains and controls all elements of the software configuration, such as documentation, source listings, data, and magnetic media; helps collect and format software productivity data; catalogs and indexes "revisable" software modules; and assists the teams in research, evaluation, and document preparation. The importance of a librarian cannot be overemphasized. The librarian acts as a controller, coordinator, and potentially, an evaluator of the software configuration.

The primary goal of the software development team is to approach a project as a joint effort. The team fosters the concept of "egoless programming" [14] that causes "my program" to become "our program." By helping to eliminate ego attachment to software, the team can foster more thorough review, increased learning through side-by-side work, and improved software quality.

In Section 4.10.1 we discussed the people-work relationships. The increased communication that is inherent in any team project would seem to mitigate against improved development productivity when software development teams are used. However, a significant percentage of effort in the software engineering process must be expended on communication (e.g., planning, analysis, and reviews) regardless of project organization. Although a team will increase the need for internal communication, structured modes of review can reduce the number of errors introduced during design and code. As a result, test effort will be reduced, thereby making a team more productive. The team approach is controversial and will continue to be debated until definitive data substantiates or invalidates the concept.

4.12 THE SOFTWARE PLAN

Each step in the software engineering process should produce a deliverable that can be reviewed and acts as a foundation for the steps that follow. The *Software Plan* is produced at the culmination of the planning step. It provides baseline cost and scheduling information that will be used throughout the software life cycle.

The *Software Plan* is a relatively brief document that is addressed to a diverse audience. It must (1) communicate scope and resources to software management, technical staff, and the requester, (2) define cost and schedule for management review, and (3) provide an overall approach to software development to all people associated with the project. The following document outline may be used as a guide.

SOFTWARE PLAN

1.0 Scope
   1.1 Project Objectives

A presentation of cost and schedule will vary with the audience to whom it is addressed. If the plan is used only as an internal document, the results of each costing technique can be presented. When the plan is disseminated outside the organization, a reconciled cost breakdown (containing a synthesis of results from both costing techniques) is provided. Similarly, the degree of detail contained within the schedule section may vary with the audience and formality of the plan.

The *Software Plan* need not be a lengthy, complex document. Its purpose is to help establish the viability of the software development effort. The *Software Plan* concentrates on a general statement of *what* and a specific statement of *how much* and *how long*. Subsequent steps in the software engineering process will concentrate on *how*.

4.13 SUMMARY

Software planning is the second step in the planning phase for computer-based systems and the first step of the software engineering process. During planning, the scope of the software effort is established and resources, cost and schedule are estimated.

Each task associated with the software planning step attempts to impress a systematic (rather than haphazard) approach to software project estimating. Risk will always exist. But by applying multiple costing techniques and scheduling guidelines, the planner can minimize estimation uncertainty and provide a usable "prediction" of the future.

REFERENCES

1. Brooks, F., *The Mythical Man-Month,* Addison-Wesley, 1975.
2. McCabe, T., "A Complexity Measure," *IEEE Transactions on Software Engineering,* December 1976, pp. 308–320.
3. Basili, V., and M. Zelkowitz, "Analyzing Medium Scale Software Development," *Proceedings of the Third International Conference on Software Engineering,* IEEE, 1978, pp. 116–123.

4. Walston, C., and C. Felix, "A Method of Programming Measurement and Estimation," *IBM Systems Journal,* vol. 16, no. 1, 1977, pp. 54–73.
5. Basili, V., *Models and Metrics for Software Management and Engineering,* IEEE Computer Society Press, 1980, pp. 4–9.
6. Putnam, L., "A General Empirical Solution to the Macro Software Sizing and Estimating Project," *IEEE Transactions on Software Engineering,* vol. 4, no. 4, 1978, pp. 345–361.
7. Norden, P., "Useful Tools for Project Management," in *Software Cost Estimating and Life Cycle Control,* L. Putnam (ed.), IEEE Computer Society Press, 1980, pp. 216–225.
8. Esterling, R., "Software Manpower Costs: A Model, " *Datamation,* March 1980, pp. 164–170.
9. Putnam, L., *Software Cost Estimating and Life Cycle Control,* IEEE Computer Society Press, 1980, pp. 324–328.
10. Wiest, J., and F. Levy, *A Management Guide to PERT/CPM,* 2d ed., Prentice-Hall, 1977.
11. Riggs, J., *Production Systems Planning, Analysis and Control,* 3d ed., Wiley, 1981, pp. 205–228.
12. Shniederman, B., *Software Psychology,* Winthrop Publishers, 1980, pp. 124–132.
13. Baker, F. T., "Chief Programmer Team Management of Production Programming," *IBM Systems Journal,* vol. 11, no. 1, 1972, pp. 56–73.
14. Weinberg, G., *The Psychology of Computer Programming,* Van Nostrand, 1971, pp. 47–66.

PROBLEMS AND POINTS TO PONDER

4-1 Software project complexity is discussed briefly in Section 4.1. Develop a list of software characteristics (concurrent operation, graphical output, etc.) that affect the complexity of a program. Prioritize the list.

4-2 Consider a software project on which you have recently worked. Write a bounded description of the software scope and present it for criticism. Can the scope you have established be misinterpreted? Have you bounded the system?

4-3 Performance is an important consideration during planning. Discuss how the interpretation of performance can vary depending on the software application area.

4-4 In Section 4.4 we discuss human, software, and hardware resources. Are there others?

4-5 The "make-buy" decision is an important management prerogative. You are manager of a software organization that has an average software development cost of $20.00/LOC. You are considering the purchase of a 5000-LOC software package that will cost $50,000. Initially, your technical staff indicates that no modifications will be required for the package to meet your specifications. However, your software development group wants to develop similar software in-house. Should you make or buy?

4-6 Reconsider the situation of Problem 4-5. After further study, your technical group now finds that at least 1000 LOC will have to be modified or added to make the package viable. Should you make or buy? Carefully state any assumptions you have made in making your decision.

4-7 The study by Walston and Felix [4] is only one of a number of sources for software productivity data. Write a paper outlining the results of other studies (see *Further Readings*). Is there commonality among the results?

4-8 Collect software productivity data for two to five projects on which you have worked. Basic information should include cost (students: if applicable), LOC, effort (person-months), a complexity indicator (scale 1 to 10), and chronological time to completion. Combine your data with information from other students and colleagues. Use a statistical technique such as multiple regression analysis to derive a static single- and multivariable cost per effort models for the combined data. Do the data correlate well? Do new data fit the model?

4-9 Using the reference works of Basili [5] or Putnam [6, 9] as a guide, write a brief paper outlining the derivation of the Putnam estimation model [equation (4-1)].

4-10 How well do the data collected as part of Problem 4-8 fit the Putnam model? Recall that the model was originally developed for very large projects.

4-11 Specify, design, and develop a program that implements the Esterling model discussed in Section 4.6.3. Using Esterling's article [8] as a guide, extend the program so that it can be used as a planning tool.

4-12 Given a project on which you are currently working or a project description assigned by your instructor, apply the LOC costing technique described in Section 4.7. Develop a complete cost table, using derived productivity data or "average data" specified by your instructor (e.g., $18.00/LOC average or 400 LOC/person-month average).

4-13 Using the results obtained in Problem 4-12, indicate potential deviation in cost and end date; assign a probability estimate to these numbers.

4-14 For the project noted in Problem 4-12, apply the effort per task costing technique. Develop a table similar to that shown in Figure 4.14. Use a burdened rate structure for wages that averages $4200/person-month.

4-15 Specify, design, and implement an abbreviated interactive software costing system. The system should incorporate modeling and the techniques described in Sections 4.7 and 4.8.

4-16 Are there circumstances under which people can be added late in a software project without incurring Brooks's law?

4-17 Develop and present a tutorial on PERT/CPM. Alternatively, write a paper on the subject. Are there other scheduling methods that can be adapted to software development?

4-18 Many software development projects are so large that many development teams (chief programmer teams) are required. Recommend a management structure for coordinating multiple teams. What are some of the potential problems that can arise?

4-19 Develop a detailed questionnaire that can be used for the collection of software productivity data in a development organization. See Basili's work [5] for guidelines.

4-20 Suggest practical methods by which a manager can monitor compliance with costs and schedules defined in the software plan.

4-21 It seems odd that cost and schedule estimates are developed during software planning—before detailed software requirements analysis (Chapter 5) have been conducted. Why do you think this is done? Are there circumstances when it should not be done?

FURTHER READINGS

Putnam's tutorial on software cost estimating [9] is a current and comprehensive study of the subject. The reference contains an 11-chapter technical presentation of his modeling technique and reprints of selected papers.

Joel Aron ("Estimating Resources for Large Programming Systems," in *Software Engineering: Concepts and Techniques,* Van Nostrand Reinhold, 1976) describes a costing technique that is similar to the LOC method but attempts to incorporate measures of complexity. A relatively complex but promising task scheduling approach is proposed by Tausworth in the *Journal of Systems and Software* ("The Work Breakdown Structure in Software Project Management," vol. 1, 1980). He describes a "work breakdown structure" that can be used to quantitatively predict the project task breakdown and number of milestones required to achieve a desired level of scheduling accuracy.

A major source for software productivity data is a database maintained by the Rome Air Development Center (RADC) at Griffiss Air Force Base in New York. Data from hundreds of software development projects have been entered in the database. Belady and Lehman ("The Characteristics of Large Systems," in *Research Directions in Software Technology,* MIT Press, 1979) provide other data for large projects.

Among recent books that discuss organizational considerations for software management (and many other topics) are:

Donaldson, H., *A Guide to the Successful Management of Computer Projects,* Halsted (Wiley), 1978.
Gunther, R. C., *Management Methodology for Software Product Engineering,* Wiley, 1978.
Metzger, P. W., *Managing a Programming Project,* 2d ed., Prentice Hall, 1980.

Each of these books has a distinct management emphasis.

An extremely thorough treatment of software management issues may be found in *Software Engineering Economics* (B. Boehm, Prentice-Hall, 1981). Boehm introduces a detailed software costing methodology and proposes a number of useful quantitative methods that may be used for scheduling, risk assessment, and benefits analysis.

FIVE

SOFTWARE REQUIREMENTS ANALYSIS

A complete specification of software requirements is essential to the success of a software development effort. No matter how well designed or well coded, a poorly specified program will disappoint the user and bring grief to the developer.

The requirements analysis task is a process of discovery and evaluation. The software scope, initially established during software planning, is refined in detail. Alternative solutions are analyzed and allocated to various software elements.

Both the developer and the requester take an active role in requirements specification. The requester attempts to reformulate a sometimes nebulous concept of software function and performance into concrete detail. The developer acts as interrogator, consultant, and problem solver.

Requirements analysis and specification may appear to be a relatively simple task, but appearances are deceiving. Communication content is very high. Chances for misinterpretation or misinformation abound. The dilemma that confronts a software engineer may best be understood by repeating the statement of an anonymous (infamous?) requester: *"I know you believe you understood what you think I said, but I am not sure you realize that what you heard is not what I meant. . . ."*

5.1 THE REQUIREMENTS ANALYSIS STEP

Requirements analysis is the last step in the planning phase of the software life cycle. Figure 5.1 illustrates the flow of events during the planning phase. Using

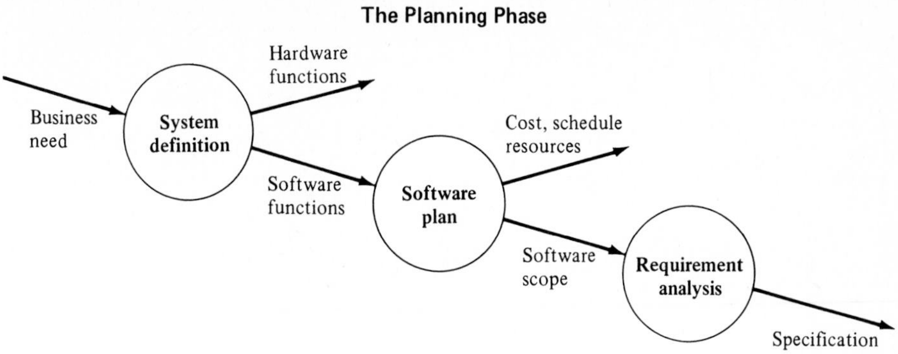

The Planning Phase

Figure 5.1

the software scope as a guide, software requirements analysis attempts to satisfy the following objectives:

- Provide a foundation for software development by uncovering the flow and structure of information
- Describe the software by identifying interface details, providing an in-depth description of functions; determining design constraints and defining software validation requirements
- Establish and maintain communication with the user and the requester so that the above two objectives may be satisfied

To achieve these objectives, the requirements analysis step encompasses a series of tasks to be discussed below.

5.1.1. Analysis Tasks

Software requirements analysis may be divided into four areas of effort: (1) problem recognition; (2) evaluation and synthesis; (3) specification; and (4) review.

Initially, the analyst (discussed in Section 5.1.2) studies the *System Specification* (if one exists) and the *Software Plan.* It is important to understand software in a system context and to review the software scope that was used to generate planning estimates. Next, communication for analysis must be established so that *problem recognition* is ensured.

The communication paths required for analysis are illustrated in Figure 5.2. The analyst must establish contact with management and technical staff of the user-requester organization and the software development organization. The project manager can serve as a coordinator to facilitate establishment of communication paths. The goal of the analyst is recognition of the basic problem elements as perceived by the user-requester.

Problem *evaluation and solution synthesis* is the next major area of effort for analysis. The analyst must evaluate the flow and structure of information, refine

Communication for Analysis

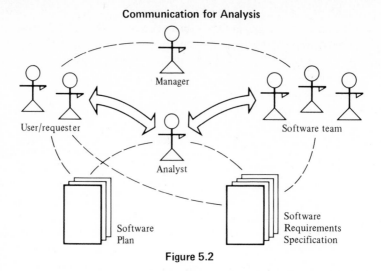

Figure 5.2

all software functions in detail, establish system interface characteristics, and uncover design constraints. Each of these tasks serves to describe the problem so that an overall approach or solution may be synthesized. For example, an inventory control system is required for a major supplier of plumbing supplies. The analyst finds that problems with the current manual system include (1) inability to obtain the status of a component rapidly, (2) 2- or 3-day turnaround to update the card file, and (3) multiple reorders to the same vendor because there is no way to associate vendors with components. On evaluating each problem, the analyst begins to synthesize one or more solutions. An on-line terminal-based system will solve one set of problems, but does it fall within the scope outlined in the *Software Plan*? A database management system would seem to be required, but is the user-requester's need for associativity justified? The process of evaluation and synthesis continues until both analyst and requester feel confident that software can be adequately specified for the development phase.

The tasks associated with *specification* strive to provide a representation of software that can be reviewed and approved by the requester. In an ideal world, the requester develops a *Software Requirements Specification* in its entirety. This is rarely the case in the real world. At best, the specification is developed as a joint effort including developer and requester.

Once basic functions, performance, interfaces, and information are described, validation criteria are specified to demonstrate understanding of a successful software implementation. These criteria serve as a basis for testing during software development. A formal requirements specification is written to define characteristics and attributes of the software. In addition, a *Preliminary User's Manual* is drafted.

It may seem odd that a user's manual is developed so early in the software engineering process. In fact, the draft-copy user manual forces the analyst (developer) to take a user's view of the software (particularly important in interactive systems). The manual encourages the user-requester to review the software from a human-engineering perspective and often elicits the comment: "The idea is OK, but this isn't the way I thought we'd do this." Better to uncover such comments early in the process!

Once the specification and the user's manual have been developed, review by the user-requester and developer is essential. The requirements review (discussed in Section 5.7) almost always results in modification. The impact of detailed requirements information on cost and schedule estimates (the *Software Plan*) is also reviewed. When necessary, estimates are modified to reflect new knowledge.

5.1.2 The Analyst

Entire textbooks have been dedicated to the role and duties of the *analyst*. Atwood [1] provides a workable job description: "The system analyst is expected to analyze and design systems of optimum performance. That is, the analyst must produce . . . an output that fully meets management objectives. . . ." The analyst is known by various aliases: *system analyst, system engineer, chief system designer, programmer-analyst,* and so on. Regardless of the job title, the analyst must exhibit the following character traits:

- The ability to grasp abstract concepts, reorganize into logical divisions, and synthesize solutions based on each division
- The ability to absorb pertinent facts from conflicting or confused sources
- The ability to understand the user-requester environments
- The ability to apply hardware and/or software system elements to the user-requester environments
- The ability to communicate well in written and verbal form
- The ability "to see the forest for the trees"

It is probably the last trait that separates truly outstanding analysts from the pack. Individuals who become mired in detail too early frequently lose sight of the overall software objective. Software requirements must be uncovered in a top-down manner—major functions, interfaces, and information must be fully understood before successive layers of detail are specified.

The analyst performs or coordinates each task associated with software requirements analysis (Section 5.1.1). During recognition tasks, he or she communicates with user-requester staff to ascertain characteristics of the existing environment. The analyst calls on development staff during evaluation and synthesis tasks so that characteristics of the software are correctly defined. The analyst is generally responsible for development of a *Software Requirements Specification* and participates in all reviews.

It is important to note that the analyst must also understand all phases of the software life cycle and appreciate the software engineering steps that are applied during later phases. Many implicit software requirements (e.g., design for main-

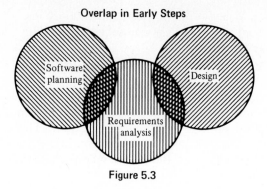

Overlap in Early Steps

Figure 5.3

tainability) are incorporated into a requirements specification only if the analyst understands the software life cycle.

5.2 ANALYSIS—A PROBLEM-SOLVING APPROACH

Like all steps in the software engineering process, there are no sharp boundaries that separate software planning, requirements analysis, and even design. To specify scope, the planner must determine top-level requirements. The analyst synthesizes solutions by beginning to design the software, and frequently the designer uncovers requirements that were missed during the specification task. Figure 5.3 illustrates the overlap among early software engineering steps.

In this section we concentrate on the evaluation and synthesis tasks that form the kernel of software requirements analysis. Once recognition is complete, the analyst must describe the software in a way that is amenable to evaluation.

5.2.1 Fundamental System Model

A computer-based system transforms information. The system accepts input in a variety of forms, applies system elements to transform input into output, and

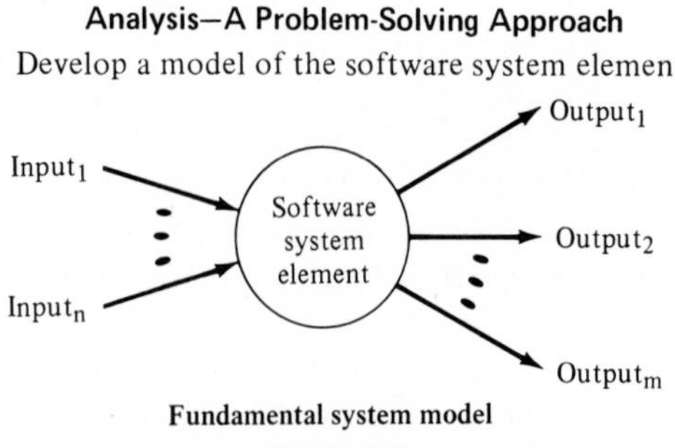

Analysis—A Problem-Solving Approach
● Develop a model of the software system element.

$Input_1$

$Input_n$

Software system element

$Output_1$

$Output_2$

$Output_m$

Fundamental system model

Figure 5.4

The Key—Information!

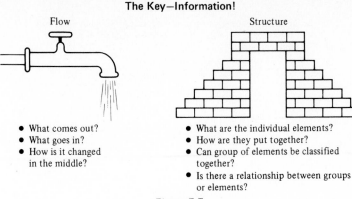

Flow

- What comes out?
- What goes in?
- How is it changed
  in the middle?

Structure

- What are the individual elements?
- How are they put together?
- Can group of elements be classified
  together?
- Is there a relationship between groups
  or elements?

Figure 5.5

produces output in various forms. Input may be a control signal transmitted by a transducer, a series of numbers typed by a human operator, a "packet" of information transmitted on a network link, or a voluminous data file retrieved from secondary storage. The transform(s) may comprise a single logical comparison, a complex numerical algorithm, or a combinatorial state-space search. Output may light a single light-emitting diode (LED) or produce a 200-page report. In effect, the model can be applied to any computer-based system regardless of size and complexity.

One technique for representing a *fundamental system model* is illustrated in Figure 5.4. The overall function of the system is represented as a single *information transform,* noted as a "bubble" in the figure. One or more inputs, shown as labeled arrows, drive the information transform to produce output information. It should be noted that the model may be applied to the entire system or to the software element only. The key is to represent the information fed into and produced by the software.

Successful analysis always considers the nature of information in a system. In the following sections we discuss techniques for representing both information *flow* and *structure* (Figure 5.5).

5.3 INFORMATION FLOW

As information moves through software, it is modified by a series of transformations. A *data flow diagram* is a graphical technique that depicts information flow and the transforms that are applied as data move from input to output. The basic form of a data flow diagram is illustrated in Figure 5.6. The diagram is similar in form to other activity flow diagrams (e.g., production flow diagrams [2]) and has been incorporated into analysis and design techniques proposed by Yourdon and

Information Flow

... As information moves through software, it is modified by a series of transformations. ... A *data flow diagram* is a graphical technique for representing flow. ...

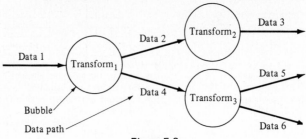

Figure 5.6

Constantine [3] and DeMarco [4]. It is also known as a *data flow graph* or a *bubble chart*.

A fundamental system model may be represented as a data flow diagram. The entire software element is depicted as a single bubble with input and ouput data indicated by incoming and outgoing arrows, respectively. In general, the fundamental model is refined into a series of bubbles, each representing a transform that occurs along the information flow path(s) from input to output.

As a simple example of a data flow diagram, consider information flow for a typical telephone call (Figure 5.7). Referring to the figure, we see that two input flow paths may be represented—the keyed phone number and the speaker's voice. The human motion to depress a key (bottom) is transformed by the keypad and associated electronic components into a series of frequencies (tones). The frequencies flow to a switching system that performs requisite routing and establishes a link from sender to receiver. The human voice is transformed by a vibration transducer that produces a signal as output. The switching system moves the voice signal to a receiver that transforms it back to sound.

Although the above example is a gross oversimplification, the flow of infor-

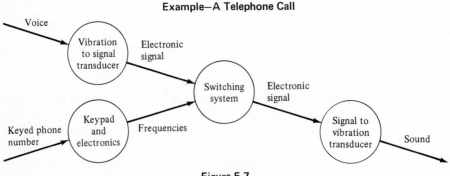

Figure 5.7

mation, represented by the data flow diagram, is easy to discern. Each transform in the diagram (the bubbles) could be refined still further to provide greater detail about keypad processing, transducers, or the switching system. That is, the diagram may be *layered* to show any desired level of detail.

It is important to note that no explicit indication of the sequence of events (e.g., is phone number keyed before or after voice input?) is supplied by the diagram. Procedure or sequence may be implicit in the diagram, but explicit procedural representation is generally delayed until software design.

5.3.1 Data Flow Diagram

The data flow diagram has three attributes that are important to note:

- Information flow in any system—manual, automated, or hybrid—can be represented.
- Each bubble may require significant refinement to establish complete understanding.
- Flow of data, rather than flow of control, is emphasized.

The graphical tools used to depict the data flow diagram are quite simple. Information (i.e., data flow) is represented by a labeled arrow. Processes (transformations) are represented by appropriately labeled bubbles. Information *sources* and *sinks* are noted as labeled boxes, and stored information (e.g., a data file) is represented by a double horizontal line. An information source is a location where data originates (e.g., a human, a transducer, or a machine). An information sink is the final destination of data as it moves through the system.

A data flow diagram using all the above graphical characteristics is shown in Figure 5.8. In the example, a travel agent (the information source) provides data to an airline travel system, depicted by the three transforms (bubbles) shown.

An Example

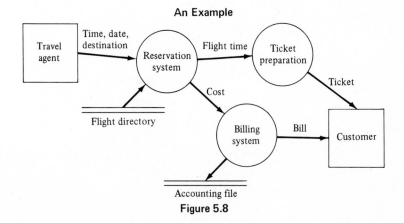

Figure 5.8

Travel data (time, date, and destination arrow) are transformed to a ticket and bill that flow to the customer (an information sink). Stored data (flight directory and accounting file) provide other information flow paths.

As we noted earlier, each bubble may be refined or layered to depict more detail. Figure 5.9 illustrates this concept. A fundamental model for system **F** indicates that the primary input is A and the ultimate output is B. We refine the **F** model into transforms f_1 to f_7. Note that *information continuity* must be maintained, that is, input and output to the refinement must remain the same. Further refinement of f_4 depicts detail in the form of transforms f_{41} to f_{45}. Again, the input (X, Y) and output (Z) remain unchanged.

5.3.2 A Detailed Example

As a further illustration of the use of data flow diagrams, we consider information flow for a "patient-monitoring system" (PMS) to be installed in a hospital. A PMS, illustrated with a fundamental system model in Figure 5.10, monitors vital signs of all patients in a ward, maintains records by updating a patient log, notifies nursing staff if anything goes awry, and produces a patient report on request.

Conducting requirements analysis for the system, we can refine information flow as shown in Figure 5.11. The fundamental model has been refined to show four major functions: local monitoring performed by a bedside monitor; central monitoring performed at the nurse's station; patient log update; and generation of reports at the nurse's station. Information sources and sinks remain unchanged. The nurse becomes both a source and a sink for information. The patient log file has been refined to depict new data flow among transforms (functions). An internal file, "patient bounds," is shown and used to indicate safe bounds (limits) for vital signs. Even without a supporting narrative, a reader of the PMS data flow diagram can discern the overall operation of the system.

Information Flow Refinement

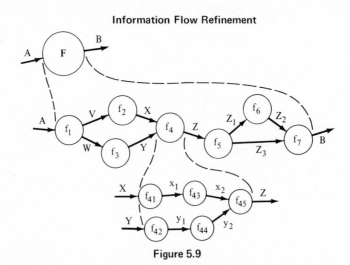

Figure 5.9

An Example—PMS

... A distributed, microprocessor based *patient monitoring system* is to be developed for a hospital ....

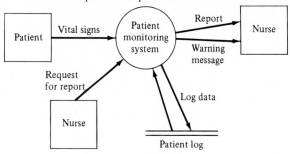

Figure 5.10

PMS data flow is further refined in Figure 5.12. The central monitoring bubble shown in Figure 5.11 has been refined to indicate greater detail. Note that continuity of information remains unchanged; that is, all incoming and outgoing arrows in the original central monitoring bubble (and all relevant files) appear in the refined data flow diagram. Refinement does, however, indicate an internal clock that supplies date and time information used as part of patient record keeping. Examining Figure 5.12, we see that a patient's vital signs are "unpacked" and compared with bounding values for vital signs. Bounds violation results in a warning message. In all cases patient data are combined with clock data for log update preparation.

Figures 5.10, 5.11, and 5.12 depict three distinct layers of information flow.

Refining the Model

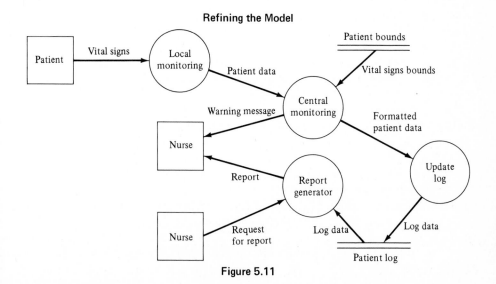

Figure 5.11

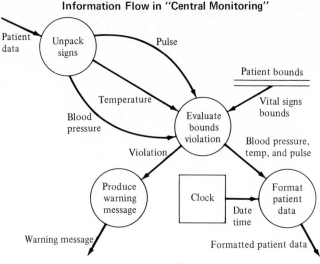

Figure 5.12

Each layer indicates that progressively more detailed requirements analysis is being conducted.

5.3.3 Guidelines and Comments

The data flow diagram is a graphical tool that can be very valuable during software requirements analysis. However, the diagram can cause confusion if its function is confused with the flowchart. A data flow diagram depicts information flow *without explicit notation of control* (e.g., conditions or loops). It is not a flowchart with rounded edges!

A few simple guidelines can aid immeasurably during the derivation of software-oriented data flow: (1) the first data flow diagram layer should always be the *fundamental system model;* (2) primary input/output (I/O) files should be carefully noted; (3) all arrows and bubbles should be labeled (with meaningful names); (4) *information continuity* must be maintained; and (5) one bubble at a time should be refined. There is a natural tendency to overcomplicate the data flow diagram. This occurs when the analyst attempts to show control procedure in lieu of information flow.

During requirements analysis, the analyst may discover that certain aspects of the system "are subject to change" or "will be enhanced in the future" or are nebulously defined by the requester. Alternatively, an analyst may be working on existing software that is about to undergo modification. In either case the data flow diagram allows easy isolation of the *domain of change,* as shown in Figures 5.13 and 5.14. By clearly understanding the flow of information across the domain of change boundary, better preparation can be made for future modification, or

Data Flow Diagrams (DFDs) for Existing Systems

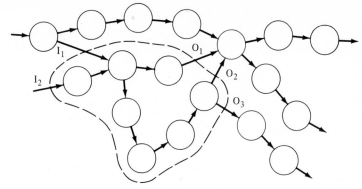

Identify the "domain of change"
Figure 5.13

Re-Model

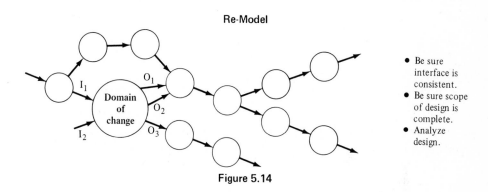

Figure 5.14

current modification can be conducted without upsetting other elements of the system.

5.4 INFORMATION STRUCTURE

Information structure is a representation of the logical relationship among individual elements of data. Because the structure of information will invariably affect the final design of software, a consideration of information structure is essential for successful software requirements analysis.

Data structure dictates the organization, methods of access, degree of associativity, and processing alternatives for information. Entire texts [e.g., 5, 6] have been dedicated to these topics, and a complete discussion is beyond the scope of this book. However, it is important to understand the classic methods available for organizing information and the concepts that underlie information hierarchies.

5.4.1 Classic Data Structures

The organization and complexity of a data structure are limited only by the ingenuity of the designer. There are, however, a limited number of classic data structures that form the building blocks for more sophisticated structures. These classic data structures are illustrated in Figure 5.15.

A *scalar item* is the simplest of all data structures. As its name implies, a scalar item represents a single element of information that may be addressed by an identifier; that is, access may be achieved by specifying a single address in storage. The size and format of a scalar item may vary within bounds that are dictated by a programming language. For example, a scalar item may be a logical entity 1 bit long, an integer or real number that is 8 to 64 bits long, or a character string that is hundreds or thousands of bits long.

When scalar items are organized as a list or contiguous group, a *sequential vector* is formed. Vectors are the most common of all data structures and open the door to variable indexing of information. To illustrate, we consider a simple FORTRAN example:

```
DIMENSION VECTOR (50)
   DO 10 I = 1, 50
     N = 50−(I−1)
     VECTOR(I)=VECTOR(I)+VECTOR(N)
10 CONTINUE
```

In the above example a sequential vector of 50 scalar elements, VECTOR(50), is defined. Access to each element may be *indexed* [e.g., VECTOR(I)] so that elements of the data structure are referenced in a defined order.

When the sequential vector is extended to two, three, and ultimately, an arbitrary number of dimensions, an *n-dimensional space* is created. The most common *n*-dimensional space is the two-dimensional matrix. In most programming languages, an *n*-dimensional space is called an *array*.

Items, vectors, and spaces may be organized in a variety of formats. A *linked list* is a data structure that organizes noncontiguous scalar items, vectors, or spaces in a manner (called *nodes*) that enables them to be processed as a list. Each node contains the appropriate data organization (e.g., a vector) and one or more pointers that indicate the address in storage of the next node in the list. Nodes may be added at any point in the list by redefining pointers to accomodate the new list entry.

Other data structures incorporate or are constructed by using the fundamental data structures described above. For example, a *hierarchical data structure* is implemented by using multilinked lists that contain scalar items, vectors, and, possibly, *n*-dimensional spaces. A hierarchical structure is commonly encountered in applications that require information categorization and associativity. The term "categorization" implies a grouping of information by some generic category (e.g., all subcompact automobiles manufactured in the United States or all 8-bit micro-

Classic Data Structures

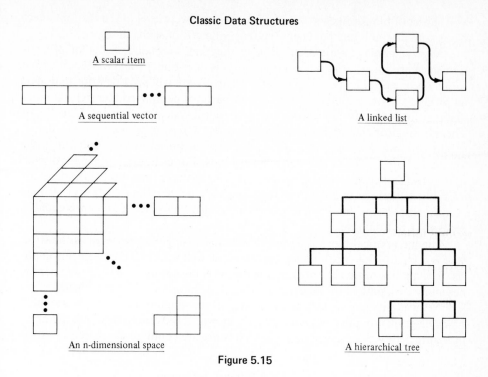

Figure 5.15

processors with S-100 bus capability). The term "associativity" implies the ability to associate information from different categories, such as to find all entries in the microprocessor category that cost less than $100.00 (cost subcategory), run at 4 MHz (cycle time subcategory), and are made by U.S. vendors (vendor subcategory).

5.4.2 Data Structure Representation

During software requirements analysis, a hierarchical information structure is often encountered. Because this information structure can have a significant impact on software design requirements, the analyst must represent the hierarchy in a readable, unambiguous manner. Two methods for representation of hierarchical data structures, the *hierarchical block diagram* and the *Warnier diagram,* are discussed in this section. It is interesting to note that these diagrammatic forms may be used to represent both data and software.

Hierarchical block diagram. The hierarchical block diagram depicts information as a series of multilevel blocks organized as a tree structure. At the top level of the structure, a single block is used to represent the entire hierarchy. Succeeding levels contain blocks that represent various categories of information that may be viewed as a subset of blocks further up the tree. At the lowest level in the diagram, each block contains individual data entities (e.g., numeric or string data).

As an example of a hierarchical block diagram, we shall consider an information structure for a computer company that is developing software requirements for an on-line product retrieval system. The software will provide information on all products marketed by the company. A partially completed hierarchical block diagram for information required by the retrieval system is shown in Figure 5.16. The information hierarchy is represented by a *vendor products* block that is subdivided into *hardware, software,* and *service* categories. These three categories are further subdivided as the hierarchy expands. For example, software is divided into *system* and *applications* categories. Moving to the bottom level of the diagram, each block represents an information quantity (rather than category). Codes, model numbers, availability dates, costs, and other "hard" data are represented by blocks at a bottom level.

The hierarchical block diagram depicts increasingly more detail as the structure is refined. This mode of representation is well suited to requirements analysis. The analyst begins by categorizing top-level information. Refinement continues along each path in the diagram until all information detail is established.

Associativity among information categories and quantities of the hierarchical block diagram is implied but not explicitly shown. If the vendor products hierarchy in Figure 5.16 was properly implemented, software could be developed to satisfy

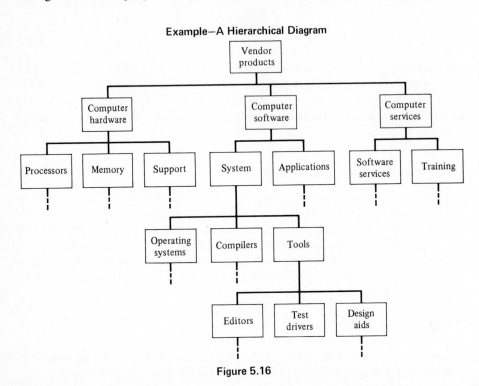

Example—A Hierarchical Diagram

Figure 5.16

Example—A Warnier Diagram

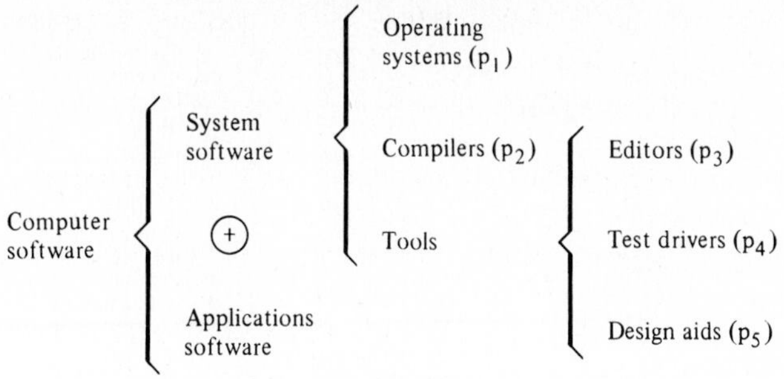

Figure 5.17

association requests like: Obtain model numbers for all processors with a delivery availability of less than 60 days or determine processor *xxxx* compatible system software cost.

However, the technical means by which the above requests would be satisfied are not indicated. The block diagram provides little information about the physical characteristics of the data structure. File and record indicators, data format, and internal attributes are not specified. A detailed model of the data structure is normally developed as part of software design.

Warnier diagram. The Warnier diagram [7] is an alternative approach for representing an information hierarchy. Like the hierarchical block diagram, the Warnier approach depicts information as a treelike data structure (tilted on its side). However, the Warnier approach also provides additional descriptive features.

The *logical organization* of information may be indicated with a Warnier diagram. That is, the repetitive nature of a specific information category or quantity may be specified. Conditional occurrences of information within a category may be shown. Because repetitive and conditional constraints are cornerstones to the specification of software procedure, the Warnier diagram can be converted to a software design description with little difficulty.

Figure 5.17 illustrates the use of a Warnier diagram. The figure depicts the software category of the computer products example discussed earlier. In the diagram a brace ({) is used to differentiate levels of the information hierarchy. All names contained within a brace correspond to information categories or quantities. The *exclusive-or* symbol ($\oplus$) indicates conditional occurrence of a category or quantity, and notation in parentheses under or next to a name indicates the number of times (repetitions) it occurs in the structure.

Given the above conventions for notation, the Warnier diagram in Figure 5.17 can be read in the following way: A software product entry consists of information about system software and applications software. There are p_1 operating systems, p_2 compilers, and a software tools subcategory. The braces following "tools" on the diagram contain further refinement for editors, test drivers, and design aids.

Output Data Structure

During requirement analysis, the following
report is requested as output:

AJAX PUMP COMPANY FOR FISCAL YEAR 1977

JULY	SALES	PROFIT
DIVISION I		
SECTION A	213.11	76.90
SECTION B	378.33	127.21
•	•	•
•	•	•
TOTAL FOR DIVISION I	1,265.66	432.93
DIVISION II		
•	•	•
•	•	•
TOTAL FOR JULY	3,811.93	1,409.30
AUGUST	SALES	PROFIT
•	•	•
•	•	•
GRAND TOTAL	36,217.98	9,182.17

*(Source: D.A. Higgins, Program Design and
Construction, Prentice-Hall, 1975.)*

(a)

Logical Output Structure

LIST OF DATA ELEMENTS
fiscal year number
month name
"SALES"
"PROFIT"
division name
section name
section sales
section profit
"TOTAL FOR"
division name
division total sales
division total profit
"TOTAL FOR"
month name
monthly total sales
monthly total profit
"GRAND TOTAL"
grand total sales
grand total profit

REPORT HIERARCHY–WARNIER DIAGRAM

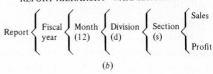

(b)

Warnier Representation

Financial Report {
    Fiscal Year {
        "AJAX PUMP COMPANY"
        "FOR FISCAL YEAR"
        fiscal year number
        Month (12) {
            month name
            "SALES" "PROFIT"
            Division (1, d) {
                division name
                Section (1, s) {
                    section name
                    section sales
                    section profit
                }
                "TOTAL FOR"
                division name
                division total sales
                division total profit
            }
            "TOTAL FOR"
            month name
            monthly total sales
            monthly total profit
        }
        "GRAND TOTAL"
        grand total sales
        grand total profit
    }
}

(c)

*(Source: D. A. Higgins, Program Design and Construction, © 1979, reprinted by permission of Prentice-Hall, Inc.
Englewood Cliffs, N.J.)*

Figure 5.18

In his text on program design, Higgins [8] presents a useful example of the Warnier diagram applied to an output financial report format for a mythical Ajax Pump Company. The required report data elements, and Warnier diagram are shown in Figure 5.18*a, b, c*. Figure 5.19 extrapolates the Warnier representation to a proposed physical record format that can be used to build an information file.

5.5 DATABASE REQUIREMENTS

Requirements analysis for a database incorporates tasks that are identical to software requirements analysis. Extensive contact with the user-requester is necessary; identification of functions and interfaces is essential; specification of information flow, structure, and associativity is required; and a formal requirements document must be developed.

A complete discussion of database analysis is beyond the scope of this book. Excellent texts by Martin [9], Wiederhold [10], or Cardenas [11] will provide the reader with a good foundation. Our goal in this section is to provide an overview of topics to be considered when a software development project includes requirements for a database.

5.5.1 Database Characteristics

The term "database" has become one of many catchwords in the computing field. Although many elegant definitions exist, we shall define a database as *a collection of information organized in a way that facilitates access, analysis, and reporting.*

A database contains information entities that are related through organization and association. The logical architecture of a database is defined by a *schema* that represents definitions of relationships among information entities. The physical

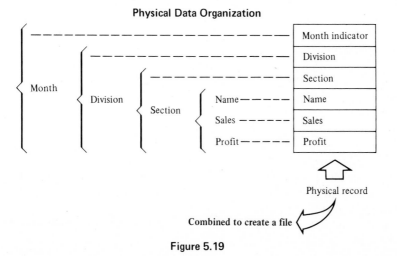

Figure 5.19

architecture of a database depends on the host hardware configuration. However, both schema (logical description) and organization (physical description) must be tuned to satisfy functional and performance requirements for access, analysis, and reporting.

A large number of database management systems (DBMS) are available for purchase. Although no industry standard exists, the CODASYL DTBG 1971 report [12] may eventually become a basis for some future standard for DBMS.

5.5.2 Analysis Steps

The flow of events for database analysis is illustrated in Figure 5.20. Before an evaluation of database requirements can commence, the analyst must understand the global objectives and scope of the system for which the database is to be developed. A complete and highly refined *information model* is then developed.

The information model includes information structure diagrams (discussed in Section 5.4) and a comprehensive *data dictionary*. The data dictionary defines all information quantities in terms of information that is used to develop the quantity. For example, profit (a dollar quantity) could be defined by using other derived quantities:

Profit = (sales + other income) − (operating expense + debt service + taxes)

The next steps in database analysis define the logical and physical characteristics of the database. With the information model and system specification as a guide, the analyst, working in conjunction with a database designer, defines a logical data organization. The *logical organization* must accommodate requirements for data access, modification, associativity, and other system-oriented concerns. Once the logical data organization is established, *physical organization* may be developed (Figure 15.20b). The physical database organization defines file structure, record formats, hardware dependent processing features, and database management system characteristics. Finally, a complete review of the schema and physical characteristics is conducted.

A series of complex interrelationships exist among the factors that are considered during database analysis. Referring to Figure 5.21, we see that no single factor can be changed without potential impact on other factors. The trade-offs that can impact the final database design include specialization versus generalization, degree of associativity, potential for expansion, and operational characteristics.

The degree of information associativity and the potential for expansion (of both size and information content) are actually elements of a broader issue—the degree of specialization assigned to the database during requirements analysis and design. A specialized database addresses specific information requirements for a system. The information structure is designed to accommodate required associativity and predicted expansion. A generalized database is amenable to a broader

Database Analysis—I

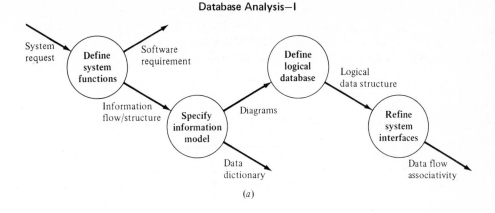

(a)

Database Analysis—II

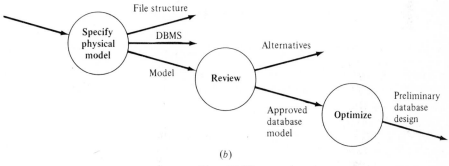

(b)

Figure 5.20

class of information requirements. However, generality is achieved at the expense of more software processing at the information interface, more overhead associated with adaptability to a broader range of problems, and greater internal complexity in data structure organization.

Operational characteristics follow from the preceding trade-offs. Database structure, size, and logical design can have a significant impact on physical organization, hardware, access methods, and performance. The impact of these and other characteristics on organization, hardware, and software is summarized in Figure 5.22.

5.5.3 An Analysis Tool

A number of tools are available for use during database analysis. In this section we present a brief overview on one such tool—the *transaction matrix*.

Analysis Considerations

... A series of complex interrelationships exist among
database organization, hardware implementation,
and database software ...

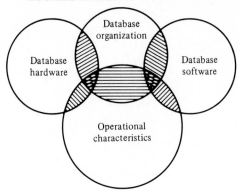

Figure 5.21

The *transaction matrix* is used to identify all requests for database access
(transactions) and relate each request to information categories or quantities
(elements) within the database. In effect, the transaction matrix helps the analyst
to answer questions such as:

- What combinations of data elements are required for each major transaction?
- What combination of data should be grouped within the same physical record/
  block?
- Can transactions be modified to:
  - Reduce frequency of access?

Interrelationships

	Organization	Hardware	Software
As sizes goes up	Structure must have low overhead	Multiple devices may be required	Performance of searches/ sorts/ compression is critical
As content becomes complex	Structure overhead increases	Performance becomes critical	Software becomes more complex
If cost must be minimal	Organization must be simple	Single device should be used	Acquire a simple DBMS
If performance is critical	Organization should be tailored to application	High speed devices are essential	Custom DBMS should be acquired; designed

Figure 5.22

Refining the Database Model

... Identify all major transactions and determine their
relationship to data elements ...
... A transaction is any event that requires database
information to be accessed ...

Transaction Matrix

Characteristic	Transactions
Type	On-line, batch, software originated, human source
Frequency	Number of transactions/month
Use	Read, modify, add, delete
Data element list	Relationship to each transaction

Figure 5.23

- Eliminate redundant requests for information?
- Improve projected performance?

The transaction matrix takes the form illustrated in Figure 5.23. Each transaction is characterized by type, frequency of access, and use (read, modify, add,
and delete). Data elements that are required for each transaction are noted in the
bottom half of the table.

To illustrate the use of a transaction matrix, we recall the Acme Pump
Company example, presented in Section 5.4.2 (Figure 5.18*a, b, c*). Asssuming that
the Warnier diagram in Figure 5.18*c* describes a simple database, five transactions,
T_1 through T_5, can be defined as shown in Figure 5.24. Based on these transactions,
a matrix (Figure 5.25) is created. Referring to the figure, each transaction is
characterized by type (e.g., batch, O/L (on-line)), frequency of access, and use.
Characteristic data elements are listed in the lower part of the matrix. The
relationship of each element to each transaction is also shown. By examining the
lower right-hand quadrant of the matrix, the analyst may be able to organize
information in a way that optimizes transaction processing.

Recall the ACME Pump Company

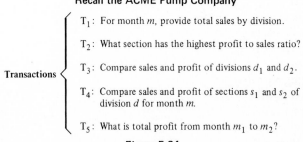

Transactions

T_1: For month m, provide total sales by division.

T_2: What section has the highest profit to sales ratio?

T_3: Compare sales and profit of divisions d_1 and d_2.

T_4: Compare sales and profit of sections s_1 and s_2 of
division d for month m.

T_5: What is total profit from month m_1 to m_2?

Figure 5.24

Transaction Matrix

Characteristic	T_1	T_2	T_3	T_4	T_5
Type	batch	on-line	on-line	on-line	batch
Frequency	4	300	4000	2000	20
Use	R	R	R	R	R
Month indicator	RK				RK
Division	RK		RK	RK	
Section		RK		RK	
Name					
Sales	R	R	R	R	
Profit		R	R	R	R

R = read; K = data element used as a "key."

Figure 5.25

5.6 SOFTWARE REQUIREMENTS SPECIFICATION

The deliverable that is developed as part of requirements analysis is the *Software Requirements Specification*. The specification extends scope (identified in the *Software Plan*) by establishing a complete information description, a detailed functional description, appropriate validation criteria, and other data pertinent to requirements. The following outline may be used as a framework for the specification.

SOFTWARE REQUIREMENTS SPECIFICATION

1. Introduction
2. Information Description
   a. data flow diagrams
   b. data structure representation
   c. data dictionary
   d. system interface description
   e. internal interfaces
3. Functional Description
   a. functions
   b. processing narrative
   c. design contraints
4. Validation Criteria
   a. performance bounds
   b. classes of tests

c. expected software response
d. special considerations
5. Bibliography
6. Appendix

The *Introduction* states the goals and objectives of the software, describing it in the context of the computer-based system. Actually, the Introduction may be nothing more than the software scope of the planning document.

The *Information Description* provides a detailed description of the problem that the software must solve. Both information flow and structure are documented. Hardware, software, and human interfaces are described for external system elements and internal software functions.

The procedural details for each function required to solve the problem are described in the *Functional Description.* A processing narrative is provided for each function; design constraints are stated and justified, and one or more block diagrams are included to graphically represent the overall structure of the software and interplay among software functions and other system elements.

The fourth section of the *Software Requirements Specification* is probably the most important and, ironically, the most often neglected! Validation may be best explained by the following short fable:

A much-harried software development manager, D. O. Loop, is about to embark on a major project. Suddenly, an evil-looking gremlin appears on Loop's desk.

"I'll deliver the system you want, free of charge," sneers the gremlin.

"Great!" says Loop. "When can you have it for me?"

"Tomorrow," says the gremlin as he disappears.

Loop's enthusiasm dissipates rapidly. Can he trust the gremlin to deliver and, more importantly, how will he recognize a successful system if it is dropped on his desk tommorrow?

Mr. Loop's last question is the concern of the *Validation Criteria* section of the *Software Requirements Specification.* How do we recognize a successful implementation? What classes of tests must be conducted to validate function, performance, and constraints? We neglect this section because completing it demands a thorough understanding of software requirements—something that we seldom have.

The Validation Criteria section acts as an implicit review of information and functional requirements. It is essential that time and attention be given to this section. Considerations for an explicit specification review are discussed in the next section.

Finally, the *Software Requirements Specification* includes a bibliography and an appendix. The bibliography contains references to all documents that relate to the software. These include other planning-phase documentation, technical references, vendor literature, and standards. The appendix contains information that supplements the specification. Tabular data, detailed description of algorithms, charts, graphs, and other material are presented as appendices.

When requirements for human interactive software are developed, it is often useful to prepare a *Preliminary User's Manual* as a supplement to the requirements document. The user manual serves two purposes:

1. Preparation of the manual forces the analyst to view software from the user's perspective. Therefore, early consideration is given to human-engineering of the interface.
2. The user-requester can review an active document that describes the human-machine interface explicitly.

The *Preliminary User's Manual* presents the software as a *black box*. That is, heavy emphasis is placed on user input and resultant output. The manual can serve as a valuable tool for uncovering problems at the human-machine interface.

5.7 SPECIFICATION REVIEW

A review of the *Software Requirements Specification* is conducted by both software developer and user-requester. Because the specification forms the foundation of the development phase, extreme care should be taken in conducting the review.

The format of the review may best be understood by considering some of the questions that must be answered:

- Do stated goals and objectives for software remain consistent with system goals and objectives?
- Have important interfaces to all system elements been described?
- Are information flow and structure adequately defined for the problem domain?
- Are diagrams clear? Can each stand alone without supplementary text?
- Do major functions remain within scope? Has each been adequately described?
- Are design constraints realistic?
- What is the technological risk of development?
- Have alternative software requirements been considered?
- Have validation criteria been stated in detail? Are they adequate to describe a successful system?
- Do inconsistencies, omissions, or redundancy exist?
- Is the user-requester contact complete?
- Has the user reviewed the *Preliminary User's Manual?*
- How are the *Software Plan* estimates affected?

Once the review is complete, the *Software Requirements Specification* is "signed-off" by both user-requester and developer. The specification becomes a "contract" for software development. Changes in requirements requested after the specification is finalized may still occur. But the user-requester should note that each after-the-fact change is an extension of software scope and thus can increase cost and/or protract the schedule.

Even with the best review procedures in place, a number of common specification problems persist. The specification is difficult to "test" in any meaningful way; therefore, inconsistencies or omissions may pass unnoticed. During the review, changes to the specification may be recommended. It is extremely difficult to assess the global impact of a change; that is, how does a change in one function affect requirements for other functions? *Automated specification tools* have been developed to help solve these problems.

5.8 REQUIREMENTS ANALYSIS TOOLS

Requirements analysis tools have been developed to provide a set of procedures that guide an analyst through requirements specification. In this section we consider examples of two classes of tools—predominantly manual and predominantly automated.

Predominantly manual tools provide the analyst with a well-defined technique (usually accompanied by some mode of graphical representation) that enables the requirements analysis task to be performed systematically. Although the technique may be supported by one or more automated aids, analysis and specification are effected manually. Structured analysis and design technique (SADT—a trademark of Softech, Inc.), is a representative tool in this category and is discussed in Section 5.8.1.

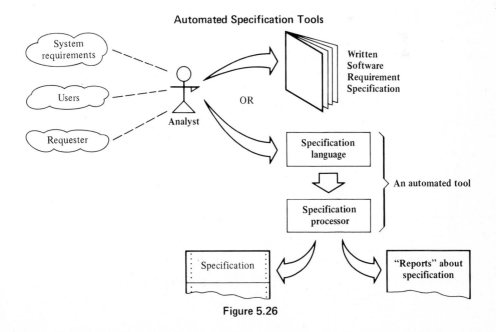

Figure 5.26

Predominantly automated tools provide the analyst with an option, illustrated in Figure 5.26. Requirements can be described with a specification language that combines keyword indicators with a natural language (e.g., English) narrative. The specification language is fed to a processor that produces a requirements specification and, more importantly, a set of diagnostic reports about the consistency and organization of the specification. Software requirements engineering methodolgy (SREM) and problem statement language/problem statement analyzer (PSL/PSA) are representative automated tools and are discussed in Section 5.8.2.

5.8.1 SADT

SADT (a trademark of Softech, Inc.) is a system analysis and design technique that has been widely used as a tool for system definition, software requirements analysis, and system and software design [13]. It consists of methods that allow the analyst to decompose software (or system) functions; a graphical notation, the SADT *actigram,* which communicates the relationships of information to function within software; and project control guidelines for applying the methodology.

Using SADT, the analyst develops a *model* comprised of many hierarchically defined actigrams. A simple actigram of the early steps in the planning phase of the software life cycle is illustrated in Figure 5.27 [14]. Each box within the actigram can be further refined in much the same way that a data flow diagram undergoes refinement.

The SADT methodology encompasses technical tools and a well-defined organizational harness through which the tools are applied. Reviews and milestones are specified, allowing validation of developer-requester communication.

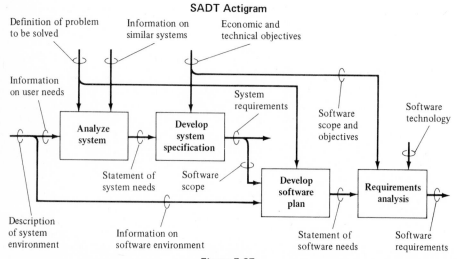

Figure 5.27

Staff responsibilities are similar to those found on the chief programmer team (Chapter 4), stressing a team approach to analysis, design, and review.

5.8.2 Automated Tools

A number of automated tools for requirements specification have been proposed over the past decade. An automated approach has been precipitated by the difficulty that is encountered in validating the consistency and completeness of manually described systems. Automated requirements tools, like the ones discussed below, are in their infancy. As automated systems mature, they may become an important supplemental tool for all analysts.

SREM. SREM [15] is an automated requirements analysis tool that makes use of a *requirements statement language* (RSL) to describe "elements, attributes, relationships, and structures." *Elements* (in SREM terminology) comprise the set of objects and concepts that are used to develop a requirements specification. *Relationships* between objects are specified as part of RSL, and *attributes* are used to modify or qualify elements. *Structures* are used to describe information flow. These RSL primitives are combined with narrative information to form the detail of a requirements specification.

The power of an automated requirements tool may be measured by the support software that has been developed to analyze the specification. SREM applies a *requirements engineering and validation system* (REVS). REVS software uses a combination of reports and computer graphics to study information flow, determine consistency in the use of information throughout the system, and simulate dynamic interrelationships among elements.

Like SADT (Section 5.8.1), SREM incorporates a set of procedures that guide the analyst through the requirements step. These procedures include:

1. *Translation.* An activity that transforms initial software requirements described in a system specification into a more detailed set of data descriptions and processing steps.
2. *Decomposition.* An activity that evaluates information at the interface to the software element and results in a complete set of computational (functional) requirements.
3. *Allocation.* An activity that considers alternative approaches to the requirements that have been established; trade-off studies and sensitivity analyses are conducted.
4. *Analytical feasibility demonstration.* An activity that attempts to simulate critical processing requirements to determine feasibility.

RSL is used heavily in the first two procedures, and REVS is used to accomplish procedures 3 and 4.

SREM was initially developed for embedded computer systems. As described in Chapter 1, an embedded system is integrated directly into a larger product or

PSL Source Listing

PSA Version A4.2R1   78.278   13.44.26
UNIVERSITY OF SASKATCHEWAN

Input Source Listing

Parameters: DB=PSADB.DBF   INPUT=* SOURCE-LISTING NOCROSS-REFERENCE   UPDATE
DATA-BASE-REFERENCE

```
LINE  S T M T                                                              ID FIELD

  1 >    /*  This top-down PSL program describes the following aspect of
  2 >         the example payroll processing system:
  3 >
  4 >                  Data Structure
  5 >
  6 >
  7 > INPUT employee-information;
  8 >    CONSISTS OF operation-code, required-information;
  9 >
 10 > ELEMENT operation-code;
 11 >    VALUES ARE 1 THRU 3;
 12 >
 13 > GROUP required-information;
 14 >
 15 > INPUT time-cards;
 16 >    CONSISTS OF a-time-card;
 17 >
 18 > GROUP a-time-card;
 19 >    CONSISTS OF employee-number, regular-hours, overtime-hours;
 20 >
 21 > OUTPUT cheque;
 22 >    CONSISTS OF employee-name, net-pay, deduction-stub;
 23 >
 24 > GROUP employee-name;
 25 >    CONSISTS OF last-name, initials;
 26 >
 27 > GROUP deduction-stub;
 28 >    CONSISTS OF gross-pay, income-tax, unemployment-insurance,
 29 >                canada-pension, union-dues, net-pay;
 30 >
 31 > SET old-master-file, new-master-file;
 32 >    CONSISTS OF number-of-employees master-file-record;
 33 >    SUBSETTING-CRITERIA ARE province;
 34 >
 35 > ENTITY master-file-record;
 36 >    CONSISTS OF record-key, employee-number, employee-name,
 37 >               hourly-wage, tax-code;
 38 >    IDENTIFIED BY record-key;
 39 >
 40 > ELEMENT hourly-wage;
 41 >    VALUES ARE 5 THRU 20;
 42 >
 43 > ELEMENT employee-number, last-name, initials, tax-code,
 44 >         regular-hours, overtime-hours, gross-pay, income-tax,
 45 >         unemployment-insurance, canada-pension, union-dues,
 46 >         net-pay, record-key, province;
 47 >
 48 > EOF
```

(Source: PSL/PSA Primer, ISDOS Project, University of Michigan, reproduced with permission.)

Figure 5.28

system (in this case, a missile defense system). SREM also provides techniques for the specification of a real-time environment.

PSL/PSA. PSL/PSA was developed by the ISDOS project [16] at the University of Michigan and is part of a larger system called the *computer-aided design and specification analysis tool* (CADSAT). PSL/PSA provides an analyst with capabilities that include (1) description of information systems, regardless of application area, (2) creation of a database containing descriptors for the information system, (3) addition, deletion, and modification of descriptors, and (4) production of formated documentation and various reports on the specification.

PSA Report

PSA Version A4.2R1   7E.272   15.12.05

UNIVERSITY OF SASKATCHEWAN

Data Base Summary

Parameters: DB=PSADB.DBF   PERCENT   SYNONYM   DESCRIPTION   NORESPONSIBLE-PPOPLEM-DEFINER
NOSOURCE   NOSECURITY   NOKEYWORD   NOATTRIBUTE

NAME TYPE	COUNT	NUMBER WITH SYNONYM	PERCENT WITH SYNONYM	NUMBER WITH DESC	PERCENT WITH DESC
ATTRIBUTE	3	0		0	
ATTRIBUTE-VALUE	2	0		0	
CONDITION	1	0		1	100.00
ELEMENT	16	0		2	12.50
ENTITY	1	0		0	
EVENT	3	0		8	
GROUP	4	0		1	25.00
INPUT	2	0		0	
INTERFACE	2	0		2	100.00
INTERVAL	2	0		0	
KEYWORD	1	0		0	
OUTPUT	1	0		0	
PROCESS	4	1	25.00	1	25.00
SET	7	0		1	14.29
SYSTEM-PARAMETER	3	0		0	
** TOTAL **	52	1	1.92	8	15.38

(Source: PSL/PSA Primer, ISDOS Project, University of Michigan, reproduced with permission.)

Figure 5.29

The PSL model structure is developed with the use of *descriptors* for system information flow, system structure, data structure, data derivation, system size and volume, system dynamics, system properties, and project management. Figure 5.28 illustrates a typical PSL program [17].

Once a complete PSL description for the system is established, a *problem statement analyzer* (PSA) is invoked. The PSA produces a number of reports that include a record of all modifications made to the specification database, reference reports that present database information in varying formats (e.g., see Figures 5.29 and 5.30), summary reports that provide project management information, and analysis reports that evaluate characteristics of the database.

The automated approach provided by PSL/PSA (and other tools) is not a panacea, but it does provide benefits that include:

- Documentation quality is improved through standardization and reporting.
- Coordination among analysts is improved because the database is available to all.
- Gaps, omissions, and inconsistencies are more easily uncovered through cross-reference maps and reports.
- The impact of modifications can be more easily traced.
- Maintenance costs for the specification are reduced.

The CADSAT system is representative of current work and goals for automated tools like PSL/PSA and SREM. Requirements analysis tools will be coupled with design techniques and various other software tools to establish an all-encompassing software development system.

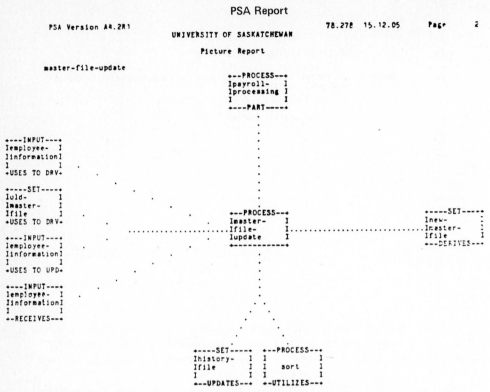

(Source: PSL/PSA Primer, ISDOS Project, University of Michigan, reproduced with permission.)

Figure 5.30

5.9 SUMMARY

Software requirements analysis is a crucial step in the planning phase of the software engineering process. It is at this point that a nebulous concept of software is translated into a concrete specification that is the foundation for software development.

Analysis tasks concentrate on a description of information, function, and performance. Each characteristic is refined by an analyst who acts as a consultant to the user-requester and a liaison to the software developer. Software characteristics are modeled by using tools like the data flow diagram for information flow, hierarchical or Warnier diagrams for information structure, transaction matrices for database evaluation, or PSL/PSA for an automated approach.

The *Software Requirements Specification* is the deliverable for this step. Review is an essential element of analysis. Unfortunately, even with the best of methods, the problem is that the problem keeps changing.

REFERENCES

1. Atwood, J. W., *The Systems Analyst,* Hayden, 1977.
2. Riggs, J., *Production Systems: Planning, Analysis and Control,* 3d ed., Wiley, 1981.
3. Yourdon, E., and L. Constantine, *Structured Design,* Prentice-Hall, 1979.
4. De Marco, T., *Structured Analysis and System Specification,* Prentice-Hall, 1979.
5. Tremblay, J. P., and P. G. Sorenson, *An Introduction to Data Structures with Applications,* McGraw-Hill, 1976.
6. Lewis, T., and M. Smith, *Applying Data Structures,* Houghton-Mifflin, 1976.
7. Warnier, J. D., *Logical Construction of Programs,* Van Nostrand, 1974.
8. Higgins, D. A., *Program Design and Construction,* Prentice-Hall, 1979.
9. Martin, J., *Principles of Data Base Management,* Prentice-Hall, 1976.
10. Wiederhold, G., *Database Design,* McGraw-Hill, 1977.
11. Cardenas, A. F., *Data Base Management Systems,* Allyn & Bacon, 1979.
12. CODASYL, "Data Base Task Group (DBTG) Report, 1971," ACM, New York, 1971.
13. Ross, D., and K. Schoman, "Structured Analysis for Requirements Definition," *IEEE Transactions on Software Engineering,* vol. 3, no. 1, January 1977, pp. 6–15.
14. Freeman, P., "Requirements Analysis and Specification," *Proceedings of the International Computer Technology Conference,* ASME, San Francisco, August 1980.
15. Davis, C., and C. Vick, "The Software Development System," *IEEE Transactions on Software Engineering,* vol. 3, no. 1, January 1977, pp. 69–84.
16. Teichroew, D., and E. Hershey, "PSL/PSA: A Computer Aided Technique for Structured Documentation and Analysis of Information Processing Systems," *IEEE Transactions on Software Engineering,* vol. 3, no. 1, 1977, pp. 41–48.
17. Wig, E. D., *PSL/PSA Primer* (version A.4.2), University of Michigan, 1978.

PROBLEMS AND POINTS TO PONDER

5-1 Software requirements analysis is unquestionably the most communication intensive step in the software engineering process. Why does the communication path frequently break down?

5-2 There are frequently severe political repercussions when software requirements analysis (and/or system analysis) begins. For example, workers may feel that job security is threatened by a new automated system. What causes such problems? Can the analysis task be conducted so that politics is minimized?

5-3 Discuss your perceptions of the ideal training and background for a systems analyst.

5-4 Draw a fundamental system model for five systems with which you are familiar. The systems need not be computer-based. Using a few paragraphs for each system, describe input, processing, and output for each system.

5-5 Using the systems described in Problem 5-4, refine each into three to seven major functions (transforms) and develop a data flow diagram for each. Remember to specify all information flow by labeling all arrows between bubbles. Use meaningful names for each transform.

5-6 Select a computer-based system with which you are familiar. Develop a detailed set of data flow diagrams for the system, beginning with the fundamental system model and ending with detailed representations of all functions. Sources, sinks, and all information files should be shown.

5-7 Discuss the difference between information flow and information structure. Are there systems in which there is no information flow? Are there systems in which there is no information structure?

5-8 Complete the data flow diagrams for the PMS described in Section 5.3.2. Make appropriate assumptions about the system. Also, represent the information structure for PMS, using a hierarchical diagram or a Warnier diagram.

5-9 Write a paper surveying the topic of data structures. Survey the classic algorithms that are applied to data structures as well as the structures themselves.

5-10 Present a tutorial on requirements analysis techniques for database systems. Use references provided at the end of this chapter and other sources as appropriate.

5-11 Select a database with which you are familiar (or a description of a database provided by your instructor). Develop a transaction matrix for the major information elements of the database.

5-12 Referring to the *Software Requirements Specification* outline presented in Section 5.6, discuss each entry in the outline in some detail. Determine a concensus with regard to the contents and format of each section. Do you feel that some sections are unnecessary or that additional information should be added?

5-13 Software for a microprocessor-based word processing system is to be developed. The system will make use of a full screen editing format. Do a few hours of research on the application area and develop a list of questions that you, as an analyst, would ask a requester. Attempt to structure your questions so that major topics are addressed in a rational sequence.

5-14 Software for a real-time test monitoring system for gas turbine engines is to be developed. Proceed as in Problem 5-13.

5-15 Software for a manufacturing control system for an automobile assembly plant is to be developed. Proceed as in Problem 5-13.

5-16 Software for a new operating system to support a 32-bit microcomputer for multiuser, interactive applications is to be developed. Proceed as in Problem 5-13.

5-17 Assuming a reasonable set of answers to the questions posed in Problems 5-13 through 5-16 or using a functional definition provided by your instructor, develop a set of validation criteria for the system you have chosen.

5-18 Write a paper on the latest progress in the area of automated requirements analysis tools. Use recent conference proceedings and journal articles or papers as your primary source of information.

5-19 Some people advocate building of a software prototype in lieu of developing a *Software Requirements Specification.* Discuss the positive and negative aspects of this idea.

FURTHER READINGS

De Marco's text [4] on system analysis is probably the best exposition of the information flow-oriented approach. In addition, the author presents useful chapters on data dictionary techniques, process specification, and system modeling. A recent text by Millington [*Systems Analysis and Design for Computer Applications,* Halsted (Wiley), 1981] describes a systems analysis technique developed by the National Computing Centre in Great Britain.

A number of excellent IEEE Computer Society publications address various issues related to software requirements analysis:

Miller, E., *Automated Tools for Software Engineering,* IEEE Computer Society Press, 1979.
Reifer, D., *Software Management,* IEEE Computer Society Press, 1979.
Riddle, W., and J. Wileden, *Tutorial on Software Design; Description and Analysis,* IEEE Computer Society Press, 1980.
Thurber, K., *Computer System Requirements,* IEEE Computer Society Press, 1980.

These publications are tutorials. Each includes original work by the author and an anthology of important papers from experts in the field. Miller's tutorial is recommended for its coverage of automated tools for requirements analysis.

SIX

THE SOFTWARE DESIGN PROCESS

Design is the first step in the development phase for any engineered product or system. It may be defined as *the process of applying various techniques and principles for the purpose of defining a device, a process, or a system in sufficient detail to permit its physical realization* [1].

The designer's goal is to produce a model or representation of an entity that will later be "built." The process by which the model is developed combines the following: intuition and judgment based on experience in building similar entities; a set of principles and/or heuristics that guide the way in which the model evolves; a set of criteria that enable "goodness" to be judged; and a process of iteration that ultimately leads to a final design representation.

Computer software design, like engineering design approaches in other disciplines, continually undergoes a process of evolution. Unlike mechanical or electronic design, software design is at a relatively early stage in its evolution. We have given serious thought to software design (as opposed to "programming" or "writing code") for little more than a decade. Therefore, software design methodology lacks the depth, flexibility, and quantitative nature that is normally associated with more classical engineering design disciplines. However, techniques for software design do exist; criteria for design goodness and qualitative analysis approaches are available, and design notation can be applied.

This chapter contains a brief overview of the software design process and a discussion of design documentation and reviews. Chapters 7 through 10 contain an in-depth presentation of various aspects of software design.

6.1 THE DEVELOPMENT PHASE

The central phase in the software life cycle is development. Beginning once software requirements have been established, the development phase is comprised of four distinct steps:

- Preliminary design
- Detailed design
- Coding
- Testing

Each step transforms information in a manner that ultimately results in validated computer software.

The flow of information during the development phase is illustrated in Figure 6.1. Software requirements and information flow or structure feed the preliminary design step. With the use of one of a number of design methodologies (discussed in later chapters), *software structure* is developed. Software structure, also called software architecture, defines the relationship among major elements of the program. Detailed design transforms structural elements into a procedural description of the software. Source code is generated, and preliminary testing is conducted during the code and unit test step. Detailed integration and validation testing are performed in the final step of the development phase.

The development phase absorbs at least 75 percent of the cost of new software. It is here that we make decisions that will ultimately affect the success of software implementation and, equally important, the ease with which software will be maintained.

6.2 THE DESIGN PROCESS

Software design is a process through which requirements are translated into a *representation* of software. Initially the representation depicts a holistic view of

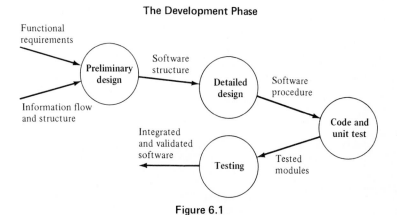

The Development Phase

Figure 6.1

software. Subsequent refinement leads to a design representation that is very close to source code in procedural detail.

In order to evaluate the "goodness" of a design representation, we must establish criteria for good design. In Chapter 7 qualitative measures of good software design are established. For the time being, we present the following guidelines:

1. A design should exhibit a *hierarchical organization* that makes intelligent use of control among elements of software.
2. A design should be *modular;* that is, the software should be logically partitioned into elements that perform specific functions and subfunctions.
3. A design should lead to modules (e.g., subroutines or procedures) that exhibit *independent functional characteristics.*
4. A design should be derived using a repeatable method that is driven by information obtained during software requirements analysis.

The above characteristics of a good design are not achieved by chance. The software engineering design process encourages good design through systematic methodology and thorough review.

The flow of events during software design is illustrated in Figure 6.2. Preliminary and detailed design steps are joined by a *preliminary design review* (PDR) and a *detailed design review* (DDR) or a *design walkthrough.* Each review applies criteria for good design and results in modifications that improve quality, strengthen correspondence to requirements, and enhance maintainability.

6.2.1 The Evolution of Software Design

The evolution of software design is a continuing process that has spanned the past two decades. Early design work concentrated on criteria for the development of

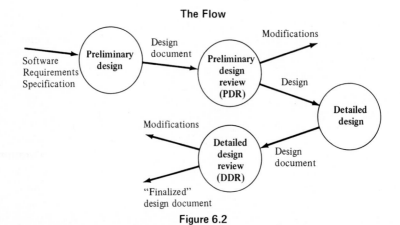

Figure 6.2

modular programs [2] and methods for refining software architecture in a top-down manner [3]. Procedural aspects of design definition evolved into a philosophy called *structured programming* [4,5]. Later work proposed methods for the translation of data flow [6,7] or data structure [8,9] into a design definition.

In the sections that follow, brief abstracts of some of the more important design methods, philosophies, and strategies are presented. Chapters 7 through 10 contain an in-depth presentation of various aspects of design.

6.2.2 Stepwise Refinement—A Top-Down Design Technique

Stepwise refinement is an early top-down design strategy proposed by Niklaus Wirth [3]. The architecture of a program is developed by successively refining levels of procedural detail. A procedural hierarchy is developed by decomposing a macroscopic statement of procedure into programming language statements. An overview of the approach is provided by Wirth [3]:

> In each step (of the refinement), one or several instructions of the given program are decomposed into more detailed instructions. This successive decomposition or refinement of specifications terminates when all instructions are expressed in terms of any underlying computer or programming language. . . . As tasks are refined, so the data may have to be refined, decomposed, or structured, and it is natural to refine the program and the data specifications in parallel.
>
> Every refinement step implies some design decisions. It is important that . . . the programmer be aware of the underlying criteria (for design decisions) and of the existence of alternative solutions. . . .

The process of program refinement proposed by Wirth is analogous to the process of refinement that transforms a fundamental system model (Chapter 5) into a detailed data flow diagram. Like data flow refinement that begins with a macroscopic model of flow (the fundamental system model), stepwise refinement begins with a high-level representation of software procedure. Initially, a software control program (the *main* or *driver* program) is defined; then each task invoked by the driver is expanded in a top-down fashion; additional levels of refinement occur until source code level detail has been achieved.

6.2.3 Structured Programming

Of all software approaches, the concept of *structured programming* has received the most press, instigated the widest debate, and finally, seen the broadest adoption in the industry. Formalized by Edsgar Dijkstra [4], structured programming proposes a limited number of *logical constructs* that tend to minimize the complexity of program flow and keep each element of a program manageably small.

The foundation of structured programming is built on the three logical constructs that comprise a structured program. Only three procedural forms (with some permutations) are recognized:

- *Sequence.* The execution of one task followed immediately by another task.
- *If-then-else.* The execution of a "then-task" when a decision is true, or alternatively, the execution of an "else-task" when the decision is false.
- *Repetition.* A task that is executed repetitively until a predefined condition is met.

The mathematical basis of structured programming and the correctness of resultant designs is addressed in papers by Mills [5] and others, and in many books [e.g., 10] on the subject. A further discussion of this design method is presented in Chapter 10.

6.2.4 Data-Oriented Design Techniques

A number of software design techniques are predicated on the relationship between information flow and structure and software architecture. Data flow–oriented design [6,7], presented in Chapter 8, specifies a series of steps that allow a designer to map information flow in a system into a representation of software. Data structure–oriented design [8,9], presented in Chapter 9, links input and output information structures with the organization of program procedure.

6.3 PRELIMINARY DESIGN—AN INTRODUCTION

In the early days of software development, "writing programs" was the thing to do. After an explanation of the problem, a period of questions and answers, and research into the "nuts and bolts" of a method, the programmer began his or her work. Starting with that portion of the problem that was well understood, lines of FORTRAN, COBOL, or ALGOL would begin to appear. As time passed additional portions were coded until the entire program was "complete." Design was often conducted implicitly, if at all!

The problem with the above approach was that the forest remained hidden while we spent time and energy searching for trees. We rarely considered the software as a whole, because we built it bottom up with no formal design as a guide.

The preliminary design step is an attempt to develop software beginning from the top down. Information flow or structure, determined from requirements, becomes a tool that leads to an overall representation of software. This representation, called *software structure* or *architecture,* may be evaluated, refined, and/or modified very early in the development phase.

In addition to software structure, preliminary design results in the definition of interfaces among internal software elements and external system elements, functional descriptions of each software element, data structure details, and special packaging considerations. These concepts are discussed in Section 6.5 and later chapters.

6.4 DETAILED DESIGN—AN INTRODUCTION

Detailed design provides a blueprint for coding. With the use of a design representation that may be graphical, tabular, or textual, a detailed procedural specification for the software is created. Like the blueprint, the detailed design specification should provide sufficient information for someone other than the designer to develop resultant source code.

It is not unfair to ask why detailed design is necessary. Won't an English-language description of a subroutine, function, or procedure suffice as a prelude to coding? The answer lies in the following statement: "a lack of ambiguity in a natural language is not natural!" Detailed design provides tools for procedural specification in an unambiguous, highly structured manner.

6.5 DESIGN DOCUMENTATION

The technical aspects of software design are considered in Chapters 7 through 10. In this section we consider the primary deliverable for software design—the *Design Specification.* Design documentation evolves in much the same way as the technical effort associated with design. Early versions of the *Design Specification* concentrate on the software architecture, while later versions depict detail for each software element.

The *Design Specification* serves a dual-purpose, providing a guide to software implementation (coding) and test and assisting the maintainer after software has been released. The specification can undergo considerable change during the software life cycle. Therefore, it is essential to control and review design documentation at each step in the development phase.

6.5.1 Documentation Outline

The document outline that follows can be used as a model for a *Design Specification.* Each section is comprised of numbered paragraphs that address different aspects of the design representation.

SOFTWARE DESIGN SPECIFICATION

1.0. Scope
    1.1. System objective and software's role as a system element
    1.2. Hardware, software, and human interfaces
    1.3. Major software functions
    1.4. Externally defined database
    1.5. Major design constraints and limitations

2.0. Reference Documents
    2.1. Existing software documentation
    2.2. System documentation
    2.3. Vendor (hardware or software) documents
    2.4. Technical references
3.0. Design Description
    3.1. Data description
        3.1.1. Review of information flow
        3.1.2. Review of information structure
    3.2. Derived software structure
    3.3. Interfaces within structure
4.0. Modules
    For each module:
    4.1. Processing narrative
    4.2. Interface description
    4.3. Design language (or other) description
    4.4. Modules used
    4.5. Data organization
    4.6. Comments
5.0. File Structure and Global Data
    5.1. External file structure
        5.1.1. Logical structure
        5.1.2. Logical record description
        5.1.3. Access method
    5.2. Global data
    5.3. File and data cross-reference
6.0. Requirements Cross-Reference (see Figure 6.3)

6.0 Requirements Cross-Reference

Requirement paragraph \ Module name	Module A	Module B	Module C	⋯	Module Z
Paragraph 3.1.1	√			√	
Paragraph 3.1.2		√	√		
Paragraph 3.1.3		√			
⋮					
Paragraph 3.m.n			√	√	

Figure 6.3

7.0. Test Provisions
    7.1. Test guidelines
    7.2. Integration strategy
    7.3. Special considerations
8.0. Packaging
    8.1. Special program overlay provisions
    8.2. Transfer considerations
9.0. Special Notes
10.0. Appendices

6.5.2 Documentation Content

The documentation outline (Section 6.5.1) presents a complete design description of the software. The numbered sections of the *Design Specification* are completed as the designer refines his or her representation of the software.

The overall scope of the design effort is described in Section 1.0 (section numbers refer to *Design Specification* outline). Much of the information contained in this section is derived from the *System Specification* and software planning phase documents. Specific references to supporting documentation are made in Section 2.0.

Section 3.0, the *design description,* is completed as part of preliminary design. We have noted that design is *information driven*—that is, flow and/or structure of data will dictate the architecture of software. In this section data flow diagrams or structure diagrams, developed during requirements analysis, are refined and used to derive software structure. Because information flow is available, interface descriptions may be developed for elements of the software.

Sections 4.0 and 5.0 evolve as preliminary design moves into detailed design. *Modules*—separately addressable elements of software such as subroutines, functions, or procedures—are initially described with an English-language *processing narrative.* The processing narrative explains the procedural function of a module. Later, a detailed design tool (described in Chapter 10) is used to translate the narrative into a structured description.

A description of data organization is contained in Section 5.0. File structures maintained on secondary storage media are described during preliminary design; global data (e.g., Fortran COMMON) are assigned, and a cross-reference that associates individual modules to files or global data is established.

Section 6.0 of the *Design Specification* contains a *requirements cross-reference.* The purpose of this cross-reference matrix is to (1) establish that all functional requirements (listed in the left hand column) are satisfied by the software design and indicate which modules (listed across the top row) are critical to the implementation of specific requirements.

The first stage in the development of test documentation is contained in Section 7.0 of the design document. Once software structure and interfaces have been established, we can develop guidelines for testing of individual modules and integration of the entire package. Although a detailed specification of test procedure is not completed until later in the development phase, development of test strategy and special considerations for testing (e.g., special hardware or simulation software) are developed as the *Design Specification* evolves.

Design constraints, such as physical memory limitations or the necessity for high performance, may dictate special requirements for assembling or packaging of software. Special considerations caused by the necessity for program overlay, virtual memory management, high-speed processing, or other factors may cause modification in design derived from information flow. Requirements and considerations for software packaging are presented in Section 7.0. Section 7.0 also describes the approach that will be used to transfer software to a user-requester site (e.g., magnetic tape or floppy disks).

Sections 9.0 and 10.0 of the *Design Specification* contain supplementary data. Algorithm descriptions, alternative procedures, tabular data, excerpts from other documents, and other relevant information are presented as a special note or as a separate appendix. It may be advisable to develop a *Preliminary Operations/Installation Manual* and include it as an appendix to the design document.

6.6 DESIGN REVIEWS

The flow of the software design process is punctuated with reviews. In fact, thoughtful, well-planned review is as important to software design as technical design methods themselves. Two design review philosophies coexist and are applied at different points in the design process. The philosophies reside at opposite ends of a *formality spectrum.* At one end we require a formal review with carefully prepared slides, an invited audience, and a planned agenda. At the other end we conduct impromptu meetings with a few colleagues to discuss (review) the efficacy of a design. Rather than selecting one end of the formality spectrum as an exclusive design approach, the degree of formality can be tailored both to the design organization and the point in time at which the review is conducted.

6.6.1 Cost-Benefit Considerations

The obvious benefit of design reviews is the early discovery of *software defects* so that each defect may be corrected prior to coding, test, and release. A number of industry studies (TRW, Nippon Electric, Mitre Corporation, etc.) indicate that the software design step introduces between 50 and 65 percent of all errors (defects) during the development phase of the software life cycle. However, effective review techniques can uncover a large percentage of these errors and substantially reduce the cost of subsequent steps in the development and maintenance phases.

To illustrate the cost impact of early error detection, we consider a series of relative costs that are based on actual cost data collected for large software projects [11]. Assume that an error uncovered during design will cost 1 monetary unit to correct. Relative to this cost, the same error uncovered just before testing commences will cost 6.5 units; during testing 15 units; and after release 67 units.

Defect Amplification Model

Development step

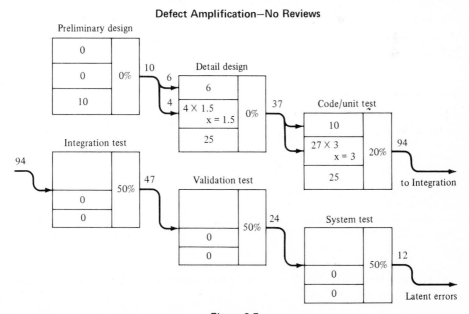

Figure 6.4

A *defect amplification model* [11] can be used to illustrate the generation and detection of errors during preliminary design, detailed design, and coding steps of the software engineering process. The model is illustrated schematically in Figure 6.4. A box represents a software development step. During the step, errors may be inadvertently generated. Review may fail to uncover newly generated errors and errors from previous steps, resulting in some number of errors that are passed through. In some cases errors passed through from previous steps are amplified (amplification factor *x*) by current work. The box subdivisions represent each of these characteristics and the percent efficiency for detecting errors, a function of the thoroughness of review.

Figure 6.5 illustrates a hypothetical example of defect amplification for a software development process in which no reviews are conducted and no defects are uncovered during design and code. Referring to the figure, each test step is

Figure 6.5

assumed to uncover and correct 50 percent of all incoming errors without introducing any new errors (an optimistic assumption!). Ten preliminary design defects are amplified to 94 errors before testing commences. Twelve latent errors are released to the field. Figure 6.6 considers the same conditions except that reviews are conducted as part of each development step. In this case, ten initial preliminary design errors are amplified to 24 errors before testing commences. Only three latent errors exist.

Recalling the relative costs associated with detection and correction of errors, overall cost (with and without review for our hypothetical example) can be established. Referring to Table 6.1, it can be seen that total cost for development and maintenance when reviews are conducted is 783 cost units. When no reviews are conducted, the total cost is 2177 units—nearly three times more costly.

To conduct reviews, a developer must expend time, effort, and money. However, the results of the preceding example leave little doubt that we have encountered a "pay now or pay much more later" syndrome. Design and code reviews provide a demonstrable cost-benefit. They should be conducted.

6.6.2 Criteria for Design Reviews

A software design is reviewed by representatives of management, technical development, and other constituencies such as user-requester, quality assurance, or

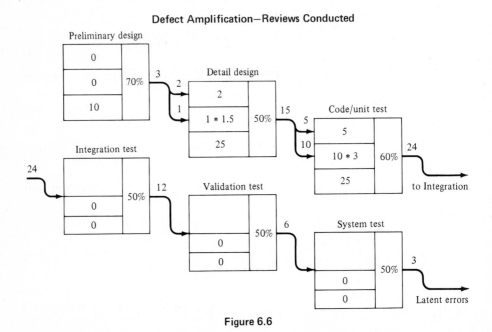

Figure 6.6

Table 6.1 Development cost comparison

Errors found	Number	Cost unit	Total
Reviews conducted			
During design	22	1.5	33
Before test	36	6.5	234
During test	15	15	315
After release	3	67	201
			783
No reviews conducted			
Before test	22	6.5	143
During test	82	15	1230
After release	12	67	804
			2177

software support. Although each participant will view the design from his or her own perspective, selected review criteria will be of importance to all participants:

1. *Traceability.* Does the software design address all facets of the *Software Requirements Specification?* Is each element of the software traceable to a specific requirement?
2. *Risk.* Will implementation of the design require high risk; that is, is the design achievable without technological breakthrough?
3. *Practicality.* Is the design a practical solution to the problem identified in requirements?
4. *Maintainability.* Has the design been developed in a way that will lead to an easily maintainable system?
5. *Quality.* Does the design exhibit qualitative characteristics of "good" software (Chapter 7)?
6. *Interfaces.* Have external and internal interfaces been adequately defined?
7. *Technical clarity.* Is the design expressed in a manner that can easily be translated to code?
8. *Alternatives.* Have design alternatives been considered? What criteria were used to select the final choice?
9. *Limitations.* Are software limitations realistic and consistent with requirements?
10. *Special interests.* Is the software design human-engineered, testable, consistent with other elements of the system, and well documented?

Each participant in a design review may want to emphasize one or more of the above criteria. However, a thorough review is complete only after all criteria are examined.

6.7 APPROACHES TO DESIGN REVIEW

A number of different philosophies and approaches to software design review may be applied in the software engineering context. In the sections that follow, three common review techniques are discussed.

6.7.1 Formal Reviews

Formal design reviews are normally conducted to evaluate the structure and interfaces established for software. Reviews of this type are characterized by significant preparation by both designer and reviewer, a fairly large number of reviewers with varying degrees of interest in the software development project, and high management and technical visibility.

The general sequence of events for a formal design review is illustrated in Figure 6.7. As we have already noted, formal design reviews are scheduled and included in the *Software Plan*. At least 2 weeks prior to the scheduled review date, design documentation is disseminated to all reviewers. Unfortunately, many reviewers may not spend enough time reviewing the documentation. For this reason, the project manager may request a written response, thereby "forcing" each reviewer to give the design a modicum of attention. The formal review process culminates with the design presentation—an audiovisual disclosure of the software design.

The format of the design presentation is established on a case-by-case basis. However, the following topics are always presented:

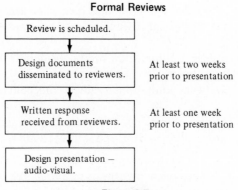

Figure 6.7

- Software identification and design responsibility
- System objectives
  - Overview of all elements
  - Major software functions
  - Validation characteristics
- Software requirements overview
  - System model
  - Data flow diagram
- Software structure
- Modules presented by function
- Data structure
- Requirements cross-reference
- Summary

Because formal reviews are normally conducted as part of the preliminary design step, there is relatively little emphasis on procedural detail within the software.

The objective of a formal review should be to evaluate the design, not the designer(s). Because reviewers and presenters are human, a clash of personalities can cause a review to degenerate into an inquisition. This should not be allowed to happen! A design review must be planned and managed in much the same way as other steps in the software engineering process.

A time limit and schedule should be established for presentation and discussion of major software functions. The agenda is enforced by a *review manager,* who should ensure that the following guidelines are followed:

1. Written notes of all reviewers' comments should be taken. It is easy for the developer to forget (by mistake or by design!) many constructive suggestions during a review. Notes can serve as a checklist of action items for a developer and for management.
2. A design review should raise issues but need not necessarily resolve them. A formal review is not a brain-storming session; therefore, problem-solving should be carefully controlled and a debate atmosphere should be discouraged.
3. The number of review participants should be limited.

Formal reviews act as important milestones for large software development efforts. However, there is a growing trend toward less formal and more frequent reviews during the design process.

6.7.2 Informal Reviews

The team approach to software development encourages an on-going process of peer review. *Informal reviews* run a gamut from impromptu get-togethers called at a moment's notice to a more structured review with colleagues. In this section we consider the *structured walkthrough*—a planned review that is less formal than reviews described in Section 6.7.1, but no less effective.

The participants in a design walkthrough are essentially the same people who attend the more formal preliminary design review. Yourdon [12] defines generic categories for walkthrough participants that include: a *coordinator* who is responsible for planning and organizing walkthrough activities; a *producer* who has developed the design to be reviewed; a *secretary* who maintains a record of walkthrough events; and others, such as representatives from maintenance, test, standards, and the user-requester.

The sequence of events for a design walkthrough is illustrated in Figure 6.8. Because the announcement to presentation time span is only two or three days, far less preparation is required by both producer and reviewers.

In general, the number of participants and time duration of a design walkthrough are small. Where a formal review might involve 8 to 12 people, a walkthrough can be conducted with two or three participants. Where a formal review might require days or even weeks to complete, a walkthrough is limited to 1 or 2 hours. The objective of the walkthrough, therefore, is to consider a specific aspect of software in an informal atmosphere.

Obviously, a design walkthrough is not a substitute for more formal review procedures. The walkthrough is used in conjunction with formal reviews as indicated in Figure 6.9. After early stages of design, a formal preliminary design (PDR) review is conducted. The PDR approves a modular definition of software that is subsequently refined in detailed design tasks $t_1, t_2, \ldots, t_n$. Walkthroughs $w_1, w_2, \ldots, w_n$ are conducted for each detailed design (alternatively, for each logical grouping of modules). Larger, more formal walkthroughs W_I, W_{II} may also be conducted as illustrated in Figure 6.9. Finally, a formal design completion review, R, may be conducted at the culmination of design steps.

6.7.3 Inspections

Another approach to design (and code) review has been developed and implemented by IBM [13]. The *inspection* is characterized by elements of both formal and informal reviews described in the preceding sections. The inspection methodology is quite formal—specific responsibilities, activities, deliverables, checklists,

Walkthrough Chronology

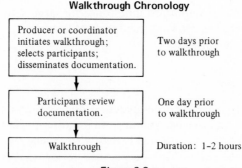

Figure 6.8

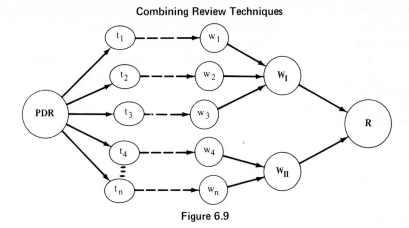

Figure 6.9

and control are specified in advance. However, the people involved and their interaction have many attributes of small group informality.

The inspection methodology incorporates a number of reviews (and related activities). An inspection team, comprised of a *moderator,* the designer, a *coder-implementer,* and a *tester,* conducts the inspection. The moderator, a specially trained individual, coordinates other members of the team and guides the progress of the inspection. The designer presents his or her design to the coder-implementer—the individual who will be responsible for translation of the design to source code, and the tester—the individual who will conduct software tests.

The inspection process begins with an overview in which the designer presents the procedural logic, paths, and interdependencies of the design to the inspection team. The moderator may flag certain areas of the design for special scrutiny. Individual inspection team members then individually prepare for the inspection by studying the design. The whole team conducts the inspection by appointing a *reader* who describes the design and how it will be implemented (the reader is not the designer). Questions are raised and errors are uncovered, but not resolved.

After the conclusion of the inspection, the moderator produces a report that specifies errors uncovered (errors are formally recorded by type) and requirements for rework and follow-up review. Rework is conducted by the designer and/or the coder-implementer, and problems uncovered are resolved. Follow-up is conducted to assure that each error has been corrected.

6.8 SUMMARY

Design—the first activity in the development phase of the software life cycle—is the technical kernel of software engineering. During design, progressively refined representations of software are developed, reviewed, and documented.

Design is driven by information gathered during requirements analysis and represented as data flow or structure. Systematic methods and tools, available for both preliminary and detailed design, translate an information representation into software structure and procedure. A detailed description of software concepts related to design and a detailed presentation of methodology are reserved for the chapters that follow.

Documentation for software design evolves as the development process progresses. The *Design Specification* provides a means for representing a holistic view of software, a detailed description of each module, and other important related data.

Design review evaluates the "goodness" of a representation of software. Reviews may be conducted formally, with invited reviewers and prepared presentations. Later, reviews may be conducted informally with members of a development team. Regardless of the degree of formality, review is absolutely essential to the success of a development effort.

REFERENCES

1. Taylor, E. S., *An Interim Report on Engineering Design,* Massachusetts Institute of Technology, Cambridge, MA, 1959.
2. Dennis, J., "Modularity," in *Advanced Course on Software Engineering,* F. L. Bauer (ed.), Springer-Verlag, New York, 1973, pp. 128–182.
3. Wirth, N., "Program Development by Stepwise Refinement," *CACM,* vol. 14, no. 4, 1971, pp. 221–227.
4. Dahl, O., E. Dijkstra, and C. Hoare, *Structured Programming,* Academic Press, London, 1972.
5. Mills, H. D., "Mathematical Foundations for Structured Programming," Technical Report FSC 71-6012, IBM Corporation, Federal Systems Division, Gaithersburg, MD, 1972.
6. Stevens, W., G. Myers, and L. Constantine, "Structured Design," *IBM Systems Journal,* vol. 13, no. 2, 1974, pp. 115–139.
7. Yourdon, E., and L. Constantine, *Structured Design,* Prentice-Hall, 1979.
8. Jackson, M., *Principles of Program Design,* Academic Press, 1975.
9. Warnier, J., *Logical Construction of Programs,* Van Nostrand Reinhold, 1974.
10. McGowan, C., and J. Kelly, *Top Down Structured Programming,* Petrocelli, New York, 1975.
11. "Implementing Software Inspections," course notes, IBM Systems Sciences Institute, IBM Corporation, 1981.
12. Yourdon, E., *Structured Walkthroughs,* Prentice-Hall, 1979, pp. 31–36.
13. Fagan, M., "Design and Code Inspections to Reduce Errors in Program Development," *IBM Systems Journal,* vol. 15, no. 3, 1976, pp. 182–211.

PROBLEMS AND POINTS TO PONDER

6-1 Do you design software when you "write" a program? What makes software design different from coding?

6-2 Use an example to illustrate your current understanding of preliminary and detailed design (much more on these steps will be presented in subsequent chapters). Are there situations in which preliminary design may not be necessary?

6-3 Research the techniques associated with functional decomposition and stepwise refinement. Show the step-by-step refinement of the software design for one or more of the following problems:

(*a*) Given an arbitrarily long text string, develop a module or modules that will find the occurrence of a specified substring and replace it with another substring of different length.

(*b*) Develop a check writer that, given any numeric dollar amount, will print the word amount that is normally required on a check.

(*c*) Iteratively solve for the roots of a transcendental equation.

(*d*) Develop a simple round robin scheduling algorithm for an operating system.

6-4 Structured programming is sometimes erroneously referred to as "gotoless" programming. Read some of the early literature on the subject and describe why it became known by this name and discuss some of the controversy that surrounded it.

6-5 Discuss each section of the *Design Specification.* Provide examples to illustrate the contents of each section of the outline.

6-6 Conduct a design walkthrough, using the following guidelines:

(*a*) Develop an algorithm to solve a "simple" problem assigned by your instructor.

(*b*) Represent your solution as a detailed flowchart.

(*c*) Walk through your design (using the format discussed in Section 6.7.2).

(*d*) Keep close count of the errors uncovered.

(*e*) Determine a class average for number of errors uncovered.

6-7 (*a*) Using the defect amplification model discussed in Section 6.6.1, determine rough bounds on the benefits accrued by using reviews. First, assume that all design and code reviews are only 20 percent efficient. Compute total development cost, using relative costs given in the text. Next, assume an 80 percent efficiency for design and code reviews. Assume that 10 errors are introduced during preliminary design, with amplification factors as in the hypothetical example and 50 percent efficiency for all test steps.

(*b*) The next time you develop a program, keep track of all errors that are made and subsequently uncovered. Build a defect amplification model for your work.

6-8 Review the literature and write a paper summarizing current quantitative data on the costs and benefits of design review.

6-9 Research the Yourdon [12] concept of a design walkthrough and the IBM concept [13] of a design inspection. Discuss in detail the similarities and differences between them.

FURTHER READINGS

An excellent survey of software design is contained in *Software Design Techniques,* 3d ed. (Freeman, P., and A. Wasserman, IEEE Computer Society Press, 1980). This tutorial on design contains a broad anthology of papers. A paper by Wasserman ("Information System

Design Methodology," reprinted in *Software Design Techniques*) presents a concise history and survey of design and includes a comprehensive bibliography. Further readings on the technical aspects of software design are presented at the conclusion of Chapters 7, 8, 9, and 10.

An interesting discussion of design documentation is contained in Chapter 7 of Yourdon's book, *Managing the Structured Techniques* (2d ed., Prentice-Hall, 1979). Yourdon outlines techniques for documenting software structure (architecture) and software procedure.

The group processes associated with design review are discussed in an excellent book by Gerald Weinberg and Daniel Freeman, the *Ethnotech Review Handbook* (Ethnotech, Lincoln, Nebraska). Peter Freeman ("Toward Improved Review of Software Design," reprinted in *Software Design Techniques*) introduces the concept of design "rationalization" to improve our ability to review designs.

IBM has published a series of manuals (manual nos. GC20-2000-0, TR21.601, TR21.629, and TR21.630) on high-level and low-level design inspection, code inspection, and test inspection. The manuals contain useful guidelines, forms, and examples that can be extrapolated for use in any design review environment.

SOFTWARE CONCEPTS

Among the many attributes that characterize an engineering discipline is the ability to define meaningful measures of a system. Lord Kelvin recognized this when he said:

> When you can measure what you are speaking about, . . . you know something about it. When you cannot . . . your knowledge is of a meager and unsatisfactory kind. It may be the beginning of knowledge, but you have scarcely in your thoughts advanced to the stage of science.

We are "at the beginning of knowledge" when available measures for computer software are considered.

In this chapter we consider fundamental measures of software that are applied during design. Such measures are generally qualitative in nature, but do provide a basis for a "scientific" approach to software engineering. In addition, we survey current work on the development of quantitative measures for software. This research and experimentation may someday allow us to advance to the stage of science.

7.1 QUALITIES OF GOOD SOFTWARE

Characteristics of "good" software design were described in Chapter 6. In a broader sense, we must understand the qualities of good software as well. The pragmatist might say that a good program is one that works! Michael Jackson, a leading authority on software design, comments on the pragmatic view in the following way: "the beginning of wisdom for a programmer is to recognize the difference between getting a program to work and getting it right."

In fact, when the entire software life cycle is considered, "getting it right" may be the ultimate arbiter of success.

Good software exhibits three qualities that make it right: (1) the software works according to specified requirements—it is as fast, efficient, and functional as is required; (2) the software is maintainable—it can be diagnosed and modified without great difficulty; and (3) the software is more than code—it is a configuration of documents that assures that the first two qualities are achieved. The driving force behind good software is good design, and good design can be gauged by applying the measures and heuristics discussed in the following sections.

7.2 SOFTWARE STRUCTURE AND PROCEDURE

Software may be represented structurally or procedurally. In this section we discuss the difference between these forms of representation. An understanding of the difference between structure and procedure is a prerequisite to an understanding of preliminary and detailed design.

7.2.1 Structure

Software structure is a hierarchical representation that indicates the relationship between elements (called *modules*) of a software solution to a problem implicitly defined by requirements analysis. The evolution of software structure begins with a problem definition. Solution occurs when each part of the problem is solved by one or more software elements. This process, symbolically represented in Figure

Evolution of Structure

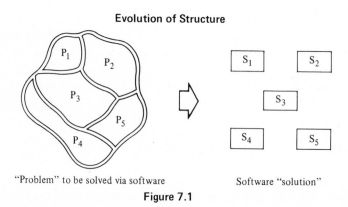

"Problem" to be solved via software　　　　Software "solution"

Figure 7.1

7.1, represents a transition between software requirements analysis and design.

Software structure represents a program architecture that implies a hierarchy of control. It does not represent procedural aspects of software such as sequence of processes, occurrence and order of decisions, or repetition of operations. In fact, an interesting analogy can be drawn between software structure and a human organizational structure.

A classic organizational chart for a company is shown in Figure 7.2. Chaos would reign if, rather than a multileveled management structure, all company personnel reported directly to the president. Decisions would be delayed indefinitely, overall efficiency would decline, and besides, what justification would there be for different-sized offices! For all its faults, a management hierarchy in a human organization distributes control so that decisions can be made close to the point at which work is conducted. At top levels of the structure, decision making (control) is the primary function and affects the organization globally. At bottom levels, production or processing (work) is conducted. An organization with these characteristics is said to be *factored.*

Software structure, like human organizations, can be factored. By distributing control in a top-down fashion, design and implementation are simplified, testability is enhanced, and maintenance can be approached in a more efficient manner.

Referring to Figure 7.3, it can be seen that a "problem" may be satisfied by many different candidate structures. Chapters 8 and 9 discuss software design methodologies that derive software structure. Because each is based on different philosophies, each design method will result in a different structure for the same set of software requirements. There is no easy answer to the question, "Which is best?" We have not yet advanced to that stage of science. However, there are characteristics of a structure that can be examined. We discuss these later in this chapter.

Structure in Human Organizations

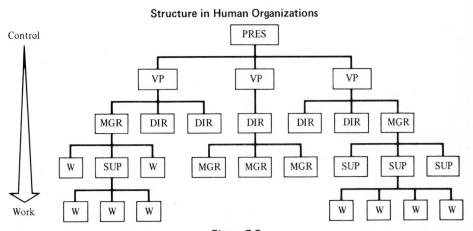

Figure 7.2

Software Structure

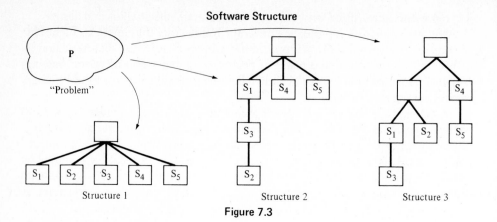

Figure 7.3

7.2.2 Structural Definitions

In order to facilitate later discussions of structure, we define a few simple measures and terms. Each of the boxes contained in a structure diagram represents one *module*—a separately addressable element of a program. Referring to Figure 7.4, *depth* and *width* provide an indication of the number of levels of control and overall span of control, respectively. *Fan-out* is a measure of the number of modules that are directly controlled by another module. *Fan-in* indicates how many modules directly control a given module.

Other "Measures" for Structure

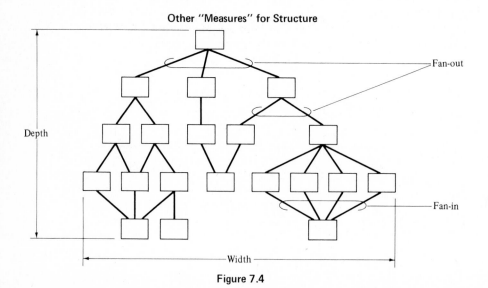

Figure 7.4

The control relationship among modules is expressed in the following way: a module that controls another module is said to be *superordinate* to it, and conversely, a module controlled by another is said to be *subordinate* to the controller [1]. For example, in Figure 7.5 module C is superordinate to modules Q, R, and S. Module V is subordinate to module S and ultimately subordinate to module C. Width-oriented relationships (e.g., between modules U and W), although possible to express in practice, need not be defined with explicit terminology.

7.2.3 Software Procedure

Software structure provides a representation of the entire software architecture without regard to the sequence of processing and decisions. *Software procedure* (Figure 7.6) focuses on the processing details of each module individually. Procedure must provide a precise specification of processing, including sequence of events, exact decision points, repetitive operations, and even data organization and structure.

There is, of course, a relationship between structure and procedure. Processing indicated for each module must include a reference to all modules subordinate to the module being described. That is, a procedural representation of software is *layered* as illustrated in Figure 7.7.

7.3 MODULARITY

The concept of *modularity* in computer software has been espoused for almost two decades. Structure, as it has been described in Section 7.2.1, embodies modularity; that is, software is divided into separately named and addressable elements, called modules, that are integrated to satisfy problem requirements.

Super- and Subordinate Modules

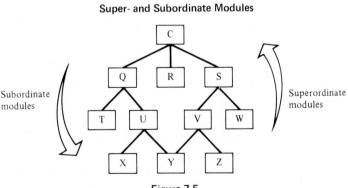

Figure 7.5

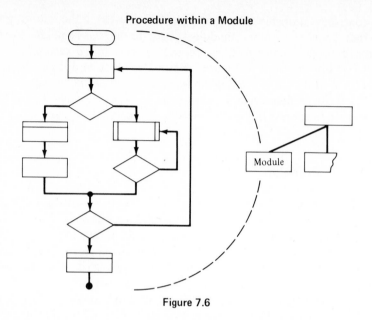

Figure 7.6

It has been stated that "modularity is the single attribute of software that allows a program to be intellectually manageable" [2]. Monolithic software (i.e., a large program comprised of a single module) cannot be easily grasped by a reader. The number of control paths, span of reference, number of variables, and overall complexity would make understanding close to impossible. To illustrate this point, consider the following argument based on observations of human problem solving.

Let $C(x)$ be a function that defines the perceived complexity of a problem x and $E(x)$ be a function that defines the effort (in time) required to solve a problem x. For two problems, p_1 and p_2, if

$$C(p_1) > C(p_2) \tag{7-1a}$$

it follows that

$$E(p_1) > E(p_2) \tag{7-1b}$$

As a general case, this result is intuitively obvious. It does take more time to solve a difficult problem.

Another interesting characteristic has been uncovered through experimentation in human problem solving; that is

$$C(p_1 + p_2) > C(p_1) + C(p_2) \tag{7-2}$$

Inequality (7-2) implies that the perceived complexity of a problem that combines p_1 and p_2 is greater than the perceived complexity when each problem is considered separately.

Procedure is layered

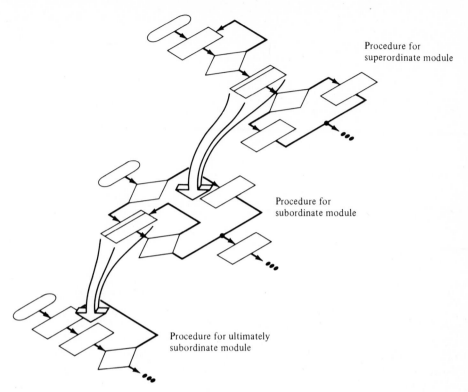

Procedure for
superordinate module

Procedure for
subordinate module

Procedure for ultimately
subordinate module

Figure 7.7

Considering inequality (7-2) and the condition implied by inequalities (7-1), it follows that

$$E(p_1 + p_2) > E(p_1) + E(p_2) \qquad (7\text{-}3)$$

This leads to a "divide and conquer" conclusion—it's easier to solve a complex problem when you break it into manageable pieces. The result expressed in inequality (7-3) has important implications with regard to modularity and software. It is, in fact, an argument for modularity.

It is possible to conclude from inequality (7-3) that if we subdivide software indefinitely, the effort required to develop it will become negligibly small! Unfortunately, other forces come into play, causing this conclusion to be (sadly) invalid. Referring to Figure 7.8, the effort (cost) to develop an individual software module does decrease as the total number of modules increases. Given the same set of requirements, a greater number of modules means smaller individual module size. However, as the number of modules grows, the effort (cost) associated with

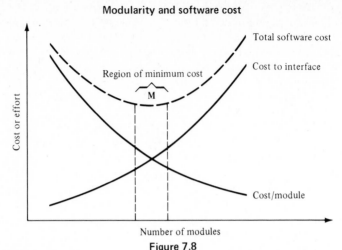

Figure 7.8

interfacing the modules also grows. These characteristics lead to a total cost or effort curve shown in Figure 7.8. There is a number M of modules that would result in minimum development cost, but we do not have the necessary sophistication to predict M with assurance.

The curves shown in Figure 7.8 do provide useful guidance when modularity is considered. We should modularize, but care should be taken to stay in the vicinity of M. Undermodularity or overmodularity should be avoided. But how do we know "the vicinity of M"? How modular should we make software? The size of a module will be dictated by its function and application. In sections that follow, design measures that help determine the appropriate number of modules for software are presented.

It is important to note that a system may be designed modularly, even if its implementation must be "monolithic." There are situations (e.g., real-time software and microprocessor software) in which the relatively minimal speed and memory overhead introduced by *subprograms* (i.e., subroutines and procedures) is unacceptable. In such situations software can and should be designed with modularity as an overriding philosophy. Code may be developed in-line. Although the program source code may not appear modular at first glance, the philosophy has been maintained, and the program will provide the benefits of a modular system.

7.3.1 Abstraction

When we consider a modular solution to any problem, many *levels of abstraction* can be posed. At the highest level of abstraction, a solution is stated in broad terms, using the language of the problem environment. At lower levels of abstraction, a more procedural orientation is taken. Problem-oriented terminology is coupled with implementation-oriented terminology in an effort to state a solution.

Finally, at the lowest level of abstraction, the solution is stated in a manner that can be directly implemented. Wasserman [3] provides a useful definition:

> The psychological notion of "abstraction" permits one to concentrate on a problem at some level of generalization without regard to irrelevant low level details; use of abstraction also permits one to work with concepts and terms that are familiar in the problem environment without having to transform them to an unfamiliar structure. . . .

Each step in the software engineering process is a refinement in the level of abstraction of the software solution. During system definition, software is described as a complete system element in the context of the entire system. During software planning and requirements analysis, the software solution is stated in terms "that are familiar in the problem environment." As we move from preliminary to detailed design, the level of abstraction is reduced. Finally, the lowest level of abstraction is reached when source code is generated.

To illustrate software defined by three different levels of abstraction, we consider the following problem:

Develop software that will perform all functions associated with a two-dimensional (2-D) drafting system for low-level computer-aided design (CAD) applications.

Abstraction I. The software will incorporate a computer graphics interface that will enable visual communication with the draftsperson and a digitizer interface that replaces the drafting board and the square. All line and curve drawing, all geometric computations, all sectioning and auxiliary views will be performed by the CAD software. . . .

At this level of abstraction, the solution is stated in terms of the problem environment.

Abstraction II.

```
CAD software tasks:
    user interaction task;
    2-D drawing creation task;
    graphics display task;
    drawing file management task;
end.
```

At this level of abstraction, each of the major software tasks associated with the CAD software is noted. Terms have moved away from the problem environment but are still not implementation specific.

Abstraction III.

```
procedure: 2-D drawing creation;
    repeat until (drawing creation task terminates)
```

```
    do while (digitizer interaction occurs)
        digitizer interface task;
        determine drawing request case;
        line: line drawing task;
        circle: circle drawing task;
            *
            *
            *
    end;
    do while (keyboard interaction occurs)
        keyboard interaction task;
        process analysis/computation case;
        view: auxiliary view task;
        section: cross sectioning task;
            *
            *
            *
    end;
        *
        *
        *
    end repetition;
end procedure.
```

At this level of abstraction, a preliminary procedural representation exists. Terminology is now software-oriented (e.g., the use of constructs such as *do while*, and an implication of modularity begins to surface.

The concepts of *stepwise refinement* (Chapter 6) and modularity are closely aligned with abstraction. As the software design evolves, each level of modules in software structure represents a refinement in the level of abstraction of the software. In reality, a *factored* (Section 7.2.1) structure distributes levels of control and decision making, that is, levels of abstraction.

7.3.2 Information Hiding

The concept of modularity leads every software designer to a fundamental question: "How do we decompose a software solution to obtain the best set of modules?" The principle of *information hiding* [4] suggests that modules be "characterized by design decisions that (each) hides from all others." In other words, modules should be specified and designed so that information (procedure and data) contained within a module are inaccessible to other modules that have no need for such information.

The term "hiding" implies that effective modularity can be achieved by defining a set of *independent* modules that communicate with one another only that information that is necessary to achieve software function. Abstraction helps to define the procedural (or informational) entities that comprise the software.

Hiding defines and enforces access constraints to both procedural detail within a module and any local data structure used by the module [5].

The use of information hiding as a design criteria for modular systems provides greatest benefits when modifications are required during testing and later, during software maintenance. Because most data and procedure are "hidden" from other parts of the software, inadvertent errors introduced during modification are less likely to propagate to other locations within the software.

7.3.3 Module Types

Abstraction and information hiding are used to define modules within a software structure. Both of these attributes must be translated into module operational features that are characterized by time history of incorporation, activation mechanism, and pattern of control.

Time history of incorporation refers to the time at which a module is included within a source language description of the software. For example, a module defined as a *compile time macro* is included as in-line code by the compiler when an appropriate reference is made. A conventional subprogram (e.g., a subroutine or procedure) is included through generation of branch and link code.

Two *activation mechanisms* are encountered. Conventionally, a module is invoked by *reference* (e.g., a "call" statement). However, in real-time applications, a module may be invoked by *interrupt;* that is, an outside event causes a discontinuity in processing that results in passage of control to another module. Activation mechanics are important because they can affect software structure.

The *pattern of control* of a module describes the manner in which it is executed internally. Conventional modules have a single entry and exit and are executed sequentially as part of one user task. More sophisticated patterns of control are sometimes required. For example, a module may be *reentrant.* That is, a module is designed so that it does not in any way modify itself or the local addresses that it references. Therefore, the module may be used by more than one task concurrently.

Within a software structure, a module may be categorized as:

- A *sequential* module that is referenced and executed without apparent interruption by the applications software.
- An *incremental* module that can be interrupted prior to completion by applications software and subsequently restarted at the point of interruption.
- A *parallel* module that executes simultaneously with another module in concurrent multiprocessor environments.

Sequential modules are most commonly encountered and are characterized by compile time macros and conventional subprograms—subroutines, functions, or procedures. Incremental modules, often called *coroutines,* maintain an entry pointer that allows the module to restart at the point of interruption. Such modules are extremely useful in interrupt-driven systems. Parallel modules, sometimes called *conroutines,* are encountered when high-speed computation (e.g., pipeline processing) demands two or more CPUs working in parallel.

A typical control hierarchy (a factored structure) may not be encountered when coroutines or conroutines are used. Such nonhierarchical or *homologous* structures require special design approaches that are in early stages of development.

7.4 MODULE INDEPENDENCE

The concept of *module independence* is a direct outgrowth of modularity and the concepts of abstraction and information hiding. In landmark papers on software design, Parnas [4] and Wirth [6] allude to refinement techniques that enhance module independence. Later work by Stevens et al. [7] solidified the concept.

Module independence is achieved by developing modules with "single-minded" functions and an "aversion" to excessive interaction with other modules. Stated another way, we want to design software so that each module addresses a specific subfunction of requirements and has a simple interface when viewed from other parts of the software structure.

It is fair to ask why independence is important. Software with effective modularity, that is, independent modules, is easier to develop because function may be compartmentalized and interfaces are simplified (consider ramifications when development is conducted by a team). Independent modules are easier to maintain (and test) because secondary effects caused by design and code modification are limited, error propagation is reduced, and "plug-in" modules are possible. To summarize, module independence is a key to good design, and design is the key to software quality.

Independence is measured using two qualitative criteria: cohesion and coupling. *Cohesion* is a measure of the relative functional strength of a module. *Coupling* is a measure of the relative interdependence among modules.

7.4.1 Cohesion

Cohesion is a natural extension of the information hiding concept described in Section 7.3.2. A cohesive module performs a single task within a software procedure, requiring little interaction with procedures being performed in other parts of a program. Stated simply, a cohesive module should (ideally) do just one thing.

Cohesion may be represented as a "spectrum," as shown in Figure 7.9. We always strive for high cohesion, although the midrange of the spectrum is often acceptable. The scale for cohesion is nonlinear. That is, low-end cohesiveness is much "worse" than middle range, which is nearly as "good" as high-end cohesion.

To illustrate (somewhat facetiously) the low end of the spectrum, we relate the following story:

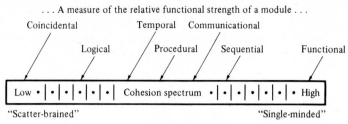

Figure 7.9

In the late 1960s most data processing managers began to recognize the worth of modularity. Unfortunately, many existing programs were monolithic, e.g., 6 to 20,000 lines of undocumented FORTRAN with one 2500-line subroutine!

To bring his environment to the state of the art, a manager asked his staff to modularize such a program that underwent maintenance continuously. This was to be done "in your spare time."

Under the gun, one staff member asked (innocently) the proper length for a module. "Seventy-five lines of code," came the reply. She then obtained a red pen and a ruler, measured the linear distance taken by 75 lines of source code, and drew a red line, then another and another. Each red line indicated a module boundary.

This technique is akin to developing software with coincidental cohesion!

Figure 7.10 provides examples of software that has relatively low cohesion—an undesirable form of modularity. A module that performs a set of tasks that relate to each other loosely, if at all, is termed *coincidentally cohesive.* A module that performs tasks that are related logically (e.g., a module that produces all

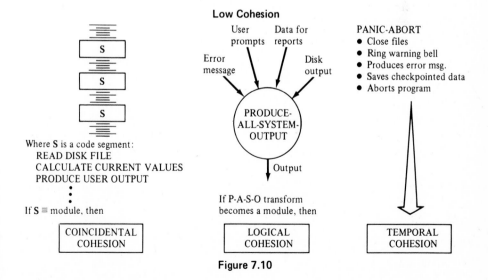

Figure 7.10

output regardless of type) is *logically cohesive.* When a module contains tasks that are related by the fact that all must be executed within the same span of time, the module exhibits *temporal cohesion.*

As an example of low cohesion, consider a module that performs error processing for an engineering analysis package. The module is called when computed data exceed prespecified bounds. It performs the following tasks: (1) computes supplementary data based on original computed data; (2) produces an error report (with graphical content) on the user terminal; (3) performs follow-up calculations requested by the user; (4) updates a database; and (5) enables menu selection for subsequent processing. Although the preceding tasks are loosely related, each is an independent functional entity that might best be performed as a separate module. Combining the functions into a single module can serve only to increase the likelihood of error propagation when a modification is made to one of the processing tasks noted above.

Moderate levels of cohesion are relatively close to one another in the degree of module independence. When processing elements of a module are related and must be executed in a specific order, *procedural cohesion* exists. When all processing elements concentrate on one area of a data structure, *communicational cohesion* is present.

High cohesion is characterized by a module that performs one distinct procedural task. To illustrate degrees of high cohesion, we consider the data flow diagram shown in Figure 7.11. If a module combines all transforms indicated by the outer dashed boundary, it is *sequentially cohesive.* That is, each processing

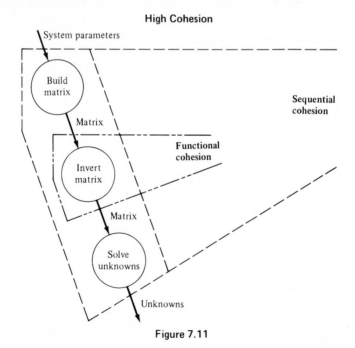

Figure 7.11

element is closely related to the same function and must be executed in sequence. If a module, INVERT-MATRIX, is defined, the highest level of cohesion, *functional cohesion,* is present. INVERT-MATRIX performs one and only one function—inverting a matrix; therefore, it exhibits a purely functional relationship with one element of processing.

The following excerpt from Stevens et al. [7] provides a set of simple guidelines for establishing the degree of cohesion (called *binding* in this reference):

A useful technique in determining whether a module is functionally bound is writing a sentence describing the function (purpose) of the module, and then examining the sentence. The following tests can be made:

1. If the sentence has to be a compound sentence, contains a comma, or contains more than one verb, the module is probably performing more than one function; therefore, it probably has sequential or communicational binding.
2. If the sentence contains words relating to time, such as "first," "next," "then," "after," "when," "start," etc., then the module probably has sequential or temporal binding.
3. If the predicate of the sentence doesn't contain a single specific object following the verb, the module is probably logically bound. For example, Edit All Data has logical binding: Edit Source Statement may have functional binding.
4. Words such as "initialize," "clean-up," etc., imply temporal binding.

Functionally bound modules can always be described by way of their elements using a compound sentence. But if the above language is unavoidable while still completely describing the module's function, then the module is probably not functionally bound.

In practice, it is unnecessary to determine the precise level of cohesion. Rather, it is important to strive for high cohesion and recognize low cohesion so that software design can be modified to achieve greater module independence.

7.4.2 Coupling

Coupling is a measure of interconnection among modules in a software structure. Like cohesion, coupling may be represented on a spectrum as shown in Figure 7.12. Coupling depends on the interface complexity between modules, the point at

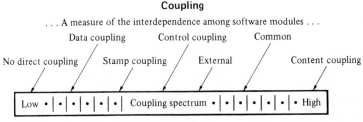

Figure 7.12

which entry or reference is made to a module, and which data pass across the interface.

In software design we strive for *lowest* possible coupling. Simple connectivity among modules results in software that is easier to understand and less prone to a "ripple effect" [7] caused when errors occur at one location and propagate through a system.

Figure 7.13 provides examples of modules residing in a structure with low coupling. Modules 1 and 2 are subordinate to different modules. Each is unrelated, and thus no direct coupling occurs. Module 3 is subordinate to module 2 and is accessed by means of a conventional argument list through which data are passed. As long as a simple argument list is present (i.e., simple data are passed; a one-to-one correspondence of items exists), low coupling (*data coupling* on the spectrum) is exhibited in this portion of structure. A variation of data coupling, called *stamp coupling*, is found when a portion of a data structure (rather than simple arguments) is passed through a module interface.

At moderate levels coupling is characterized by passage of control between modules. *Control ·coupling*, which is very common in most software designs, is illustrated in Figure 7.14. In its simplest form, control is passed by means of a "flag" on which decisions are made in a subordinate or superordinate module.

Relatively high levels of coupling occur when modules are tied to an environment external to software. For example, I/O couples a module to specific devices, formats, and communication protocols. External coupling is essential but should be limited to a small number of modules within a structure. High coupling also occurs when a number of modules reference a global data area. *Common coupling*, as this mode is called, is shown in Figure 7.15. Modules C, F, and N each access a data item in a global data area (e.g., a disk file, Fortran COMMON). Module C reads the item, invoking F, which recomputes and updates the item. Let's assume that an error occurs and F updates the item incorrectly. Much later in processing, module N reads the item, attempts to process it, and fails, causing the software to abort. The apparent site and cause of abort is module N; the actual cause, module

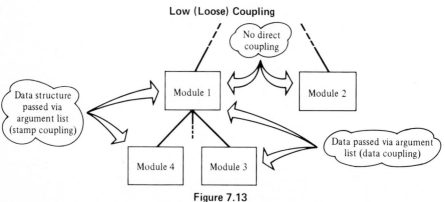

Figure 7.13

Moderate Coupling

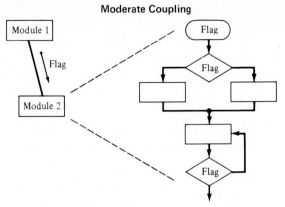

Control coupling occurs when module 1 passes control data to module 2.

Figure 7.14

F. Diagnosing problems in structures with considerable common coupling is time consuming and difficult. However, this does not mean that the use of global data is necessarily "bad." It does mean that a software designer must be aware of potential consequences of common coupling and take special care to guard against them.

The highest degree of coupling, *content coupling,* occurs when one module makes use of data or control information maintained within the boundary of another module. Content coupling also occurs when branches are made into the "middle" of a module. This mode of coupling can and should be avoided.

The coupling modes discussed above occur because of design decisions made when structure was developed. Variants of external coupling, however, may be introduced during coding. For example, compiler coupling ties source code to specific (and often nonstandard) attributes of a compiler; operating system cou-

High Coupling

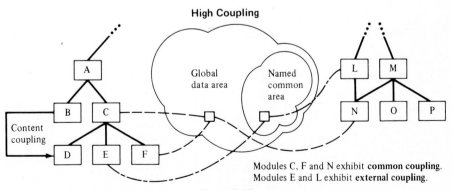

Modules C, F and N exhibit **common coupling**.
Modules E and L exhibit **external coupling**.

Figure 7.15

pling ties design and resultant code to operating system "hooks" that can create havoc when operating system changes occur.

7.5 SOFTWARE MEASUREMENT

Software engineering is in its formative years. The measures that we have discussed in previous sections are qualitative and have no formal mathematical basis. Yet, a relationship between concepts such as module independence and software quality is logically presumed to exist.

In an excellent survey of software measurement, Curtis [8] describes three major uses for *software metrics:* (1) management information tools; (2) measures of software quality; and (3) feedback to the software engineer.

Management information tools are currently applied in the planning phase of the software life cycle. Productivity data (discussed in Chapter 4) provides one of few quantitative metrics that can be applied today.

Metrics for software quality are more elusive. Figure 7.16 presents a synthesis [8] of work conducted by Boehm et al. [9] and McCall et al. [10] that attempts to provide useful measures for software quality. Boehm's primitive constructs and McCall's criteria may ultimately be reduced to a set of metrics that can be measured in a quantitative manner. The hierarchy of quality measures shown on both sides of Figure 7.16 is useful as a means for qualitative evaluation.

Additional work in software metrics has concentrated on software complexity [11], control structures, *interconnectedness* (another term for module independence), and Halstead's [12] theory of software science. *Complexity* is categorized in terms of computational complexity—a formal specification of algorithm structure, efficiency, and application, and psychological complexity—a measure of human factors that affect software development. Software control structures use graph theory [13] to measure internal procedural characteristics such as number of branches or processing paths. In the sections that follow, two important quantitative approaches to software measurement are presented.

7.5.1 Halstead's Software Science

Halstead's theory of software science [12] is "probably the best known and most thoroughly studied . . . composite measures of (software) complexity" [8]. Software science proposes the first analytical "laws" for computer software.

Software science is a relatively new area of research that assigns quantitative laws to the development of computer software. Halstead's theory is derived from one fundamental assumption [12]: "The human brain follows a more rigid set of rules (in developing algorithms) than it has been aware of. . . ." Software science uses a set of primitive measures that may be derived after code is generated or estimated once design is complete. These are listed at the top of p. 166.

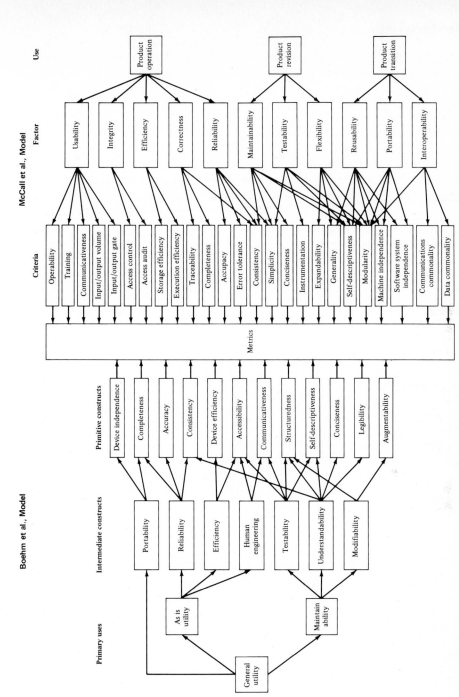

Figure 7.16

(*Source: William Curtis, Management and Experimentation in Software Engineering, Proceedings of the IEEE, Vol. 68, No. 9, September 1980, p. 1147. Reprinted with permission.*)

n_1—the number of distinct operators that appear in a program
n_2—the number of distinct operands that appear in a program
N_1—the total number of operator occurrences
N_2—the total number of operand occurrences

To illustrate how these primative measures are obtained, refer to the simple SORT program [14] shown in Figure 7.17.

Halstead uses the primitive measures to develop expressions for the overall program *length;* potential minimum *volume* for an algorithm; the actual volume (number of bits required to specify a program); the *program level* (a measure of software complexity); *language level* (a constant for a given language); and other features such as development effort, development time, and even the projected number of faults in the software.

Halstead shows that length N can be estimated

$$N = n_1 \log_2 n_1 + n_2 \log_2 n_2 \qquad (7\text{-}4)$$

and program volume may be defined

$$V = N \log_2(n_1 + n_2) \qquad (7\text{-}5)$$

It should be noted that V will vary with programming language and represents the volume of information (in bits) required to specify a program. For the SORT module shown in Figure 7.17, it can be shown [14] that the volume for the FORTRAN version is 204. Volume for an equivalent assembler language version would be 328. As we would suspect, it takes more effort to specify a program in assembler language.

Theoretically, a minimum volume must exist for a particular algorithm. Halstead defines a volume ratio L as the ratio of volume of the most compact form of a program to the volume of the actual program. In actuality, L must always be less than one. In terms of primitive measures, the volume ratio may be expressed as

$$L = \frac{2}{n_1} \cdot \frac{n_2}{N_2} \qquad (7\text{-}6)$$

Halstead proposed that each language may be categorized by language level, l, which will vary among languages. Halstead theorized that language level is constant for a given language, but recent work [15] indicates that language level is a function of both language and programmer. The following language level values have been empirically derived for common languages:

Language	Mean l
English prose	2.16
PL/1	1.53
ALGOL/68	2.12
FORTRAN	1.14
Assembler	0.88

Operators and Operands for a Simple Program

Interchange Sort Program

```
SUBROUTINE SORT (X, N)
DIMENSION X(N)
IF (N.LT.2) RETURN
DO 20 I = 2,N
    DO 10 J = 1,I
    IF (X(I).GE.X(J)) GO TO 10
        SAVE = X(I)
        X(I) = X(J)
        X(J) = SAVE
10 CONTINUE
20 CONTINUE
    RETURN
    END
```

Operators of the interchange sort program

	Operator	Count
1	End of statement	7
2	Array subscript	6
3	=	5
4	IF ( )	2
5	DO	2
6	,	2
7	End of program	1
8	.LT.	1
9	.GE.	1
$n_1 = 10$	GO TO 10	1
		$28 = N_1$

Operands of the interchange sort program

	Operand	Count
1	X	6
2	I	5
3	J	4
4	N	2
5	2	2
6	SAVE	2
$n_2 = 7$	1	1
		$22 = N_2$

(Source: A. Fitzsimmons and T. Love, A Review and Evaluation of Software Science, ACM Computing Surveys, Vol. 10, No. 1, March 1978. © 1978, Association of Computing Machinery, Inc. Reprinted with permission.)

Figure 7.17

It appears that language level implies a level of abstraction in the specification of procedure. High-level languages allow specification of code at a higher level of abstraction than does assembler (machine-oriented) language.

Unlike many software metrics, Halstead's work is amenable to experimental verification. A large body of research has been conducted to investigate software science. A discussion of this work is beyond the scope of this text, but it can be said that surprisingly good agreement has been found between analytically predicted and experimental results [e.g., 14].

Quantitative metrics proposed by Halstead have had only limited application in actual practice [16]. However, software science shows promise as a quantitative tool for software reliability, software development effort estimation, software maintenance effort estimation, and as a formal measure of complexity and modularity.

7.5.2 McCabe's Complexity Measure

A complexity measure of software proposed by Thomas McCabe [11] is based on a control flow representation of a program. A *program graph*, illustrated in Figure 7.18, is used to depict control flow. Each circled letter represents a processing task (one or more source code statements); flow of control (branching) is represented with connecting arrows. Therefore, for the graph G in Figure 7.18, processing task a may be followed by tasks b, c, or d, depending on conditions tested as part of a. Processing task b is always followed by e, and both may be executed as part of a doubly nested loop (the curved arrows moving upward to b and a, respectively).

McCabe defines a software complexity measure that is based on the *cyclomatic complexity* of a program graph for a module. One technique that may be used to compute the cyclomatic complexity metric, $V(G)$, is to determine the number of

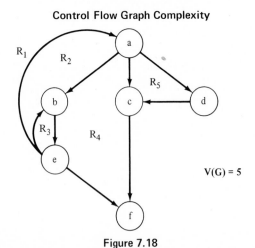

Control Flow Graph Complexity

$V(G) = 5$

Figure 7.18

regions in a planar graph (see McCabe [11] or for more detail, Bondy and Murty [13]). A *region* may be informally described as an enclosed area on the plane of the graph. The number of regions is computed by counting all bounded areas and the unbounded area outside the graph. The graph in Figure 7.18 has five regions (noted as R_1 through R_5) and thus has a cyclomatic complexity metric, $V(G) = 5$.

Because the number of regions increases with the number of decision paths and loops, the McCabe metric provides a quantitative measure of testing difficulty and an indication of ultimate reliability. Experimental studies [e.g., 17, 18] indicate distinct relationships between the McCabe metric and the number of errors existing in source code, as well as time required to find and correct such errors.

McCabe [11] also contends that $V(G)$ may be used to provide a quantitative indication of maximum module size. Collecting data from a number of actual programming projects, he has found that $V(G) = 10$ appears to be a practical upper limit for module size. When the cyclomatic complexity of modules exceeded this number, it became extremely difficult to adequately test a module (see Chapter 12 for a discussion of test techniques).

The McCabe and Halstead metrics are representative of a growing "quantitative" approach to the measurement of computer software. Automated tools that assist in the computation of both metrics have been developed. The McCabe measure may be applied earlier in the software engineering process (after detailed design is complete) than the Halstead approach (requires code). Therefore, cyclomatic complexity offers an evaluation tool for software testability and reliability that may ultimately become an important criterion for the review of module "goodness."

7.6 DESIGN HEURISTICS

Software concepts introduced in this chapter form the basis for design heuristics (guidelines) that may be applied regardless of the specific design methodology being used. Modifying an earlier figure, we can now say that the software design process is driven by considerations shown in Figure 7.19.

In this section we shall examine a number of important design heuristics. By

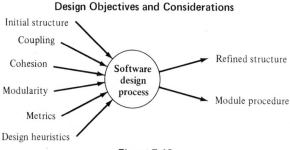

Figure 7.19

coupling these guidelines with notions such as modularity and independence, we provide a foundation for design methods to be discussed in the chapters that follow.

I. Evaluate the preliminary software structure to reduce coupling and improve cohesion. Once software structure has been developed, modules may be *exploded* or *imploded* with an eye toward improving module independence (Figure 7.20). The processing description of each module is examined to determine if a common process component can be exploded from two or more modules and redefined as a separate cohesive module. When high coupling is expected, modules can sometimes be imploded to reduce passage of control, reference to global data, and interface complexity.

II. Attempt to minimize structures with high fan-out; strive for fan-in as depth increases. The structure shown on the left-hand side of Figure 7.21, does not make effective use of factoring. In general, a more reasonable distribution of control is shown in the right-hand structure of the figure. The structure takes an oval shape, indicating a number of layers of control and highly utilitarian modules at lower levels.

III. Keep scope of effect of a module within the scope of control of that module. The *scope of effect* of a module *m* is defined as all other modules that are affected by a decision made in module *m*. The *scope of control* of module *m* is all modules that are subordinate and ultimately subordinate to module *m*. Figure 7.22 illustrates a violation of heuristic III and a modification that satisfies the heuristic.

Design Heuristics

1. Evaluate the preliminary structure to reduce coupling and improve cohesion.

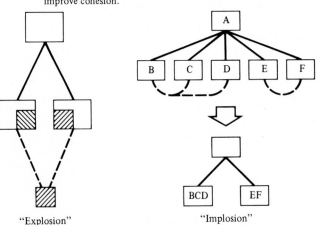

"Explosion" "Implosion"

Figure 7.20

Design Heuristics

2. Attempt to minimize high fan-out; strive for high fan-in as depth increases.

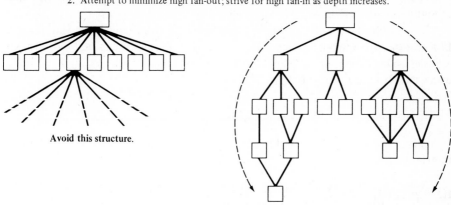

Avoid this structure.

Strive for this structure.

Figure 7.21

IV. Evaluate module interfaces to reduce complexity and redundancy and improve consistency. Module interface complexity is a prime cause of software errors. Interfaces should be designed to pass information simply and should be consistent with the function of a module. To illustrate interface complexity, consider the following source code:

```
TBL(1) = A
TBL(2) = B
TBL(3) = C


CALL QUAD-ROOT (TBL,X);
```

Design Heuristics

3. Keep the *scope-of-effect* of a module within the *scope-of-control* of that module.

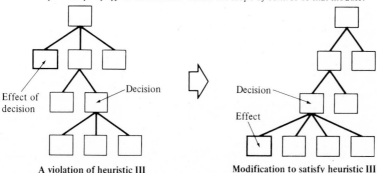

A violation of heuristic III

Modification to satisfy heuristic III

Figure 7.22

The module QUAD-ROOT computes the root of a quadratic equation with coefficients passed via the TBL array and returns roots by way of the X array. Can the interface to QUAD-ROOT be simplified?

The use of TBL and X could cause confusion (particularly) during maintenance and errors during development. A simpler interface might be

CALL QUAD-ROOT (A,B,C,ROOT1, ROOT2);

Interface inconsistency (i.e., seemingly unrelated data passed via an argument list or other technique) is an indication of low cohesion. The module in question should be reevaluated.

V. Define modules whose function is predictable, but avoid modules that are overly restrictive. A module is *predictable* when it can be treated as a black box; that is, the same external data will be produced regardless of internal processing details. Modules that have internal "memory" can be unpredictable unless care is taken in their use. The procedural flow shown in Figure 7.23 illustrates a module that "remembers" an internal flag and uses the flag to select processing options. Because the flag is invisible to superordinate modules, confusion can arise.

A module that restricts processing to a single subfunction exhibits high cohesion and is viewed with favor by a designer. However, a module that arbitrarily restricts size of a local data structure, options within control flow, or modes of external interface will invariably require maintenance to remove such restrictions.

VI. Strive for single-entry, single-exit modules, avoiding "pathological connections." This design heuristic warns against content coupling. Software is easier to understand and hence easier to maintain when modules are entered at the

Design Heuristics

5. Avoid *restrictive* modules, but define modules whose function is *predictable.*

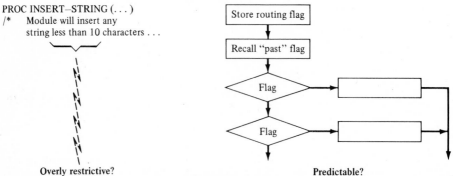

PROC INSERT–STRING (. . .)
/*   Module will insert any
      string less than 10 characters . . .

Overly restrictive?

Store routing flag

Recall "past" flag

Flag

Flag

Predictable?

Figure 7.23

top and exited at the bottom. The term *pathological connection* refers to branches or references into the middle of a module.

VII. Package software based on design constraints and portability requirements. *Packaging* alludes to the techniques used to assemble software for a specific processing environment or to ship software to a remote location. Design constraints sometimes dictate that a program *overlay* itself in memory. When this must occur, the design structure may have to be reorganized to group modules by degree of repetition, frequency of access, and interval between calls. In addition, optional or "one-shot" modules may be separated in the structure so that they may be effectively overlaid. An excellent discussion of packaging considerations for software design is presented in Yourdon and Constantine [1].

VIII. Select the size of each module so that independence is maintained. Nearly every discussion of modularity leads to the question: "What is the correct size for a module?" The answer must consider three characteristics: the concept of module independence; the necessity to reduce complexity; and the need for a quantitative recommendation. In almost all cases an attempt to achieve a high level of cohesion will result in a relatively small module. By reducing coupling, the complexity of a module is also reduced.

But what about size? How many modules should be defined for a given application? Or stated another way, is there an average number of source lines that is recommended? Many recommendations about average number of source lines have been made. A good guideline is: A module should be coded so that it may be read without turning a page in the source listing (i.e., module size can range from 50 to 100 source lines, on the average).

Recalling our earlier discussion of software science, Halstead has attempted to derive an expression for the optimal number of modules M, given other software characteristics. The criterion in his derivation is equal *length* for all modules:

$$\text{Program length} = (\text{module length}) \times M$$

which is expanded in the following way:

$$p = \frac{n - n'}{M}$$

$$n \log \frac{n}{2} = M(p + n') \log \frac{p}{2}$$

where n is program vocabulary $n = n_1 + n_2$, n' is a common vocabulary in all modules, and M is the number of modules.

The above transcendental equation may be solved for M. Halstead [12] derives a similar expression for M as a function of program volume.

McCabe's work indicates that control flow complexity has an important bearing on module size (Section 7.5.2). A detailed design should be evaluated to ensure that $V(G) < 10$.

Quantitative heuristics based on Halstead and McCabe metrics have been applied in only a limited number of practical applications. However, such work may lead to a more precise view of "good" modularity, allowing us to pinpoint the precise number of modules that should be developed for a set of software requirements.

7.7 SUMMARY

The concepts presented in this chapter serve as a precursor to more detailed discussions of software design. Software structure depicts a control hierarchy among all modules and provides an architectural view of the software. Procedure describes the internal details of a module and is layered as control passes from one module to the next.

Modularity is an essential attribute of all programs, but modular software by itself is not enough. Modularity is characterized by levels of abstraction that may be used to describe a software solution and by information hiding, a concept that is an important aspect of module independence. Modules must also exhibit independence in the form of high cohesion and low coupling. These quantitative measures of design "goodness" provide excellent guidance to the software designer.

Quantitative measures of software are in their infancy. Software science and cyclomatic complexity, probably the best developed of software measures, show promise as predictors for effort estimation, testing, reliability, and maintenance.

Design heuristics have been presented as generic guidelines to software development. Each of these guidelines can be applied to refine and improve preliminary design representations.

REFERENCES

1. Yourdon, E., and L. Constantine, *Structured Design,* Prentice-Hall, 1979
2. Myers, G., *Composite Structured Design,* Van Nostrand, 1978.
3. Wasserman, A., "Information System Design Methodology," in *Software Design Techniques,* 3d ed., IEEE Computer Society Press, 1980, p. 27.
4. Parnas, D. L., "On Criteria to Be Used in Decomposing Systems into Modules," *CACM,* December 1972, pp. 1053–1058.
5. Ross, D., J. Goodenough, and C. Irvine, "Software Engineering: Process, Principles and Goals," *Computer, IEEE,* May 1975.
6. Wirth, N., "Program Development by Stepwise Refinement," *CACM,* vol. 14, no. 4, April 1971, pp. 221–227.
7. Stevens, W., G. Myers, and L. Constantine, "Structured Design," *IBM System Journal,* vol. 13, no. 2, 1974.
8. Curtis, W., "Management and Experimentation in Software Engineering," *Proceedings of the IEEE,* vol. 68, no. 9, September 1980.

9. Boehm, B. et al., *Characteristics of Software Quality,* North Holland Publishing Company, 1978.
10. McCall, T. et al., *Factors in Software Quality,* (GE-TIS-77CIS02), General Electric Company, 1977.
11. McCabe, T., "A Software Complexity Measure," *IEEE Transactions on Software Engineering,* vol. 2, December 1976, pp. 308–320.
12. Halstead, M., *Elements of Software Science,* North Holland, 1977.
13. Bondy, J., and U. Murty, *Graph Theory with Applications,* North Holland, New York, 1976.
14. Fitzsimmons, A., and T. Love, "A Review and Evaluation of Software Science," *ACM Computing Surveys,* vol. 10, no. 1, March 1978, pp. 3–18.
15. Private communication from M. Zelkowitz, University of Maryland, June 1981.
16. Elshoff, J., "A Review of Software Measurement Studies at GM Research Laboratory," *Proceedings of the 2d IEEE Software Life Cycle Management Workshop,* 1978.
17. Green, T. et al., "Program Structures, Complexity and Error Characteristics," in *Computer Software Engineering,* Polytechnic Press, New York, 1976, pp. 139–154.
18. Curtis, W. et al., "Measuring the Psychological Complexity of Software Maintenance Tasks with the Halstead and McCabe Metrics," *IEEE Transactions on Software Engineering,* vol. 5, March 1979, pp. 96–104.

PROBLEMS AND POINTS TO PONDER

7-1 Lord Kelvin's statement, contained in the introduction to this chapter, is a cause for serious concern. Will our understanding of the characteristics of software ever achieve "the stage of science"? What as yet undeveloped quantitative measures would you like to see for computer software?

7-2 The analogy between a human organization chart and software structure can be carried further than we have done in Section 7.2.1. Attempt to draw parallels between concepts such as a matrix organization and certain types of software structures, "working through channels" and pathological connections, and other similarities you recognize. Where does the analogy fail?

7-3 How do the concepts of stepwise refinement (Chapter 6), layered procedure, and abstraction relate to one another?

7-4 Is there a case when inequality (7-2) may not be true? How might such a case affect the argument for modularity?

7-5 When should a modular design be implemented as monolithic software? How can this be accomplished? Is performance the only justification for implementation of monolithic software?

7-6 Describe the concept of abstraction for software in your own words.

7-7 Develop at least five levels of abstraction for one of the following software problems:
    (*a*) A full-screen editor for a CRT
    (*b*) A 3-D transformation package for computer graphics
    (*c*) A BASIC language interpreter
    (*d*) A payroll system
    (*e*) A 2-degree of freedom robot controller
    (*f*) Any problem mutually agreeable to you and your instructor

As the level of abstraction decreases, your focus may narrow so that at the last level (source code) only a single task need be described.

7-8 Obtain the original Parnas paper [4] and summarize the software example that he uses to illustrate decomposition of a system into modules. How is information hiding used to achieve the decomposition?

7-9 Discuss the relationship between the concept of information hiding as an attribute of effective modularity and the concept of module independence.

7-10 Review some of your recent software development efforts and grade each module (on a scale of 1, low to 7, high). Bring in samples of your "best" and "worst" work.

7-11 Is there a relationship between the degree of cohesion in a module and the module's cyclomatic complexity? Explain your reasoning and attempt to show counterexamples.

7-12 Is there a relationship between the degree of cohesion and a module's location in a factored structure? Explain your reasoning.

7-13 A number of high-level programming languages support the "internal" procedure as a modular construct. How does this construct affect coupling? Information hiding?

7-14 How are the concepts of coupling and software portability related? Provide examples to support your discussion.

7-15 As a class project, research Halstead's software science. Develop (using software engineering principles, of course) an automated processor that will accept a high-level language program (e.g., FORTRAN or PASCAL) and provide values for n_1, n_2, N_1, and N_2. From these primitive measures, compute other pertinent values as described in Halstead's book [12].

7-16 Using Halstead's book [12] as a guide, derive the expression given for the optimal number of modules M in a system. Is this expression useful in a practical sense?

7-17 Write a paper describing the results of studies that have attempted to validate Halstead's work, that have attempted to relate his work to other software characteristics such as reliability, and that consider the psychological aspects of software science.

7-18 Draw a program graph for each of the structured programming constructs described in Chapter 6. What is the value of $V(G)$ for each? A module m contains four if-then-else constructs following one another in sequence and contained inside two nested repeat-until constructs. What is $V(m)$? Is the module too complex?

7-19 Attempt to draw a program graph (consult [11] or [13] for guidance) for a module that you have recently developed. Determine the cyclomatic complexity for the module.

7-20 Discuss the impact of characteristics such as hiding, coupling, cohesion, Halstead's length, and McCabe's complexity measure on the *testability* of a module. Can you develop design guidelines that will ensure that a module can be easily tested?

FURTHER READINGS

A good discussion of qualitative software concepts such as structure, procedure, cohesion, and coupling (as well as many other design-related topics) can be found in Yourdon and

Constantine [1] and Myers [2]. Each book presents useful examples and opinions concerning the relationship of these concepts to good design.

Mathematically rigorous treatments of computer software and concepts related to design may be found in:

Horowitz, E., and S. Sahni, *Fundamentals of Computer Algorithms,* Computer Science Press, Potomac, MD, 1978.

Jones, C. B., *Software Development: A Rigourous Approach,* Prentice-Hall, 1980.

Knuth, D. E., *The Art of Computer Programming,* 2d ed., vol. 1, *Fundamental Algorithms,* Addison-Wesley, 1973.

Wulf, W. A. et al., *Fundamental Structures of Computer Science,* Addison-Wesley, 1981.

Each of these texts helps to supply a necessary theoretical foundation for our understanding of computer software.

An excellent collection of papers on software metrics is contained in *Models and Metrics for Software Management and Engineering* (Basili, V., IEEE Computer Society Press, 1980). Many of the references noted for this chapter are reprinted in this tutorial. A voluminous survey of the current status of software metrics research is contained in *Draft Software Metrics Panel Final Report* (A. J. Perlis et al., Eds., Yale University, Report No. 182/80, June 1980).

EIGHT

DATA FLOW–ORIENTED DESIGN

Design has been described as a multistep process in which representations of software structure and procedure are synthesized from information requirements. This description is extended by Freeman [1]:

> Design is an activity concerned with making major decisions, often of a structural nature. It shares with programming a concern for abstracting information representation and processing sequences, but the level of detail is quite different at the extremes. Design builds coherent, well planned representations of programs that concentrate on the interrelationships of parts at the higher level and the logical operations involved at the lower levels. . . .

As we have noted in preceding chapters, design is information-driven. Software design methodologies have been derived from consideration of information flow or information structure.

A data flow–oriented design method is presented in this chapter. The objective of the method is to provide a systematic approach for the development of software structure—an architectural view of software and the underpinning of the preliminary design step.

8.1 DESIGN AND INFORMATION FLOW

Information flow is a key consideration during the requirements analysis step of software engineering. Beginning with a fundamental system model (Chapter 5), information may be represented as a continuous "flow" that undergoes a series of transforms (processes) as it evolves from input to output. The data flow diagram

(DFD) is used as a graphical tool to depict information flow. Data flow–oriented design defines a number of different "mappings" that transform information flow into software structure.

8.1.1 Contributors

Data flow–oriented design (and software design generally) has its origins in earlier design concepts that stressed modularity [2], top-down design [3], and structured programming [4, 5]. However, the data flow–oriented design approach extended these procedural techniques by explicitly integrating information flow into the design process. Stevens et al. [6] were early proponents of software design based on the flow of data through a system. Early work was refined and presented in books by Myers [7] and Yourdon and Constantine [8]. The methods presented in this chapter are a synthesis of this material.

8.1.2 Areas of Application

Each software design methodology has strengths and weaknesses. An important judgmental factor for a design method is the breadth of applications to which it can be applied. Data flow–oriented design is amenable to a broad range of application areas. In fact, because all software can be represented by a data flow diagram, a design method that makes use of the diagram could theoretically be applied in every software development effort.

A data flow–oriented approach to design is particularly powerful when no formal data structure exists. For example, microprocessor control applications; complex, numerical analysis procedures; process control; and many engineering and scientific software applications do not require sophisticated data structures and are difficult to model with data structure–oriented design. A data flow approach solves this difficulty nicely.

Data flow–oriented design can also be applied to conventional data processing and other applications (e.g., CAD or operating systems) where distinct data structures do exist. In fact, most tutorials [e.g., 8] on the subject use case studies taken from the commercial data processing world.

An extension of data flow–oriented design, called MASCOT [9], adapts the approach to real-time, interrupt-driven applications. Using an information flow representation of concurrent processes, MASCOT provides intercommunication data areas that permit definition of interprocess communication. Heavy emphasis in real-time applications must be on interfaces among various processes. MAS-COT allows the designer to specify interfaces and coordinate communication with synchronizing primitives.

8.2 DESIGN PROCESS CONSIDERATIONS

Data flow–oriented design allows a convenient transition from information representations, the data flow diagram (DFD), contained in a *Software Requirements*

Specification to a preliminary design description of software structure. The transition from information flow to structure is accomplished as part of a five-step process: (1) information flow category is established; (2) flow boundaries are indicated; (3) DFD is mapped into software architecture; (4) control hierarchy is defined by factoring; and (5) resultant structure is refined by the use of design measures and heuristics. The information flow category is the *driver* for the mapping approach required in step 3. In the following paragraphs we examine two flow types.

8.2.1 Transform Flow

Recalling the fundamental system model (Chapter 5), information must enter and exit software in an "external world" form. For example, data typed on a terminal keyboard, tones on a telephone line, and pictures on a computer graphics display are all forms of external world information. Such externalized data must be converted into an internal form for processing.

The time history of data is illustrated in Figure 8.1. Information enters the system along paths that transform external data into an internal form. Flow along such incoming paths is called *afferent*. At the kernel of the software, a transition occurs. Incoming data are passed through a *transform center* and begin to move along paths that now lead "out" of the software. Flow along such outgoing paths is called *efferent*. When a segment of a data flow diagram exhibits these characteristics, *transform flow* is present.

8.2.2 Transaction Flow

The fundamental system model implies transform flow; therefore, it is possible to characterize all information flow in this category. However, information flow is

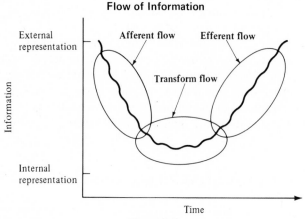

Figure 8.1

often characterized by a single data item, called a *transaction,* that triggers other data flow along one of many paths. When a DFD takes the form shown in Figure 8.2, *transaction flow* is present.

Transaction flow is characterized by data moving along a *reception path* that converts external world information into a transaction. The transaction is evaluated, and based on its value, flow along one of many *action paths* is initiated. The hub of information flow from which many action paths emanate is called a *transaction center.*

It should be noted that within a DFD for a large system, both transform and transaction flow may be present. For example, in a transaction-oriented flow, information flow along an action path may have transform flow characteristics.

8.2.3 A Process Abstract

The overall approach to data flow–oriented design is illustrated in Figure 8.3. Design begins with an evaluation of the data flow diagram. The information flow category (i.e., transform or transaction flow) is established, and flow boundaries that delineate the transform or transaction center are defined. Based on the location of boundaries, transforms (the DFD bubbles) are mapped into software structure as modules. The precise mapping and definition of modules is accomplished by factoring the structure and applying design measures and heuristics discussed in Chapter 7.

Figure 8.3 illustrates a step-by-step approach to design. However, variation can and does occur. Above all, software design demands human judgment that can often transcend the "rules" of a method.

Transaction Flow

. . . Characterized by an individual information item, called a *transaction,* that results in information flow along one of many action paths . . . .

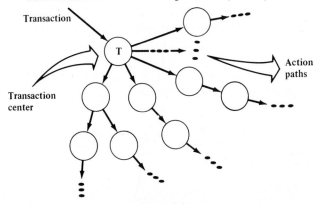

Transaction

Transaction center

Action paths

Figure 8.2

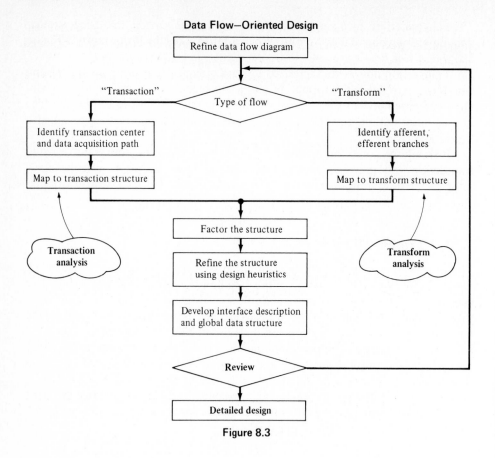

Figure 8.3

8.3 TRANSFORM ANALYSIS

Transform analysis is a set of design steps that allows a DFD with transform flow characteristics to be mapped into a predefined template for software structure. In this section transform analysis is described by applying design steps to an example system.

Many good examples of transform analysis have been drawn from commercial data processing applications [8]. As a change of pace, we consider an application from the domain of embedded microcomputer-based systems.

8.3.1 An Example

The era of "intelligent" products is upon us. Programmable calculators, microwave ovens, TV games, cameras, and typewriters—the list is endless—each require software (or firmware) development.

In such products, software is embedded in ROM and becomes a permanent part of the device. As an example of transform analysis in data flow–oriented design, we consider an integrated digital dashboard for an automobile.

Depicted in Figure 8.4, our hypothetical dashboard will perform the following functions:

- Microcomputer interface through analog-to-digital (A/D) conversion with transducers at engine, drivetrain, and chassis locations
- Data displayed on LED panels
- Indicators for miles per hour (mph), odometer, miles per gallon (mpg), cost per mile, trip cost, and other optional features
- An "overspeed" indicator that rings a chime synchronized to the difference between current speed (if > 55) and 55 mph
- Motorist selectable functions through a button array (to be discussed later)

Each of the above features and others would have to be thoroughly evaluated and documented during software requirements analysis. The fundamental system diagram and data flow diagrams accrue.

8.3.2 Design Steps

The above example will be used to illustrate each step in transform analysis. The steps begin with a reevaluation of work done during requirements analysis and then move to the development of software structure.

Step 1. Review the fundamental system model. In actuality the design step begins with an evaluation of both the *System Specification* and the *Software Requirements*

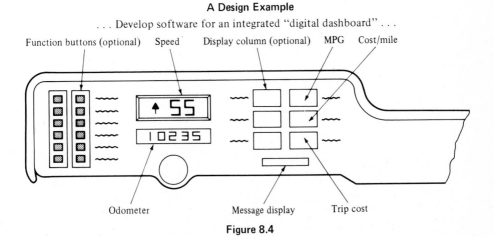

A Design Example

. . . Develop software for an integrated "digital dashboard" . . .

Function buttons (optional) Speed Display column (optional) MPG Cost/mile

Odometer Message display Trip cost

Figure 8.4

Specification. Both documents describe information flow and structure at the software interface.

Step 2. Review and refine data flow diagrams for the software. Using information obtained from a *Software Requirements Specification,* a data flow diagram derived from the digital dashboard is shown in Figure 8.5. Incoming flow at the upper left is a converted rotation signal that is read and converted into signals per second. Time average and change in signal [measured in signals per second (sps)] are used to drive speedometer functions and to indicate acceleration or deceleration, respectively.

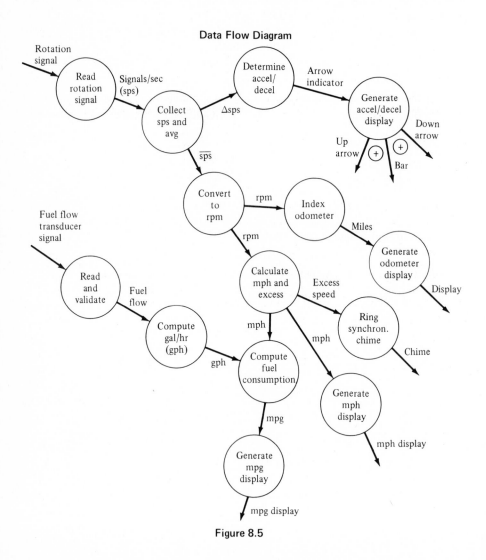

Figure 8.5

Once average sps is converted to rpm, speed (in mph) is developed and used to ring a synchronous chime (if speeding!), to generate mph display, and as one data item required to compute fuel consumption in mpg. The odometer function also uses rpm as incoming data. All of these functions lead to a display on the dashboard.

Acceleration and deceleration are indicated by an arrow to the left of the speed display (Figure 8.4). An up arrow indicates acceleration, a bar indicates steady speed, and a down arrow indicates deceleration. Finally, a second incoming path collects fuel flow data, converting it to gallons per hour for fuel efficiency calculation and display.

The data flow diagram shown in Figure 8.5 contains sufficient detail for a "first cut" at preliminary design of software structure. Therefore, we proceed without further refinement.

Step 3. Determine whether the DFD has transform or transaction characteristics. In general, information flow within a system can always be represented as transform. However, when an obvious transaction characteristic (Figure 8.2) is encountered, a different design mapping is recommended. In this step, the designer selects a global (software-wide) flow characteristic based on the prevailing nature of the DFD. In addition, local regions of transform or transaction flow are isolated. These *subflows* can be used to refine software structure derived from a global characteristic described above.

Evaluating the dashboard DFD (Figure 8.5), we see data entering the software along two incoming paths (rotation signal and fuel flow transducer signal) and exiting at five display (or chime) paths. No distinct transaction center is implied (although the transform *calc mph and excess* could be perceived as such). Therefore, an overall transform characteristic will be assumed for information flow.

Step 4. Isolate the transform center by specifying afferent and efferent flow boundaries. In the preceding section afferent or incoming flow was described as a path in which information is converted from external to internal form; efferent or outgoing flow converts from internal to external form. Afferent and efferent flow boundaries are open to interpretation. That is, different designers may select slightly different points in the flow as boundary locations. In fact, alternative design solutions can be derived by varying the placement of flow boundaries. Although care should be taken when boundaries are selected, a variance of one bubble along a flow path will generally have little impact on the final software structure.

Flow boundaries for the digital dashboard example are illustrated in Figure 8.6. The transforms (bubbles) that comprise the transform center lie within the two boundaries that run from top to bottom in the figure. An argument can be made to readjust a boundary [e.g., an afferent flow boundary separating *read and validate* and *compute gal/hr (gph)* could be proposed]. The emphasis in this design step should be on selecting reasonable boundaries, rather than lengthy iteration on placement of divisions.

DFD with Flow Boundaries

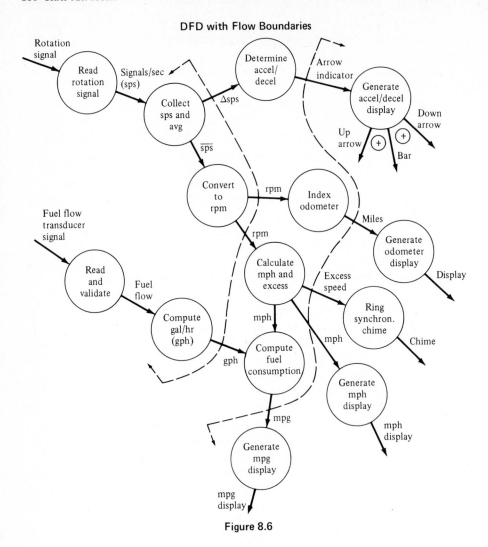

Figure 8.6

Step 5. Perform "first-level factoring." Software structure represents a top-down distribution of control. Factoring, as described in Chapter 7, is a process that distributes control.

When transform flow is encountered, a DFD is mapped to a specific structure that provides control for afferent (incoming), transform, and efferent (outgoing) information processing. This *first-level factoring* is illustrated in Figure 8.7. A control module C_m resides at the top of the software structure and serves to coordinate the following subordinate control functions:

- An afferent information processing controller C_a, that coordinates receipt of all incoming data

Design Approach

Step 5. Perform first-level factoring.

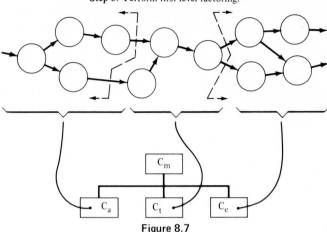

Figure 8.7

- A transform center controller C_t, that supervises all operations on data in internalized form (e.g., a module that invokes various "number crunching" procedures)
- An efferent information processing controller C_e, that coordinates production of output information.

Although a three-pronged structure is implied by Figure 8.7, complex flows in large systems may dictate two or more control modules for each of the generic control functions described above. The number of modules at the first level should be limited to the minimum that can accomplish control functions and still maintain good coupling and cohesion characteristics.

Continuing the digital dashboard example, first-level factoring is illustrated as a structure in Figure 8.8. Each control module is given a name that implies the function of subordinate modules it controls.

Step 6. Perform "second-level factoring." Second-level factoring is accomplished by mapping individual transforms (bubbles) of a DFD into appropriate modules of software structure. Beginning at the transform center boundary and moving outward along afferent and then efferent paths, transforms are mapped into subordinate levels of the software structure. The general approach to second-level factoring is illustrated in Figure 8.9.

Although Figure 8.9 illustrates a one-to-one mapping between DFD transforms and software modules, different mappings frequently occur. Two or even three bubbles can be combined and represented as one module (recalling potential problems with cohesion) or a single bubble may be expanded to two or more modules. Practical considerations and measures of design "goodness" dictate the outcome of second-level factoring.

First-Level Factoring

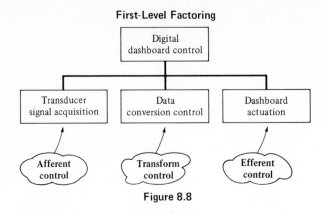

Figure 8.8

Design Approach

Step 6. Perform second-level factoring by moving "outward" from transform center on DFD. Develop afferent, transform, and efferent segments of structure separately.

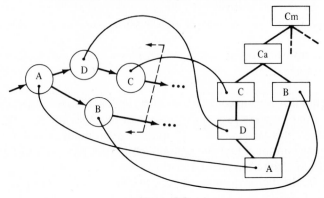

Figure 8.9

Software structure derived from the afferent flow paths of the DFD (Figure 8.6) is shown in Figure 8.10. A simple one-to-one mapping of bubbles to modules can be observed by following flow backward from the transform center boundary. Review and refinement may lead to changes in this structure, but it can serve as a "first-cut" design.

Second-level factoring for the transform center of digital dashboard software is shown in Figure 8.11. Each data conversion or calculation transform of the DFD is mapped into a module subordinate to the transform controller. Finally, efferent flow is mapped into software structure as illustrated in Figure 8.12. Factoring is again accomplished by moving outward from the transform center boundary.

Each module shown in Figures 8.10, 8.11, and 8.12 represents an initial design

Unrefined Afferent Structure

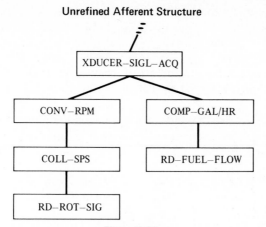

Figure 8.10

Unrefined Transform Structure

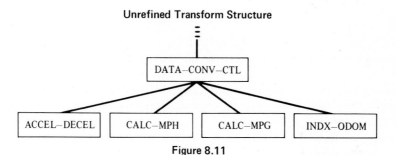

Figure 8.11

Unrefined Efferent Structure

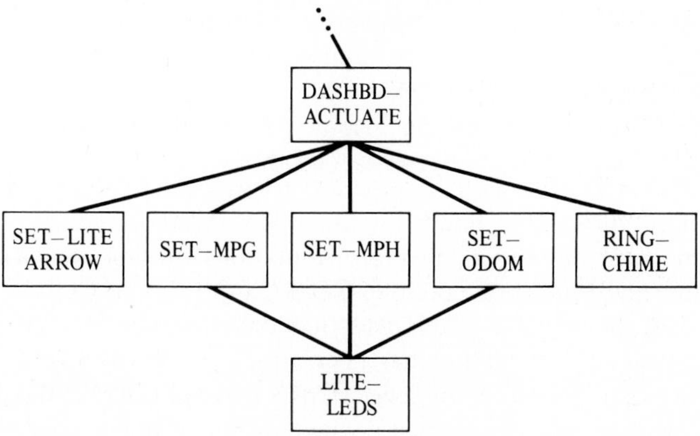

Figure 8.12

of software structure. Although modules are named in a manner that implies function, a brief processing narrative should be written for each. The narrative describes:

- Information that passes into and out of the module (an interface description)
- Information that is retained by a module; for example, data stored in a local data structure
- A procedural narrative that indicates major decision points and tasks
- A brief discussion of restrictions and special features (e.g., file I/O, hardware dependent characteristics, and special timing requirements).

The narratives serve as a first-generation *Design Specification.* However, further refinement and additions occur regularly during this period of design.

Step 7. Refine the first-cut software structure by using design measures and heuristics. A first-cut software structure can always be refined by applying concepts of module independence. Modules are exploded or imploded to produce sensible factoring, good cohesion, minimal coupling, and most importantly, a structure that can be implemented without difficulty, tested without confusion, and maintained without grief.

Refinements are dictated by practical considerations and common sense. There are times, for example, when an afferent controller is totally unnecessary, when some input processing is required in a module subordinate to the transform controller, when high coupling due to global data cannot be avoided, or when optimal fan-out or fan-in cannot be achieved. Software requirements coupled with human judgment is the final arbiter.

Many modifications can be made to the first-cut structure developed for the digital dashboard example. Some of the many possibilities are as follows:

- Modules CONV-RPM and COLL-SPS in the afferent structure branch can be imploded. Collection of transducer signals and conversion to an RPM measure are sequentially cohesive and make sense in this context.
- Module ACCEL-DECEL can be placed subordinate to CALC-MPH. This arrangement reduces coupling by simplifying information transfer through the transform controller, DATA-CONV-CTL.
- Module SET-LITE-ARROW can also be placed subordinate to SET-MPH to conform to the structural change described above.

The refined software structure for the digital dashboard is shown in Figure 8.13. Design constraints (e.g., memory limitations or time performance) may dictate further revisions. For example, RD-ROT-SIGL and CONV-RPM could be imploded (at the expense of relatively low cohesion), or DATA-CONV-CTL could be removed and control functions performed by DIG-DASH-CTL.

The objective of the preceding seven steps is to develop a global representation of software. That is, once structure is defined, we can evaluate and refine software architecture by viewing it as a whole. Modifications made at this time require little

Refined Structure

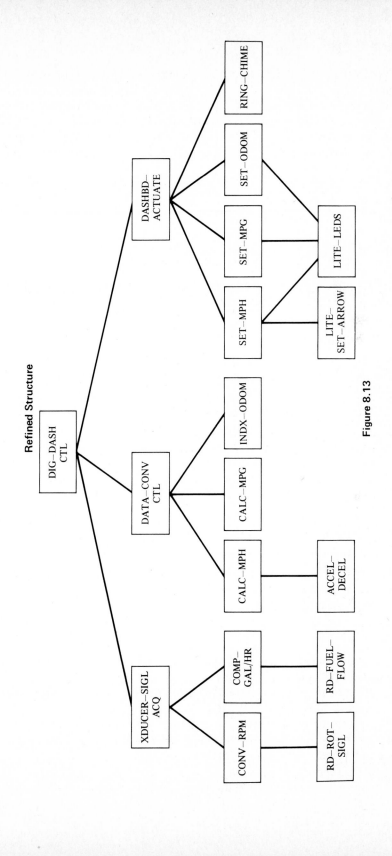

Figure 8.13

additional work, yet can have a profound impact on software quality and maintainability.

The reader should pause for a moment and consider the difference between the design approach described above and the process of "writing programs." If code is the only representation of software, the developer will have great difficulty evaluating or refining at a global or holistic level and will, in fact, have difficulty "seeing the forest for the trees."

8.4 TRANSACTION ANALYSIS

Information flow frequently represents a data item that on evaluation triggers additional flow along one of a number of selected paths. The data item, called a *transaction,* and its corresponding flow characteristics were discussed in Section 8.2.2. In this section we consider design steps used to treat transaction flow.

8.4.1 An Example

Transaction analysis will be illustrated by considering an extension of the digital dashboard software presented in the previous section. The basic dashboard system has optional features that include an *electronic key* and a *function selection/display* facility. An ignition start-up sequence of numbers is keyed through a button array (Figure 8.4) and replaces the ignition key. The array is also used to initiate the following functions:

Button	Function Selected
1	Initiate ignition start-up sequence
2	Activate radar detector (available only where legal!)
3	Activate display of various engine functions including oil pressure, temperature, etc.
4	Initiate data input and subsequent output for "trip computer"
5	Clear "trip computer"
6	Cancel previous key (clear)

During requirements analysis for the dashboard, a data flow diagram is developed for these optional features (Figure 8.14).

Referring to Figure 8.14, the array button or "function key" hit is a primary input that drives subsequent flow. After the key is validated, flow moves along one of a number of paths that are entered on determination of which button was pressed. In the figures, paths for buttons 1 and 2 are shown in detail, while other paths are indicated with single transforms (of course, these bubbles would need refinement) to simplify the drawing.

It should be noted that information flow along both paths 1 and 2 incorporates

Data Flow Diagram

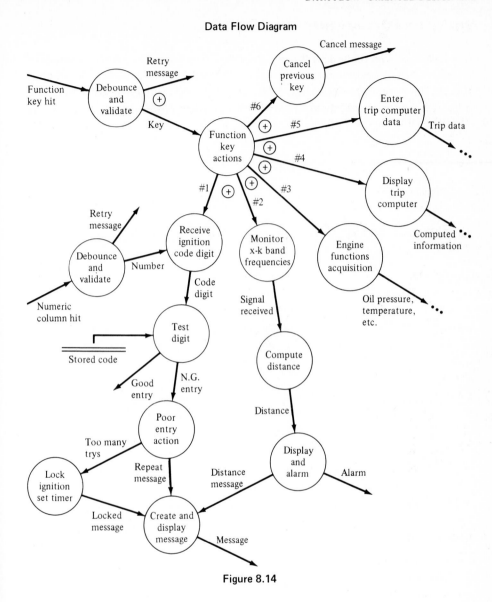

Figure 8.14

additional incoming data. Each path also produces displays, messages, and/or alarms.

8.4.2 Design Steps

Design steps for transaction analysis are similar and in some cases identical to steps for transform analysis (Section 8.3). A major difference lies in the mapping of DFD to software structure.

Step 1. Review the fundamental system model.

Step 2. Review and refine data flow diagrams for the software.

Step 3. Determine whether the DFD has transform or transaction characteristics.
Steps 1, 2, and 3 are identical to corresponding steps in transform analysis. The DFD shown in Figure 8.14 has a classic transaction flow characteristic. However,

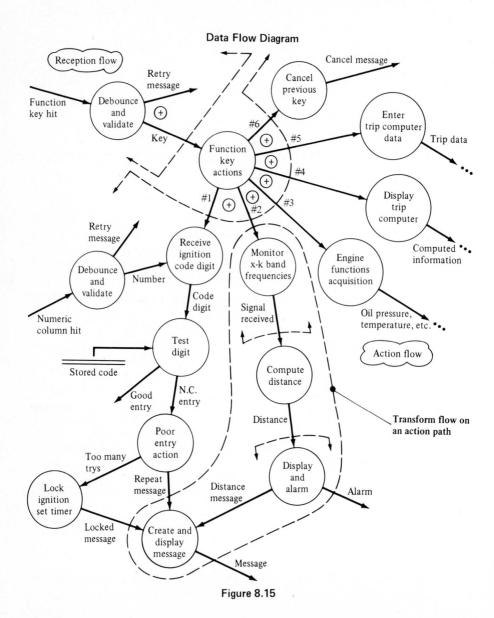

Figure 8.15

flow along each information path emanating from the "function key actions" bubble appears to have transform flow characteristics. Therefore, flow boundaries must be established for both flow types.

Step 4. Identify the transaction center and the flow characteristics of each action path. The location of the transaction center can be immediately discerned from the DFD. The transaction center lies at the origin of a number of information paths that flow radially from it. For dashboard flow shown in Figure 8.14, the function key actions bubble is the *transaction center.*

The *reception path* (i.e., the flow path along which a transaction is received) and all *action paths* must also be isolated. Boundaries that define a reception path and action paths are shown in Figure 8.15. Each action path must be evaluated for its individual flow characteristic. For example, the radar detection path (shown enclosed by a dashed curve in Figure 8.15) has transform characteristics. Afferent, transform, and efferent flow are indicated with dashed boundaries.

Step 5. Map the DFD into a software structure amenable to transaction processing. Transaction flow is mapped into a software structure that contains a *reception branch* and a *dispatch branch.* Structure for the reception branch is developed in much the same way as transform analysis. Starting at the transaction center boundary, bubbles along the reception flow path are mapped into modules. The structure of the dispatch branch contains a dispatcher module that controls all subordinate action modules. Each action flow path of the DFD is mapped to a structure that corresponds to its specific flow characteristics. This process is illustrated in Figure 8.16.

Considering the digital dashboard flow, first-level factoring for step 5 is shown

Design Approach

STEP 5 . Map the transaction flow into a structure that contains a reception branch and a dispatch branch.

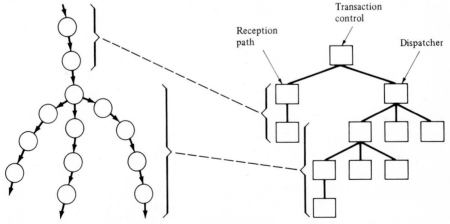

Figure 8.16

Map the Transaction Structure

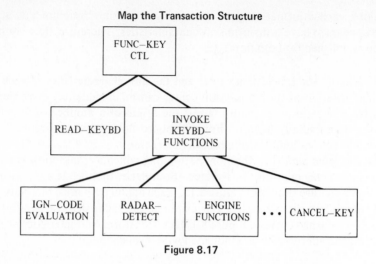

Figure 8.17

in Figure 8.17. Module READ-KEYBD performs all reception operations passing the transaction (a function key hit) through the transaction controller, FUNC-KEY-CTL, to the dispatcher module, INVOKE-KEYBD-FUNCTIONS. Subordinate to the dispatcher, modules IGN-CODE-EVALUATION, RADAR-DETECT, and others act as control modules for each action.

Step 6. Factor and refine the transaction structure and the structure of each action path. Each action path of the data flow diagram has its own information flow characteristics. We have already noted that transform or transaction subflows may be encountered. The action-path-related substructure is developed by using the design steps discussed in this and the preceding section.

Develop Action-Path Structure

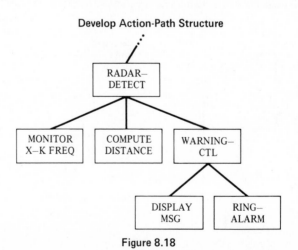

Figure 8.18

As an example, consider the radar detector information flow shown (inside dashed boundary) in Figure 8.15. The flow exhibits classic transform characteristics. Frequencies are monitored (afferent flow), producing input to a transform center when a signal is received. An alarm and warning message (efferent flow) are then produced. The structure for the resultant action path is shown in Figure 8.18.

A RADAR-DETECT module serves as the main controller. The afferent (incoming) flow is mapped into a MONITOR-X-K-FREQ module. Module COMPUTE-DISTANCE performs transform functions, and WARNING-CTL acts as the efferent (outgoing) branch controller. To maintain high cohesion, two modules, DISPLAY-MSG and RING-ALARM, perform reporting functions as subordinates to the efferent controller. The DFD transform *create and display message* is mapped into a utility module (i.e., a module with fan-in) that is used by two action structures.

The overall software structure is illustrated in Figure 8.19. Ignition code and radar detection functions are factored to illustrate development of action branches. It should be noted that within each transform substructure input is acquired and output is produced. The DISPLAY-MSG module is subordinate to two action paths, exhibiting fan-in, a common feature of transaction structures.

Step 7. Refine the first-cut software structure by using design measures and heuristics. This step for transaction analysis is identical to the corresponding step for transform analysis. In both design approaches, criteria such as module independence, practicality (efficacy of implementation and test), and maintainability must be carefully considered as structural modifications are proposed.

8.5 STRUCTURAL BUILDING BLOCKS

Transform and transaction analysis are frequently applied to different portions of the same DFD for a large system. The resultant substructures form building blocks that can be used to develop a large software architecture. The building block concept has been implied by the design example in Section 8.4.2.

To further illustrate the concept of structural building blocks, we consider the DFD shown in Figure 8.20. (*Note:* Generally a DFD of this size would be layered on separate sheets; a combined representation is used for illustrative purposes only.) Labeling has been deleted and regions of flow are indicated with boxed letters. Two options arise when the flow is evaluated (steps 1, 2, and 3 of the design approach):

1. *Transform analysis may be applied.* Regions A and B are afferent (incoming) paths; flow in the neighborhood of C, D, and E is assumed to be the transform center, and flow in region F and to the right of regions C and D is efferent (outgoing).
2. *Transaction analysis may be applied.* Region A contains reception flow paths;

Transaction Structure

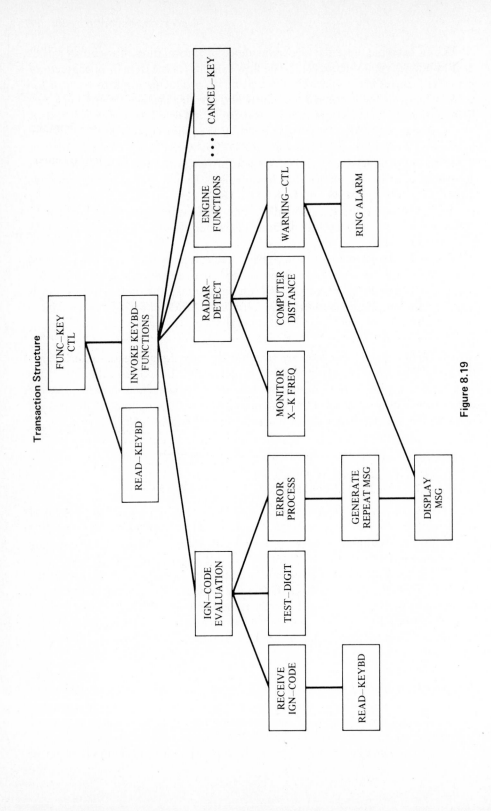

Figure 8.19

the transaction center is the bubble "southwest" of *C* and above *E;* and action paths reside in regions *B, C, D, E,* and *F.*

Which approach do we pursue? Is there one overriding flow characteristic that will dictate the approach? Can we view the flow as having combined characteristics?

We could select either design approach to develop software structure from the DFD. If flow does not divide dramatically, it is generally best to apply transform analysis. If, on the other hand, flow divides to form a classic transaction center, that analysis technique should be used. In complex flows such as that shown in Figure 8.20, both flow characteristics often occur.

To help illustrate the above points, the reader is urged to conduct the following exercise:

1. Number all bubbles in Figure 8.20.
2. Select an overriding flow characteristic.
3. Assume flow boundaries for the main flow and subflows.
4. Develop a software structure by using steps indicated in Sections 8.3 and 8.4.

It will become obvious that the overall software structure for the system in Figure 8.20 will be comprised of a framework structure and many building block substructures. Many unnecessary control modules will be specified if transform and

Complex Data Flow

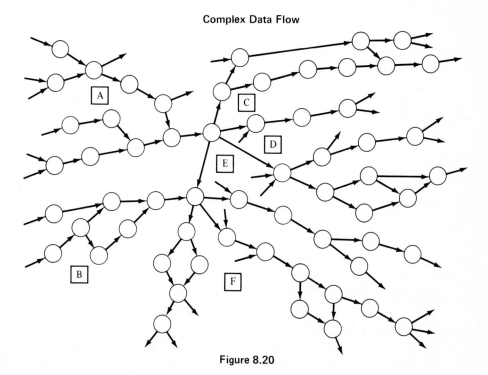

Figure 8.20

transaction mappings are followed explicitly. These modules can and should be eliminated when no useful purpose is being served.

8.6 DESIGN POSTPROCESSING

Successful application of transform or transaction analysis is supplemented by additional documentation that is required as part of preliminary design. After structure has been developed and refined, the following tasks must be completed:

- A processing narrative must be developed for each module.
- An interface description is provided for each module.
- Local and global data structures are defined.
- All design restrictions and limitations are noted.
- A preliminary design review (PDR) is conducted.
- "Optimization" is considered (if required and justified).

A processing narrative is (ideally) an unambiguous, bounded description of processing that occurs within a module. The narrative describes major tasks, decisions, and I/O and concentrates on important aspects of processing. The following narrative might be used for the RADAR-DETECT module shown in Figure 8.18:

> RADAR-DETECT is a control module for the radar detection function. The module invokes monitoring of X-K band frequencies, polling a monitoring module for occurrence of signal. If an occurrence is detected, RADAR-DETECT first invokes a distance computation and then passes control to warning generation modules. . . .

This narrative serves as a top-level procedural description that will subsequently be refined during detailed design.

An interface description provides a list of all data that enter and exit a module. The description should include data that move across an argument list, external world I/O, and information items acquired from global data areas. In addition, subordinate and superordinate modules are noted. As an example, consider an interface description for a digital dashboard module, CALC-MPG:

calling protocol: CALL CALC-MPG (MPH, GPH, MPG)
where
   MPH—miles per hour (real, input)
   GPH—gallons per hour (real, input)
   MPG—miles per gallon (real, output)
no external I/O or global data are used
called by: DATA-CONV-CTL
calls: no subordinates

The design of data structures can have a profound impact on software structure and the procedural details for each module (in fact, design techniques that are driven by data structure rather than data flow are discussed in Chapter 9).

Module Data Structure

Consider the example module DISPL–TRIP–COMP:

Data Structure

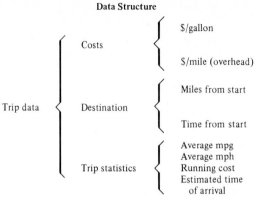

Figure 8.21

Both local and global data structures must be defined after software structure has been established. Hierarchical or Warnier diagrams (Chapter 5) may be used to represent the organization of data. Figure 8.21 illustrates local data required for module DISPL-TRIP-COMP of the digital dashboard system.

Restrictions and/or limitations for each module are also documented. Typical topics for discussion include restriction of data type or format, memory or timing limitations, bounding values or quantities of data structures, special cases not considered, and specific characteristics of an individual module.

The purpose of a restrictions-limitations section is to reduce the number of errors introduced because of "assumed" functional characteristics. As an example, consider the following excerpt from restrictions-limitations of module RING-CHIME: ". . . chime frequency (number of chimes per second) is a function of automobile speed . . . chime frequency has a lower limit of 0.5 Hz at 56 mph and an upper limit of 3.0 Hz at 80 mph. . . ." This excerpt specifies bounding values that restrict the function of the module.

Once preliminary design documentation is complete, a preliminary design review (PDR) is conducted (PDR criteria and format are discussed in Chapter 6). The review emphasizes traceability to software requirements, quality of software structure, interface descriptions, data structure descriptions, implementation, test practicality, and maintainability.

8.7 DESIGN OPTIMIZATION

Any discussion of design optimization should be prefaced with the following comment: "Remember that an 'optimal design' that doesn't work has questionable merit!" The software designer should be concerned with developing a representation of software that will meet all functional and performance requirements and merit acceptance based on design measures and heuristics.

Refinement of software structure during early stages of design is to be encouraged. Alternative representations may be derived (e.g., see Section 8.5), refined, and evaluated for the "best" approach. This approach to optimization is one of the true benefits derived by developing a representation of software architecture.

It is important to note that structural simplicity often reflects both elegance and efficiency. Design optimization should strive for the smallest number of modules that is consistent with effective modularity and the least complex data structure that adequately serves information requirements.

For time critical applications, it may be necessary to optimize during detailed design and, possibly, during coding. The software developer should note, however, that a relatively small percentage (typically 10 to 20 percent) of a program often accounts for a large percentage (50 to 80 percent) of all processing time. It is not unreasonable to propose the following approach for time critical software:

1. Develop and refine software structure without concern for time critical optimization.
2. During detailed design, select modules that are suspect "time hogs" and carefully develop procedures (algorithms) for time efficiency.
3. Code in a high-level language.
4. Instrument the software to isolate modules that account for heavy processor utilization.
5. If necessary, redesign or recode in machine-dependent language to improve efficiency.

This approach follows a dictum that will be further discussed in a later chapter: "Get it to work, then make it fast."

8.8 SUMMARY

Data flow–oriented design is a methodology that uses information flow characteristics to derive software structure. A data flow diagram is mapped into software structure by using one of two design analysis techniques—transform analysis or transaction analysis.

Transform analysis is applied to an information flow that exhibits distinct boundaries between incoming and outgoing data. The DFD is mapped into a structure that allocates control to input, processing, and output along three separately factored module hierarchies.

Transaction analysis is applied when an information item causes flow to branch along one of many paths. The DFD is mapped into a structure that allocates control to a substructure that acquires and evaluates a transaction. Another substructure controls all potential processing actions based on a transaction.

The techniques presented in this chapter lead to a preliminary design description of software. Modules are defined, interfaces are established, and data structure is developed. These design representations form the basis for all subsequent development work.

REFERENCES

1. Freeman, P., "The Context of Design," in *Software Design Techniques,* P. Freeman and A. Wasserman (eds.), *IEEE Computer Society Press,* 3d ed., 1980, pp. 2–4.
2. Dennis, J. B., "Modularity," in *Advanced Course on Software Engineering,* F. L. Bauer (ed.), Springer-Verlag, New York, 1973, pp. 128–182.
3. Wirth, N., "Program Development by Stepwise Refinement," *CACM,* vol. 14, no. 4, 1971, pp. 221–227.
4. Dahl, O., E. Dijkstra, and C. Hoare, *Structured Programming,* Academic Press, 1972.
5. Mills, H., *Mathematical Foundations for Structured Programming,* Technical Report FS71-6012, IBM Corporation, Federal Systems Division, Gaithersburg, MD, February 1972.
6. Stevens, W., G. Myers, and L. Constantine, "Structured Design," *IBM System Journal,* vol. 13, no. 2, 1974, pp. 115–139.
7. Myers, G., *Composite Structured Design,* Van Nostrand, 1978
8. Yourdon, E., and L. Constantine, *Structured Design,* Prentice-Hall, 1979.
9. Simpson, H. R., and K. Jackson, "Process Synchronization in MASCOT," *The Computer Journal,* vol. 22, no. 4, 1979, pp. 332–345.

PROBLEMS AND POINTS TO PONDER

8-1 Write a paper that tracks the progress of software design methodologies from 1970 to the present. A starting point for reference material could be the contributors noted in Section 8.1.1.

8-2 Some designers contend that all data flow may be treated as transform oriented. Discuss how this contention will affect the software structure that is derived when a transaction-oriented flow is treated as transform. Use an example flow to illustrate important points.

8-3 If you haven't done so, complete Problem 5-8 (in Chapter 5). Use the design methods described in this chapter to develop a software structure for the PMS.

8-4 Propose an approach to the design of real-time software applications that makes use of data flow–oriented techniques. To begin your discussion, list problems with real-time systems (e.g., interrupt-driven) that make direct application of data flow–oriented design somewhat unwieldy.

8-5 Using a data flow diagram and a processing narrative, describe a computer-based system that has distinct transform flow characteristics. Define flow boundaries and map the DFD into a software structure, using the technique described in Section 8.3.

8-6 Using a data flow diagram and a processing narrative, describe a computer-based system that has distinct transaction flow characteristics. Define flow boundaries and map the DFD into a software structure, using the technique described in Section 8.4.

8-7 Using requirements that are derived from class discussion or which you derive yourself, complete the DFD and design of the digital dashboard software used as an example in Sections 8.3 and 8.4. Assess the cohesion of each module and the coupling of the system. Develop preliminary design documentation for each module.

8-8 This project is intended for readers with a background in compiler design. Develop a DFD for a simple compiler; assess its overall flow characteristic, and derive a software structure, using the techniques described in this chapter. Provide processing narratives for each module.

8-9 How does the concept of *recursive modules* (i.e., modules that invoke themselves) fit into the design philosophy and techniques presented in this chapter?

8-10 Using the DFD shown in Figure 8.20, apply transaction analysis to the DFD and derive a software structure. Assume flow characteristics along the action paths to be transform in regions *C* and *D* and transaction in region *F*. Label all bubbles and map, using a one-to-one correspondence with modules.

8-11 Discuss the relative merits and difficulties of applying data flow oriented design in the following areas:
  (*a*) Embedded microprocessor applications
  (*b*) Engineering-scientific analysis
  (*c*) Computer graphics
  (*d*) Operating system design
  (*e*) Business applications
  (*f*) Database management system design
  (*g*) Communications software design
  (*h*) Compiler design
  (*i*) Process control applications
  (*j*) Combinatorial applications

8-12 Given a set of requirements provided by your instructor (or a set of requirements for a problem on which you are currently working), develop a complete preliminary design including all design documentation. Conduct a preliminary design review to assess the quality of your design. This problem may be assigned to a team, rather than an individual.

8-13 The data flow–oriented design approach does not address (directly) a key element in the design of software. What is it?

8-14 List at least three attributes of software that sometimes require optimization, and describe how a systematic design method that derives software structure can assist in such optimization.

FURTHER READINGS

A complete presentation of data flow–oriented design may be found in Myers [7] and Yourdon and Constantine [8]. These books are dedicated to design alone and provide a comprehensive tutorial in the data flow approach. Both texts contain numerous examples of data flow design application and are strongly recommended for those readers who are interested in software design.

An interesting presentation of software design is provided by Enos and Van Tilburg in Chapter 3 of Jensen and Tonies' book, *Software Engineering* (Prentice-Hall, 1979). The authors cover a broad range of design topics and emphasize the use of data flow–oriented design with a number of worthwhile examples.

NINE

DATA STRUCTURE–ORIENTED DESIGN

The intimate relationship between software and data can be traced to the origins of computing. The original concept behind the stored program computer was that programs could be viewed as data and data interpreted as programs. The structure of information, called *data structure,* has been shown to have an important impact on the complexity and efficiency of algorithms designed to process information.

As software design methods have evolved over the past decade, one school of thought [1] holds that *"The identification of the inherent data structure (for a computer-based system) is vital, and the structure of data (input and output) can be used to derive the structure (and some details) of a program."* In many areas of application a distinct, hierarchical information structure exists. Input data, internally stored information (i.e., a database), and output data may each have a unique structure. Data structure–oriented design makes use of these structures as a foundation for development of software.

9.1 DESIGN AND DATA STRUCTURE

Data structure affects the design of both structural and procedural aspects of software. Repetitive data are always processed with software that has control facilities for repetition; alternative data (i.e., information that may or may not be present) precipitate software with conditional processing elements; a hierarchical data organization frequently has a remarkable resemblance to software that uses the data. In fact, the structure of information is an excellent predictor of software structure.

Data structure–oriented design transforms a representation of data structure into a representation of software. Like data flow–oriented techniques (Chapter 8), developers of a data structure–oriented design have defined a set of "mapping" procedures that use information (data) structure as a guide.

9.1.1 Contributors

The origins of data structure–oriented design can be found in technical discussions on the fundamentals of data structures [e.g., 2], computer algorithms [e.g., 3], the structure of control and data [4], and the concept of data abstractions [5]. More pragmatic treatments of software design and its relationship to data structure have been proposed by Jackson [6], Warnier [7,8], and more recently by Chand and Yadav [9].

The Jackson methodology, one of the most widely used software design methods, takes the view that "paralleling the structure of input data and output (report) data will ensure a quality design" [1]. Jackson emphasizes practicality, developing pragmatic techniques to transform data to program structure.

Logical construction of programs (LCP), a design methodology developed by Jean Dominique Warnier [7], provides a more rigorous method for software design. Drawing on fundamental concepts in computer science, Warnier develops a set of techniques that accomplish a mapping from input/output (I/O) data structure to a detailed procedural representation of software.

A technique called *logical construction of software* (LCS) [9] is representative of a synthesis of data flow- and data structure-oriented design approaches. The developers of the method contend that "logical design can be described explicitly if the software is viewed as a system of data sets and data transforms" [9]. Although LCS is not purely data structure–oriented, it may be correctly viewed within this class of design techniques.

9.1.2 Areas of Application

Data structure–oriented design may be successfully applied in applications that have a well-defined, hierarchical structure of information. Typical examples include:

Business and financial applications. Input and output have distinct structure (e.g., input files and output reports); the use of a hierarchical database is common.

Systems applications. The data structure for operating systems is comprised of many tables, files, and lists that have well-defined structure.

CAD/CAM applications. Computer-aided design and computer-aided manufacturing systems require sophisticated data structure for information storage, translation, and processing.

In addition, applications from the engineering-scientific domain, computer-aided instruction, combinatorial problem solving, and many other areas may be amenable to data structure–oriented design.

As we have already noted, a data flow–oriented design approach may always be used. However, data structure–oriented design can also produce good results when the proper information characteristics are present.

9.1.3 Data Structure versus Data Flow Technique

Before considering differences between data structure– and data flow–oriented design, it is important to note that both are information-driven, attempt to transform information into a software representation, and are based on separately derived concepts of "good" design.

Data structure–oriented design does not make explicit use of a data flow diagram. Therefore, transform and transaction flow classifications have little relevance to the data structure–oriented design method. More importantly, the ultimate objective of data structure–oriented methods is to produce a procedural description of the software. The concept of software structure is not explicitly considered. Modules are considered as a by-product of procedure, and a philosophy of module independence is given little emphasis.

Data structure–oriented design makes use of a hierarchial diagram or Warnier diagram to represent information structure. Therefore, the emphasis during software requirements analysis must be placed on these modes of representation.

The above paragraphs imply a number of significant differences in design philosophy. An obvious question arises: "Which method is best?" Controversy surrounds the answer. In Section 9.5 we consider different points of view.

9.2 DESIGN PROCESS CONSIDERATIONS

Software requirements analysis remains the foundation for data structure–oriented design. The description of information structure contained in the *Software Requirements Specification* foreshadows software architecture that is to be developed during design. Each design method provides a set of "rules" that enables the designer to transform data structure into a representation of software.

Each data structure–oriented method has its own set of rules. However, the following design tasks are always conducted: (1) data structure characteristics are evaluated; (2) data are represented in terms of elementary forms such as sequence, selection, and repetition; (3) data structure representation is mapped into a control hierarchy for software; (4) software hierarchy is refined by using guidelines defined as part of a method; and (5) a procedural description of software is ultimately developed.

A clean division between preliminary and detailed design steps (as they have been described as part of the software life cycle) is not evident in data structure–

oriented methods. Both Jackson and Warnier move quickly to a procedural representation.

9.3 THE JACKSON METHODOLOGY

The essence of the Jackson methodology may be stated by paraphrasing its developer, Michael Jackson: "Problems should be decomposed into hierarchical structures of parts that may be represented by three structural forms." The "structural forms" that Jackson alludes to are sequence, condition, and repetition—in actuality, *procedural constructs* (in the terminology of this book) that are the foundation of the structured programming philosophy (Chapter 6).

Jackson has developed a data structure notation that closely resembles the data structure (hierarchical) diagram. In addition, the methodology proposes a set of mapping or transformation procedures. It is through these procedures that the method may be adapted to variations in data structure and nonconformity between input and output data structures.

An overview of the Jackson methodology is presented in this section. Many of the examples used are adapted from Jackson's text [6].

9.3.1 Data Structure Notation

A simple representation of Jackson's data structure notation is shown in Figure 9.1. Following the hierarchical diagram, a collection of data A is comprised of multiple occurrences (denoted by *) of data substructure B. Substructure B includes multiple occurrences of C and another substructure D that contains data item E or F (alternative data are denoted by an *o*). Jackson's block diagrammatic representation of information hierarchy may be applied to input, output, or database structures with equal facility.

Data Structure Notation

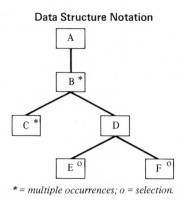

* = multiple occurrences; o = selection.

Figure 9.1

As a more concrete example of this notation, we consider software to be developed for a credit card accounting system (grossly simplified), shown in Figure 9.2. A payment file, containing customer numbers (CNO), payment date (DATE), and amount paid (AMT), is to be reconciled with a customer master file that contains CNO and outstanding balance. The payment file is presorted in customer number groupings (CNO-GROUP) so that all payments by an individual are contained within a single record. The data structure for both files, described in Jackson notation, is shown in Figure 9.2.

An output report format for the credit card accounting system and the resultant data structure diagram is shown in Figure 9.3. The report implies a hierarchy that includes customer data (CUST-DATA) and master totals. Sub-structures indicate information contained with the hierarchy.

9.3.2 Program Structure Derivation

Jackson contends that processing hierarchy for software maps directly from input and/or output data structure. Unfortunately, he calls processing hierarchy *structure*, thus causing confusion with earlier definitions used in this book.

Using a direct mapping of the data structure shown in Figure 9.3, a processing hierarchy (Jackson's "program structure") for the credit card system can be derived. Referring to Figure 9.4, we see that the structure of data (Figure 9.3) and program are identical. Unlike data flow–oriented design, the boxes of a processing

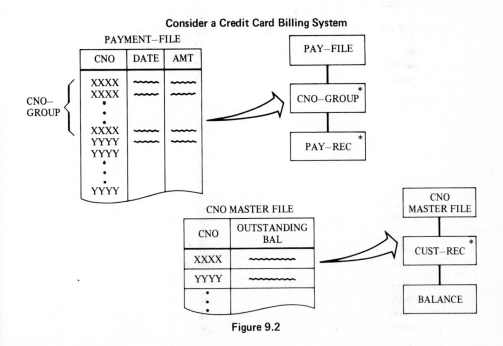

Figure 9.2

System Output

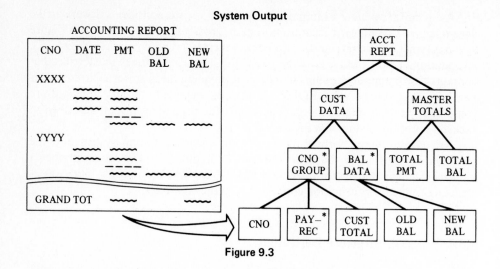

Figure 9.3

hierarchy do not necessarily delineate modules. In fact, Jackson takes a mixed view (a view not shared by this author) of modularity, foreseeing potential problems during software integration and maintenance.

Unfortunately, information structure for many systems is not amenable to the direct mapping approach described above. In such cases Jackson describes a set of supplementary techniques (discussed in Section 9.3.4) that makes the design approach more flexible.

Resultant Program Structure

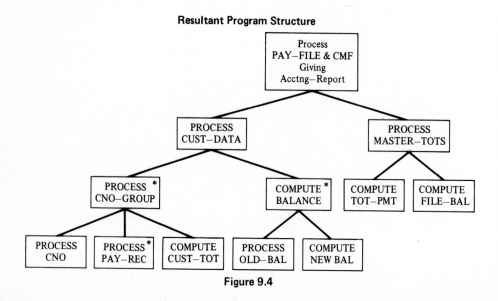

Figure 9.4

9.3.3 Procedural Representation

The Jackson methodology derives a processing hierarchy as the primary design representation. A natural extension of the processing hierarchy is a procedural representation of the program in *pseudocode,* a programming language–like notation. A more detailed discussion of pseudocode is presented in Chapter 10.

A pseudocode development of a substructure of the credit card system processing hierarchy is shown in Figures 9.5 and 9.6. As noted earlier, Jackson

Procedural Representation

Consider the substructure PROCESS–CUST–DATA:

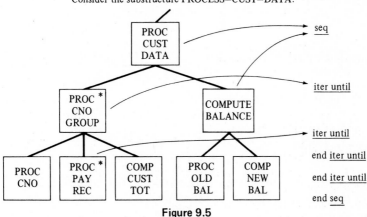

Figure 9.5

Jackson's Procedural Representation

```
PROC–CUST–DATA seq.
    open PAY–FILE; open C–M–F;
    PROC–CNO–GROUP iter until EDF–PAY–FILE;
        read PAY–FILE;
        PROC–CNO; {reads C–M–F, finds old balance }
        PROC–PAY–REC iter until end CNO group;
            write report line;
            compute total payments
            read PAY–FILE;
        end PROC–PAY–REC;
        COMP–CUST–TOT;
        COMP–BAL seq.
            PROC–OLD–BAL;
            COMP–NEW–BAL;
            write report line;
        end COMP–BAL;
    end PROC–CNO–GROUP;
end PROC–CUST–DATA;
```

Figure 9.6

makes use of three procedural building blocks: sequence; condition; and repetition (called *iteration*) that follow directly from his data structure notation. In order to process customer data (PROC-CUST-DATA in Figure 9.5), a sequence (*seq*) of procedural steps is initiated. Each CNO-GROUP is processed until (*iter until*) an end of file is encountered. Within each group, payment records are processed until the end of the CNO-GROUP is reached. The pseudocode shown in Figure 9.6 begins to approximate a programming language source listing, where PROC-OLD-BAL and COMP-NEW-BAL are references to separate modules.

The Jackson procedural representation is more closely aligned with detailed design description (rather than preliminary design description). The holistic representation of software structure, discussed in Chapter 8, is not evident in this method.

9.3.4 Supplementary Techniques

The Jackson methodology supports a number of supplementary techniques that broaden its applicability and enrich the overall design approach. A complete discussion of each of these techniques is best left to Jackson himself [6]. However, an overview of the more important supplementary concepts is presented in the following paragraphs.

Data validity and error processing. The problem of erroneous data (or data that are out of sequence) is a difficult one to resolve in data structure–oriented design. The data structure diagram does not represent erroneous data because such information should not exist in the structure. Realistically, the occurrence of erroneous data must be anticipated. To quote Jackson: "the program structure (processing hierarchy) must have consistent rules for allocating responsibility for testing data validity. . . ." The following rules are stated:

- Every module specification (as modules are derived from procedural representations) must have a defined range of valid data.
- Every module is designed with the assumption that data supplied to it are valid.
- If module B is subordinate to module A, then A is responsible for ensuring that data passed to B are valid.

These rules cannot be directly derived from data structure. Unlike data flow-oriented methods that transform error processing shown in a DFD, the Jackson approach does not "map" such design characteristics. In some cases, however, tests for data invalidity and/or error processing can be built in. As an example, we consider the credit card accounting system discussed earlier.

Recalling that each CNO-GROUP contains payment records that indicate payment amount and date, we now assume that only chronologically ordered payment records are to be processed. That is, if date($i + 1$) < date(i), the record is rejected. To reflect this change, the PAY-REC portion of the data structure may

Error Processing

Modifying the PAY–REC portion of the data structure:

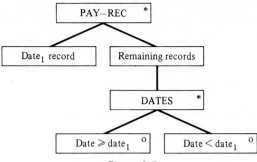

Figure 9.7

be modified as shown in Figure 9.7. Using procedural constructs for sequence, condition, and repetition, a pseudocode representation may be derived.

Backtracking. Jackson recognizes that during program execution, a processing path is often chosen based on poor or nonexistent evidence. That is, we assume a path to be correct and backtrack when later evidence indicates that the path is not the correct one. To help in the design of such backtracking situations, Jackson proposes three new "constructs" for procedural pseudocode.

Posit is used to indicate that processing is to occur on the basis of a hypothesis of correctness. The program state is stored on entry to a *posit* construct. *Quit* indicates that the hypothesis fails, and control is passed to an *admit* construct that provides an alternative processing path. The program state is restored unconditionally on entry to *admit*. Only "virtual" input and output are performed during *posit* so that all files may be restored if *quit* is invoked.

To illustrate backtracking, we use the following example from Jackson's book:[1]

A program component is to be written to process a single card.

The card contains three fields—F1, F2 and F3. F1 should be numeric in the range 1 through 99 and if so, it can be used to retrieve an entry from a table. The entry contains two limit values and a multiplier to give a disk address. The record at the disk address contains a character string. F3 should be equal to a substring of this character string. If so, its prefix in the string is to be printed.

We therefore have the following situation. Each of the fields F1, F2 and F3 may be good data or error data. There are three processes, P1, P2 and P3, which may be carried out on F1, F2 and F3 respectively:

P1 retrieves the entry from the table;

[1] Jackson, M., *Principles of Program Design,* Academic Press Ltd., London, 1975, pp. 117–123. Reprinted with permission.

P2 accesses the disk record;
P3 prints the prefix of F3 in the character string.
The program component should carry out the following operations:
if all the fields are good, *then* print the prefix of F3, *else* execute the error routine
PX.
if Fn is not good, *then* process Pn cannot be executed ($n = 1,2,3$).

A data structure and resulting pseudocode representation for the above example is shown in Figure 9.8 (reproduced from Jackson [6]). Note that *posit* assumes a "good" card, quitting if an error is detected.

Structure clash. In many software applications input information has little or no structural correspondence to output information. Jackson terms this situation a *structure clash* and proposes a series of detailed design maneuvers to overcome it. To outline the approach:

1. Characteristics of the input structure are defined by using data structure diagram notation.
2. Software is designed to decompose the input data structure into elements that form some transient *intermediate data structure.*
3. The output data structure is described.
4. Software is designed to build the output structure from the intermediate structure.

For complicated structure clashes, the designer may synthesize a number of intermediate data structures. Each resultant software design must be integrated to form a single program.

Other design procedures. Jackson proposes additional design procedures that help to mitigate the structure clash problem. *Program inversion* and a more complicated variant called *multithreading* may be applied during design to eliminate the use of intermediate data structure.

Myers [10] describes the process of inversion in the following manner:

Data Structure and Procedure

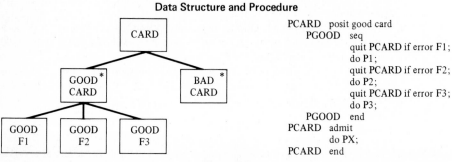

Figure 9.8

Although the use of intermediate files resolves the structure clashes, it adds obvious inefficiencies and is also conceptually unnecessary. If there was a way to multiprogram (concurrently execute) and synchronize the two programs, the intermediate file would be unnecessary. This is because the first program sequentially reads it. Therefore, the file could then be replaced with a single-record buffer. Whenever the first program would have written a record, it would wait until the buffer is empty and then place the record in the buffer; whenever the second program would have read a record, it would wait until a record is placed into the buffer and then move it out and process it.

Once we convince ourselves that the two programs can work successfully this way, we can achieve the same effect, without the buffer and the multiprogramming, by directly linking the programs. This is done by "inverting" one of the programs and having the other program call it. Inverting a program does not substantially change its function but does, in a sense, invert its function. . . .

Optimization in the Jackson methodology is a topic that is approached with care. The following comment on optimization sets the tone for its application [6]:

The word "optimization" is ill-chosen. Its Latin derivation implies that to optimize a program is to make it as good as it can be; but what we mean by an optimized program is one that is as small or as fast as it can be. In making it small or fast, or if we can, both, we are liable to make it bad in various ways: it may become harder to understand, harder to maintain and more prone to error.

Although Jackson provides examples of optimization in his writings, no general approach or criterion is stated. Rather, a case-by-case attempt to reduce program size appears to be the goal of his procedures.

9.3.5 Summary—The Jackson Methodology

The Jackson methodology uses data structure as a driver for a procedurally oriented design approach. Circumventing the software structure representation used in data flow–oriented design, Jackson moves directly to procedural constructs that include sequence, condition, and repetition. Supplementary constructs and techniques are used to accommodate backtracking situations, resolve structure clash, and optimize the software.

Jackson's writings make heavy use of examples (a commendable approach) but often lack sufficient explanatory text to give meaning to each example. In order to appreciate the merit of Jackson's work, careful reading (and probably some supplementary training) is required.

9.4 LOGICAL CONSTRUCTION OF PROGRAMS

Logical construction of programs (LCP), begins with a representation of data structure; moves to a formal representation of procedure; and culminates with systematic methods for pseudocode generation, verification, and optimization.

Warnier, an information scientist, developed his method under the assumption that "programs can be constructed logically and verified rigorously using tools derived from the study of informatics (computer science). [7]"

LCP is presented as a series of "rules" and "laws" that govern the structure of information and the resultant organization of derived software. Unlike other design methods discussed in this book, LCP is derived from theoretical foundations and is clearly the most rigorous method in its treatment of design development and verification.

A complete discussion of LCP is beyond the scope of this book. In this section we consider some of the important characteristics of the methodology. For additional information, the reader is urged to study Warnier's texts [7,8].

9.4.1 The Warnier Diagram

Data structure notation used in LCP is the *Warnier diagram* (introduced in Chapter 5). Like Jackson's hierarchical diagram, the Warnier representation of data depicts hierarchy as well as explicit repetitive and conditional information. Basic diagram characteristics are illustrated in Figure 9.9. Referring to the figure, a data file contains three record types (1, 2, and 3) that are encountered 4 times, 0 or 1 time, and n times, respectively. Data record 1 contains items a, b, and c. Data record 2 contains item f and an item g that may or may not be present (occurs 0 or 1 time). Data record 3 always contains item e and may contain n items that are comprised of m occurrences of element i.

A "rule" stated by Warnier indicates that "any set of information must be

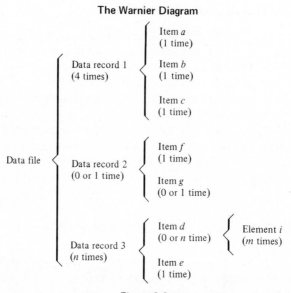

Figure 9.9

subdivided into subsets . . ." [7]. The Warnier diagram accomplishes this subdivision with additional specification of the number of occurrences of data elements. In addition, data that appear conditionally are indicated with a "(0 or 1 time)" qualifier.

9.4.2 LCP Design Approach

The LCP design approach begins with specification of both input and output data structures with the use of Warnier diagrams. Like other design methods, a thorough evaluation of software requirements is a precursor to a derivation of a software representation. Warnier takes the classic view that "programs, like data (input) and results, are information files." Therefore, the next step of LCP is to represent software processing with the Warnier diagram.

A processing hierarchy for a program is derived from the structure of input data. For example, the data file shown in Figure 9.9 can be processed by a program such as that illustrated in Figure 9.10. Note that a bar above an entry in the diagram indicates a *not* condition, e.g., the bar above *process g* indicates that *g* may not be processed.

The Warnier diagram representation of software may be transformed into a more conventional flowchart representation shown in Figure 9.11. Examining the flowchart, we see that repetition in the data structure is translated into a *repeat-until* construct and conditional occurrence into the *if-then-else* construct. It is possible to interpret each box of the flowchart as a module. However, Warnier (like Jackson) takes a procedural view that circumvents software structure and direct definition of modules.

LCP Processing Hierarchy

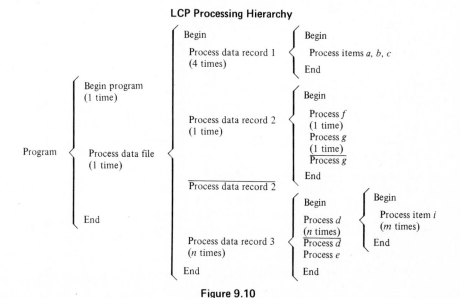

Figure 9.10

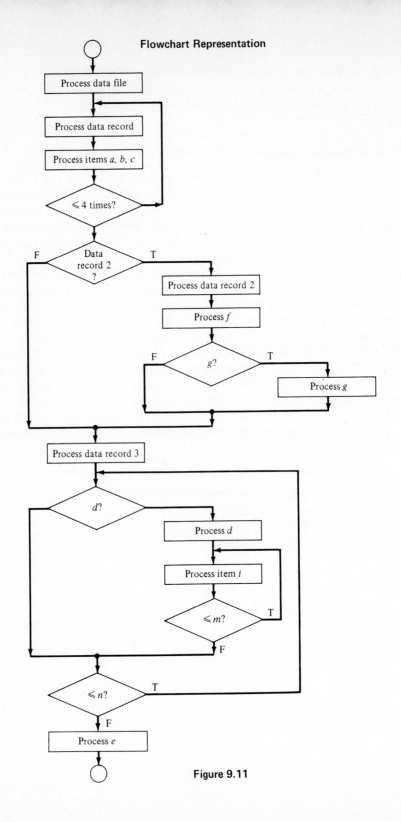

Flowchart Representation

Process data file

Process data record

Process items a, b, c

≤ 4 times?

Data record 2 ?

F   T

Process data record 2

Process f

F g?   T

Process g

Process data record 3

d?

Process d

Process item i

$\leq m$?   T

F

$\leq n$?   T

F

Process e

Figure 9.11

As an example of the LCP design approach, applied through the development of a flowchart representation, we consider an application discussed in Warnier's text [7]:

A periodic report of customer's accounts is to be produced. The input file contains for each customer a header record followed by "movement" (transaction) records. In other words, there are 0, 1 or many movements (transactions) for each customer.

The overall organization of an output report for the above application and a description of input records are given in Figure 9.12. The "code" field of the second input record indicates whether a movement (MVT) is credit or a debit.

Warnier diagrams that describe the information hierarchy of the output report and the input data records are shown in Figure 9.13. It should be noted that the output diagram implies the conditional occurrence of levels 4 and 5. (A customer may have initiated no transactions.) The input records (Figure 9.12) are included in the Warnier diagram. Again, levels 4 and 5 occur only when a transaction has been made.

Processing hierarchy is developed from the input information structure. A Warnier diagram representation of the program is shown in Figure 9.14. A flowchart derived from the diagram is shown in Figure 9.15. The numbers to the left of each processing block in the flowchart are used in the development of *detailed organization.*

An Example

The layout of the output report is:

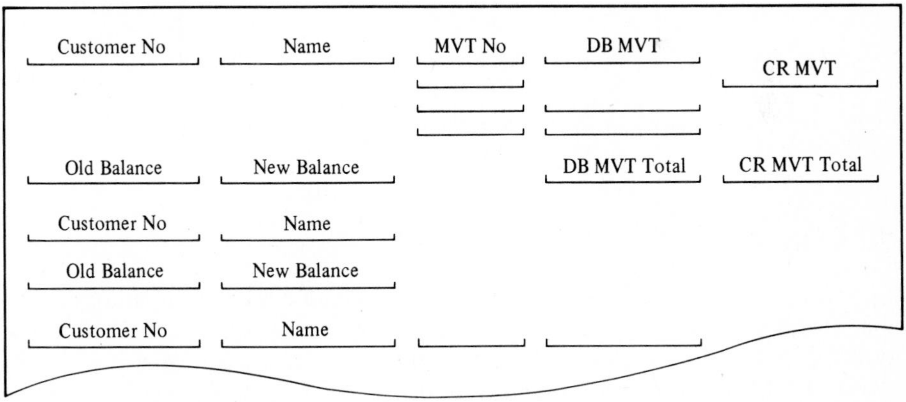

Customer No	Name	MVT No	DB MVT	
				CR MVT
Old Balance	New Balance		DB MVT Total	CR MVT Total
Customer No	Name			
Old Balance	New Balance			
Customer No	Name			

The layouts of the input records are:

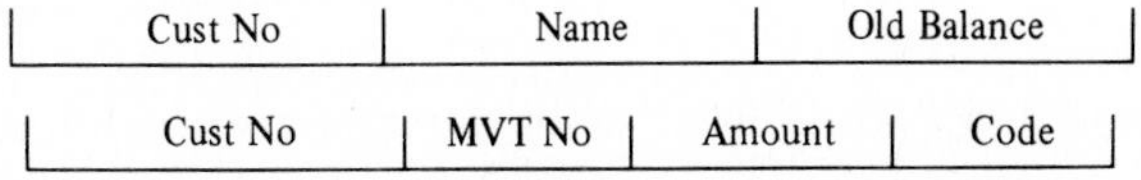

Cust No	Name	Old Balance	

Cust No	MVT No	Amount	Code

(Source: J. D. Warnier, Logical Construction of Programs. Copyright 1974, Les Editions d'Organisation, reprinted with permission Van Nostrand Reinhold Company.)

Figure 9.12

Information Structure

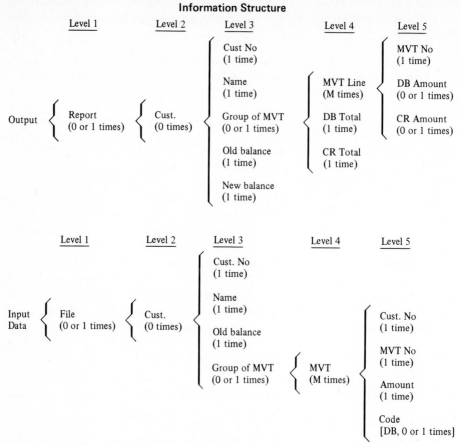

(Source: J. D. Warnier, Logical Construction of Programs. Copyright 1974, Les Editions d'Organisation, reprinted with permission Van Nostrand Reinhold Company.)

Figure 9.13

9.4.3 Detailed Organization

Logical construction of programs attempts to extend design methodology into a domain that other methods avoid. Warnier has developed a technique, called *detailed organization,* in which a set of detailed instructions can be systematically developed from the logical organization of the program (e.g., Figures 9.14 and 9.15). Of course, other design methods set a foundation for specification of detailed instructions, but Warnier has proposed a step-by-step process for deriving such instructions.

Warnier defines the following types (or classes) of instructions:

- Input and input preparation
- Branching and branching preliminaries

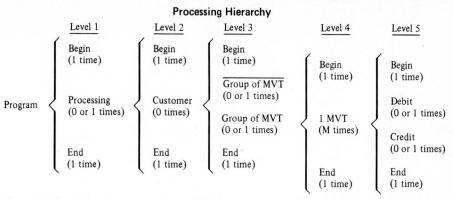

(Source: J. D. Warnier, Logical Construction of Programs. Copyright 1974, Les Editions d'Organisation, reprinted with permission Van Nostrand Reinhold Company.)

Figure 9.14

- Calculations
- Output and output preparation
- Subprogram (module) calls

A detailed organization is developed by generating lists of instructions by type. The instruction is written and correlated to the appropriate processing block with a numeric indication (e.g., the number to the left of each block in Figure 9.15). A list for each instruction type is prepared.

After instruction lists are prepared, instructions with the same processing block identifier are grouped and organized in an input-processing-output sequence. For the customer accounts software discussed in Section 9.4.2, the corresponding instruction lists [7] are shown in Figure 9.16. An example of sorted instructions is illustrated in Figure 9.17.

Detailed organization provides the designer with a technique for developing a detailed design description in a systematic way. The nonsequential nature of the approach may seem a bit unusual (bizarre!), but the method does work.

9.4.4 Complex Structures

As the logical organization of a program becomes complex, additional design techniques are required to represent, and ultimately simplify, conditions and corresponding processing. LCP recommends the usage of *Boolean algebra* and/or *Karnaugh mapping* to help reduce logical complexity, thereby aiding the design in specification of detailed organization.

Although a detailed discussion of logical simplification techniques is beyond the scope of this text,[2] we shall consider a brief example [7] to illustrate Warnier's

---

[2] For further information, see works by Warnier [7], Bartee [11], and Roth [12].

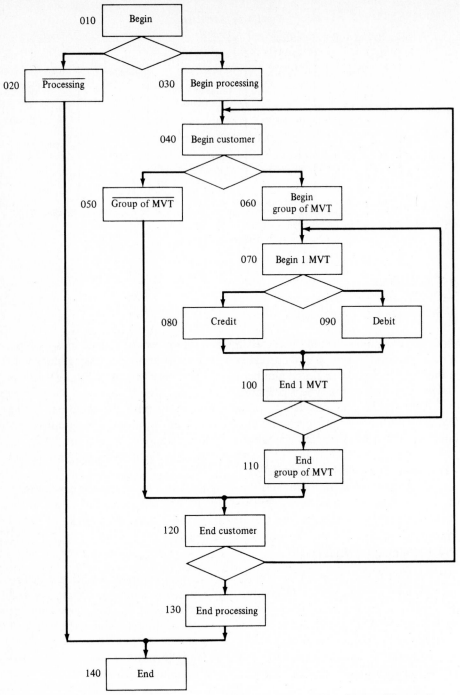

(Source: J. D. Warnier, Logical Construction of Programs. Copyright 1974, Les Editions d'Organisation, reprinted with permission Van Nostrand Reinhold Company.)

Figure 9.15

Instruction Lists

List of branch instructions:
- 010 – if not end of file ($\overline{EOF}$)   030
- 020 –   140
- 040 – if Cust No read = Cust No processed   060
- 050 –   120
- 070 – if code DB   090
- 080 –   100
- 100 – if Cust No read = Cust No processed   070
- 120 – if not end of file ($\overline{EOF}$)   040

Preparation of branch instructions:
- 040 – transfer Cust No to Reference Cust No field

Calculations:
- 040 – Transfer old balance to working field
- 060 – Clear debit total field
- 060 – Clear credit total field
- 090 – Add debit to debit total
- 080 – Add credit to credit total
- 110 – Subtract debit total from working field
- 110 – Add credit total to working field

Outputs:
- 030 – Spaces to print area
- 040 – Transfer old balance to reference field
- 040 – Edit cust. heading
- 040 – Output and restore print area
- 070 – Edit MVT No
- 090 – Edit debit amount
- 080 – Edit credit amount
- 100 – Output and restore print area
- 110 – Edit debit total
- 110 – Edit credit total
- 120 – Edit old balance from reference field
- 120 – Edit new balance from reference field
- 120 – Output and restore print area

Inputs:
- 010 : read
- 040 : read
- 100 : read

(Source: J. D. Warnier, Logical Construction of Programs. Copyright 1974, Les Editions d'Organisation, reprinted with permission Van Nostrand Reinhold Company.)

Figure 9.16

approach. A tabular representation of four data items, A, B, C, and D, and corresponding processing actions V, W, X, Y, Z, and $\overline{R}$ (not R) is given in Figure 9.18. This *truth table* indicates under what circumstances processing actions will be executed. For example, from the third row, actions V and Y will be executed when data item C is encountered. It is possible to execute V under eight different sets of conditions and to execute Y under two different sets of conditions. Applying Boolean algebra, we obtain

$$V = \overline{A} \cdot \overline{B} \cdot C \cdot \overline{D} + \overline{A} \cdot \overline{B} \cdot C \cdot D + \overline{A} \cdot B \cdot C \cdot \overline{D} + \overline{A} \cdot B \cdot C \cdot D + A \cdot \overline{B} \cdot C \cdot \overline{D} + A \cdot \overline{B} \cdot C \cdot D + A \cdot B \cdot C \cdot \overline{D} + A \cdot B \cdot C \cdot D$$

where in Boolean notation "·" indicates *logical and* and "+" indicates *logical or*. Applying rules of logic simplification, we obtain the equations shown on p. 225:

Sorted Instructions

The sorted list of instructions:

010 – Read		
If EOF	030	
020 –	140	
030 – Spaces to print area		
040 – Cust No to Reference Cust No		
Old balance to working field		
Old balance to ref field		
Edit Cust No		
Print and restore print area		
Read		
If Cust No = Ref. Cust No	060	
050 –	120	
060 – Clear debit total		
Clear credit total		
070 – Edit MVT No		
If code DB	090	

080 – Add credit to CR total	
Edit credit	100
090 – Add debit to DB total	
Edit debit	
100 – Print and restore print area	
Read	
If Cust No = ref Cust No	070
110 – Subtract DB total from	
working field	
Add CR total to working field	
Edit DB total	
Edit CR total	
120 – Edit old balance	
Edit new balance	
Print and restore print area	
If EOF	040

(Source: J. D. Warnier, Logical Construction of Programs. Copyright 1974, Les Editions d'Organisation, reprinted with permission Van Nostrand Reinhold Company.)

Figure 9.17

A Truth Table

	DATA A B C D	V	W	X	Y	Z	$\overline{R}$
	0 0 0 0						X
	0 0 0 1						X
	0 0 1 0	X			X		
	0 0 1 1	X			X		
	0 1 0 0						X
	0 1 0 1						X
Complex	0 1 1 0	X				X	
Alternatives	0 1 1 1	X				X	
	1 0 0 0						X
	1 0 0 1						X
	1 0 1 0	X	X	X			
	1 0 1 1	X	X	X			
	1 1 0 0						X
	1 1 0 1						X
	1 1 1 0	X	X				
	1 1 1 1	X	X				

(Source: J. D. Warnier, Logical Construction of Programs. Copyright 1974, Les Editions d'Organisation, reprinted with permission Van Nostrand Reinhold Company.)

Figure 9.18

$V = \bar{A} \cdot \bar{B} \cdot C(\bar{D}+D) + \bar{A} \cdot B \cdot C(\bar{D}+D) + A \cdot \bar{B} \cdot C(\bar{D}+D) + A \cdot B \cdot C + (\bar{D}+D)$

$\quad = \bar{A} \cdot \bar{B} \cdot C + \bar{A} \cdot B \cdot C + A \cdot \bar{B} \cdot C + A \cdot B \cdot C$

$\quad = \bar{A} \cdot C(\bar{B}+B) + A \cdot C(\bar{B}+B)$

$\quad = \bar{A} \cdot C + A \cdot C = C(\bar{A}+A)$

$\quad = C$

and similarly

$X = A \cdot \bar{B} \cdot C \cdot \bar{D} + A \cdot \bar{B} \cdot C \cdot D$

$\quad = A \cdot \bar{B} \cdot C(\bar{D}+D)$

$\quad = A \cdot \bar{B} \cdot C$

Therefore, V will be executed whenever C is encountered, and X will be executed when A and C are present and B is not present.

From the table in Figure 9.18, the following additional simplifications can be made for other processing actions:

$V = C$
$W = C \cdot A$
$X = C \cdot A \cdot \bar{B}$

Resulting Program Structure

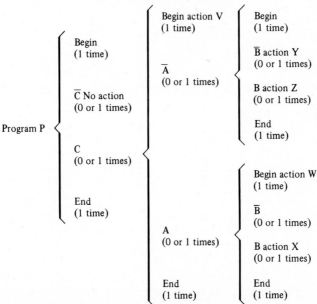

(Source: J. D. Warnier, Logical Construction of Programs. Copyright 1974, Les Editions d'Organisation, reprinted with permission Van Nostrand Reinhold Company.)

Figure 9.19

$Y = C \cdot \bar{A} \cdot \bar{B}$
$Z = C \cdot \bar{A} \cdot B$
$\bar{R} = \bar{C}$

Using these simplified logical conditions, a Warnier diagram for processing hierarchy can be developed as shown in Figure 9.19.

The LCP approach to logical simplification requires a fairly rigorous evaluation of actions and conditions. However, redundant tests are eliminated from the procedure, thereby improving the efficiency of the software design. These techniques, called *complex alternative structure evaluation* by Warnier, may be combined with techniques discussed earlier in this section to develop composite solutions for complex sets of software requirements.

Logical simplification may also be used during maintenance of existing, "unstructured" software. Many older programs have rambling control flow that is difficult to understand and impossible to maintain. Warnier suggests an approach for *restructuring* such programs with the use of complex alternative structures:

1. Develop a flowchart for the software.
2. Write a Boolean expression for each processing sequence.

An Example

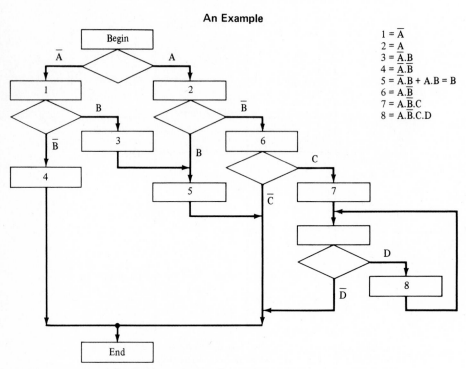

$1 = \bar{A}$
$2 = A$
$3 = \bar{A}.B$
$4 = \bar{A}.\bar{B}$
$5 = \bar{A}.B + A.B = B$
$6 = A.\bar{B}$
$7 = A.\bar{B}.C$
$8 = A.\bar{B}.C.D$

(Source: J. D. Warnier, Logical Construction of Programs. Copyright 1974, Les Editions d'Organisation, reprinted with permission Van Nostrand Reinhold Company.)

Figure 9.20

3. Compile a truth table.
4. Reconstruct the software, using techniques for complex alternative structures; add modifications as required.

As an example [7], we consider the unstructured flowchart and resultant truth table shown in Figures 9.20 and 9.21. Maintenance requires that the modifications ("amendments") shown in Figure 9.21 be applied. After amending the truth table and simplifying, a Warnier diagram for processing hierarchy may be developed by using the simplification techniques described above. This leads to the structured procedural design shown in Figure 9.22.

9.4.5 Summary—Logical Construction of Programs

Logical construction of programs offers a second data structure–oriented design methodology. Using a set of rules developed from computer science foundations, LCP developer Jean Warnier proposes a rigorous design approach that is driven by

Resultant Truth Table

E A B C D	1	2	3	4	5	6	7	8
0 0 0 0	X			X				
0 0 0 1	X			X				
0 0 1 0	X			X				
0 0 1 1	X			X				
0 1 0 0	X		X		X			
0 1 0 1	X		X		X			
0 1 1 0	X		X		X			
0 1 1 1	X		X		X			
1 0 0 0		X				X		
1 0 0 1		X				X		
1 0 1 0		X				X	X	
1 0 1 1		X				X	X	X
1 1 0 0		X			X			
1 1 0 1		X			X			
1 1 1 0		X			X			
1 1 1 1		X			X			

The amendments required for this program sub-set are the following:
- action 9 = A. This action must be executed at the end of the processing of A.
- action 10 = A.B.C.D. This action must be executed once for the group D at the end, but not at all if D contains no elements.

(Source: J. D. Warnier, Logical Construction of Programs. Copyright 1974, Les Editions d'Organisation, reprinted with permission Van Nostrand Reinhold Company.)

Figure 9.21

Amended, Structured Program

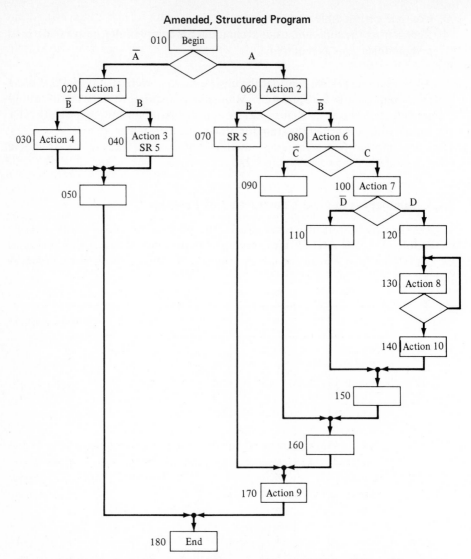

(Source: J. D. Warnier, Logical Construction of Programs. Copyright 1974, Les Editions d'Organisation, reprinted with permission Van Nostrand Reinhold Company.)

Figure 9.22

information hierarchy. Warnier offers a set of techniques that extend software design into detailed procedural specification, logic simplification, and even restructuring of existing software.

9.5 DATA DESIGN

Data structure–oriented design methods imply that data organization is a dominant characteristic in software design. The potential benefits of *data design* were recognized early in the evolution of software design, but formal integration within the design methods presented in this book has not yet occurred. The concepts of *information hiding* and *data abstractions* (Chapter 7) provide the foundation for an approach to data design.

Most software design methods concentrate on structural (architectural) or procedural considerations. We run the risk of having a formal consideration of data design "fall into the cracks" during the software development process.

The process of data design is summarized by Wasserman [13]:

> The primary activity during data design is to select logical representations of *data objects* (data structures) identified during the requirements definition and specification phase. The selection process may involve algorithmic analysis of alternative structures in order to determine the most efficient design or may simply involve the use of a set of modules (a "package") that provide the desired operations upon some representation of an object.
>
> An important related activity during design is to identify those program modules that must operate directly upon the logical data structures. In this way the scope of effect of individual data design decisions can be constrained.

Regardless of the design techniques to be used, well-designed data can lead to better software structure, module independence, and reduced procedural complexity.

Wasserman [13] has proposed a set of principles that may be used to specify and design data. In actuality, the design of data is often encountered as part of the requirements specification task described in Chapter 5. Recalling that requirements analysis and design often overlap, we consider the following set of principles [13] for data specification:

1. *The systematic analysis methods applied to software should also be applied to data.* We spend much time and effort deriving, reviewing, and specifying software requirements and preliminary design. Representations of data flow and structure (the DFD, hierarchical, or Warnier diagram) should also be developed and reviewed, alternative data organizations should be considered, and the impact of data design on software design should be evaluated. For example, specification of a multiringed linked list may nicely satisfy data requirements but may also lead to an unwieldy software design. An alternative data organization may lead to better results.

2. *All data structures and the operations that are to be performed on each should be identified.* The design of an efficient data structure must take the operations to be performed on the data structure into account [e.g., 2]. For example, consider a data structure made up of a set of diverse data elements. The data structure is to be manipulated in a number of major software functions. On evaluation of the operation performed on the data structure, an *abstract data type* [5] is defined for use in subsequent software design. Specification of the abstract data type may simplify software design considerably.

3. *A data dictionary should be established and used to define both data and software design.* The concept of a *data dictionary* has been introduced in Chapter 5. A

data dictionary explicitly represents the relationship among data and the constraints on the elements of a data structure. Algorithms that must take advantage of specific relationships can be more easily defined if a dictionarylike data specification exists.

4. *Low-level data design decisions should be deferred until late in the design process.* A process of *stepwise refinement* may be used for the design of data. That is, overall data organization may be defined during requirements analysis, refined during preliminary design work, and specified in detail during the detailed design step. The top-down approach to data design provides benefits that are analogous to a top-down approach to software design—major structural attributes are designed and evaluated first so that the architecture of the data may be established.

5. *The representation of a data structure should be known only to those modules that must make direct use of the data contained within the structure.* As we have seen in Chapter 7, the concept of information hiding and the related concept of coupling provide important insight into the quality of a software design. Principle 5 alludes to the importance of these concepts as well as "the importance of separating the logical view of a data object from its physical view" [13].

6. *A library of useful data structures and the operations that may be applied to them should be developed.* Data structures and operations should be viewed as a resource for software design. Just as subroutine packages can greatly reduce the development time for utility software, a library of data structure *templates* can reduce both specification and design effort for data.

7. *A software design and programming language should support the specification and realization of abstract data types.* The implementation (and corresponding design) of a sophisticated data structure can be made exceedingly difficult if no means for direct specification of the structure exists. For example, implementation (or design) of a linked list structure or a multilevel heterogeneous array would be difficult if the target programming language was FORTRAN because the language does not support direct specification of these data structures.

The principles described above form a basis for a data design approach that can be integrated into either data flow–oriented design or data structure–oriented design. As we have noted elsewhere in this book, a clear definition of information is essential to successful software development.

9.6 A COMPARISON OF DESIGN METHODOLOGIES

In Chapters 8 and 9 we have considered data flow– and data structure–oriented design methodologies. An obvious question arises: "How do we choose the best method?" This simple question can be rephrased to address a number of very complex issues, such as:

- How do we establish criteria for selecting a best method?
- Is one method applicable in all software application areas?
- Do we know enough about software design to answer the above questions intelligently?

To help answer these and other questions, a comparison of design methodologies [14] is presented in the following section. It should be noted, however, that software design comparisons are inherently subjective, and many of the conclusions might meet with (violent) opposition from other quarters.

9.6.1 One View on Design Methodologies

"A Comparison of Design Methodologies," prepared by Simpact Systems, Ltd., appeared in the ACM Sigsoft *Software Engineering Notes* in October 1978. The article compares each of the design methods presented in this book as well as other popular techniques. Major excerpts from the paper (edited to conform to the style of this book) follow to page 237.

Introduction. The objective of this section is to compare several design methodologies and attempt to come to some conclusions as to which, in objective terms, is the "right one." Seven methodologies have been selected:

1. Modular programming (MP)
2. Top-down design based on functional decomposition (TDD)
3. Composite design (CD) developed by Glenford J. Myers
4. Structured design (SD) developed by Larry L. Constantine
5. Structured analysis design technique (SADT) developed by Douglas Ross of Softech
6. The logical construction of programs (LCP) and its sister methodology, the logical construction of systems (LCS), developed by Jean Dominique Warnier.
7. The Michael Jackson structured design method (MJSD), developed by Michael Jackson.

Modular programming is included, not as a candidate, but to provide a basis for comparison and a starting point.

[*Author's note:* CD and SD are analogous to the data flow–oriented design approach discussed in Chapter 8. The discussion of SADT is not thorough enough and has been deleted.]

Definition of terms. Before embarking on the comparison itself, several terms used need to be explained:

Methodology. A methodology provides reasons for all steps in a process which may be understood without reference to a particular application.

Vertical modularity. Concerned with the isolation of data structures in discrete modules and the identification of processes.

Horizontal modularity. Arising from successive breakdowns of modules, usually along functional lines.

Common modularity. The generalizing of functions; in effect, extending the language used for problem solution.

Pragmatic modularity. Determined by such factors as programmer availability and skill, the economics of compilation, and so on.

The Comparison. The comparison is considered under two main headings: structural factors and peripheral factors. The criteria for the examination of structural factors are:

1. *Basis.* What are the fundamental tenets of the methodology?
2. *Complexity.* What are the means by which complexity is recognized and its effect on design contained?
3. *Modularity.* What types of modularity are recognized? What are the criteria of modular separation?
4. *Scale.* What provisions are made for program and system design? How are they integrated?
5. *Structural integrity.* Those attributes of a design methodology which ease maintenance and enhancement.

Criteria for the examination of peripheral factors are (1) the design stages and their documentation, (2) project control, (3) testing, and (4) portability and external compatibility.

Evaluation of structural factors

1. Basis Modular programming (MP) is the division of a task, which is always less than a system, and often no more than a program, into pragmatic modules. There are two exceptions to this pragmatic subdivision: the *control module*—the skeleton of the main or only process; and *common modules*—which replace repeated in-line code. MP has no governing principle as such; all but the control and common modules represent some state or states of one or more processes. Therefore, most are variable-state subroutines which require access to global data and data computed by earlier invocations. The result of this arbitrary approach is that structural distinctions are represented by switches or similar devices.

Top-down design (TDD) is modular programming to which functional decomposition has been added. The subdivision into modules is determined by pragmatic criteria to which the top-down principle has been applied. Although the processes themselves are obscured by this approach, it does avoid the worst excesses of arbitrary module demarcation, and the single-entry, single-exit requirement of structured programming is satisfied by the use of invocation to refer to lower-level modules.

Composite design (CD) has two main principles: modules should be weakly coupled to each other and strongly bound internally. These concepts are not easily defined, indeed CD is unable to provide any quantitative measure but merely provides examples going from worst to best. The rules of strength are curious in that they rely on a verbal expression of function—the clause structure and so forth. The best level of strength (functional) is one in which the module task is expressible in a simple subject-object statement (e.g., remove redundant blanks from input record). The coupling rules are based on the way nonlocal data are referenced. The "best" level of coupling, called *data coupling,* occurs when all data required by a module are explicitly passed to and from as parameters.

This insistence on data coupling elevates maintainability above correctness, when, in truth, correctness is a prerequisite of maintainability. The other problem with these rules is that they are applied after the design has been done.

Levels of abstraction are applied to the principal input and output streams. This is done by tracing through the successive transformations required to reduce input and the converse for the output. This builds up a source-process-sink model for each instance of an entity and the addition of a multiplicity of entities means that each transform becomes a program or a process. This technique introduces some formality into an activity which is essentially intuitive.

Structured design (SD) has basic principles similar to those of CD, but has added a greater degree of formalism and a good deal of different terminology. For example, "strength" is renamed *cohesion,* and now the coupling factors are used to provide better module division rather than to calibrate a scale.

Additionally, the source-process-sink model is translated into *afferent* and *efferent* transformations, and the levels of abstraction are formalized into a technique called *transform analysis.* An alternative method to transform analysis, known as *transaction analysis,* is also offered. This technique appears to be orthogonal to transform analysis in that it starts by identifying actions to be performed rather than following the way the data flow. Indeed, the weakness of SD is that it offers these two techniques with little guidance on which one to use and when!

The only principle of the LCP/LCS (Warnier's method) methodology is that it is necessary to base the program on hierarchical structures of data from which the program structure is formed. The procedural approach epitomized by functional decomposition is rejected and replaced by (in LCP, at least) a detailed set of rules to take a design from tree structure to structured flowchart with a list of executable operations.

LCS is based on an insistence on establishing the total information content of a proposed system as a set of static relationships between a finite number of hierarchies. This is seen as a prerequisite to a determination of the dynamic relationships necessitated by the seriality of processing. This dynamic modeling (LCE) forms a bridge between LCS and LCP and claims to ensure that the whole gamut of systems and program design is covered.

MJSD is similar in concept to LCP. Although it does not address itself to the problem of total system design, it compensates by providing the program designer with an insight into the real causes of complexity in logic. There are two major achievements:

1. *Backtracking.* This technique enables the correspondence of data and program structure to be maintained in those cases where the serial nature of reading an input stream prohibits the making of decisions when they are required.
2. *Structure clashes.* LCP confines itself to designing programs from one data structure, or a set of structures, which do not differ significantly. MJSD provides the means to recognize cases where the constituent data structures are, for example, wrongly ordered, decouple them, design simple programs around each, and link them at implementation time. It is the recognition of these situations or the potential for these situations to occur that leads to vertical modularity.

2. Complexity Complexity can usefully be defined as the presence of anything which cannot be traced back, as a whole, to a corresponding factor in the problem or one of the implementation constraints which modify it. MP makes no explicit reference to complexity, whereas TDD introduces a spurious simplicity because the process of breaking down systems or programs into small, manageable pieces seems so eminently reasonable.

CD and SD improve on TDD by giving measures of independence, but are unable to prevent the complexity that comes from being unable to recognize all types of process. LCP/LCS enforces noncomplex solutions, but its capacity is limited—it can prevent complexity if the system is simple enough. MJSD can handle the complexity which LCS/LCP avoids and is thus best able to prevent spurious complexity. But—is the LCS/LCP emphasis on simple data structures at system level a better approach than MJSD's concentration on program design, where many clashes introduced at the system design level may need to be resolved?

3. Modularity This factor is inseparable from the structural basis of the methodologies already outlined. Attempting to consider it in its own right, there are two separate ideals for modularity: modules of the solution should correspond one-to-one with the major structural components of the database of the problem, and physical modules should exhibit the minimum possible interdependence. The ideal process of modularization could be summarized as:

- Ascertain vertical modularity (define the processes).
- Ascertain common modularity (define the extensions to the base language).
- Divide modules for practical reasons if necessary.

MP relies almost entirely on pragmatic criteria for modularity; any common modularity is ad hoc. TDD works on the scale of a single program emphasizing horizontal modularity, but with poor detection of common modularity. CD deals well with common, and better than TDD or MP on vertical modularity as it, at least, recognizes the need to divide processes from each other. SD recognizes, by including transaction analysis, that there is more to vertical modularity than the recognition of transformations, but fails to exploit it.

LCP/LCS includes comprehensive tools to define data structure, but does not emphasize common modularity. MJSD places no emphasis on horizontal modularity, because it ceases to be a difficulty, but common modularity is ignored as is the pragmatic division of large vertical modules.

4. Scale System and program design are distinct activities, so any methodology need not provide equally for both; if it possesses an ideal system design capability, the omission of program design is not crucial, but a program design methodology is of little use if the programs are wrongly defined.

- MPP/TDD are not concerned with system design.
- CD/SD try to ensure by their strength-cohesion and coupling rules that the internal design of modules will not have an iterative effect on system design.
- LCS/LCP cover both fully, but only for simple systems.
- MJSD makes program design more automatic than any other methodology, but has not yet capitalized on this in the system design area.

5. Structuring integrity Structural integrity is the most important single attribute a system should possess. A system has structural integrity if an outsider ignorant of its development history can deduce the problem it solves, by inspection of the design negotiations or compilable code, and, further, cannot tell whether it has been amended.

- MP, TDD, CD, SD, being solution-oriented methodologies, cannot reveal correctness by inspection, but CD/SD do ensure that "patches" do not show if the strength-cohesion and coupling rules are followed.
- LCS/LCP and MJSD provide insufficient insight for the full effects of any proposed amendment to be worked out and any necessary structural changes made.

Evaluation of peripheral factors

1. The design stages and their documentation The requirements for design stages and documentation are (1) the stages needed should be a strict succession, invariable for all types of problems, (2) each stage should have a documented record without which progress to the next stage is impossible, and (3) the documentation of any stage should be a total statement of the problem-solution (depending on the stage).

MP has no significant design stages after the initial modular division and no de facto standards of documentation. TDD recognizes the problem of documentation and attempts to overcome it by having small modules, which are easily understood. Often used with TDD are HIPO charts, which consist of a hierarchy chart and associated input, process, and output charts. In summary, the three requirements laid down above are largely satisfied, given the imprecision of the design principles.

CD uses only the hierarchy chart but supplements it with special symbols in an attempt to convey the dynamic relationship of modules, which fail to convey precise information because they are merely notational addenda to a static module hierarchy chart. SD has notations similar to those of CD, but also has a bubble chart showing the major transformations (or programs). This diagram is the predecessor to the hierarchy chart stage. Neither is a sufficient record to support the design stage which follows it.

LCP's and MJSD's design stages are very similar; both methodologies create data structure diagrams, although MJSD is clearer, the crucial difference being the extra design stage in MJSD which combines the input and output data structures to form the program structure. Once the program structure (MJSD) or the flowchart (LCP) has been drawn, it is a more or less mechanical task to form pseudocode. In both techniques, operations are listed and appended to the program-structure flowchart and are then written into the pseudocode. MJSD has the best defined stages of all the methodologies (in the program design area) and comes closest of all to satisfying the three requirements stated as the ideal.

2. Project control The only thing that project control wants from a design methodology is the means to quantify real progress. This quantification may be reduced to three factors: (1) noniterative, small design stages; (2) self-contained documentation; and (3) an objective measure of completeness for each stage.

Both LCP and MJSD answer well to factor 1. None of the techniques adequately satisfy factor 2. Only MJSD offers any prospect of satisfying factor 3, while CD/SD do not, in the program design area, because of their iterative approach: divide; measure the quality; and try again.

3. Testing Testing is always of two kinds: The first seeks to ascertain whether the components function reliably in their operational contexts and is, therefore, indifferent to component structure. It is thus scarcely relevant to this comparison. The second kind seeks to prove that a component operates correctly in terms of specification. There are two questions to ask:

• What approximation of exhaustiveness is possible?
• How necessary is this internal testing?

Testing is exhaustive if all the distinct cases are exercised (given that we have defined what a "case" is). The obstacle to the achievement of exhaustiveness is an acceptable set of criteria which will ensure that testing is nondiscretionary.

The functional decomposition school cannot hope to do this because it addresses a pattern of modules and not the logic paths within modules. Hence the possible control paths are deducible only by laborious inspection.

Although MJSD does make all the control paths in a program enumerable, it does not insist on the independence of data items in data structures, which would be the only way of guaranteeing that all the paths were operationally possible. However, MJSD questions the need for extensive internal testing. It argues that since the testing of all possible paths in a component may be impossible, it is better to ensure that the components are structurally separate, so that the combinations become meaningless as independent sources of malfunction.

Evidence from the use of MJSD cannot directly substantiate the claim that so-called exhaustive testing is a waste of time, but the simple circumstantial evidence of drastically reduced numbers of test shots and increased levels of operational reliability is very compelling.

4. Portability and external compatibility All the methodologies ensure portability in their own way, either by not descending to the level of detail where it matters or by causing code to be generated in a language-independent form as pseudocode. With external compatibility, there is the irony that the more a methodology differs from conventional modularity in the systems it creates, the more difficult it is to interface with existing systems. MJSD certainly suffers in this way as a systems design tool.

Conclusion. On the basis of the criteria established for this comparison, it would appear that the data-structure/process orientated approach is the one that has the best prospects for the system and program design in the future.

Examining the two data-structured approaches available today, that of Jackson appears to be further developed and clearer than that of Warnier, and despite its identified shortcomings, the Jackson methodology must be the recommended design technique. However, we should not lose sight of the lessons on module independence that we have learned from Myers and Constantine.[3]

9.6.2 Additional Comments on Design Comparison

The excerpts from the Simpact paper in Section 9.6.1 represent one view of software design methods. Many other viewpoints [e.g., 1, 15], "goodness" criteria, and conclusions can be found in the literature. Freeman [16] defines five general operations that are always encountered during the software design process: operationalization; abstraction; elaboration; verification; and decision making.

The term *operationalization* refers to a process of specification that we have called *software requirements analysis. Abstraction* is the middle ground between analysis and design. Here, requirement concepts are translated into an abstract

---

[3] "A Comparison of Design Methodologies," Simpact Systems Ltd., John Parker (ed.), ACM Sigsoft *Software Engineering Notes*, October 1978. Reprinted with permission.

representation. *Elaboration* fills in design detail. Structure is transformed into procedure; abstractions become concrete, and implementation considerations are evaluated. *Verification* is a process of review and modification. The goal of this operation is to ascertain design correctness. The process of *decision making* is applied during all preceding operations.

Each of these operations is directed toward the achievement of a design goal or criterion. The design goal for most methodologies is to achieve a functionally correct system. However, to quote Freeman [16]:

> The obvious goal in most design situations is to create a system that provides certain functions. All too often in software design, this seems to be the only goal to which much attention is paid.
> There are other very important goals for many systems, however, such as reliability, user centeredness, maintainability, efficiency, and security. Increasingly, these other goals are seen to be at least as important as the goal of providing certain functions.

Perhaps, a comparison of design methodologies should concentrate on "other" goals of design and how well a particular method achieves them.

Another worthwhile comparison of design methodologies has been proposed by Peters and Tripp [1]. Table 9.1 summarizes their findings. A number of important conclusions are drawn by these investigators:

Table 9.1 A comparison of design methods

				Attribute		
Method	Specialized graphics	Defined procedure(s)	Requirements traceability	Compatibility with other techniques and schemes	Area of application	Evaluation (quality) criteria
Structured design	Use structure charts for system architecture	An iterative framework which guides the solution development	Designer's responsibility	Usable with any module design strategy	Systems whose data flow can be communicated graphically	A well-defined set of design heuristics
The Jackson methodology	Treelike charts for data structures	Loosely defined guidelines to address various problems	Designer's responsibility	Usable with other data-structuring methods	Business and other systems with well-understood data structure(s)	Verify compliance with basic assumptions
Logical construction of programs	Use Warnier chart for data structure	Well-defined set of procedures at all levels of detail	Designer's responsibility	Procedural nature would limit compatibility	Business and other systems with well-understood data structure(s)	Verify compliance with basic assumptions

- There is no single method that is applicable across all application areas.
- Established criteria for "good" design are based on assumptions that are generally not provable.
- Design is, above all else, a problem-solving task. And problem solving is an intensely personal issue. What works for one designer may not work for another.
- Methods are important, but their successful application occurs only in a supportive environment [1].

9.7 SUMMARY

The underlying concepts and techniques of data structure–oriented design have been presented in this chapter. The Jackson methodology and Warnier's LCP both rely on the hierarchical organization of input and output data, both circumvent a design derivation of modular structure, both move directly toward a processing hierarchy followed by a detailed procedural representation, and both provide supplementary techniques for more complex problems. The methods differ in notation and rigor, but are otherwise similar.

Data design is an issue that complements the design of software. Data structures and the operations performed on them must be specified and analyzed in the context of software design.

A thorough comparison of software design techniques is crucial to the selection of a "right" design approach for a given application area. Although software design comparisons are inherently subjective, they can provide important insights into the process of design.

REFERENCES

1. Peters, L. J., and L. L. Tripp. "Comparing Software Design Methodologies," *Datamation,* November, 1977.
2. Tremblay, J. P., and P. G. Sorenson, *An Introduction to Data Structures with Applications,* McGraw-Hill, 1976.
3. Horowitz, E., and S. Sahni, *Fundamentals of Computer Algorithms,* Computer Science Press, 1978.
4. Wulf, W., et al., *Fundamental Structures of Computer Science,* Addison-Wesley, 1981.
5. Guttag, J., "Abstract Data Types and the Development of Data Structures," *CACM,* vol. 20, no. 6, June 1977, pp. 396–404.
6. Jackson, M., *Principles of Program Design,* Academic Press, 1975.
7. Warnier, J. D., *Logical Construction of Programs,* Van Nostrand, 1974.
8. Warnier, J. D., *Logical Construction of Systems,* Van Nostrand, 1981.
9. Chand, D. R., and S. B. Yadav, "Logical Construction of Software," *CACM,* vol. 23, no. 10, October 1980, pp. 546–555.
10. Myers, G., *Composite Structured Design,* Van Nostrand, 1978.
11. Bartee, T., *Digital Computer Fundamentals,* 4th ed., McGraw-Hill, 1977.
12. Roth, C., *Fundamentals of Logic Design,* 2d ed., West Publishing, 1979.

13. Wasserman, A., "Principles of Systematic Data Design and Implementation," in *Software Design Techniques,* 3d ed., P. Freeman and A. Wasserman, (eds.), IEEE Computer Society Press, 1980, pp. 287–293.
14. "A Comparison of Design Methodologies," Simpact Systems Ltd., John Parker, (ed.), ACM Sigsoft *Software Engineering Notes,* vol. 3, no. 4, October 1978.
15. Griffiths, S., "Design Methodologies—A Comparison," in *Tutorial: Software Design Strategies,* G. Bergland and R. Gordon, (eds.), IEEE Computer Society Press, 1979, pp. 189–213.
16. Freeman, P., "The Nature of Design," in *Software Design Techniques,* 3d ed., P. Freeman and A. Wasserman, (eds.), IEEE Computer Society Press, 1980, pp. 46–53.

PROBLEMS AND POINTS TO PONDER

9-1 Using a number of "data structures" textbooks as references, propose a library of data *templates* and corresponding software as proposed in Section 9.5.

9-2 Propose a text notation for the specification of hierarchical data structures. Alternatively, research the topic and present a summary of existing forms of notation for data structures.

9-3 You have been asked to design inventory control software for an automobile dealership that markets both new and used cars. Using requirements that you derive yourself, provide a complete description of a data structure that will support the inventory system.

9-4 Explain how modules are defined as part of the Jackson design method. Can structure and procedure be separated by use of Jackson's approach?

9-5 Using the backtracking design primitives described in Section 9.3.4, develop a design description for a simple problem-solving board game such as tick-tack-toe.

9-6 Describe the concept of a structure clash in your own words. Give three applications examples in which a structure clash might be encountered.

9-7 Represent the data structure developed for Problem 9-3, using the Jackson notation.

9-8 Represent the data structure developed for Problem 9-3, using the Warnier diagram.

9-9 Given a set of requirements provided by your instructor or requirements of a project on which you are currently working, apply the LCP approach and attempt to derive a procedural design. Show Warnier diagrams for input and output data and the program itself. Use a structured flowchart to define procedure.

9-10 This project is intended for those readers who are unfamiliar with Boolean simplification. Obtain an introductory text in logic design [e.g., 12]. Review chapters on Boolean algebra and simplification and prepare a brief summary of important concepts and theorems. Reread Section 9.4.4 of this book and show how expressions for W, Y, Z, and $\bar{R}$ were derived.

9-11 A word processor produces an output file that contains formatting information for document production. All documents contain header information that includes margin specification, line spacing, font selection, and so on. The text file may (or may not contain) other margin modification information, always contains paragraph indicators, end-of-text block indicators, and other text specific commands. Use the LCP approach to define the output data structure and the resultant program procedural organization for document production software. Optionally, continue by developing detailed organization, using a known word processing system as a guide.

9-12 Select a fairly complex module that was not developed by use of the structured constructs. (These are seldom difficult to find!) Apply Warnier's simplification approach to generate a structured representation of the same program.

9-13 Search the literature for other comparisons of software design methods and write a short paper summarizing criteria for comparison and recommendations of the authors.

9-14 Write a paper describing a design technique that has not been discussed in this book. Attempt to compare it to the data flow/data structure–oriented techniques that you have studied.

9-15 Which design approach (i.e., data flow or data structure) would be (1) easier to review, (2) easier to control from a management standpoint, and (3) easier to apply to a broad range of applications?

9-16 This is intended as a major class project. Define full specifications and develop an "automated design tool" that would assist in the application of a data flow/data structure–oriented design technique. The tool should be interactive, mechanize some or all of the design mappings, and provide graphical output as well as other reports that might help the designer assess his or her design. The tool should also support "hooks" for one or more of the detailed design tools to be discussed in Chapter 10.

FURTHER READINGS

Texts by Jackson [6] and Warnier [7] are required material for those readers who are interested in data structure–oriented design. The Jackson text is difficult because of its style. It does, however, provide many excellent examples of the Jackson methodology. The Warnier text is much more readable and also presents many worthwhile examples.

Another good tutorial on software design may be found in *Software Design Strategies* (Bergland, G., and R. Gordon, IEEE Computer Society Press, 1979). This tutorial contains sections on both Jackson and Warnier techniques (and others) and reprints of three software design comparisons. It also contains an excellent bibliography.

A complete survey of data structure–oriented design would not be complete without reference to design techniques for databases and database management systems. Worthwhile papers are reprinted in *Software Design Techniques, Software Design Strategies,* and *Software Methodologies*—all IEEE tutorials. Among many good texts on database design are References 9, 10, and 11 in Chapter 5.

Kenneth Orr (*Structured Requirements Specification* Orr Associates, Inc., Topeka, Kansas, 1981) has attempted to resolve both data flow- and data structure–oriented design methods into one all-encompassing approach. Orr uses "functional mappings" developed with DFD techniques to derive Warnier diagrams, a data structure–oriented tool.

TEN

DETAILED DESIGN TOOLS

The software engineering methodology proposed in this book approaches software design in two distinct steps. First, a preliminary design establishes the modular structure of software. Second, a detailed design step completes all necessary procedural detail. At the culmination of the second step, there should exist a design representation from which source code may be directly and simply derived.

In an ideal world, the procedural specification required in the detailed design step would be stated in a natural language such as English. After all, members of a software development organization all speak a natural language (in theory, at least!); people outside the software domain could more readily understand the specification, and no new learning would be required.

Unfortunately, there is one small problem. A detailed design must specify procedural detail unambiguously, and unambiguity in a natural language is not natural. Using a natural language, we can write a set of procedural steps in too many different ways. We frequently rely on context to get a point across. We often write as if a dialogue with the reader were possible (it isn't). For these and many other reasons, a more constrained mode for representing procedural detail must be used.

10.1 TOOLS FOR DESIGN

During the preliminary design step, each module is defined as part of a holistic view of software. In addition to a structure chart and interface descriptions, a processing narrative for each module is developed. The processing narrative is a natural language description of module function and performance. It is, at best, a concise unambiguous description of general processing steps. Design representation tools are required to transform the narrative into a precise, structured description of procedure.

Design tools are applied during each step of the software development process. Figure 10.1 depicts three classes of tools. Data representation tools are used during software requirements analysis for specification of information flow or structure. Requirements can be transformed into tools for representation of software structure. Finally, tools for specification of procedural detail complete the design description.

Tools for the specification of procedure, called *detailed design tools,* may be categorized in the following manner:

Graphical tools. Procedural detail is represented as part of a "picture" in which logical constructs take specific pictorial forms.
Tabular tools. Procedural detail is represented by using a table that depicts actions and corresponding conditions or alternatively, input, processing, and output information.
Language tools. Procedural detail is represented with a pseudocode representation that closely resembles a programming language.

Regardless of category, a design tool should indicate flow of control, processing function, data organization (many tools fail in this regard), and implementation detail.

Tool Classes

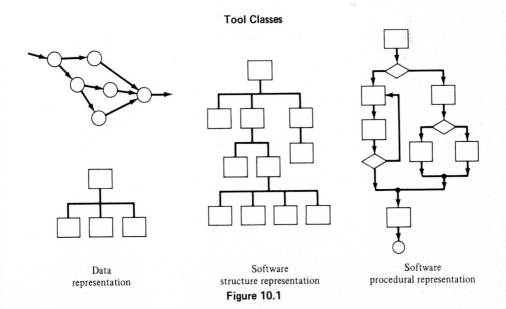

| Data representation | Software structure representation | Software procedural representation |

Figure 10.1

In the following sections a number of common detailed design tools are presented. First, however, we must consider the logical foundation of detailed design—the *structured constructs.*

10.2 THE STRUCTURED CONSTRUCTS

The foundations of detailed design began in the early 1960s and were solidified with the work of Edsgar Dijkstra and his colleagues [1–4]. In the late 1960s Dijkstra and others proposed a set of logical constructs from which any program could be formed. The constructs emphasized "maintenance of functional domain." That is, each construct had a predictable logical structure, was entered at the top, and exited at the bottom.

The constructs, introduced earlier in the book (Chapter 6), are *sequence, condition,* and *repetition.* Sequence implements processing steps that are essential in the specification of any algorithm. Condition provides the facility for selected processing based on some logical occurrence, and repetition provides for looping. These three constructs are fundamental to *structured programming*—an important technique in the broader field that we have learned to call *software engineering.*

The structured constructs were proposed to limit the procedural design of software to a small number of predictable operations. McCabe's complexity metric (Chapter 7) indicates that the use of the structured constructs reduces program complexity and thereby enhances readability, testability, and maintainability. The use of a limited number of logical constructs also contributes to a human understanding process that psychologists call "chunking." To understand this process, consider the way in which you are reading this page. You do not read individual letters, but rather, recognize patterns or "chunks" of letters that form words or phrases. The structured constructs are logical chunks that allow a reader to recognize procedural elements of a module, rather than reading the design or code line by line. Understanding is enhanced when readily recognizable logical forms are encountered.

Any program, regardless of application area or technical complexity, can be designed and implemented by using *only* the three structured constructs. It should be noted, however, that dogmatic use of only these constructs can sometimes cause practical difficulties. Section 10.3.1 considers this issue in further detail.

10.3 GRAPHICAL DESIGN TOOLS

"A picture is worth a thousand words," but as Carl Machover (a leading computer graphics expert) says, "it's rather important to know which picture and which 1000 words." There is no question that graphical tools, such as the flowchart or box diagram, provide excellent pictorial patterns that readily depict procedural detail. However, if graphical tools are misused, the wrong picture may lead to the wrong software.

10.3.1 Flowcharts

The *flowchart* is the most widely used method for design representation of software. Unfortunately, it is the most widely abused method as well.

The flowchart is quite simple pictorially. A box is used to indicate a processing step. A diamond represents a logical condition and arrows show the flow of control. Figure 10.2 illustrates the three structured constructs discussed in Section 10.2. Sequence is represented as two processing boxes connected by a line (arrow) of control. Condition, also designated *if-then-else*, is depicted as a decision diamond which if true causes *then-part* processing to occur, and if false, invokes *else-part* processing. Repetition is represented by using two slightly different forms. The *do-while* tests a condition and executes a *loop task* repetitively as long as the condition holds true. A *repeat-until* executes the loop task first, then testing a condition and repeating the task until the condition fails. The selection (or *select-case*) construct shown in Figure 10.2 is actually an extension of the *if-then-else*. A parameter is tested by successive decisions until a true condition occurs and a *case-part* processing path is executed.

The structured constructs may be *nested* within one another as shown in Figure 10.3. Referring to the figure, a *repeat-until* forms the then-part of an *if-then-else* (shown enclosed by the outer dashed boundary). Another *if-then-else* forms the else-part of the larger condition. Finally, the condition itself becomes a second

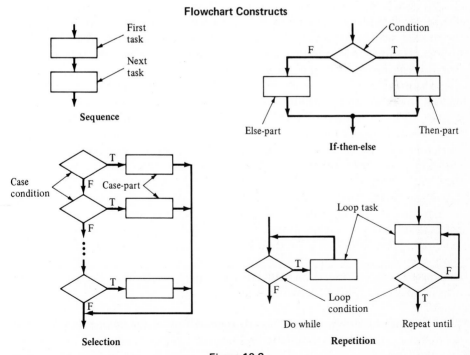

Flowchart Constructs

Sequence

If-then-else

Selection

Repetition

Do while   Repeat until

Figure 10.2

Nesting Constructs

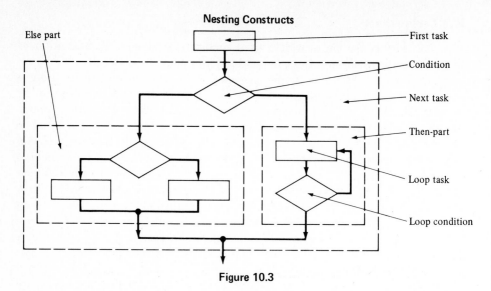

Figure 10.3

block in a sequence. By nesting constructs in this manner, a complex logical schema may be developed. It should be noted that any one of the blocks in Figure 10.3 could reference another module, thereby accomplishing *procedural layering* implied by software structure.

A more detailed structured flowchart is shown in Figure 10.4. As an exercise, the reader should attempt to box each construct. On completion of the exercise, two things will be apparent. The entire procedure is constructed by using the constructs shown in Figure 10.3, and as the constructs are "boxed," boundaries of the boxes never cross. That is, *all constructs have a single entry and single exit.*

The use of only structured constructs can at times introduce complications in logical flow. For example, assume that as part of process i (Figure 10.4) a condition z may arise that requires an immediate branch to process j. A direct branch violates the logical constructs by escaping from the functional domain of the *repeat-until* of which process i is a part. To implement the above branch without violation, tests for condition z must be added to x_7 and x_8. These tests would occur repeatedly, even if the occurrence of z is rare. We have introduced additional complication and execution inefficiency.

In general, the dogmatic use of only the structured constructs can introduce inefficiency when an escape from a set of nested loops or nested conditions is required. More importantly, additional complication of all logical tests along the path of escape can cloud software control flow, increase the possibility of error, and have a negative impact on readability and maintainability. What can we do?

The designer is left with two options:

1. The procedural representation is redesigned so that the escape branch is not required at a nested location in the flow of control.
2. The structured constructs are violated in a controlled manner; that is, a constrained branch out of the nested flow is designed.

A Structured Flowchart

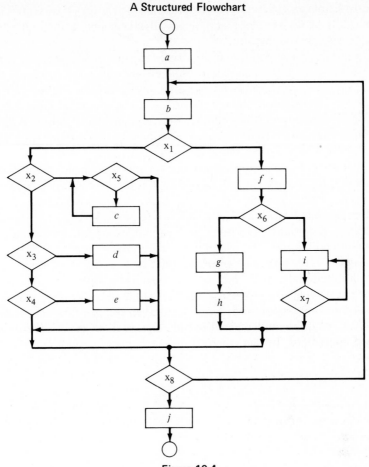

Figure 10.4

Option 1 is obviously the ideal approach, but option 2 can be accommodated without violating of the spirit of structured programming [5]. We shall see that some detailed design tools do not provide facilities for violation of the constructs, while others provide limited constructs to escape nests. Flowcharts, on the other hand, have "the arrow"—giving a designer *carte blanche* to violate functional domain without regard for the spirit of structured programming. However, if the temptation of the arrow is avoided, the flowchart can serve as a useful design tool.

10.3.2 Box Diagrams

The *box diagram* evolved from a desire to develop a graphical design tool that would not allow violation of the structure constructs. Developed by Nassi and Shneiderman [6] and extended by Chapin [7], the diagrams (also called *Nassi-Shneiderman charts,* or *N-S charts,* or *Chapin charts*) have the following character- istics: (1) *functional domain* (i.e., the scope of a specific construct) is well defined and clearly visible as a pictorial representation; (2) arbitrary transfer of control is impossible; (3) the scope of local and/or global data can be easily determined; and (4) recursion is easy to represent.

The graphical representation of structured constructs using the box diagram is illustrated in Figure 10.5. The fundamental element of the diagram is a box. To represent sequence, two or more boxes are connected bottom to top. To represent an *if-then-else,* a condition box is followed by a then-part and an else-part box. Repetition is depicted with a bounding pattern that encloses the process (do-while-part or repeat-until-part) to be repeated. Finally, selection is represented using the graphical form shown at the bottom of Figure 10.5.

The box diagram may appear unusual (or unreadable) to a reader who has encountered it for the first time. In actuality, it is no more complex (in a pictorial sense) than a flowchart. Like flowcharts, a box diagram is layered on multiple pages as processing elements of a module are refined. A "call" to a subordinate module can be represented by a box with the module name enclosed by an oval.

Figure 10.6 illustrates the use of a box diagram to represent flow of control that is identical to the flowchart given in Figure 10.4. To illustrate the relative ease with which functional domain may be discerned, refer to the *repeat-until* loop on condition x_8. All logical constructs contained within the loop are readily apparent because of the boundary pattern. Note also that an escape branch (as described in Section 10.3.1) can be implemented in only one way—by strict adherence to the structured constructs. In fact, there is no mechanism for violation of the constructs.

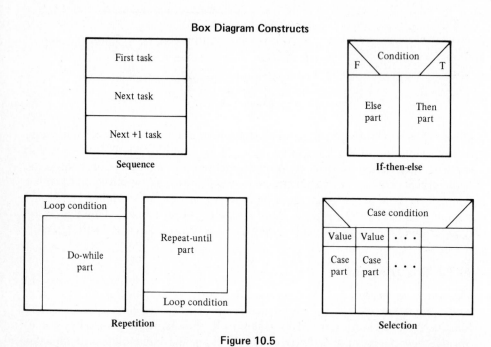

Box Diagram Constructs

Sequence

If-then-else

Repetition

Selection

Figure 10.5

Box Diagram*

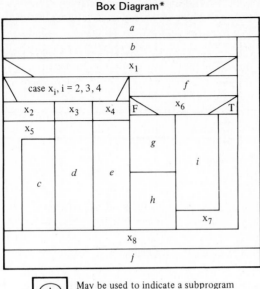

A | May be used to indicate a subprogram
reference (i.e., a call to module A).

*Identical to flowchart procedure, Figure 10.4.

Figure 10.6

As a summary of this technique, consider the words of Nassi and Shneiderman [6]: "Programmers who first learn to design programs with these symbols (box diagrams) never develop the bad (procedural design) habits which other flowchart notations permit. . . ." The use of structured constructs is a state of mind. If a design tool enforces only the structured constructs, this mode of thinking is continuously reinforced and eventually becomes natural.

10.4 DECISION TABLES

In many software applications, a module may be required to evaluate a complex combination of conditions and select appropriate actions on the basis of these conditions. *Decision tables* provide a tool that translates actions and conditions (described in a processing narrative) into a tabular form. The table is difficult to misinterpret and may even be used as a machine readable input to a "table-driven" algorithm. In a comprehensive treatment of this design tool, Michael Montalbano [8] states: "for the systems analyst (and the software designer), the decision table can be the start toward a tool kit that will . . . introduce order, regularity and intelligibility into the chaotic world. . . ."

Decision table organization is illustrated in Figure 10.7. Referring to the figure, heavy lines divide the table into four sections. The upper left-hand quadrant contains a list of all conditions. The lower left-hand quadrant contains a list of all

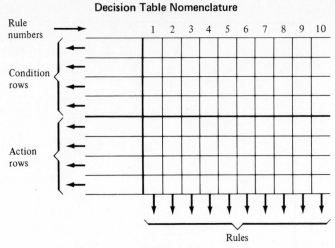

Decision Table Nomenclature

Figure 10.7

actions that are possible on the basis of combinations of conditions. The right-hand quadrants form a matrix that indicates condition combinations and the corresponding actions that will occur for a specific combination. Therefore, each column of the matrix may be interpreted as a processing *rule*.

The following steps are applied to develop a decision table:

1. List all actions that can be associated with a specific procedure (or module).
2. List all conditions (or decisions made) during execution of the procedure.
3. Associate specific sets of conditions with specific actions eliminating impossible combinations of conditions; alternatively, develop every possible permutation of conditions.
4. Define *rules* by indicating what action(s) occurs for a set of conditions.

Resultant Decision Table

		1	2	3	4	5
	Fixed rate account	T	T	F	F	F
	Variable rate account	F	F	T	T	F
Conditions	Consumption < 100 KWH	T	F	T	F	
	Consumption ≥ 100 KWH	F	T	F	T	
	Minimum monthly charge	X				
	Schedule A billing		X	X		
Actions	Schedule B billing				X	
	Other treatment					X

Figure 10.8

To illustrate the use of a decision table, consider the following excerpt from a processing narrative for a public utility billing system:

> If the customer account is billed using a fixed rate method, a minimum monthly charge is assessed for consumption of less than 100 KWH (kilowatt-hours). Otherwise, computer billing applies a Schedule A rate structure. However, if the account is billed using a variable rate method, a Schedule A rate structure will apply to consumption below 100 KWH, with additional consumption billed according to Schedule B.

Figure 10.8 illustrates a decision table representation of the preceding narrative. Each of the five rules indicates one of five viable conditions (e.g., a "T" (true) in both fixed rate and variable rate accounts makes no sense in the context of this procedure).

The previous example illustrates that a decision table is a concise, unambiguous representation of this processing narrative. Unfortunately, there is no simple way to incorporate other processing characteristics such as sequence, repetition, or

Example*

Rules

		1	2	3	4	5	6	7	8	9	10	11	12	13	
	x_1	T	T	T	T	T	F	F	F	F	F	F	F	F	F
	x_2						T	T	F	F	T	T	F	F	
	x_3								T	F			T	F	
	x_4									T				T	
Conditions	x_5							T				T			
	x_6	T	T	T	F	F									
	x_7		T	T											
	x_8				T	F	T				T	T	T	T	
	a	x	x	x	x	x	x	x	x	x	x	x	x	x	x
	b	x	x	x	x	x	x	x	x	x	x	x	x	x	x
	c							x				x			
	d								x				x		
	e									x				x	
Actions	f	x	x	x	x	x									
	g				x	x									
	h				x	x									
	i	x	x	x											
	j	x	x	x	x	x	x	x	x	x	x	x	x	x	x

*Depicts actions and conditions for flowchart example, Figure 10.4.

Figure 10.9

timing. As a general-purpose design tool, therefore, a decision table has significant failings. To illustrate this point, we once again consider the example design (Figure 10.4) represented by use of a decision table in Figure 10.9. It is not possible to discern the overall control flow with this tool alone; supplementary information is required.

As a general rule, the decision table can be effectively used to supplement other detailed design tools. It is possible to systematically evaluate completeness and consistency [8] of a table and to simplify complex alternatives by use of an approach described in Chapter 9 (Section 9.4.4).

10.5 IPO CHARTS

Input-processing-output (IPO) charts evolved from a software design and documentation technique developed by IBM [9]. The most important feature of the IPO chart is its inherent ability to represent the relationship between input/output data (both external data and internal data flow may be represented) and software procedure. An extended version of the chart, called the *IPO/DB* [10] *diagram*, is shown in Figure 10.10.

Procedure is specified in a central processing box and is "connected" to input, output and database information. This allows a designer to explicitly associate information flow with procedural flow. Processing is typically specified with a list

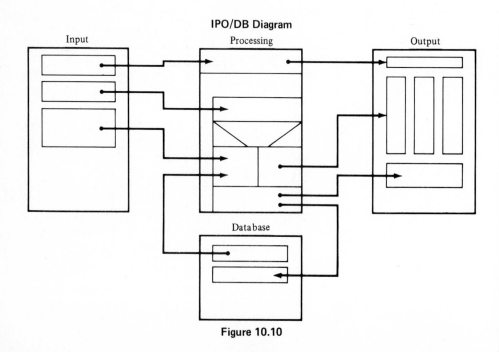

Figure 10.10

Example of a Software Costing System Design Document

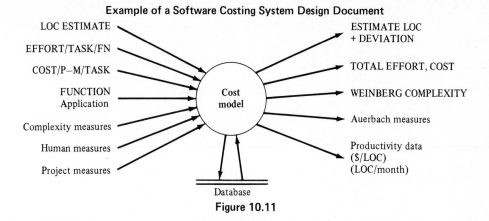

Figure 10.11

of steps, but may also be represented by a flowchart, box diagram, or *design language* (to be discussed).

To provide a brief illustration of the IPO chart as a tool for detailed design, we consider an excerpt of design documentation for a software costing system. Figure 10.11 shows a fundamental system model for the system. An IPO chart that depicts top-level processing functions is given in Figure 10.12

10.6 PROGRAM DESIGN LANGUAGE

Program design language (PDL), called pseudocode in earlier chapters, is a "pidgin" language in that it uses the vocabulary of one language (e.g., English) and the overall syntax of another (i.e., a structured programming language)" [11]. In this chapter PDL is used as a generic reference for a design language. It should be noted, however, that PDL often is used to describe a specific design language developed by Caine and Gordon [11].

At first glance PDL looks like PL/1, PASCAL, or ALGOL. The difference between PDL and a real high-level programming language lies in the use of narrative text (e.g., English) embedded directly within PDL statements. Given the combined use of narrative text and a formal procedural form, PDL cannot be compiled (at least not yet!). However, PDL "processors" currently exist to help in the development of detailed design. Such processors format PDL text, produce nesting maps, a design operation index, cross-reference tables, and various other features.

A program design language may be a simple transposition of a language such as PL/1 or a product purchased specifically for procedural design. Regardless of origin, a design language should have the following characteristics:

• A fixed syntax of KEYWORDS that provide for all structured constructs, data declarations, and modularity characteristics

SOFTWARE COSTING SYSTEM
DESIGN DOCUMENT

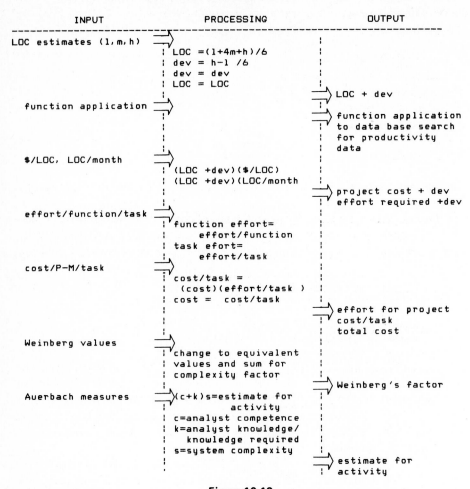

Figure 10.12

- A free syntax of a natural language that describes processing features
- Data declaration facilities that should include both simple (scalar and array) and complex (linked list or hierarchical) data structures
- Subprogram definition and calling techniques that support various modes of interface description

The design language should be programming–language–independent. A design described with PDL can be translated to assembly language, FORTRAN, or PASCAL (although not with equal facility).

10.6.1 A Typical Design Language

As an example of PDL, we consider a design language modeled after any of the more common structured programming languages such as PL/1, ALGOL, or PASCAL. Basic PDL forms include:

- Data declarations
- Techniques for *block structuring*
- Condition constructs
- Repetition constructs
- Subprogram definitions
- Interface descriptions
- I/O constructs

The format and semantics of the example PDL are presented in the paragraphs below.

During earlier discussions of design, we emphasized the importance of data structure on both a local (per module) and global (program-wide) scale. PDL contains a construct that enables the design to represent both local and global data structure:

```
DECLARE ⟨variable-names⟩ AS ⟨qualifier-1⟩⟨qualifier-2⟩
where
    ⟨variable-names⟩ is a list of all variables
            contained within a module
    ⟨qualifier-1⟩ indicates the specific data organization
            and includes keywords like:
                SCALAR
                ARRAY
                LIST
                CHAR
                STRUCTURE
    ⟨qualifier-2⟩ indicates how the variable names are
            to be used in the context of a module
            or program.
```

PDL also allows the specification of *abstract data types* [12] that are problem specific. For example,

```
DECLARE table.1 AS symboltable
```

would be useful in the detailed design of modules for a compiler. The abstract data type *symboltable* would be defined in terms of other data types at some other location in the design.

Referring to an earlier example of a patient-monitoring system (PMS), we can use PDL to define a patient-record that must be globally available to many modules. The record is comprised of different data types in a specfic hierarchy and is thus characterized as a *heterogeneous structure.* Using PDL, we have

```
DECLARE patient-record AS STRUCTURE GLOBAL
   level 01 patient-id CHAR
   level 01 identification information
      level 02 patient-name CHAR
      level 02 address CHAR
         level 03 street CHAR
         level 03 town CHAR
      level 02 age SCALAR
   level 01 medication-history ARRAY
   level 01 physician-information
         .
         .
         .
```

In addition to KEYWORDS used above, we could add specific sizes, "dimensions," or qualifying characteristics. Once the details of this *heterogeneous structure* have been defined, it is possible to use *patient-record* as an abstract data type or as a single occurrence of an identifier.

The procedural elements of PDL are *block-structured;* that is, pseudocode may be defined in blocks that are executed as a single entity. A block is delimited in the following manner:

```
BEGIN ⟨block-name⟩
   ⟨pseudocode statements⟩
END
```

where ⟨block-name⟩ may be used (but is not required) to provide a mode for subsequent reference to a block and ⟨pseudocode statements⟩ are a combination of all other PDL constructs. For example:

```
BEGIN ⟨draw-line-on-graphics-terminal⟩
   get end-points from display list
   scale physical end-points to screen coordinates
   DRAW a line using screen coordinates
END
```

The above block makes use of pseudocode statements that describe appropriate processing. The use of a specialized keyword, DRAW, illustrates the manner in which a PDL may be customized to address a specific application.

The condition construct in PDL takes a classic *if-then-else* form:

```
IF ⟨condition-description⟩
   THEN ⟨block or pseudocode statement⟩
   ELSE ⟨block or pseudocode statement⟩
ENDIF
```

where ⟨condition-description⟩ indicates the logical decision that must be made to invoke either then-part or else-part processing. For example, the following PDL segment describes a decision sequence for a payroll system:

```
IF year.to.date.FICA < maximum
   THEN BEGIN
      calculate FICA.deduction (see formula No. 30-1)
         IF (year.to.date.FICA + FICA.deduction) > maximum
            THEN set FICA.deduction = maximum − year.to.date.FICA
            ELSE skip
            ENDIF
         END
      ELSE
      set FICA.deduction = 0
ENDIF
```

Two nested IFs are shown in the PDL segment above. The then-part of the outer IF contains a block that combines the inner IF with pseudocode statements. ELSE *skip* indicates that else-part processing is skipped. The ENDIF is used to eliminate unambiguous termination of the IF construct and is particularly useful when nested IFs are represented. The END following the first ENDIF terminates the block that processes FICA information.

The selection (or *select-case*) construct, actually a degenerate set of nested IFs, is represented:

```
CASE OF ⟨case-variable-name⟩
   WHEN⟨case-condition-1⟩SELECT⟨block or pseudocode statement⟩
   WHEN⟨case-condition-2⟩SELECT⟨block or pseudocode statement⟩
   .
   .
   .
   WHEN⟨last-case-condition⟩SELECT⟨block or pseudocode statement⟩
      ⟨default or error case:block or pseudocode statement⟩
ENDCASE
```

In general, this construct tests a specific parameter, the *case-variable,* against a set of conditions. On satisfaction of a condition, a block or an individual pseudocode statement is invoked. As an example of the CASE construct in PDL, we consider a segment for system I/O processing:

```
CASE OF communication-status-bits (csb)
   WHEN csb = clear-to-send SELECT
      BEGIN
         select channel path
         initiate.message.transmission
      END
   WHEN csb = clear-to-receive SELECT initiate.buffer.management
```

```
    WHEN csb = busy SELECT set queuing bit
    process csb content error
ENDCASE
```

Figure 10.13 illustrates repetition constructs that are offered by a typical PDL. The classic structured constructs, DO WHILE and REPEAT UNTIL, are augmented with an indexing *do-loop* construct and nested loop escapes called EXIT and NEXT. As an example of repetition, consider the following analysis loop that tests for convergence of two calculated values:

```
epsilon = 1.0
no.of.tries = 0
DO WHILE (epsilon > 0.001 AND no.of.tries < 100)
   calculate value.1 = f(x,y,z)
   calculate value.2 = g(x,y,z)
   epsilon = ABSVAL (value.1 − value.2)
   increment no.of.tries by 1
ENDDO
```

It should be noted that the loop condition must be defined so that escape from the loop is guaranteed. The no.of.tries counter is established for this purpose.

There are situations (as discussed in Section 10.3.1) in which an escape from nested loops is required. The PDL constructs EXIT and NEXT provide constrained violation of purely structured constructs as shown in Figure 10.14. Referring to the figure, EXIT causes a branch to the statement immediately following the repetition construct in which it is contained. NEXT causes further loop processing to be discontinued, but restarts repetition on the next loop cycle. By labeling outer loops, EXIT and NEXT can be used to escape from nesting as shown by

```
ELSE NEXT loop-y
```

Repetition Constructs

```
DO WHILE <condition>
    <block or other constructs>
ENDDO

REPEAT UNTIL <condition>
    <block or other constructs>
ENDREP
```

$$DO\ FOR\ I = \left\{ \begin{array}{l} x\ TO\ y\ BY\ z \\ list\ of\ items \end{array} \right\}$$

```
    <block or other constructs>
ENDDO
```

Unstructured loop facilities: NEXT, EXIT

Figure 10.13

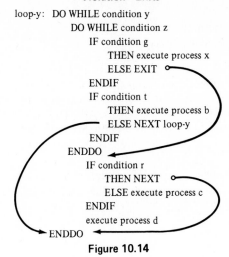

"Violation" Exits

```
loop-y:  DO WHILE condition y
            DO WHILE condition z
               IF condition g
                  THEN execute process x
                  ELSE EXIT
               ENDIF
               IF condition t
                  THEN execute process b
                  ELSE NEXT loop-y
               ENDIF
            ENDDO
            IF condition r
               THEN NEXT
               ELSE execute process c
            ENDIF
            execute process d
         ENDDO
```

Figure 10.14

that causes a branch to an outer loop labeled *loop-y*.

Subprograms and corresponding interfaces are defined by using the following PDL constructs:

PROCEDURE ⟨subprogram-name⟩ ⟨attributes⟩
INTERFACE ⟨argument-list⟩
   ⟨blocks and/or pseudocode statements⟩
RETURN
END

where ⟨attributes⟩ of a subprogram describe its reference characteristics (e.g., an *internal* or *external* module) and other implementation (programming language)-dependent attributes (if any). INTERFACE is used to specify a module *argument list* that contains identifiers for all incoming and outgoing information. An example procedure is described in the next section.

Input/output specification is highly variable among design languages. Typical forms include:

READ/WRITE TO ⟨device⟩ **LIST** ⟨I/O-list⟩

or

ASK ⟨query⟩**ANSWER**⟨response-options⟩

where ⟨device⟩ indicates the physical I/O device (e.g., CRT, tape, printer, or disk) and ⟨I/O list⟩ contains variables to be transmitted. ASK-ANSWER is used for human interactive design in which a question-answer format is appropriate. For example:

ASK "select processing option" ANSWER "cost", "schedule"

I/O specification is frequently expanded to include special characteristics such as audio output or graphical display.

10.6.2 PDL Examples

Two examples are presented to illustrate the use of PDL as a design tool. The first, shown in Figure 10.15, depicts a design segment for the flowchart example presented earlier in this chapter. PDL represents the flowchart procedure in a concise manner.

The second example is a PDL design representation (Figure 10.16) of a processing module for a text editor. The PROCEDURE and INTERFACE

Example*

.
.
.

execute process a
REPEAT UNTIL condition x_8
    execute process b
    IF condition x_1
        THEN BEGIN
            execute process f
            IF condition x_6
                THEN
                    REPEAT UNTIL condition x_7
                        execute process i
                    ENDREP
                ELSE BEGIN
                    execute process g
                    execute process h
                END
            ENDIF
        ELSE CASE OF x_i
            WHEN condition x_2 **SELECT**
            DO WHILE condition x_5
                execute process c
            ENDDO
            WHEN condition x_3 **SELECT** process d
            WHEN condition x_4 **SELECT** process e
        ENDCASE
        ENDIF
    ENDREP
execute process j
END

Identical to flowchart procedure, Figure 10.4.

Figure 10.15

A PDL Design Representation

```
PROCEDURE FIND (string, char, len, occurrence, positions)
        this procedure finds the number of occurrences of a character, char, in an alphanumeric string and
        stores a 1 in the corresponding bit position of a positions array
        DECLARE    string (len) AS STRING ARG
                        char AS CHAR ARG
                        len AS SCALAR ARG
                        occurrence AS SCALAR ARG
                        positions AS BIT ARRAY ARG
        index = 0
        set positions to 0
        occurrence = 0
        DO WHILE string (index) ≠ end-of-string
            IF string (index) = char
                THEN BEGIN
                        occurrence = occurrence + 1
                        set position (index) to 1
                            END
                ELSE skip
            ENDIF
            increment index
        ENDDO
        RETURN
END FIND
```

Figure 10.16

statements have been combined into a more common "procedure name followed by argument list" format.

10.7 COMPARISON OF DESIGN TOOLS

Any comparison of design tools must be predicated on the premise that any tool for detailed design, if used correctly, can be an invaluable aid in the design process; conversely, even the best tool, if poorly applied, adds little to understanding. With this thought in mind, we examine criteria that may be applied to compare tools.

A detailed design tool should lead to a procedural representation that is easy to understand and review. In addition, the tool should enhance *code-to* ability so that code does, in fact, become a natural by-product of design. Finally, the design representation must be easily maintainable so that design always represents the program correctly.

The following attributes of design tools have been established in the context of the general characteristics described above:

Modularity. A design tool should support the development of modular software (e.g., direct specification of procedures and block structuring) and provide a means for interface specification.

Overall simplicity. A design tool should be relatively simple to learn, relatively easy to use, and generally easy to read.

Ease of editing. The detailed design may require modification during the design step, during software testing, and finally, during the maintenance phase of the software life cycle. The ease with which a design representation can be edited can help facilitate each of these software engineering steps.

Machine readability. There is a growing trend toward automated software development techniques. A tool that can be input directly into a computer-based development system may offer enormous potential benefits.

Maintainability. Software maintenance is the most costly phase of the software life cycle. Maintenance of the software configuration nearly always means maintenance of the detailed design representation.

Structure enforcement. The benefits of a design approach that uses structured programming concepts have already been discussed. A design tool that enforces the use of only the structured constructs promotes good design practice.

Automatic processing. A detailed design contains information that can be processed to give the designer new or better insights into the correctness and quality of a design. Such insight can be enhanced with "reports" provided by an automatic processor.

Data representation. The ability to represent local and global data is an essential element of detailed design. Ideally, a design tool should represent such data directly.

Logic verification. Automatic verification of design logic is a goal that is paramount during software testing. A tool that enhances the ability to verify logic greatly improves testing adequacy.

Code-to ability. The software engineering step that follows detailed design is coding. A tool that may be converted easily to source code reduces effort and error.

A natural question that arises in any discussion of design tools is: "What tool is really best, given the attributes noted above?" An answer to this question is admittedly subjective and is open to debate. However, it appears that program design language offers the best combination of characteristics. PDL may be embedded directly into source listings, thus improving documentation and making design maintenance less difficult. Editing can be accomplished with any text editor or word processing system; automatic processors already exist [11], and the potential for automatic code generation is good.

However, it does not follow that other design tools are necessarily inferior to PDL or are "not good" in specific attributes. The pictorial nature of flowcharts and box diagrams provides a perspective on control flow that many designers prefer. The precise tabular content of decision tables is an excellent tool for table-driven applications. The IPO diagram provides a useful connection between information flow and procedure. In the final analysis, the choice of a design tool may be more closely related to human factors [13] than to technical attributes.

10.8 SUMMARY

Tools for detailed design representation span three broad categories—graphical, tabular, and language. Graphical and language tools apply the logical constructs of structured programming, providing a foundation from which code can be generated directly. Tabular tools, like the decision table, provide a concise, unambiguous specification of actions that occur as a result of complex combinations of conditions.

The need for tools results from a compelling need for unambiguous, easily coded-to procedural design specifications. Each of the tools discussed in this chapter enables a designer to successfully address this need.

REFERENCES

1. Dijkstra, E., "Programming Considered as a Human Activity," in *Proceedings of the 1965 IFIP Congress,* North Holland Publishing Company, 1965.
2. Bohm, C., and G. Jacopini, "Flow Diagrams, Turing Machines and Languages with Only Two Formation Rules," *CACM,* vol. 9, no. 5, May 1966, pp. 366–371.
3. Dijkstra, E., "GO TO Statement Considered Harmful," *CACM,* vol. 11, no. 3, March 1968, letter to the editor.
4. Dijkstra, E., "Structured Programming," in *Software Engineering, Concepts and Techniques,* J. Buxton, et al., (eds.), Van Nostrand, 1976.
5. Knuth, D., "Structured Programming with Goto Statements," *ACM Computing Surveys,* vol. 6, no. 4, December 1974, pp. 261–301.
6. Nassi, I., and B. Shneiderman, *Flowchart Techniques for Structured Programming,* SIGPLAN Notices, ACM, August, 1973.
7. Chapin, N., "A New Format for Flowcharts," *Software—Practice and Experience,* vol. 4, no. 4, 1974, pp. 341–357.
8. Montalbano, M., *Decision Tables,* Science Research Associates (SRA), 1973.
9. Stay, J. F., "HIPO and Integrated Program Design," *IBM Systems Journal,* vol. 15, no. 2, 1976, pp. 143–154.
10. Orr, K., *Structured Systems Development,* Yourdon Press, New York, 1977.
11. Caine, S., and K. Gordon, "PDL—A Tool for Software Design," in *Proceedings of the National Computer Conference,* AFIPS Press, 1975, pp. 271–276.
12. Morris, J., "Programming by Successive Refinement of Data Abstractions," *Software—Practice and Experience,* vol. 10, no. 4, April 1980, pp. 249–263.
13. Shepard, S., and E. Kruesi, "The Effects of Symbology and Special Arrangement of Software Specifications in a Coding Task," *Proceedings of Trends and Applications 1981: Advances in Software Technology,* IEEE, Gaithersburg, MD, 1981.

PROBLEMS AND POINTS TO PONDER

10-1 An enormous volume of literature has evolved on the topic of structured programming. Write a brief paper that highlights the published arguments—pro and con—about the exclusive use of structured constructs.

Problems 10-2 through 10-13 may be represented by using any one (or more) of the design tools that have been presented in this chapter. Your instructor may assign specific tools to specific problems. In some of the problems you should develop a DFD and preliminary design first!

10-2 Develop a detailed design for modules that implement the following sorts: Shell-Metzner sort, heapsort, and BSST (tree) sort. Refer to a book on data structures if you are unfamiliar with these sorts.

10-3 Develop a detailed design for a module that finds the roots of a transcendental equation, using the Newton-Raphson technique. Refer to a book on numerical methods for more information.

10-4 Develop a detailed design for an interactive user interface that queries for basic income tax information. Derive your own requirements and assume that all tax computations are performed by other modules.

10-5 Develop a detailed design for garbage collection function for a variable partitioned memory management scheme. Define all appropriate data structures in the design representation. Refer to a book on operating systems for more information.

10-6 Develop a detailed design for a program that accepts an arbitrarily long text as input and produces a list of words and their frequency of occurrence as output.

10-7 Develop a detailed design of a program that will numerically integrate a function f in the bounds a to b.

10-8 Develop a detailed design for a generalized Turing machine that will accept a set of quadruples as program input and produce output as specified.

10-9 Develop a detailed design for a program that will solve the Towers of Hanoi problem. Most books on artificial intelligence discuss this problem in some detail.

10-10 Develop a detailed design for all or major portions of an LR parser for a compiler. Refer to one or more books on compiler design.

10-11 Develop a detailed design for an encryption-decryption algorithm of your choice.

10-12 This is intended as a team project. Develop requirements, preliminary design, and detailed design for software that accepts a PDL description of a module and computes the McCabe complexity metric for the input module. Refer to McCabe's original work for more information.

10-13 This is another team project. Develop requirements, preliminary design, and detailed design for a *detailed design automated tool*. For example:
(*a*) A computer graphics–based system for the generation of flowcharts or box diagrams
(*b*) A decision table analyzer (see Montalbano [8] for additional information)
(*c*) A PDL indentation aid and flow analyzer

10-14 Conduct an in-class design walkthrough for one or more of the detailed designs developed for Problems 10-2 through 10-13. Designs should be disseminated to reviewers at least 1 day prior to the review.

10-15 Can you think of extensions that might be added to the PDL presented in Section 10.6.1? Should a PDL have a user-extendable set of keywords that could be applied to suit specific application areas?

10-16 Write a paper on the "human factors" aspects of detailed design representations. Use Shepard and Kruesi's work [13] as a starting point.

10-17 Some people argue that when detailed design comes too close to the level of detail contained in source code, it might as well be eliminated as a step and replaced by coding. Debate this issue in your class.

10-18 How can a PDL be used to implement the philosophy of stepwise refinement of design?

10-19 Write a one-or two-page argument for the detailed design tool that you feel is best. Be certain to address the attributes discussed in Section 10.7.

FURTHER READINGS

The concepts behind detailed design and what others call "programming" are so closely related that no meaningful distinction can be made. Many excellent books on computer programming (particularly recent books on Ada, C, PASCAL, PL/1, and ALGOL; see Chapter 11 for references) contain many fine examples of good detailed design.

Software Tools by Kernighan and Plauger (Addison-Wesley, 1976) was written with the premise that "good programming (detailed design) is not learned from generalities, but by seeing . . . significant programs." The authors provide programming guidance and examples that are invaluable to the student and practitioner alike.

Zelkowitz, Shaw, and Gannon (*Principles of Software Engineering and Design,* Prentice-Hall, 1979) dedicate about 80 percent of their book to issues that relate to detailed design. A number of extensive examples are presented. Additional information on decision table techniques may be found in Montalbano [8] and *Programs from Decision Tables* (E. Humby, American Elsevier, New York, 1973).

Structured Programming—Theory and Practice (Linger, R., H. Mills, and B. Witt, Addison-Wesley, 1979) is a comprehensive treatment of the subject. The text contains an extremely thorough PDL as well as detailed discussions of the ramifications of structured programming.

Futayama et al. ("Development of Computer Programs by Problem Analysis Diagram (PAD)," in *Proceedings of the 5th International Conference on Software Engineering,* IEEE, 1981, pp. 325–332) describe an interesting graphical design tool called PAD. Developed by Hitachi, PAD provides an alternative graphical approach to flowcharts and box diagrams. The technique makes recognition of the structured constructs quite simple.

ELEVEN

PROGRAMMING LANGUAGES AND CODING

All software engineering steps that have been presented to this point are directed toward a final objective: to translate representations of software into a form that can be "understood" by the computer. We have (finally) reached the coding step— a process that transforms design into a programming language. Gerald Weinberg [1] expressed the true meaning of coding when he wrote: "When we talk to our computers, unhappily, we are usually speaking in different tongues. . . ." Most readers of this book will live to see the day when this quotation may be proved incorrect. Requests for computer processing services may be coded (or spoken) in a natural langue, like English. The manner in which we perform "programming" may change dramatically as automatic code generation comes into existence. For the time being, however, we "code" by use of artificial languages such as FOR-TRAN, PASCAL, COBOL, or assembler language.

When considered as a step in the software engineering process, coding is viewed as a natural consequence of design. However, programming language characteristics and coding style can profoundly affect software quality and maintainability. This chapter does not aspire to teach the reader to code. Rather, topics associated with programming languages and coding are presented in the broader context of software engineering.

11.1 THE TRANSLATION PROCESS

The coding step translates a detailed design representation of software into a programming language realization. The translation process continues when a compiler accepts *source code* as input and produces machine-dependent *object code* as output. Compiler output is further translated into *machine code*—the actual instructions that drive hardwired or microcoded logic in the central processing unit.

The initial translation step—from detailed design to programming language—is a primary concern in the software engineering context. "Noise" can enter the translation process in many ways. Improper interpretation of a detailed design specification can lead to erroneous source code [2]. Programming language complexity or restrictions can lead to convoluted source code that is difficult to test and maintain. More subtly, characteristics of a programming language can influence the way we think, propagating unnecessarily limited software designs and data structures.

For example, a design directed at a target FORTRAN implementation would be less likely to select a linked list data structure, because FORTRAN does not directly support such a structure. If the target language were PL/1 or PASCAL (both languages provide direct support for linked lists), the linked list would be a more feasible alternative.

Language characteristics have an impact on the quality and efficiency of translation. In Section 11.2 we evaluate language characteristics by considering two different views of programming languages.

11.2 PROGRAMMING LANGUAGE CHARACTERISTICS

Programming languages are a vehicle for communication between humans and computers. The coding process—communication by way of a programming language—is a human activity. As such, the psychological characteristics of a language have an important impact on the quality of communication. The coding process may also be viewed as one step in a software engineering methodology. The engineering characteristics of a language have an important impact on the success of a software development project. Finally, technical characteristics of a language can influence the quality of design (recall that practicality often dictates that detailed design be directed toward a specific programming language). Therefore, technical characteristics can affect both human and software engineering concerns.

11.2.1 A Psychological View

In his recent book on *software psychology,* Ben Shneiderman [3] observed that the role of the software psychologist is to "focus on human concerns such as ease of use, simplicity in learning, improved reliability, reduced error frequency, and enhanced user satisfaction, while maintaining an awareness of machine efficiency, software capacity, and hardware constraints." Software engineering is an intensely human activity. We still have much to learn about the human aspects of computer-based system development.

Another software psychologist, Gerald Weinberg [1], relates a story that bears repeating (in paraphrased form) when we consider characteristics of programming languages:

> It is impossible to begin a discussion of psychological principles of programming language design without recalling the story of "The Genius Tailor." It seems that a man had gone to the tailor to have a suit made cheaply, but when the suit was finished and he went to try it on, it didn't fit him at all.
>
> Complaining that the jacket was too big in back, the right arm was too long, one pant leg was too short, and three buttons were missing, the man was justifiably upset.
>
> "No problem," said the tailor, "just hunch your back, bend your arm, walk with a limp, and stick your fingers through the button holes and you'll look just fine!"
>
> The man contorted his body to fit the suit and feeling duped by the tailor, he left. He had not walked one block when he was approached by a stranger.
>
> "Who made that suit for you?" asked the stranger. "I'm in the market for a new suit myself."
>
> Surprised, but pleased at the compliment, the man pointed out the tailor's shop.
>
> "Well, thanks very much," said the stranger, hurrying off. "I do believe I'll go to that tailor for my suit. Why, he must be a genius to fit a cripple like you!"

Weinberg suggests that we could extend this parable to a story of the genius programming language designer. The designers of programming languages frequently make us contort our approach to a problem so that the approach will fit the constraints imposed by a specific programming language. Because human factors are critically important in programming language design, the psychological characteristics of a language have a strong bearing on the success of design to code translation and implementation.

A number of psychological characteristics [1] occur as a result of programming language design. Although these characteristics are not measurable in any quantifiable way, we recognize their manifestation in all programming languages. We discuss each characteristic briefly in the paragraphs that follow.

Uniformity indicates the degree to which a language uses consistent notation, applies seemingly arbitrary restrictions, and supports syntactic or semantic exceptions to the rule. For example, FORTRAN uses parentheses as delimiters for array indices, as a modifier for arithmetic precedence and as a delimiter for a subprogram argument list (to name a few!). This multiuse notation has lead to more than a few subtle errors.

Ambiguity in a programming language is perceived by the programmer. A compiler will always interpret a statement in one way, but the human reader may interpret the statement differently. Here lies psychological ambiguity. For example, psychological ambiguity arises when arithmetic precedence is not obvious:

$X = X1/X2*X3$

One reader of the source code might interpret the above as $X = (X1/X2)*X3$, while another reader might "see" $X = X1/(X2*X3)$. Another potential source of ambiguity is nonstandard use of identifiers that have default data types. For example, in FORTRAN an identifier KDELTA would be assumed (by default) to have *integer* characteristics. However, an explicit declaration, REAL KDELTA, assigns floating point attributes to KDELTA and could cause confusion due to psychological ambiguity.

A lack of uniformity and the occurrence of psychological ambiguity normally exist together. If a programming language exhibits the negative aspects of these characteristics, source code is less readable and translation from design is more error prone.

Compactness of a programming language is an indication of the amount of code-oriented information that must be recalled from human memory. Among the language attributes that serve as an index of compactness are:

- The degree to which a language supports the structured constructs (Chapter 10) and logical "chunking"
- The kinds of keywords and abbreviations that may be used
- The variety of data types and default characteristics
- The number of arithmetic and logical operators
- The number of built-in functions

APL is an exceptionally compact programming language. Its powerful and concise operators allow relatively little code to accomplish significant arithmetic and logical procedures. Unfortunately, the compactness of APL also makes the language difficult to read and understand and can lead to poor uniformity (e.g., the use of *monadic* and *dyadic* forms for the same operator symbol).

The characteristics of human memory have a strong impact on the way in which we use language. Human memory and recognition may be divided into *synesthetic* and *sequential* domains [4]. Synesthetic memory allows us to remember and recognize things as a whole. For example, we recognize a human face instantly; we do not consciously evaluate each of its distinct parts prior to recognition. Sequential memory provides a means for recalling the next element in a sequence (e.g., the next line in a song, given preceding lines). Each of these memory characteristics affect programming language characteristics that are called *locality* and *linearity*.

Locality is the synesthetic characteristic of a programming language. Locality is enhanced when statements may be combined into blocks, when the structured constructs may be implemented directly, and when design and resultant code is highly modular and cohesive (Chapter 7). A language characteristic that supports or encourages discontinuous processing (e.g., ON-condition processing in PL/1 or ERR= in extended versions of FORTRAN) violate locality.

Linearity is a psychological characteristic that is closely associated to the concept of maintenance of functional domain. That is, human perception is facilitated when a linear sequence of logical operations is encountered. Extensive branching (and to some extent, large loops) violates the linearity of processing.

Again, direct implementation of the structured constructs aids programming language linearity.

Our ability to learn a new programming language is affected by *tradition.* A software engineer with a background in FORTRAN or ALGOL would have little difficulty learning PL/1 or PASCAL. The latter languages have a tradition established by the former. Constructs are similar, form is compatible, and a sense of programming language "format" is maintained. However, if the same individual was required to learn APL or LISP, tradition is broken and time on the learning curve would be longer.

Tradition also affects the degree of innovation during the design of a new programming language. Although new languages are proposed frequently, new language forms evolve slowly. For example, PASCAL is a close relative of ALGOL. However, a major innovation in the PASCAL language [5] is an implementation of user-defined data types, a form that does not exist in earlier languages tied to PASCAL by tradition.

The psychological characteristics of programming language have an important bearing on our ability to learn, apply, and maintain them. In summary, a programming language colors the way we think about programs and inherently limits the way in which we communicate with a computer. Whether this is good or bad remains an open question.

11.2.2 A Syntactic-Semantic Model

Shneiderman [3] has developed a *syntactic-semantic model* of the programming process that has relevance in a consideration of the coding step. When a programmer applies general software development techniques (e.g., software requirements analysis methods, design methods) that are programming language–independent, semantic knowledge is tapped. Syntactic knowledge, on the other hand, is language-dependent, concentrating on the characteristics of a specific language.

Of these knowledge types, semantic knowledge is the most difficult to acquire and the most intellectually demanding to apply. All software engineering steps that precede coding make heavy use of semantic knowledge. The coding step applies syntactic knowledge that is "arbitrary and instructional" and learned by rote [3]. When a new programming language is learned, new syntactic (as well as semantic) information is added to memory. Potential confusion may occur when the syntax of a new programming language is similar but not equivalent to the syntax of another language.

When arguments about the compelling need to "generate code" arise, the listener should realize that a software crisis has not been caused by a lack of syntactic knowledge. The problem lies in the scope of our semantic knowledge and our ability to apply it. The goal of software engineering is to expand knowledge of the semantics of software development.

11.2.3 An Engineering View

A software engineering view of programming language characteristics focuses on the needs of a specific software development project. Although esoteric requirements for source code may be derived, a general set of engineering characteristics may be established: (1) ease of design to code translation; (2) compiler efficiency; (3) source code portability; (4) availability of development tools; and (5) maintainability.

The coding step begins after a detailed design has been defined, reviewed, and modified, if necessary. In theory, source code generation from a detailed design specification should be straightforward. *Ease of design to code translation* provides an indication of how closely a programming language mirrors a design representation. As we discussed in Section 11.1, a language that directly implements the structured constructs, sophisticated data structures, specialized I/O, bit-manipulation capabilities, and string handling will make translation from design to source code much easier (if these attributes are specified in design).

Although rapid advances in processor speed and memory density have begun to mitigate the need for "super efficient code," many applications still require fast, "tight" (low memory requirement) software. An on-going criticism of high-level language compilers is directed at an inability to produce fast, tight, executable code. Languages with optimizing compilers may be attractive if software performance is a critical requirement. New stack-oriented languages, such as FORTH, have been developed specifically to enhance *compiler efficiency,* that is, the ability to produce fast, tight code.

Source code portability is a programming language characteristic that may be interpreted in three different ways:

1. Source code may be transported from processor to processor and compiler to compiler with little or no modification.
2. Source code remains unchanged even when its environment changes (e.g., a new version of an operating system is installed).
3. Source code may be integrated into different software packages with little or no modification required because of programming language characteristics.

Of the three interpretations of portability, the first is by far the most common. Standardization [by International Standards Organization (ISO) and/or American National Standards Institute (ANSI)] continues to be a major impetus for improvement of programming language portability. Unfortunately, most compiler designers succumb to a compelling urge to provide "better" but nonstandard features for a standardized language. If portability is a critical requirement, source code must be restricted to the ISO or ANSI standard, even if other features exist.

Availability of development tools can shorten the time required to generate source code and can improve the quality of the code. Many programming languages may be acquired with a suite of tools that include debugging compilers, source code formatting aids, built-in editing facilities, tools for source code control, extensive subprogram libraries in a variety of application areas, cross-compilers for microprocessor development, and macroprocessor capabilities. In fact, the concept of a good *programming environment* [6] that includes both conventional and automated tools has been recognized as a key contributor to successful software engineering.

Maintainability of source code is critically important for all nontrivial software development efforts. Maintenance cannot be accomplished until software is understood. Earlier elements of the software configuration (i.e., design documentation) provide a foundation for understanding, but ultimately source code must be read and modified according to changes in design. Ease of design to code translation is an important element in source code maintainability. In addition, self-documenting characteristics of a language (e.g., allowable length of identifiers, labeling format, and data type and structure definition) have a strong influence on maintainability.

11.2.4 Choosing a Language

The choice of a programming language for a specific project must take into account both engineering and psychological characteristics. However, the problem associated with choice may be moot if only one language is available or dictated by a requester. Mack and Heath [7] suggest a general philosophy when a programming language must be chosen:

> The art of choosing a language is to start with the problem, decide what its requirements are, and their relative importance, since it will probably be impossible to satisfy them all equally well (with a single language) . . . available languages should be measured against the list of requirements. . . .

Among the criteria that are applied during an evaluation of available languages are (1) general applications area, (2) algorithmic and computational complexity, (3) environment in which software will execute, (4) performance considerations, (5) data structure complexity, and (6) knowledge of software development staff. The applications area of a project is a criterion that is applied most often during language selection. As we noted in Chapter 1, four major applications areas have evolved, and de facto standard languages may be selected for each. In the engineering-scientific area, FORTRAN remains the predominant language (although ALGOL, PL/1, and PASCAL have wide usage). Commercial applications are normally coded in COBOL or RPG (although PL/1 and some specialized languages are good alternatives). Systems and real-time applications make use of assembler language or a relatively new breed of systems/real-time languages such as BLISS, PL/S, Ada, and others. Finally, combinatorial (problem-solving) applications draw on languages from other areas, but make heavy use of the LISP language.

The proliferation of "new and better" programming languages continues. Although many of these languages are attractive, it is sometimes better to choose a "weaker" (old) language that has solid documentation and support software, is familiar to everyone on the software development team, and has been successfully applied in the past. However, new languages should be thoroughly evaluated, and transition from old to new should occur, recognizing the psychological resistance to change that is encountered in all organizations.

11.2.5 Technical Characteristics of Programming Languages

The technical characteristics of programming languages span an enormous number of topics that range from theoretical (e.g., formal language theory and specification) to pragmatic (e.g., functional comparisons of specific languages). In this section a brief discussion of the relationship of programming language characteristics to other steps of the software engineering process is presented.

During the planning step (Chapter 4), a consideration of the technical characteristics of a programming language is rarely undertaken. Planning for support tools associated with resource definition may require that a specific compiler (and associated software) or programming environment be specified. Cost and schedule estimation may require "learning curve" adjustments because of staff inexperience with a language. But a detailed evaluation of language characteristics is generally premature.

Once software requirements have been established, the technical characteristics of candidate programming languages become more important. If complex data structures are required, languages with sophisticated data structure support (e.g., PASCAL or PL/1) would merit careful evaluation. If high-performance, real-time capability is paramount, a language designed for real-time application (e.g., Ada) or memory-speed efficiency (e.g., FORTH) might be specified. If many output reports and heavy file manipulation are specified, languages such as COBOL or RPG might fit the bill. Ideally, software requirements should precipitate the selection of a language that best fits the processing to be accomplished. In practice, however, a language is often selected because "it's the only one we have running on our computer!"

The quality of a software design is established in a manner that is independent of programming language characteristics. However, language attributes do play a role in the quality of an implemented design and affect (both consciously and unconsciously) the way that design is specified.

In Chapter 7 we discussed a number of qualitative and quantitative measures of good design. The concepts of modularity and module independence were emphasized. Technical characteristics of many programming languages can affect these design concepts during the implementation of the design. To illustrate, consider the following examples:

- Modularity is supported by nearly all modern programming languages. COBOL, for example, supports a hierarchy of function that integrates various levels of procedural abstraction (Chapter 6) with the modularity concept. The hierarchy consists of division, sections, paragraphs, sentences, and finally, words. Each of these terms has a precise meaning in the language and helps to emphasize a modular implementation.
- Module independence can be enhanced or subverted by language characteristics. For example, the FORTRAN subroutine supports the concept of information hiding, while the use of internal procedures in PL/1 can lead to extensive global data that increase module coupling.

Data design (discussed in Chapter 9) can also be influenced by language characteristics. Wasserman [8] describes characteristics of a number of programming languages (CLU, Alphard, PLAIN, etc.) that support the concept of abstract data types—an important tool in data design and specification. Other more common languages, such as PASCAL, allow the definition of user-defined data types and direct implementation of linked lists and other data structures. These features provide the designer with greater latitude during the preliminary and detailed design steps.

In some cases design requirements can be satisfied only when a language has special characteristics. Per Brinch-Hansen [9] describes a set of language characteristics essential for implementation of a design that specifies distributed processes that are executing concurrently and must communicate and coordinate with one another. Languages such as concurrent PASCAL or MODULA can be used to satisfy such designs.

The effect of programming language characteristics on the steps that comprise software testing is difficult to assess. Languages that directly support the structured constructs tend to reduce the cyclomatic complexity (Chapter 7) of a program, thereby making it somewhat easier to test. Languages that support the specification of external subprograms and procedures (e.g., FORTRAN) make integration testing much less error prone than languages such as BASIC that support internal modules only. On the other hand, some technical characteristics of a language can impede testing. For example, block structuring in ALGOL can be specified in a manner that causes loss of intermediate data when exit from a block occurs, thereby making the status of a program more difficult to assess.

Like testing, the effect of programming language characteristics on software maintenance is not fully understood. There is no question, however, that technical characteristics that enhance code readability and reduce complexity are important for effective maintenance. Further discussion of software maintenance is postponed until Chapter 13.

11.3 LANGUAGE CLASSES

There are hundreds of programming languages that have been applied at one time or another to serious software development efforts. Even a detailed discussion of the five most common languages is beyond the scope of this book. The reader is referred to Pratt [10] or Tucker [11] for thorough surveys and comparisons of the most common programming languages. In this section three classes of high-level programming languages are defined and representative languages from each class are discussed.

Any categorization of programming languages is open to debate. For the purposes of this book, we develop general language categories illustrated in Figure 11.1.

There are as many machine dependent languages—normally called *assembly languages*—as there are processor architectures with custom instruction sets. From

Classes of Languages

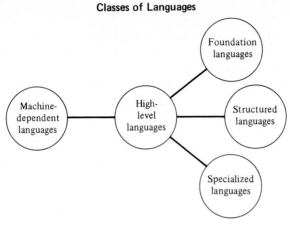

Figure 11.1

a software engineering viewpoint, such languages should be used only when a high-level language cannot meet requirements or is not supported. To help justify the preceding statement, consider recent developments in the design of processor hardware. A number of modern processors (e.g., P-code machines and Intel IAPX-432) do not support assembler language. Instead, such machines are programmed directly in a high-level language—Ada in the case of the IAPX-432. This development underlines the fact that hardware manufacturers are beginning to recognize the severe disadvantages (from a software engineering viewpoint) of using assembly language.

Three classes of high-level languages are also shown in Figure 11.1: *foundation languages, structured languages,* and *specialized languages.* It should be noted that a programming language can legitimately be categorized as a member of more than one class.

11.3.1 Foundation Languages

Foundation languages are characterized by broad usage, enormous software libraries, and widest familiarity and acceptance. There is little debate that FOR-TRAN, COBOL, ALGOL, and (to some extent) BASIC are foundation languages by virtue of their maturity and acceptance.

FORTRAN has withstood 20 years of criticism (much of it justified) to remain the premier programming language in engineering and scientific work. The original standardized version of FORTRAN (called *FORTRAN-66*) provided a powerful tool for computational problem solving, but lacked direct support of the structured constructs, had poor data typing, could not easily support string handling, and had many other deficiencies. The newer ANSI standard (called *FORTRAN-77*) corrects some of the deficiencies found in earlier versions of the language.

COBOL, like FORTRAN, has reached maturity and is the accepted standard language for commercial data processing applications. Although the language is sometimes criticized for lack of compactness, it has excellent data typing, is largely self-documenting, and provides support for a wide range of procedural techniques relevant to business data processing.

ALGOL is the forerunner of all structured languages and offers an extremely rich repertoire of procedural and data-typing constructs. ALGOL has been used extensively in Europe, but has found little support (with the exception of academic environments) in the United States. The most commonly used version of the language, correctly termed *ALGOL-60,* has been extended to a more powerful implementation, *ALGOL-68.* Both versions of the language support the notion of block structuring, dynamic storage allocation, recursion, and other characteristcs that have had a strong influence on the structured languages that have followed.

BASIC is an interpretive language that was originally designed to teach programming in a time-sharing mode. The language was moving toward obsolescence in the early 1970s, but has experienced a rebirth with the advent of personal microcomputer systems. There are hundreds of versions of BASIC, making it difficult to discuss benefits and deficiencies of the language.

11.3.2 Structured Languages

Structured languages are characterized by strong procedural and data structuring capabilities. All languages in this class directly support the structured logical constructs discussed in Chapters 6 and 10. The earliest structured language (also a foundation language), ALGOL, served as a model for other languages in this category. Its descendents, PL/1, PASCAL, C, and Ada, are being adopted as languages with potential for broad-spectrum applications (i.e., for use in engineering-scientific, commercial, and/or systems application areas).

PL/1 was the first true *broad-spectrum* language. That is, it was developed with a wide range of features that enable it to be used in many different application areas. PL/1 provides support for conventional engineering-scientific and business applications while at the same time enabling specification of sophisticated data structures, multitasking, complex I/O, list processing, and many other features. Subsets of the language have been developed to teach programming (PL/C), for use in microprocessor applications (PL/M), and for systems programming (PL/S).

PASCAL is a structured programming language developed in the early 1970s as a language for teaching modern techniques (e.g., structured programming) in software development. Since its introduction, PASCAL has found growing support from a broad audience of software developers and is used widely for engineering-scientific applications and systems programming (the language has been called "the FORTRAN of the 1980s"). PASCAL is a direct descendant of ALGOL and contains many of the same features, such as block structuring, strong data typing, direct support for recursion, and other complementary features. It has been implemented on computers of all sizes and shows particular promise as a development language for microcomputer applications.

The C programming language was developed as the primary language for the UNIX (a trademark of Bell Laboratories, AT&T) operating system, but has also been implemented independently of the UNIX system on a variety of mini- and microcomputers. C was developed for the "sophisticated" software engineer and contains powerful features that give it considerable flexibility. Like other languages in the structured category, C supports strong data typing, makes extensive use of pointers, and has a rich set of operators for computation and data manipulation.

Ada is a language developed (under the auspices of the U.S. Department of Defense) as a new standard for embedded computer systems. PASCAL-like in structure and notation, Ada supports a rich set of real-time features that include support for interrupt handling, multitasking, interprocess communication, and operations at a machine-dependent level. At the same time, Ada is high-level in structure and notation, making it much easier (than assembly language) to maintain. The language, under development since the mid-1970s, has been reviewed and evaluated by hundreds of representatives from government, academia, and industry. It may, therefore, find widespread usage in software development projects that are far removed from defense systems.

11.3.3 Specialized Languages

Specialized languages are characterized by unusual syntactic forms that have been especially designed for a distinct application. Hundreds of specialized languages are in use today. In general, such languages have a relatively small user base. The following list contains a representative sample of specialized languages:

APL. An extremely concise and powerful language designed for array and vector manipulation. The language contains little support for structured constructs or data typing. APL does provide a rich set of computational operators and has gained a small but avid following for mathematical problem solving.

APT. A programming language designed for numerically controlled machine tools. The language contains a syntax for the geometric description of parts, motion commands for cutting tools, and general-purpose statements for machine control.

BLISS. This language is designed for development of compilers and other operating system software.

FORTH. A language designed for microprocessor software development. The language supports the definition of user-defined functions that are executed in a stack-oriented manner for speed and memory efficiency.

LISP. This language is especially suited to symbol manipulation and list processing encountered in combinatorial problems. Used almost exclusively by the artificial intelligence community, the language is particularly well suited to theorem proving, tree searches, and other problem-solving activities.

SNOBOL. This language is particularly well suited to string manipulation and processing. The language supports strong character string pattern matching constructs.

From a software engineering standpoint, specialized languages provide both advantages and disadvantages. Because a specialized language has been designed to address a specific application, translation of requirements to design to code implementation can be facilitated. On the other hand, most specialized languages are far less portable and often less maintainable than foundation and structured languages.

11.4 CODING STYLE

After source code is generated, the function of a module should be apparent without reference to a design specification. In other words, code must be understandable. Coding style encompasses a coding philosophy that stresses simplicity and clarity. In their landmark text on the subject, Kernighan and Plauger [12] state:

> Writing a computer program eventually boils down to writing a sequence of statements in the language at hand. How each of those statements is expressed determines in large measure the intelligibility of the whole. . . .

The elements of style include internal (source code level) documentation, methods for data declaration, an approach to statement construction, and techniques for I/O. We consider each of these topics in the sections that follow.

11.4.1 Code Documentation

Internal documentation of source code begins with the selection of identifier (variables and labels) names, continues with placement and composition of commenting, and concludes with the visual organization of the program.

Selection of meaningful identifier names is crucial to understanding. Languages that limit variable names or labels to only a few characters inherently obscure meaning. Consider the following three statements:

```
D=V*T
DIST= HORVEL*TIME
DISTANCE:= HORIZONTAL.VELOCITY * TIME.TRAVELED.IN.SECS;
```

The BASIC language expression is undeniably concise, but the meaning of D=V*T is unclear unless the reader has prior information. The FORTRAN expression provides more information, but the meaning of DIST and HORVEL could be misinterpreted. The ALGOL statement leaves little doubt regarding the meaning of the calculation. These statements illustrate the way in which identifiers may be chosen to help document code.

It can be argued that wordy expressions (e.g., the ALGOL statement above) obscure logical flow and make modification difficult. Obviously, common sense must be applied when identifiers are selected. Unnecessarily long identifiers do indeed provide a potential for error (not to mention a backache from sitting long hours typing at a development terminal!). Studies [3] indicate, however, that even for "small" programs, meaningful identifiers improve comprehension. In terms of the syntactic-semantic model discussed in Section 11.2.2, meaningful names "simplify the conversion from program syntax to internal semantic structure" [3].

The ability to express natural language comments as part of a source code listing is provided by all general-purpose programming languages. However, certain questions arise:

- How many comments are "enough"?
- Where should comments be placed?
- Do comments obscure logic flow?
- Can comments mislead the reader?
- Are comments unmaintainable and, therefore, unreliable?

There are few definitive answers to the above questions. But one thing is clear: *software must contain internal documentation.* Comments provide the developer with one means of communicating with other readers of the source code. Comments can provide a clear guide to understanding during the last phase of the software life cycle—maintenance.

Many guidelines have been proposed for commenting. Prologue comments and functional comments are two categories that require somewhat different approaches. Prologue comments should appear at the beginning of every module. The format for such comments is:

1. A statement of purpose that indicates the function of the module
2. An interface description that includes
   a. a sample "calling sequence"
   b. a description of all arguments
   c. a list of all subordinate modules
3. A discussion of pertinent data such as important variables and their use, restrictions, and limitations, and other information
4. A development history that includes
   a. Module designer (author)
   b. Reviewer (auditor) and date
   c. Modification dates and description

An example of prologue comments is given in Figure 11.2. Subroutine NGON is a module in a large general-purpose computer graphics system developed by the

```
C
C    TITLE:      SUBROUTINE NGON
C
C    PURPOSE:   THE PURPOSE OF TO CONTROL THE DRAWING OF
C               NGONS.
C
C    SAMPLE CALL:   CALL NGON (KROW,IX,IY,KN)
C
C    INPUTS:        KROW = IS THE LINE ON THE TABLET WHERE
C                          THE NEXT LINE OF OUTPUT WILL BE
C                          PRINTED.
C                   IX   = X-COORDINATE OF THE LEFT END OF THE
C                          BOTTOM SEGMENT
C                   IY   = Y-COORDINATE PF THE LEFT END OF THE
C                          BOTTOM SEGMENT
C                   KN   = IS THE NUMBER OF THE LAST NGON
C
C    OUTPUTS:       KROW = IS THE INCREMENTED ROW COUNTER
C                   KN   = IS THE INCREMENTED NGON COUNTER
C
C    SUBROUTINES REFERENCED:      1.) DBNGON
C                                 2.) ALPHA
C                                 3.) ROWCOL
C
C    PERTINENT DATA:
C             KROW IS CHECKED TO SEE IF THE TABLET IS FULL.
C         IF IT IS THEN REPNT IS CALLED TO REFRESH THE SCREEN
C         AND PUT UP A NEW TABLET. THE NGON COUNTER (KN) IS
C         INCREMENTED AND THE POINTER ARRAY PO IS WRITTEN TO
C         THE DISPLAY FILE.
C
C             A PROMPT IS THEN ISSUED FOR THE NUMBER OF
C         OF SIDES AND THE ORIENTATION OF THE NGON WITH
C         RESPECT TP THE X-AXIS. THE ARRAY 'NG' IS LOADED
C         AND WRITTEN TO THE OBJECT FILE.
C
C             THE ROUTINE DBNGON DOES THE ACTUAL DRAWING.
C         IT REQUIRES THE NUMBER OF SIDES, THE LENGTH OF A
C         SIDE, THE ORIENTATION, AND THE COORDINATES OF THE
C         OF THE STARTING POINT AND IPEN.
C
C    AUTHOR:  M. WRIGHT
C
C    AUDITOR: D. CURRIE
C
C    DATE:    10/30/80
C
C    MODIFICATIONS:
C
C         11/29/80  D.C.
C         CHANGES MADE TO ALLOW TABLES TO BE BUILT FOR REPNT
C
C         1/7/81  R.P.S.
C         ADD ERROR CHECKING COMMON 'SPECAL' AND ERROR
C         HANDLING.
C
         SUBROUTINE NGON(KROW,IX,IY,KN)
         DIMENSION PO(10),NG(10)
         INTEGER#2 ARG1,ARG2,ARG3,RPTFLG,RPTNUM
```

Figure 11.2

Computer Aided Design and Manufacturing Center (CADMC) at the University of Bridgeport.

Descriptive comments are embedded within the body of source code and are used to describe processing functions. A primary guideline for such commenting is expressed by Van Tassel [13]: "comments should provide something extra, not just paraphrase the code." In addition, descriptive comments should:

- Describe blocks of code, rather than commenting every line
- Use blank lines or indentation so that comments can be readily distinguished from code
- Be correct; an incorrect or misleading comment is worse than no comment at all

With proper identifier mnemonics and good commenting, adequate internal documentation is assured.

When a detailed design is represented by use of a program design language (Chapter 10), design documentation can be embedded directly into the source listing as comment statements. This technique is particularly useful when implementation is to be done in assembly language and helps to ensure that both code and design will be maintained when changes are made to either.

The form of the source code as it appears on the listing is an important contributor to readability. Source code indentation indicates logical constructs and blocks of code by indenting from the left margin so that these attributes are visually offset. Like commenting, the best approach to indentation is open to debate. Manual indentation can become complicated as code modification occurs, and experiments [3] indicate that only marginal improvement in understanding accrues. Probably the best approach is to use an automatic code formatter (a tool) that will properly indent source code. By eliminating the burden of indentation from the coder, form may be improved with relatively little effort.

11.4.2 Data Declaration

The complexity and organization of data structure are defined during the design step. The style of data declaration is established when code is generated. A number of relatively simple guidelines can be established to make data more understandable and maintenance simpler.

The order of data declarations should be standardized even if the programming language has no mandatory requirements. For example, declaration ordering for a FORTRAN module might be:

1. All explicit declarations

INTEGER, REAL, DOUBLE PRECISION, . . .

2. All global data blocks

COMMON/block-name/ . . .

3. All local arrays

DIMENSION array names and dimensions

4. All file declarations

DEFINE FILE, OPEN, CLOSE

Ordering makes attributes easier to find, thus expediting testing, debugging, and maintenance.

When multiple variable names are declared with a single statement, an alphabetical ordering of names is worthwhile. Similarly, labeled global data (e.g., FORTRAN common blocks) should be ordered alphabetically.

If a complex data structure is prescribed by design, commenting should be used to explain peculiarities inherent in a programming language implementation. For example, a linked list data structure in PL/1 or a user-defined data type in PASCAL might require supplementary documentation contained in comments.

11.4.3 Statement Construction

The construction of software logical flow is established during design. The construction of individual statements, however, is part of the coding step. Statement construction should abide by one overriding rule: Each statement should be simple and direct; code should not be convoluted to effect efficiency.

Many programming languages allow multiple statements per line. The space saving aspects of this feature are hardly justified by the poor readability that results. Consider the following two code segments:

```
DO I = 1 TO N−1; T = I; DO J = I+1 TO N;
IF A(J) < A(T) THEN DO T=J; END;
IF T <> I THEN DO H=A(T); A(T)=A(I); A(I)=H; END; END;
```

The loop structure and conditional operation contained in the above segment are masked by multistatement per line construction. Reorganizing the form of the code, we obtain

```
DO I = 1 TO N−1;
  T=I;
  DO J = I+1 TO N;
    IF A(J)<A(T) THEN DO
      T=J;
      END;
```

```
    IF T <> I THEN DO
        H = A(T);
        A(T) = A(I);
        A(I) = T;
        END;
    END;
END
```

Here, simple statement construction and indentation illuminate the logical and functional characteristics of the segment.

Individual source code statements can be simplified by:

- Avoiding the use of complicated conditional tests
- Eliminating tests on "negative" conditions
- Avoiding heavy nesting of loops or conditions
- Using parentheses to clarify logical or arithmetic expressions
- Using spacing and/or readability symbols to clarify statement content
- Using only ANSI standard features
- Thinking: "Could I understand this if I was not the person who coded it?"

Each of the above guidelines strives to "keep it simple."

11.4.4 Input/Output

The style of input and output is established during software requirements analysis and design, not coding. However, the manner in which I/O is implemented can be the determining characteristic for system acceptance by a user community.

Input/output (I/O) style will vary with the degree of human interaction. For *batch-oriented* I/O, logical input organization, meaningful I/O error checking, good I/O error recovery, and rational output report formats are desirable characteristics. For *interactive* I/O, a simple, guided input scheme, extensive error checking and recovery, human-engineered output, and consistency of I/O format become primary concerns.

Regardless of the batch or interactive nature of software, a number of I/O style guidelines should be considered during design and coding:

- Validate all input data.
- Check the plausibility of important combinations of input items.
- Keep input format simple.
- Use end-of-data indicators, rather than requiring a user to specify "number-of-items."
- Label interactive input requests, specifying available choices or bounding values.
- Keep input format uniform when a programming language has stringent formatting requirements.
- Label all output and design all reports.

The style of I/O is affected by many other characteristics such as I/O devices (e.g., terminal type, computer graphics device, or digitizer), user sophistication, and communication environment. Wasserman [14] provides a comprehensive set of guidelines for "user software engineering and the design of interactive systems." These guidelines, applicable to both software design and coding, are summarized as follows:

1. Make the underlying aspects of the computer invisible to the user.
2. Make the program "bulletproof," that is, make it virtually impossible for the user to cause the program to end abnormally.
3. Notify the user if any request can have major consequences.
4. Provide on-line assistance in the use of the program.
5. Tailor input requirements to user skills.
6. Tailor output messages to the speed of output devices.
7. Distinguish among different classes of users.
8. Maintain a consistent response time.
9. Minimize extra work for the user in the event of an error.

Each of these guidelines should become automatic software requirements for all interactive systems. Software should be designed to accommodate each and coded to implement a user software-engineered interface.

11.5 EFFICIENCY

In well-engineered systems, there is a natural tendency to use critical resources efficiently. Processor cycles and primary memory locations are often viewed as critical resources, and the coding step is seen as the last point where microseconds or bits can be squeezed out of the software. Although efficiency is a commendable goal, three maxims should be stated before we discuss the topic further. First, efficiency is a *performance requirement* and should, therefore, be established during software requirements analysis. Software should be as efficient as is required, not as efficient as is humanly possible! Second, efficiency is improved with good design. Third, code efficiency and code simplicity go hand in hand. In general, don't sacrifice clarity, readability, or correctness for nonessential improvements in efficiency.

11.5.1 Code Efficiency

The efficiency of source code is directly tied to the efficiency of algorithms defined during detailed design. However, coding style can have an effect on execution speed and memory requirement. The following set of guidelines can always be applied when detailed design is translated into code:

- Simplify arithmetic and logical expressions before committing to code.
- Carefully evaluate nested loops to determine if statements or expressions can be moved outside.
- When possible, avoid the use of multidimensional arrays.
- When possible, avoid the use of pointers and complex lists.
- Use "fast" arithmetic operations.
- Don't mix data types.
- Use integer arithmetic and Boolean expressions whenever possible.

Many compilers have "optimizing" features that automatically generate efficient code by collapsing repetitive expressions, performing loop evaluation, using fast arithmetic, and applying other efficiency related algorithms. For applications in which efficiency is paramount, such compilers are an indispensable coding tool.

11.5.2 Memory Efficiency

Memory restrictions in the large machine ("mainframe") world are largely a thing of the past. Virtual memory management provides application software with an enormous logical address space. Memory efficiency for such environments cannot be equated to minimum memory used. Rather, memory efficiency must take into account the "paging" characteristics of an operating system (see the works by Denning [15] and Lorin and Deitel [16] for a discussion of virtual memory systems). In general, code locality or maintenance of functional domain through the structured constructs is an excellent method for reducing paging and thereby increasing efficiency.

Memory restrictions in the microcomputer world are a very real concern, although low-cost, high-density memory is evolving rapidly. If minimal memory is demanded by system requirements (e.g., a high-volume, low-cost product), high-level language compilers must be carefully evaluated for memory compression features, or as a last resort, assembler language may have to be used.

Unlike many other system characteristics that must be traded against one another, techniques for execution efficiency often lead to memory efficiency. For example, limiting the use of three- or four-dimensional arrays results in simple element access algorithms that are "fast" and "short." Again, the key to memory efficiency is "keep it simple."

11.5.3 Input/Output Efficiency

Two classes of I/O should be considered when efficiency is discussed: I/O directed at a human or I/O directed to another device (e.g., a disk or another computer). Input supplied by a user and output produced for a user are efficient when information can be supplied or understood with economy of intellectual effort.

Efficiency of I/O to other hardware is an extremely complicated topic and is beyond the scope of this book. From the coding (and detailed design) standpoint, however, a few simple guidelines that improve I/O efficiency can be stated:

- All I/O should be buffered to reduce communication overhead.
- For secondary memory (e.g., disk), the simplest acceptable access method should be selected and used.
- I/O to secondary memory devices should be blocked.
- I/O to terminals and printers should recognize features of the device that could improve quality or speed.
- Remember that "super efficient" I/O is worthless if it can't be understood.

As we noted earlier in this chapter, I/O design establishes style and ultimately dictates efficiency. The guidelines presented above are applicable to both design and coding steps of the software engineering process.

11.6 SUMMARY

The coding step of software engineering is a process of translation. Detailed design is translated into a programming language that is ultimately (and automatically) transformed into machine-executable instructions. Psychological and technical characteristics of a programming language affect the ease of translation from design and the effort required to test and maintain software. These characteristics may be applied to programming languages that fall into one of three classes: foundation, structured, or specialized languages.

Style is an important attribute of source code and can determine the intelligibility of a program. The elements of style include internal documentation, methods for data declaration, procedures for statement construction, and I/O coding techniques. In all cases, simplicity and clarity are key characteristics. An offshoot of coding style is the execution time and/or memory efficiency that are achieved. Although efficiency can be an extremely important requirement, we should remember that an "efficient" program that is unintelligible has questionable value.

Coding lies at the kernel of the software engineering process. Critically important steps have preceded coding, relegating it to a somewhat mechanistic translation of a detailed design specification. Equally important steps follow coding, and it is a discussion of these steps and related topics that comprise the remainder of this book.

REFERENCES

1. Weinberg, G., *The Psychology of Computer Programming,* Van Nostrand, 1971.
2. Shepard, S., E. Kruesi, and B. Curtis, "The Effects of Symbology and Spatial Arrangement on the Comprehension of Software Specifications," *International Conference on Software Engineering, IEEE,* San Diego, Cal., March 1981, pp. 207–214.
3. Shneiderman, B., *Software Psychology,* Winthrop Publishers, 1980.
4. Klatzky, R., *Human Memory,* 2d ed., W.H. Freeman, 1980.
5. Jensen, K., and N. Wirth, *PASCAL User Manual and Report,* Springer-Verlag, 1974.

6. "Programming Environments" (a series of articles), in *Computer,* A. Wasserman, (ed.), vol. 14, no. 4, April, 1981.

7. Mack, B., and P. Heath, (eds.), *Guide to Good Programming,* Halsted (Wiley), 1980.

8. Wasserman, A., "Principles of Systematic Data Design and Implementation," in *Software Design Techniques,* A. Wasserman and P. Freeman, (eds.), IEEE Computer Society Press 1980, pp. 287–293.

9. Brinch-Hansen, P., "Distributed Processes: A Concurrent Programming Concept," *CACM,* vol. 21, no. 11, November 1978, pp. 934–941.

10. Pratt, T., *Programming Languages: Design and Implementation,* Prentice-Hall, 1975.

11. Tucker, A., *Programming Languages,* McGraw-Hill, 1977.

12. Kernighan, B., and P. Plauger, *The Elements of Programming Style,* McGraw-Hill, 1974.

13. Van Tassel, D., *Program Style, Design, Efficiency, Debugging and Testing,* 2d ed., Prentice-Hall, 1978.

14. Wasserman, A., "User Software Engineering and the Design of Interactive Systems," in *Proceedings of the Fifth International Conference on Software Engineering, IEEE,* San Diego, CA, March 1981, pp. 387–393.

15. Denning, P., "Virtual Memory," *ACM Computing Surveys,* vol. 2, no. 3, September 1970, pp. 153–189.

16. Lorin, H., and H. Deitel, *Operating Systems,* Addison-Wesley, 1981.

PROBLEMS AND POINTS TO PONDER

11-1 Do some research on *semantic information processing* (most texts on artificial intelligence discuss this topic), and write a position paper on the probability of natural language programming.

11-2 through 11-13 Code and attempt to implement the detailed designs for corresponding problems in Chapter 10. You may use the programming language of your choice, but remember the style and clarity guidelines discussed in this chapter.

11-14 Much of the work in software psychology has centered on the characteristics of programming languages and their effect on the coding task. Write a paper that presents some of the more current work in this area.

11-15 Select one or more programming languages and provide examples of each of the psychological characteristics (uniformity, ambiguity, etc.) discussed in Section 11.2.

11-16 Select the one programming language that you feel best satisfies the software engineering traits that are discussed in Section 11.2.3. Would your choice change if the technical characteristics of the language were also considered?

11-17 Select one of the structured languages discussed in Section 11.3.2. Prepare a brief summary of important language characteristics, and write a small program that illustrates the language syntax.

11-18 Select any specialized language and prepare a summary of important characteristics and special features. Write a small program that illustrates language syntax.

11-19 List in order of priority those style guidelines that you feel are most important. Justify your selection.

11-20 In this chapter coding has been referred to as a *mechanistic task*. Do you feel that this is the case?

FURTHER READINGS

Programming languages are fundamental to an understanding of computer science and should be understood individually and in relationship to one another. Books by Pratt [10] and Tucker [11] satisfy both requirements nicely. A thumbnail sketch of important programming languages is provided in outline fashion by Gottfried (*A Comparison of Programming Languages*, Quantum Publishers, New York, 1973).

The Elements of Programming Style [12] is *must* reading for all individuals who intend to generate source code. The authors have provided an extensive, annotated set of rules for coding (and design) that are well worth heeding.

There is no "best" textbook that can be chosen from the hundreds that have been written about languages within any one of the three language classes. The following list contains a representative sample of source material for many of the programming languages discussed in this chapter:

FORTRAN: Chirlian, P., *Introduction to Structured Fortran*, Matrix Publishers, 1979.
COBOL: Sass, C., *COBOL Programming and Applications*, Allyn and Bacon, 1979.
ALGOL: Brailsford, D., and A. Walker, *Introductory Algol-68 Programming*, Wiley, 1979.
BASIC: Pavlovich, J., and T. Tahan, *Computer Programming in BASIC*, Holden-Day, 1971.
PL/1: Hughs, J., *PL/1 Structured Programming*, 2d ed., Wiley, 1979.
PASCAL: Gregono, P., *Programming in PASCAL*, Addison-Wesley, 1980.
C: Kernighan, B., and D. Ritchie, *The C Programming Language*, Prentice-Hall, 1978.
Ada: Wegner, P., *Programming with Ada*, Prentice-Hall, 1980.
FORTH: Katzen, H., *Invitation to FORTH*, Petrocelli, 1981.

An introduction to formal language theory can be found in *Jewels of Formal Language Theory* (Salomaa, A., Computer Science Press, 1981). This text surveys morphic representations, formal syntax specification, DOL languages, and many other topics. An equally rigorous treatment of these topics may be found in Pagan (*Formal Specification of Programming Languages*, Prentice-Hall, 1981).

TWELVE

SOFTWARE TESTING AND RELIABILITY

The importance of software testing and its implications with respect to reliability cannot be overemphasized. To quote Deutsch [1]:

> The development of software systems involves a series of production activities where opportunities for injection of human fallibilities are enormous. Errors may begin to occur at the very inception of the process where the objectives . . . may be erroneously or imperfectly specified, as well as (errors that occur in) later design and development stages . . . . Because of human inability to perform and communicate with perfection, software development is accompanied by a quality assurance activity.

Software testing is a critical element of *software quality assurance* and represents the ultimate review of specification, design, and coding.

The increasing visibility of software as a system element and the attendant "costs" associated with a software failure are motivating forces for well-planned, thorough testing. It is not unusual for a software development organization to expend 40 percent of total project effort on testing. In the extreme, testing of human-rated software (e.g., flight control or nuclear reactor monitoring) can cost 3 to 5 times as much as all other software engineering steps combined!

In this chapter we discuss three interrelated topics. The first, *software testing,* is a planned step in the software engineering process. Like other steps, deliverables derived from testing become part of the software configuration. Testing invariably leads to the second topic of discussion—*debugging.* More an art than a science, debugging diagnoses program errors and corrects them. The results of testing can also lead to a consideration of *reliability,* the third topic. We strive to guarantee reliability (as yet, an impossible goal if 100 percent reliability is desired) while at the same time developing failure prediction models to help anticipate problems. At the time of this writing, we must still rely on a series of thorough test steps as the only practical "guarantee" of software reliability.

12.1 CHARACTERISTICS OF TESTING

Testing presents an interesting anomaly for the software engineer. During earlier steps in planning and development, the engineer attempts to build software from an abstract concept to a tangible implementation. Now comes testing. The engineer creates a series of test cases that are intended to "demolish" the software that has been built. In fact, testing is the one step in the software engineering process that could be viewed (psychologically, at least) as destructive rather than constructive.

Software developers are by nature constructive people. Testing requires that the developer disregard preconceived notions of the correctness of software just developed and overcome a "conflict of interest" that occurs when errors are uncovered. Is testing really destructive? The answer to this question is *NO!* However, the objectives of testing are somewhat different than we might expect.

12.1.1 Testing Objectives

In an excellent book on software testing, Glen Myers [2] states a number of rules that can serve well as testing objectives:

1. Testing is a process of executing a program with the intent of finding an error.
2. A good test case is one that has a high probability of finding an as yet undiscovered error.
3. A successful test is one that uncovers an as yet undiscovered error.

The above objectives imply a dramatic change in viewpoint. They move counter to the commonly held view that a successful test is one in which no errors are found. Our objective is to design tests that systematically uncover different classes of errors.

Later in this chapter, four different testing steps are discussed. Each has specific objectives that are presented in forthcoming sections. However, the objectives described above provide an overriding principle that is the only clear guarantee of adequate software quality.

12.1.2 Test Information Flow

Information flow for testing follows the pattern described in Figure 12.1. Two classes of input are provided to the test process: (1) a software configuration that includes a *Software Requirements Specification,* a *Design Specification,* and source code: (2) a test configuration that includes a *Test Plan and Procedure,* test cases, and expected results. In actuality, the test configuration is a subset of the software configuration when the entire life cycle is considered.

Tests are conducted and all results are evaluated. That is, test results are compared with expected results. When erroneous data are uncovered, an error is implied and debugging commences. The debugging process (discussed in Section 12.8) is the most unpredictable part of the testing process. An "error" that indicates a discrepancy of 0.01 percent between expected and actual results can take 1 hour, 1 day, or 1 month to diagnose and correct. It is the uncertainty inherent in debugging that makes testing difficult to schedule reliably.

As test results are gathered and evaluated, a qualitative indication of software reliability begins to surface. If severe errors that require design modification are encountered with regularity, software quality and reliability are suspect and further tests are indicated. If, on the other hand, software functions appear to be working properly and errors encountered are easily correctable, one of two conclusions can be drawn: software quality and reliability are acceptable; or (2) the tests are inadequate to uncover severe errors! Finally, if testing uncovers no errors, there is little doubt that the test configuration was not given enough thought and that errors do lurk within the software. These errors will eventually be uncovered by the user and corrected by the developer during the maintenance phase (when cost per fix can be 40 times the cost per fix during the developmental phase!).

The results accumulated during testing can also be evaluated in a more formal manner. Software reliability models (discussed in Section 12.9) use error-rate data to predict future occurrence of errors and hence reliability.

Each bubble shown in Figure 12.1 represents an exceedingly complex transform. Throughout the remainder of this chapter, we examine the concepts and processes that make test information flow comprehensible and test transforms understandable.

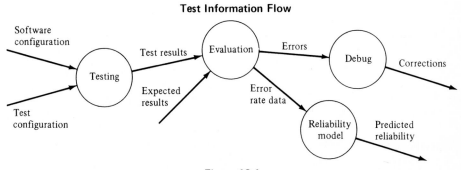

Figure 12.1

12.1.3 Black-Box versus White-Box Testing

Any engineered product (and most other things) can be tested in one of two ways: (1) if the function that a product is to perform is known, tests can be conducted that demonstrate each function to be fully operational; (2) if the internal workings of a product are known, tests can be conducted to assure that "all gears mesh," that is, that internal operation performs according to specification. The first test approach is called *black-box testing* and the second, *white-box testing*.

When computer software is considered, black-box testing alludes to tests that are conducted at the software interface. That is, test cases demonstrate that software functions are operational, that input is properly accepted and output is correctly produced, and that the integrity of external information (e.g., data files) is maintained. A black-box test examines some aspect of the fundamental system model (Chapter 5) with little regard for the internal logical structure of the software.

White-box testing of software is predicated on close examination of procedural detail. Logical paths through the software are tested by providing test cases that exercise specific sets of conditions and/or loops. The status of the program may be examined at various points to determine if the expected or "asserted" status corresponds to the actual status.

At first glance it would seem that very thorough white-box testing is the solution to "100 percent correct programs." All we need do is define all logical paths, develop test cases to exercise them, and evaluate results. Unfortunately, exhaustive testing presents certain logistical problems. For even small programs, the number of possible logical paths can be very large. For example, consider the control flow graph shown in Figure 12.2. Each circle represents a source line (or

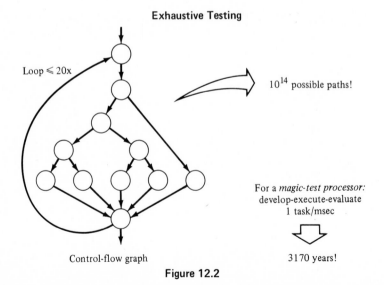

Exhaustive Testing

Loop $\leq$ 20x

10^{14} possible paths!

For a *magic-test processor:*
develop-execute-evaluate
1 task/msec

Control-flow graph

3170 years!

Figure 12.2

block of statements), arrows represent options in control flow, and the curved arrow on the left indicates a loop that may be executed no more than 20 times. There are approximately 100,000,000,000,000 possible paths that may be executed!

To put this number in perspective, we assume that a *magic-test processor* ("magic" because no such processor exists) has been developed for exhaustive testing. The processor can develop a test case, execute it, and evaluate the results in one millisecond. The processor would work for 3170 years to test the program represented in Figure 12.2. This would, undeniably, create havoc in most development schedules. Exhaustive testing is impossible for large software systems.

White-box testing should not, however, be dismissed as impractical. A limited number of "important" logical paths can be selected and exercised. Important data structures can be probed for validity. The attributes of both black- and white-box testing can be combined to provide an approach that validates the software interface and *selectively* assures that the internal workings of the software are correct.

12.1.4 Quality Assurance Issues

"Quality" is a subjective term that is extremely difficult to define precisely. How then, do we assure the quality of computer software? What is software quality assurance, and where is it encountered in the software life cycle? Pfau [3] provides a partial answer:

> Quality assurance is the name given to the activities performed in conjunction with (the development of) a software product to guarantee the product meets the specified standards. These activities reduce doubts and risks about the performance of the product in the target environment.

Software quality assurance may be viewed as a set of building blocks depicted in Figure 12.3. As reviews are conducted, planning and development tasks are tested to assure the quality of each software engineering step. In a similar manner, analysis, design, and implementation (coding) methods act to enhance quality by providing uniform techniques and predictable results. Throughout the process,

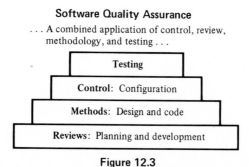

Software Quality Assurance

... A combined application of control, review, methodology, and testing ...

| Testing |
| Control: Configuration |
| Methods: Design and code |
| Reviews: Planning and development |

Figure 12.3

control applied to every element of a software configuration helps to ensure the integrity of the whole. Testing provides the last bastion from which quality can be assessed and, more pragmatically, errors can be uncovered.

Miller [4] relates software testing to quality assurance by stating that "the underlying motivation of program testing is to affirm software quality with methods that can be economically and effectively applied to both large-scale and small-scale systems." To date, economics and practical issues (that govern effectiveness) have dictated selective testing. Test cases are developed manually, and results are evaluated individually. The emphasis on quality assurance during the past decade is leading to a new generation of automatic testing tools, which are discussed later in this chapter.

Following the lead of hardware developers, a software quality assurance approach may result in a *test group* that is separated organizationally from a software development group. The primary charter of a test group is to uncover errors in software. Since this team has not participated directly in development, the psychological "conflict of interest" that a developer can encounter during testing is eliminated.

The test group concept is illustrated in Figure 12.4. During the planning and development phases, the test group participates in definition of validation criteria (requirement analysis step) and design-coding reviews to establish testability constraints. Once code has been generated, the software configuration is passed from the development group to the test group. Using a test plan and procedure (generated in parallel with development) as a guide, the test group conducts tests and evaluates results.

Separation of testing from other development tasks can produce an adversary relationship between groups. Therefore, this quality assurance approach must be managed carefully to eliminate needless squabbling and political intrigue. A

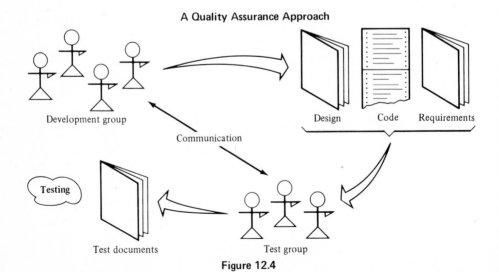

A Quality Assurance Approach

Development group

Design   Code   Requirements

Communication

Testing

Test documents   Test group

Figure 12.4

member of the development team can serve with the test group to facilitate understanding of design and code and establish built-in liaison between groups.

12.2 STEPS IN SOFTWARE TESTING

Testing within the context of software engineering is actually a series of four steps that are implemented sequentially (see Figure 12.5). Initially, tests focus on each module individually, assuring that it functions properly as a unit; hence the appellation *unit testing.* Next, modules must be assembled or integrated to form the complete software package. *Integration testing* addresses the issues associated with the dual problems of verification and assembly. Finally, validation requirements (established during the planning phase) must be tested. *Validation testing* provides final assurance that software meets all functional and performance requirements.

The last testing step falls outside the boundary of software engineering and into the broader context of computer system engineering. Software, once validated, must be combined with other system elements (e.g., hardware and information). *System testing* verifies that all elements mesh properly and that overall system function and performance are achieved.

In the sections that follow, each test step is presented. Earlier in the book we noted that the software engineering process could be viewed as a vortex. Moving in from the periphery during planning and requirements analysis, technical intensity is accelerated during design, and the "funnel" is reached as code is generated. We now reverse the vortex, moving outward as each test step is completed. As we approach the vortex, a system concept is all that exists; when we leave the vortex, operational software has been developed and is ready for integration with a larger system.

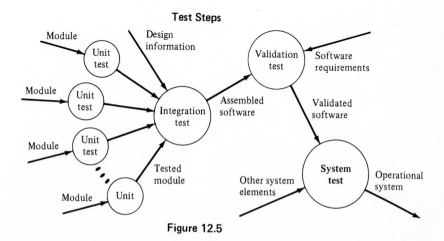

Figure 12.5

12.3 UNIT TESTING

Unit testing focuses verification effort on the smallest unit of software design—the module. With the detailed design description used as a guide, important control paths are tested to uncover errors within the boundary of the module. The relative complexity of tests and uncovered errors is limited by the constrained scope established for unit testing. The unit test is always white-box–oriented, and the step can be conducted in parallel for multiple modules.

12.3.1 Unit Test Considerations

Five primary characteristics of a module are evaluated during unit testing:

- The module interface
- Local data structure
- "Important" execution paths
- Error-handling paths
- Boundary conditions affecting all of the above

Tests of data flow across a module interface are required before any other test is initiated. If data do not enter and exit properly, all other tests are moot. In his text on software testing, Myers [2] proposes a checklist for interface tests:

1. Number of input parameters equal to number of arguments?
2. Parameter and argument attributes match?
3. Parameter and argument units system match?
4. Number of arguments transmitted to called modules equal to number of parameters?
5. Attributes of arguments transmitted to called modules equal to attributes of parameters?
6. Units system of arguments transmitted to called modules equal to units of system parameters?
7. Number of attributes and order of arguments to built-in functions correct?
8. Any references to parameters not associated with current point of entry?
9. Input only arguments altered?
10. Global variable definitions consistent across modules?
11. Constraints passed as arguments?

When a module performs external I/O, additional interface tests must be conducted. Again, from Myers:

1. File attributes correct?
2. OPEN statements correct?
3. Format specification matches I/O statement?
4. Buffer size matches record size?

5. Files opened before use?
6. End-of-file conditions handled?
7. I/O errors handled?
8. Any textual errors in output information?

The local data structure for a module is a common source of errors. Test cases should be designed to uncover errors in the following categories:

1. Improper or inconsistent declaration
2. Erroneous initialization or default values
3. Incorrect (misspelled or truncated) variable names
4. Inconsistent data types
5. Underflow, overflow, and addressing exceptions

In addition to local data structures, the impact of global data (e.g., FORTRAN COMMON) on a module should be ascertained (if possible) during unit testing.

Selective testing of execution paths is an essential task during the unit test. Test cases should be designed to uncover errors due to erroneous computations, incorrect comparisons, or improper control flow. Among the more common errors in computation are (1) misunderstood or incorrect arithmetic precedence, (2) mixed-mode operations, (3) incorrect initialization, (4) precision inaccuracy, and (5) incorrect symbolic representation of an expression. Comparison and control flow are closely coupled to one another (i.e., change of flow frequently occurs after a comparison). Test cases should uncover errors such as (1) comparison of different data types, (2) incorrect logical operators or precedence, (3) expectation of equality when precision error makes equality unlikely, (4) incorrect comparison or variables, (5) improper or nonexistent loop termination, (6) failure to exit when divergent iteration is encountered, and (7) improperly modified loop variables.

Good design dictates that error conditions be anticipated and error-handling paths set up to reroute or cleanly terminate processing when an error does occur. Yourdon [5] calls this approach *antibugging*. Unfortunately, there is a tendency to incorporate error handling into software and then never test it. A true story may serve to illustrate:

> A major interactive design system was developed under contract. In one analysis module, a practical joker placed the following error handling message after a series of conditional tests that invoked various control flow branches: ERROR! THERE IS NO WAY YOU CAN GET HERE. This "error message" was uncovered by a customer during user training!

Among the potential errors that should be tested when error handling is evaluated are:

1. Error description is unintelligible.
2. Error noted does not correspond to error encountered.

3. Error condition causes system intervention prior to error handling.
4. ON-condition processing is incorrect.
5. Error description does not provide enough information to assist in the location of the cause of the error.

Boundary testing is the last (and probably most important) task of the unit test step. Software often fails at its boundaries. That is, errors often occur when the nth element of an n-dimensional array is processed, when the ith repetition of a loop is encountered. Test cases that exercise data structure, control flow, and data values just below, at, and just above maxima and minima are very likely to uncover errors.

12.3.2 Unit Test Procedures

Unit testing is normally considered as an adjunct to the coding step. After source level code has been developed, reviewed, and verified for correct syntax, unit test case design begins. A review of design information provides guidance for establishing test cases that are likely to uncover errors in each category discussed above. Each test case should be coupled with a set of expected results.

Because a module is not a stand-alone program, *driver* and/or *stub* software must be developed for each unit test. In most applications a driver is nothing more than a "main program" that accepts test case data, passes such data to the module (to be tested), and prints relevant results. Stubs serve to replace modules that are subordinate (called by) the module to be tested. A stub or "dummy subprogram" uses the subordinate module's interface, may do minimal data manipulation, prints verification of entry, and returns control to the superordinate module.

Drivers and stubs represent *overhead*. That is, both are software that must be written (formal design is not commonly applied) but that is not delivered with the final software product. If drivers and stubs are kept simple, actual overhead is relatively low. Unfortunately, many modules cannot be adequately unit tested with "simple" overhead software. In such cases, complete testing can be postponed until the integration test step (where drivers or stubs are also used).

Unit testing is simplified when a module with a high degree of cohesion is designed. When only one function is addressed by a module, the number of test cases is reduced and errors can be more easily predicted and uncovered. Technical procedures for test case design are presented in Section 12.7.

12.4 INTEGRATION TESTING

A neophyte in the software world might ask a seemingly legitimate question once all modules have been unit tested: "If they all work individually, why do you doubt that they'll work when we put them together?" The problem, of course, is "putting them together"—interfacing. Data can be lost across an interface; one module can have an inadvertent, adverse affect on another; subfunctions, when combined, may not produce the desired major function; individually acceptable imprecision may be magnified to unacceptable levels; and global data structures can present problems. Sadly, the list goes on and on.

Integration testing is a systematic technique for assembling software while at the same time conducting tests to uncover errors associated with interfacing. The objective is to take unit-tested modules and build a software structure that has been dictated by design.

12.4.1 Top-Down Integration

Top-down integration is an incremental approach to the assembly of software structure. Modules are integrated by moving downward through the control hierarchy, beginning with the main control module ("main program"). Modules subordinate (and ultimately subordinate) to the main control module are incorporated into the structure in either a *depth-first* or *breadth-first* manner.

Referring to Figure 12.6, depth-first integration would integrate all modules on a major control path of the structure. Selection of a major path is somewhat arbitrary and depends on application-specific characteristics. For example, selecting the left-hand path, modules M_1, M_2, and M_5 would be integrated first. Next, M_8 or (if necessary for proper functioning of M_2) M_6 would be integrated. Then, the central and right-hand control paths are built. Breadth-first integration incorporates all modules directly subordinate at each level, moving across the structure horizontally. From the figure, modules M_2, M_3, and M_4 (a replacement for stub S_4) would be integrated first. The next control level, M_5, M_6, and so on follows.

The integration process is performed in a series of five steps:

1. The main control module is used as a *test driver*, and stubs are substituted for all modules directly subordinate to the main control module.
2. Depending on the integration approach selected (i.e., depth- or breadth-first), subordinate stubs are replaced one at a time with actual modules.
3. Tests are conducted as each module is integrated.

Top-Down Integration

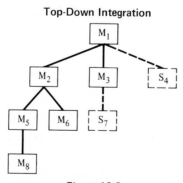

Figure 12.6

4. On completion of each set of tests, another stub is replaced with the real module.
5. *Regression testing* (i.e., conducting all or some of previous tests) may be conducted to assure that new errors have not been introduced.

The process continues from step 2 until the entire software structure is built. Figure 12.6 illustrates the process. Assuming a depth-first approach and a partially completed structure, stub S_7 is next to be replaced with module M_7. M_7 may itself have stubs that will be replaced with corresponding modules. It is important to note that at each replacement tests are conducted to verify the interface.

The top-down integration strategy verifies major control or decision points early in the test process. In a well-factored software structure, decision making occurs at upper levels in the hierarchy and is therefore encountered first. If major control problems do exist, early recognition is essential. If depth-first integration is selected, a complete function of the software may be implemented and demonstrated. For example, consider a classic transaction structure (Chapter 8) in which a complex series of interactive inputs are requested, acquired, and validated by means of a *reception path*. The reception path may be integrated in a top-down manner. All input processing (for subsequent transaction dispatching) may be demonstrated before other elements of the structure have been integrated. Early demonstration of functional capability is a confidence builder for both the developer and the requester.

Top-down strategy sounds relatively uncomplicated, but in practice, logistical problems can arise. The most common of these problems occurs when processing at low levels in the hierarchy is required to adequately test upper levels. Stubs replace low-level modules at the beginning of top-down testing; therefore, no significant data can flow upward in the software structure. The tester is left with two choices: (1) delay many tests until stubs are replaced with actual modules; or (2) integrate the software from the bottom of the hierarchy upward. The first approach causes us to lose some control over correspondence between specific tests and incorporation of specific modules. This can lead to difficulty in determining the cause of errors and tends to violate the highly constrained nature of the top-down approach. The latter approach, called *bottom-up testing,* is discussed in Section 12.4.2

12.4.2 Bottom-Up Integration

Bottom up integration testing, as its name implies, begins assembly and testing with *atomic modules* (i.e., modules at the lowest levels in the software structure). Because modules are integrated from the bottom up, processing required for modules subordinate to a given level is always available, and the need for stubs is eliminated.

A bottom-up integration strategy may be implemented with the following steps:

1. Low-level modules are combined into *clusters* that perform a specific software subfunction.
2. A driver (a control program for testing) is written to coordinate test case input and output.
3. The cluster is tested.
4. Drivers are removed and clusters are combined, moving upward in the software structure.

Integration follows the pattern illustrated in Figure 12.7. Modules are combined to form clusters 1, 2, and 3. Each cluster is tested by using a driver (shown as a dashed block). Modules in clusters 1 and 2 are subordinate to M_a. Drivers D_1 and D_2 are removed, and the clusters are interfaced directly to M_a. Similarly, driver D_3 for cluster 3 is removed prior to integration with module M_b. Both M_a and M_b will ultimately be integrated with module M_c, and so forth.

As integration moves upward, the need for separate test drivers lessens. In fact, if the top two levels of software structure are integrated top down, the number of drivers can be reduced substantially and integration of clusters is greatly simplified.

12.4.3 Comments on Integration Testing

There has been much discussion [e.g., 6,7] of the relative advantages and disadvantages of top-down versus bottom-up integration testing. In general, the advantages of one strategy tend to result in disadvantages for the other strategy. The major disadvantage of the top-down approach is the need for stubs and the attendant

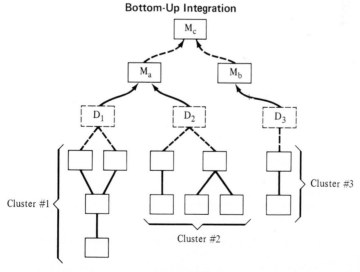

Figure 12.7

testing difficulties that can be associated with them. Problems associated with stubs may be offset by the advantage of testing major control functions early. The major disadvantage of bottom-up integration is that "the program as an entity does not exist until the last module is added" [2]. This drawback is tempered by easier test case design and a lack of stubs.

Selection of an integration strategy depends on software characteristics and sometimes, project schedule. In general, a combined approach that uses the top-down approach for upper levels of the software structure, coupled with a bottom-up approach for subordinate levels, may be the best compromise.

12.4.4 Integration Test Documentation

An overall plan for integration of the software and a description of specific tests are documented in the *Test Specification.* The specification is a deliverable in the software engineering process and becomes part of the software configuration. The following outline may be used as a framework:

TEST SPECIFICATION

1. Scope of Testing
2. Test Plan
   a. test phases
   b. schedule
   c. overhead software
   d. environment and resources
3. Test Procedure
   a. description of test phase *n*
        i. order of integration
        ii. purpose and modules to be tested
        iii. special tools or techniques
        iv. overhead software description
        v. test case data
   b. expected results for test phase *n*
4. Actual Test Results
5. References
6. Appendix

The *Scope of Testing* section summarizes specific functional, performance, and internal design characteristics that are to be tested. The scope of testing effort is bounded, criteria for completion of each test phase are described, and schedule constraints are documented.

The *Test Plan* describes the overall strategy for integration. Testing is divided into *phases* that address specific characteristics of the software. For example, integration testing for a computer graphics–oriented CAD system might be divided into the following test phases:

- User interaction
- Data manipulation and analysis
- Display processing and generation

Each of these phases delineates a broad functional category within the software and can generally be related to a specific domain of the software structure.

The following criteria and corresponding tests are applied for all test phases:

Interface integrity. Internal and external interfaces are tested as each module (or cluster) is incorporated into the structure.

Functional validity. Tests designed to uncover functional errors are conducted.

Information content. Tests designed to uncover errors associated with local or global data structures are conducted.

Performance. Tests designed to verify performance bounds established during software design are conducted.

These criteria and tests associated with them are discussed in this section of the *Test Specification.*

A schedule for integration, overhead software, and related topics are also discussed as part of the Test Plan section. Start and end dates for each phase are established, and "availability windows" for unit tested modules are defined. A brief description of overhead software (stubs and drivers) concentrates on characteristics that might require special effort. Finally, test environment and resources are described. Unusual hardware configurations, exotic simulators, special test tools, or techniques are a few of many topics that may be discussed in this section.

A detailed testing procedure that is required to accomplish the test plan (delineated above) is described in the *Test Procedure* section. Referring back to *Test Specification* outline items 3a and 3b, the order of integration and corresponding tests at each integration step are described. A listing of all test cases (annotated for subsequent reference) and expected results is also included.

A history of actual test results, problems, or peculiarities is recorded in the fourth section of the *Test Specification.* Information contained in this section can be vital during software maintenance.

Like all other elements of a software configuration, *Test Specification* format may be tailored to the local needs of a software development organization. It is important to note, however, that an integration strategy, contained in a *Test Plan,* and testing details, described in a *Test Procedure,* are essential ingredients and must appear.

12.5 VALIDATION TESTING

At the culmination of integration testing, software is completely assembled as a package; interfacing errors have been uncovered and corrected, and a final series of software tests—*validation testing*—may begin. Validation can be defined in many ways, but a simple (albeit harsh) definition is that validation succeeds when software functions in a manner that can be reasonably expected by a requester or user. At this point a battle-hardened software developer might protest: "Who or what is the arbiter of *reasonable expectations?*"

Reasonable expectations are defined in the *Software Requirements Specification*—a document (Chapter 5) that describes all user-visible attributes of the software. The specification contains a section called *Validation Criteria.* Information contained in that section forms the basis for a validation testing approach.

12.5.1 Validation Test Criteria

Software validation is achieved through a series of black-box tests that demonstrate conformity with requirements. A test plan outlines the classes of tests to be conducted, and a test procedure defines specific test cases that will be used to demonstrate conformity with requirements. Both the plan and the procedure are designed to ensure that all functional requirements are satisfied, all performance requirements are achieved, documentation is correct and human-engineered, and other requirements are met (e.g., transportability, compatibility, error recovery, and maintainability).

After each validation test case has been conducted, one of two possible conditions exist: (1) the function or performance characteristics conform to specification and are accepted; or (2) a deviation from specification is uncovered and a *deficiency list* is created. Deviation or error discovered at this stage in a project can rarely be corrected prior to scheduled completion. It is often necessary to negotiate with the requester to establish a method for resolving deficiencies.

12.5.2 Configuration Review

An important element of the validation process is a configuration review. The intent of the review, as illustrated in Figure 12.8, is to assure that all elements of the

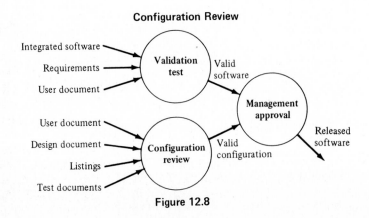

Figure 12.8

software configuration have been properly developed, are cataloged, and have the necessary detail to support the maintenance phase of the software life cycle.

12.6 SYSTEM TESTING

At the beginning of this book we stressed the fact that software is only one element of a larger computer-based system. Ultimately, software is incorporated with other system elements (e.g., new hardware and information), and a series of system integration and validation tests are conducted. These tests fall outside the scope of the software engineering process and are seldom conducted by the software developer. However, steps taken during software design and testing can greatly improve the probability of successful software integration in the larger system.

A classic system testing problem is "finger pointing." This occurs when an error is uncovered, and each system element developer blames the other for the problem. Rather than indulging in such nonsense, the software engineer should anticipate potential interfacing problems and (1) design error-handling paths that test all information coming from other elements of the system, (2) conduct a series of tests that simulate "bad data" or other potential errors at the software interface, (3) record the results of tests to use as "evidence" if finger pointing does occur, and (4) participate in planning and design of system tests to ensure that software is adequately tested.

The final step in system testing is often called the *acceptance test.* Conducted by the end user rather than the system developer, an acceptance test can range from an informal "test drive" to a planned and systematically executed series of tests. In fact, acceptance testing can be conducted over a period of weeks or months, thereby uncovering cumulative errors that might degrade the system over time.

12.7 TEST CASE DESIGN

The primary objective of test case design is to define a combination of test data that has the highest probability of uncovering an error or class of errors. We have already seen that it is impossible to test every program path. Even tests for a small subset of all paths can result in extremely large amounts of test data. Therefore, the test case designer must apply techniques that will uncover the highest possible number of errors with the minimum reasonable number of tests.

Many test case design techniques have been proposed in the literature [e.g., 8–10], but few have been widely adopted. A detailed discussion of these techniques is beyond the scope of this book. However, an overview of some of the more important approaches [2] is presented in the following sections.

12.7.1 Logic Coverage

Selective execution of program paths is the only reasonable alternative to exhaustive testing. *Logic coverage* is a generic term for a set of test procedures that result in progressively more complete degrees of path testing. The following degrees of coverage can be proposed: (1) every statement is executed at least once; (2) every decision is tested for the consequences of true and false results; or (3) more complex paths are tested by evaluating different permutations of conditions.

Test case design is predicated on a clear definition of all decision variables and combinations of data that satisfy each degree of logic coverage. Initial test cases may ensure that all statements have been executed. Such test cases leave many errors undetected and must be supplemented with more thorough decision and path testing.

High degrees of logic coverage can be achieved by creating tables of decision variables and their relationship to input data. Test cases are designed to exercise each decision alternative individually or to test specific paths that result from a combination of decisions.

Unfortunately, the number of test cases grows rapidly as the degree of coverage improves. The relationship between a decision variable and a program input may not be obvious, and the need to backtrack may discourage the designer from attempting higher degrees of coverage.

12.7.2 Equivalence Partitioning

Some of the errors encountered during software testing have been categorized in Section 12.3.1. An ideal test case single-handedly uncovers a class of errors (e.g., errors within a local data structure) that might otherwise require the execution of many cases before the general error could be observed. *Equivalence partitioning* strives to define a test case that uncovers classes of errors, thereby reducing the total number of test cases that must be developed.

Test case design for equivalence partitioning is based on an evaluation of equivalence classes for input conditions. An equivalence class represents a set of valid or invalid states for input conditions. For example, a valid equivalence class for a phone number record might be

Area code—blank or three-digit number
Prefix—three-digit number not beginning with 0 or 1
Suffix—four-digit number
Extension—up to four-digit number

An invalid equivalence class for the above record might be a two-digit area code or an area code < 100 (a special test might be defined for 800 and 900 area codes). Similar erroneous classes of data could be specified for other attributes of the valid equivalence class.

Test cases are selected so that the largest number of attributes of an equivalence class are exercised at once. Equivalence partitioning is a black-box testing technique. Only input information is used to develop a test case.

12.7.3 Boundary Value Analysis

Boundary value analysis leads to a selection of test cases that exercise bounding values. As we noted earlier in this chapter, many software errors occur just below, at, or just above the bounding value of indices, data structures, and scalar values. Test cases that exercise this domain have a high probability for uncovering errors.

Logic coverage, equivalence partitioning, and boundary value analysis are normally used in conjunction with one another. By combining white-box with black-box testing, both design internals and interface requirements can be verified.

12.7.4 Graphing Techniques

Graphical representation can often serve to clarify the logical flow of software. For software testing, a worthwhile graphical tool should (1) represent the logical relationship between conditions and corresponding actions or (2) elements of procedural flow (paths) of a program. *Cause-effect graphing* is a technique that addresses the former category, and *program graphing* (discussed later in this section) may be applied when path testing is to be considered.

Cause-effect graphing is a test technique that provides a concise representation of logical conditions and corresponding actions. This technique follows four steps:

1. *Causes* (input conditions) and *effects* (actions) are listed for a module, and an identifier is assigned to each.
2. A cause-effect graph (described below) is developed.
3. The graph is converted to a decision table.
4. Decision table rules are converted to test cases.

A simplified version of cause-effect graph symbology is shown in Figure 12.9. The left column of the figure illustrates various logical relationships between causes c_i and effects e_i. The dashed notation in the right columns indicate potential constraining relationships that may apply to either causes or effects.

To illustrate the use of cause-effect graphs, we consider a variant of the utility billing example discussed in an earlier chapter. Four causes are defined:

1: residential indicator
2: commercial indicator
3: peak consumption $\geq 1000\,\text{KWH}$
4: off-peak consumption $\geq 1000\,\text{KWH}$

On the basis of various combinations of causes, the following effects may be listed:

101: schedule A billing
102: schedule B billing
103: schedule C billing

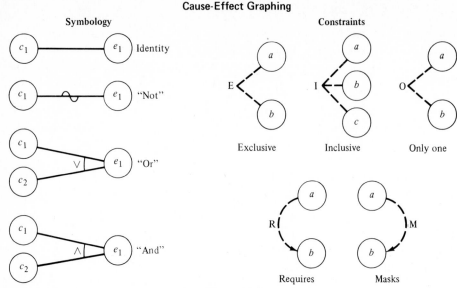

Figure 12.9

A cause-effect graph for the above example is shown in Figure 12.10. Causes 1, 2, 3, and 4 are represented along the left side and final effects 101, 102, and 103, along the right side. *Secondary causes* are identified (e.g., causes 11, 12, 13, 14, etc.) in the central part of the graph. From the cause-effect graph, a decision table (Figure 12.11) can be developed. Test case data are selected so that each rule in the table is

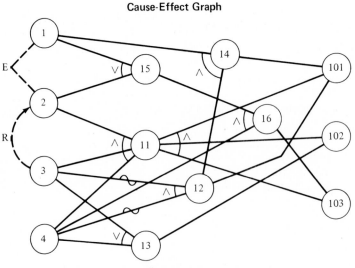

Figure 12.10

Decision Table

		1	2	3	4	5	6	7	8	9		
	1	1							0	1		
Causes	2		1		1			1	1	0		
	3	0	1	0	1	0	1	1				
	4	0	1	0	1	1	0	1	1	1		
	11		1		1			1				
	12	1		1								
Intermediate causes	13					1	1					
	14	1										
	15								1	1		
	16								1	1		
	101	1	1	1	0	0	0	0	0	0		
Effects	102	0	0	0	1	1	1	0	0	0		
	103	0	0	0	0	0	0	1	1	1		

Figure 12.11

exercised. Obviously, if a decision table has been used as a design tool, cause-effect graphing is no longer necessary.

Program graphing is actually a general-purpose tool for representation and analysis of software procedural flow. Applications of program graphs extend far beyond testing [11]; however, when used as a tool for test case design, the program graph helps isolate program paths for selective testing and logic coverage. The program graph is also a useful device for computing McCabe's cyclomatic complexity metric (Chapter 7). The McCabe metric provides an indication of the testability of software by providing an independent variable for models that correlate past testing effort with $V(G)$, McCabe's metric.

As an example of the application of program graphs for testing, we consider a simple "triangle calculator" proposed by Brown and Lipow [12]. Each executable statement in the program is numbered and the connectivity among statements is represented by a program graph shown in Figure 12.12a. Each circle represents a statement and each arrow, a connecting path. A decision is implied if two arrows emanate from one circle. By examining the program graph, we may define a set of paths (Figure 12.12b). Input test values are then selected so that each path is exercised (Figure 12.12c). Statement and/or branch coverage (see Section 12.7.1) is assured by executing paths shown in Figure 12.12d.

Program Graphing

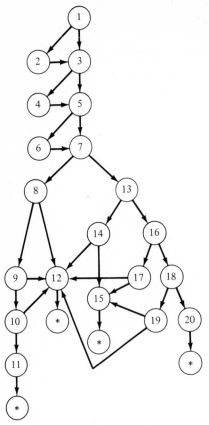

(a) Network of node-to-node branching potential

Identification Number	Path Representation
P1	1-2-3-4-5-6-7-13-16-18-20
P2	1-2-3-5-7-13-14-12
P3	1-2-3-5-7-13-14-15
P4	1-3-4-5-7-13-16-17-12
P5	1-3-4-5-7-13-16-17-15
P6	1-3-5-6-7-13-16-18-19-12
P7	1-3-5-6-7-13-16-18-19-15
P8	1-3-5-7-8-9-10-11
P9	1-3-5-7-8-9-10-12
P10	1-3-5-7-8-9-12
P11	1-3-5-7-8-12

(b) Logical paths through the program

	Input Values		
Path ID	I	J	K
P1	1	1	1
P8	2	3	4
P3	2	2	3
P4	1	2	1
P6	2	1	1
P2	1	1	2
P5	2	3	2
P7	3	2	2
P9	1	3	2
P10	3	2	1
P11	1	2	3

(c) Test case input values for path operation

Subsets of paths to guarantee usage of all statements:

P1, P8, P3, P4, P6

Subset of paths to guarantee usage of all branches:

P1, P8, P3, P4, P6, P2, P5, P7, P9, P10, P11

(d) Path subsets for program-testing coverage

(Source: J. Brown and M. Lipow, "Testing for Software Reliability," Program Testing Techniques, E. Miller (ed.), IEEE, 1977. Reproduced with permission.)

Figure 12.12

12.7.5 Summary of Techniques

Each technique discussed in Section 12.7 may be viewed as one of a combination of tools used in test case design. In practice, the most common approach combines logic coverage (a white-box approach) with equivalence partitioning and boundary analysis (black-box approaches). The use of graphical techniques, or automated derivatives of such techniques, may ultimately replace the aforementioned manually oriented methods. A number of automated software engineering tools have been developed for test case design. A discussion of these tools is postponed until Section 12.10.

12.8 THE ART OF DEBUGGING

Software testing is a process that can be systematically planned and specified. We have seen that the stated goal of testing is to uncover errors. Debugging occurs as a consequence of successful testing.

Although debugging can and should be an orderly process, it is still very much an art. A software engineer, evaluating the results of a test, is often confronted with a *symptomatic* indication of a software problem. That is, the external manifestation of the error and the internal cause of the error may have no obvious relationship to one another. The poorly understood mental process that connects a symptom to a cause of a software problem is debugging.

12.8.1 Psychological Considerations

Unfortunately, there appears to be some evidence that debugging prowess is an innate human trait. Some people are good at it, and others aren't. Although experimental evidence on debugging is open to many interpretations, large variances in debugging ability have been reported for programmers with the same educational and experiential background.

Commenting on the human aspects of debugging, Shneiderman [13] states:

> Debugging is one of the more frustrating parts of programming. It has elements of problem solving or brain teasers, coupled with the annoying recognition that you have made a mistake. Heightened anxiety and the unwillingness to accept the possibility of errors increases the task difficulty. Fortunately, there is a great sigh of relief and a lessening of tension when the bug is ultimately . . . corrected.

Although it may be difficult to "learn" debugging, a number of approaches to the problem can be proposed. We examine these in the next section.

12.8.2 Approaches to Debugging

Regardless of the approach that is taken, debugging has one overriding objective: to find and correct the cause of a software error. The objective is realized by a combination of systematic evaluation, intuition and luck. In general, three categories for debugging approaches may be proposed [2]:

- Brute force
- Cause elimination
- Backtracking

The *brute force* category of debugging is probably the most common and least efficient method for isolating the cause of a software error. If a "let the computer find the error" philosophy is used, memory dumps are taken, run-time traces are invoked, and the program is loaded with WRITE statements. Although the mass of information produced may ultimately lead to success, it more frequently leads to wasted effort and time. Thought must be expended first!

The second approach to debugging—*cause elimination*—is manifested by induction or deduction [2]. Data related to the error occurrence are organized to isolate potential causes. A *cause hypothesis* is devised, and the above data are used to prove or disprove the hypothesis. Alternatively, a list of all possible causes is developed and tests are conducted to eliminate or substantiate each cause. If initial tests indicate that a particular cause hypothesis shows promise, data are refined in an attempt to isolate the bug.

Backtracking is a fairly common debugging approach that can be used successfully in small programs. Beginning at the site where a symptom has been uncovered, the source code is traced backward (manually) until the site of the cause is found. Unfortunately, as the number of source lines increases, the number of potential backward paths may become unmanageably large.

Each of the above debugging approaches can be supplemented with *debugging tools*. We can apply a wide variety of debugging compilers, dynamic debugging aids ("tracers"), automatic test case generators, memory dumps, and cross-reference maps. However, tools are not a substitute for careful evaluation based on a complete software design document and clear source code.

In many ways, debugging of computer software is like problem solving in the business world. Brown and Sampson [14] have proposed a debugging approach, called "the method," that is an adaptation of management problem-solving techniques. The authors propose the development of a *specification of deviation* that describes a problem by delineating "what, when, where, and to what extent?" The specification is represented in the tabular format that follows:

Specification of Deviation

	Is	*Is not*
What occured?		
When?		
Where?		
To what extent?		

Each of the above questions (what, when, where, and to what extent) is divided into *is* and *is not* responses so that a clear distinction between what has occurred and what has not occurred can be made. Once information about the bug has been recorded, a cause hypothesis is developed on the basis of distinctions observed from the *is* and *is not* responses. Debugging continues with the use of a deductive or inductive approach (described earlier in this section).

Any discussion of debugging approaches and tools is incomplete without mention of a powerful ally: other people! Weinberg's "egoless programming" concept (discussed earlier in this book) should be extended to egoless debugging as well. Each of us can recall puzzling for hours or days over a persistent bug. A colleague wanders by, and in desperation we explain the problem and throw open the listing. Instantaneously (it seems), the cause of the error is uncovered. Smiling smugly, our colleague wanders off. A fresh viewpoint, unclouded by hours of frustration, can do wonders. A final maxim on debugging might be: "When all else fails, get help!"

12.9 SOFTWARE RELIABILITY

In many computer-based systems, software failure cannot be tolerated. Therefore, we strive to understand the meaning of "software reliability" and develop techniques that assure reliable programs.

12.9.1 A Definition of Software Reliability

The reliability of any technical system is measured in stochastic terms. That is, reliability is "the probability that the system performs its assigned function under specified environmental conditions for a given period of time" [15]. If we consider a computer-based system, the reliability of hardware may be measured as *mean time between failure* (MTBF) where

$$MTBF = MTTF + MTTR$$

The acronyms MTTF and MTTR are *mean time to failure* and *mean time to repair*, respectively. Hardware failure is generally caused by deterioration with time. Therefore, hardware reliability can be determined by using a combination of empirical data (derived by driving the hardware until failure occurs) and stochastic models.

Software reliability may be characterized in terms that closely parallel the definition of reliability for technical systems. Goodenough [16] defines software reliability as "the frequency and criticality of program failure where failure is an unacceptable effect or behavior under permissible operating conditions." Like hardware, software reliability can be represented by the rate at which errors are uncovered and corrected. Unlike hardware, there is less evidence that empirical error data (collected during testing and after release of the software) can be used to develop accurate predictive models of software reliability.

Attempts to develop a mathematical theory of software reliability have resulted in a number of promising models. A brief overview of work in this area is presented in the next section.

12.9.2 Reliability Models

Software reliability models normally fall into one of the following categories:

- Models derived from hardware reliability theory
- Models based on the internal characteristics of the program
- Models developed by "seeding" software with known errors and evaluating the number of seeded errors detected versus actual errors detected

Assumptions made by models in the first category is presented by Sukert and Goel [17]: (1) the debugging time between error occurrences has an exponential distribution with an error occurrence rate that is proportional to the number of remaining errors; (2) each error discovered is immediately removed, decreasing the total number of errors by 1; and (3) the failure rate between errors is constant. The validity of each of these assumptions can be questioned. For example, correction of one error may inadvertently introduce other errors in the software, thus invalidating the second assumption.

The second category for reliability models computes a predicted number of errors that exist in the software. The models, based on the quantitative relationships derived as a function of a software complexity measures (discussed in Chapter 7), relate specific design or code-oriented attributes of a program (e.g., number of operands and operators or the cyclomatic complexity) to "an estimate of the initial number of errors to be expected in a given program" [18].

Seeding models can be used as an indication of software reliability, or more practically, as a measure of the "error uncovery power" of a set of test cases. A program is randomly seeded with a number of known *calibration errors* [19]. The program is tested (using test cases T). The probability of finding j real errors of a total population of J (an unknown) errors can be related to the probability of finding k seeded errors from all K calibration errors embedded in the code.

Important work in the area of predictive models for software reliability continues [e.g., 20]. Only time will tell whether such models can evolve to be practical tools in a production software development environment.

12.9.3 Proof of Correctness

We have seen that testing can be used successfully to uncover errors, but it cannot be used to demonstrate program correctness. If an infallible program correctness prover could be developed, test effort would be reduced substantially; the need for reliability models would disappear, and one of the major contributors to the software crisis—quality that is suspect—would be no more.

Proofs of program correctness span a broad spectrum of sophistication.

Manual correctness proofs, such as the use of mathematical induction or the predicate calculus, may have some value in the evaluation of small programs, but are of little use when large software subsystems must be validated. As Anderson [21] states in his book on the subject: "We are well aware that informal (manual) correctness proofs can easily contain errors and are no panacea for preventing or discovering all program errors."

If a general-purpose method for proving software correctness is ever successfully developed, it will probably be comprised of the following:

- An easily applied and validated method for specifying assertions concerning the correct operation of the software
- A method for indicating variance from correct operation (errors)
- A technique for uncovering the cause of an error
- A fully automated approach that takes the source code or some other element of the software configuration (e.g., a design representation) as input

A number of automated approaches to proof of correctness for computer software have been developed during the past decade. Automated correctness provers, not to be confused with automatic testing tools, generally involve a formal specification of program logic. The specification can be developed by a *macrocompiler* that produces a symbolic representation of the software. Program correctness is "proved" by use of automated techniques whose foundation is derived from artificial intelligence theory and predicate calculus. Correctness provers for PASCAL and LISP have been developed and are currently being evaluated and improved. (These systems are currently limited to the evaluation of relatively small programs.) There is little argument that much work remains to be done before such systems can be practically applied to large-scale software.

12.10 AUTOMATED TESTING TOOLS

Because software testing often accounts for as much as 40 percent of all effort expended on a software development project, tools that can reduce test time (without reducing thoroughness) are very valuable. Recognizing the potential benefits, researchers and practitioners have developed a vast array of automated test tools. Miller [22] describes a number of categories for test tools:

Static analyzers. These program-analysis systems support "proving" of static allegations—weak statements about a program's structure and format.
Code auditors. These special-purpose filters are used to check the quality of software to ensure that it meets minimum coding standards.
Assertion processors. These preprocessor-postprocessor systems are employed to tell whether programmer supplied claims, called *assertions,* about a program's behavior are actually met during real program executions.

Test file generators. These processors generate, and fill with predetermined values, typical input files for programs that are undergoing testing.

Test data generators. These automated analysis systems assist a user in selecting test data that cause a program to behave in a particular fashion.

Test verifiers. These tools measure internal test coverage, often expressed in terms that are related to the control structure of the test object, and report the coverage value to the quality assurance expert.

Test harnesses. This class of tools supports the processing of tests by making it almost painless to (1) install a candidate program in a test environment, (2) feed it input data, and (3) simulate by stubs the behavior of subsidiary (subordinate) modules.

Output comparators. This tool makes it possible to compare one set of outputs from a program with another (previously archived) set to determine the difference between them.

In the following paragraphs we consider three representative testing systems. For a complete discussion of these and other automated tools, see Miller [22]

DAVE [23] is an automated test system that makes use of data flow and program graphing techniques (see Section 12.7.4). The DAVE system is capable of accurately identifying many classes on program errors and *data flow anomalies* (e.g., data are referenced before being completely specified). The system is designed to evaluate FORTRAN programs and uses a sophisticated depth-first search algorithm to trace the flow of a specific variable. DAVE processes a subject program in the manner illustrated in Figure 12.13 (reproduced from Osterweil and Fosdick [23]).

DISSECT [24] is an automated test system that symbolically evaluates a program by creating *symbolic predicates* that are derived from a representation of control flow. Software may be "dissected" into individual sets of control paths. These sets, called a *system of predicates,* are used in the validation of computations within the program. In addition, the system of predicates can be used to generate test case data.

Program mutation techniques [25] provide an automated approach for determining the adequacy of test case data. An overview of the approach is described by the following steps:

1. For a program P, a test case T is defined.
2. T is executed by P. If errors occur, the case has succeeded.
3. If no errors are uncovered by T, the program P is "mutated" by making subtle changes to the source code (e.g., a .LE. comparison is changed to .LT.); T is reexecuted.
4. If the *mutant* P' gives the same results as P for the same test case T, then T does not have the sensitivity to distinguish the error purposely introduced into the program P'.

The above sequence of steps is executed automatically. The test system produces a series of reports and other information that help to measure the adequacy of a

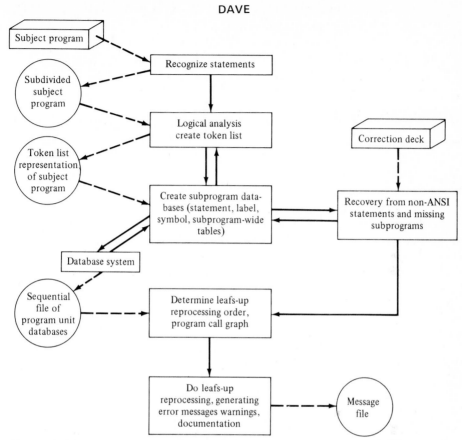

(Source: L. Osterweil and L. Fosdick, DAVE—A Validation Error Detection and Documentation System for FORTRAN Programs, Software: Practice and Experience. Reprinted with permission.)

Figure 12.13

given test case. In addition, information obtained about mutants can be used as a tool in test case design.

The widespread use of automated test tools is expected to accelerate during the 1980s. Automated systems such as those described above are currently being used in production software environments. By the end of this decade, automated provers may replace or supplement other tools, causing a radical change in the way we test software.

12.11 MANAGEMENT ISSUES

In earlier sections of this chapter we discussed the software engineering steps that are conducted as part of the testing process. It is incumbent upon the manager to review progress as each test step is initiated and to institute necessary standards and controls to assure thoroughness in testing. Goodenough [16] describes a series of questions that may be of interest to the manager:

- How can test effort be reduced without reducing the thoroughness of tests?
- How can the testing process be organized so that meaningful measures of progress are available?
- How can test effectiveness be measured effectively?
- What database tools are useful in tracking test-related information?
- What is the proper role of an independent test group?
- How does testing relate to other quality assurance issues (e.g., design reviews and code walkthroughs)?
- How should testing procedures be affected by the amount of code to be tested?
- In what sequence should programs be developed to promote efficient testing?
- How does testing fit in (to the overall software engineering methodology)?

Throughout this chapter we have attempted to address some of these questions. Others do not have easy answers. As our understanding of the technical aspects of software testing improves, we can only hope that a solid management approach evolves.

12.12 SUMMARY

Software testing accounts for the largest percentage of technical effort in the software development process. Yet we are only beginning to understand the subtleties of systematic test planning, execution, and control.

The objective of software testing is to uncover errors. To fulfill this objective, a series of test steps—unit, integration, validation, and system tests—are conducted. Unit and integration tests concentrate on functional verification of a module and incorporation of modules into a software structure. Validation testing demonstrates traceability to software requirements, and system testing validates software once it has been incorporated into a larger system.

Each test step is accomplished through a series of systematic test techniques that assist in the design of test cases. Manual techniques are most prevalent today, but a growing number of automated tools show promise for the future.

Unlike testing (a systematic, planned activity), debugging must be viewed as an art. Beginning with a symptomatic indication of a problem, the debugging activity must track down the cause of an error. Of the many resources available during debugging, the most valuable is the counsel of other members of the software development staff.

Software testing and software reliability are concurrent issues. A "theory" of software reliability is in its infancy and may be eclipsed by automated techniques that demonstrate program correctness. Each area of research discussed in this chapter has the potential to improve our confidence in the software we develop. The evolution of each should be followed. For the time being, however, the vast majority of software engineers will continue to use manual testing and reliability techniques.

REFERENCES

1. Deutsch, M., "Verification and Validation," in *Software Engineering*, R. Jensen and C. Tonies, (eds.), Prentice-Hall, 1979, pp. 329–408.
2. Myers, G., *The Art of Software Testing*, Wiley, 1979.
3. Pfau, P., "Applied Quality Assurance Methodology," in *Proceedings of the Software Quality and Assurance Workshop, ACM*, San Diego, CA, November 1978, pp. 1–8.
4. Miller, E., "The Philosophy of Testing," in *Program Testing Techniques*, E. Miller, (ed.), IEEE Computer Society Press, 1977, p. 1–3.
5. Yourdon, E., *Techniques of Program Structure and Design*, Prentice-Hall, 1975.
6. Yourdon, E., and L. Constantine, *Structured Design*, Prentice-Hall, 1979.
7. Zelkowitz, M., et al., *Principles of Software Engineering and Design*, Prentice-Hall, 1979.
8. Howden, W. E., "Theoretical and Empirical Studies of Program Testing," in *Proceedings of the Third International Conference on Software Engineering, IEEE*, 1978, pp. 99–106.
9. Huang, J. C., "An Approach to Program Testing," *ACM Computing Surveys*, vol. 7, no. 3, 1975.
10. Yeh, R., (ed.), *Current Trends in Programming Methodology*, vol. 2, Prentice-Hall, 1978.
11. Jensen, P. A., and W. Barnes, *Network Flow Programming*, Wiley, 1980.
12. Brown, J., and M. Lipow, "Testing for Software Reliability," in *Program Testing Techniques*, E. Miller, (ed.), IEEE Computer Society Press, 1977, pp. 21–30.
13. Shniederman, B., *Software Psychology*, Winthrop Publishers, 1980, p. 28.
14. Brown, A., and W. Sampson, *Programming Debugging*, American Elsevier, New York, 1973.
15. Kopetz, H., *Software Reliability*, Springer-Verlag, 1979, p. 3.
16. Goodenough, J., "A Survey of Program Testing Issues," in *Research Directions in Software Technology*, P. Wegner, (ed.), MIT Press, 1979, pp. 316–340.
17. Sukert, A., and A. Goel, "Error Modeling Applications in Software Quality Assurance," in *Proceedings of the Software Quality and Assurance Workshop, ACM*, San Diego, CA, November 1978, pp. 33–38.
18. Halstead, M., *Elements of Software Science*, North-Holland Publishing Company, 1977, p. 84.
19. Mills, H. D., *On the Statistical Validation of Computer Programs*, FSC 72:6015, IBM Federal Systems Division, 1972.
20. Musa, J., "Software Reliability Measurement," *The Journal of Systems and Software*, vol. 1, 1980, pp. 223–241.
21. Anderson, R., *Proving Programs Correct*, Wiley, 1974.
22. Miller, E., *Tutorial: Automated Tools for Software Engineering*, IEEE Computer Society Press, 1979, p. 169.
23. Osterweil, L., and L. Fosdick, "DAVE—A Validation Error Detection and Documentation System for Fortran Programs," *Software—Practice and Experience*, October-December, 1976, pp. 473–486.
24. Howden, W., "DISSECT—A Symbolic Evaluation and Program Testing System," *IEEE Transactions on Software Engineering*, vol. 4, no. 1, January 1978, pp. 70–73.
25. Budd, T. A., et al., "The Design of a Prototype Mutation System for Program Testing," in *Proceedings of the National Computer Conference, AFIPS*, vol. 47, 1978, p. 623–627.

PROBLEMS AND POINTS TO PONDER

12-1 Myers [2] uses the following program as a self-assessment for your ability to specify adequate testing:

A program reads three integer values. The three values are interpreted as representing the lengths of the sides of a triangle. The program prints a message that states whether the triangle is scalene, isosceles, or equilateral.

Develop a set of test cases that you feel will adequately test this program.

12-2 Design and implement the program (with error handling where appropriate) specified in Problem 12-1. Use logic coverage and/or program graphing to develop a set of test cases that will execute every statement in the program at least once. Execute the cases and show your results.

12-3 Can you think of any additional testing objectives that are not discussed in Section 12.1.1?

12-4 Give at least three examples in which black-box testing might give the impression that "everything's O.K.," while white-box tests might uncover an error.

12-5 Will exhaustive testing (even if it is possible for very small programs) guarantee that the program is 100 percent correct?

12-6 Describe all software engineering activities that contribute to software quality assurance.

12-7 Select one or more of the programs developed for Problems 10-2 through 10-13 and 11-2 through 11-13. Develop a test strategy and conduct unit and integration tests for the program(s) that has been selected. Outline a formal test specification for integration testing.

12-8 Add at least three additional questions to each segment of the unit test checklist presented in Section 12.3.1.

12-9 The concept of *antibugging* (Section 12.3.1) is an extremely effective way to provide built-in debugging assistance when an error is uncovered.
(*a*) Develop a set of guidelines for antibugging.
(*b*) Discuss advantages of using the techniques.
(*c*) Discuss disadvantages.

12-10 Develop an integration testing strategy for the digital dashboard software described in Chapter 8. Define test phases, note the order of integration, specify additional test software, and justify your order of integration. Assume that all modules have been unit tested and are available.

12-11 How can project scheduling affect integration testing?

12-12 Is unit testing possible or even desirable in all circumstances? Provide examples to justify your answer.

12-13 Who should perform the validation test—the software developer or the software user? Justify your answer.

12-14 Research the methods presented for test case design and present (for your class) a brief tutorial on one of the methods. Be sure to present a number of illustrative examples.

12-15 Write a paper on the relationship among software complexity measures, program testing, and the number of errors to be encountered. Use the work of Halstead and McCabe as a foundation.

12-16 As a class project, develop a *Debugging Guide* for your installation. The guide should provide language and system oriented hints that have been learned through the school of hard knocks! Begin with an ouline of topics that will be reviewed by the class and your instructor. Publish the guide for others in your local environment.

12-17 Software reliability is an extremely active area of software engineering research. Write a paper that categorizes and summarizes current work in the field.

12-18 Select a legitimate automated test tool and write a detailed report that describes its use.

12-19 Attempt to develop answers to all questions posed in Section 12.11. (This may be done in class if time permits.)

FURTHER READINGS

Those readers who are interested in software testing should read Reference 2 in its entirety. Myers has presented a comprehensive treatment of manual testing techniques that should be of interest to all software professionals. Miller's tutorial on software testing techniques [4] contains an excellent survey of the literature and is a good place to initiate research on the subject. *Computer Logic, Testing and Verification* (J. Roth, Computer Society Press, 1980) covers logic testing and verification for both hardware and software. The author introduces a notation and algorithms for software verification.

Debugging Techniques in Large Systems (R. Rustin, (ed.), Prentice-Hall, 1971) is a somewhat dated but worthwhile collection of papers on debugging. Insight into the debugging process can be gained by perusing *The Rational Manager* (Kepner, C., and B. Tragoe, McGraw-Hill, 1965). This and other management training books contain systematic approaches to problem solving that can often be extrapolated to computer software.

The literature on software reliability is extremely broad and, in some cases, difficult to understand and apply to practical problems. A paper by Littlewood ("Theories of Software Reliability: How Good Are They and How Can They Be Improved?," *IEEE Transactions on Software Engineering*, vol. 6, no. 5, September 1980, pp. 489–500) is recommended as an excellent survey and critique of current techniques. *Software Reliability* (Thayer, Lipow, and Nelson, North-Holland Publishing Company, 1978) contains an in-depth presentation of software reliability. The book contains a survey of available models and a detailed presentation and analysis of experimentally derived error data.

Program analysis and verification is another important subset of software testing and reliability. The January 1981 issue of *IEEE Transactions on Software Engineering* contains three papers that describe work in this area.

THIRTEEN

SOFTWARE MAINTENANCE

Software maintenance has been characterized [1] as an "iceberg." Wishfully, we hope that what is immediately visible is all there is to it. Realistically, we know that an enormous mass of potential problems and cost lies under the surface. The maintenance of existing software can account for over 60 percent of all effort expended by a development organization. The percentage continues to rise as more software is produced. On the horizon we can foresee a *maintenance-bound* software development organization that can no longer produce new software because it is expending all available resources maintaining old software.

Uninitiated readers may ask why so much maintenance is required; and why so much effort is expended. Rochkind [2] provides a partial answer:

> Computer programs are always changing. There are bugs to fix, enhancements to add, and optimizations to make. There is not only the current version to change, but also last year's version (which is still supported) and next year's version (which almost runs). Besides the problems whose solutions required the changes in the first place, the fact of the changes themselves creates additional problems.

Throughout this book we have discussed a software engineering methodology. A primary goal of this methodology is to reduce the amount of effort expended on maintenance. In this chapter, the final phase of the software life cycle—*software maintenance*—is presented.

13.1 A DEFINITION OF SOFTWARE MAINTENANCE

Upon reading the introduction to this chapter a reader may protest: "But I don't spend 60 percent of my time fixing mistakes in the programs I develop. . . ." Software maintenance is, of course, far more than "fixing mistakes." We may define maintenance by describing four activities that are undertaken after a program is released for use.

The first maintenance activity occurs because it is unreasonable to assume that software testing will uncover all latent errors in a large software system. During the use of any large program, errors will occur and be reported to the developer. The process that includes diagnosis and correction of one or more errors is called *corrective maintenance.*

The second activity that contributes to a definition of maintenance occurs because of the rapid change that is encountered in every aspect of computing. New generations of hardware seem to be announced on a 36-month cycle; new operating systems, or new releases of old ones, appear regularly; peripheral equipment and other system elements are frequently upgraded or modified. The useful life of application software, on the other hand, can easily surpass 10 years, outliving the system environment for which it was originally developed. Therefore, *adaptive maintenance*—an activity that modifies software to properly interface with a changing environment—is both necessary and commonplace.

The third activity that may be applied to a definition of maintenance occurs when a software package is successful. As the software is used, recommendations for new capabilities, modifications of existing functions, and general enhancements are received from users. To satisfy requests in this category, *perfective maintenance* is performed. This activity accounts for the majority of all effort expended on software maintenance.

The fourth maintenance activity occurs when software is changed to improve future maintainability or reliability or to provide a better basis for future enhancements. Often called *preventive maintenance,* this activity is still relatively rare in the software world.

The terms used to describe the first three maintenance activities were coined by Swanson [3]. The fourth term is commonly used in the maintenance of hardware and other physical systems. It should be noted, however, that analogies between software and hardware maintenance can be misleading. As we noted in Chapter 1, software, unlike hardware, does not wear out; therefore, the major activity associated with hardware maintenance—replacement of worn or broken parts— simply does not apply.

Some software professionals are troubled by the inclusion of the second and third activities as part of a definition of maintenance. In actuality, the tasks that occur as part of adaptive and perfective maintenance are the same tasks that are applied during the development phase of the software life cycle. To adapt or perfect, we must determine new requirements, redesign, generate code, and test existing software. Traditionally, such tasks have been called *maintenance.*

In fact, approximately half of all software maintenance is perfective, as

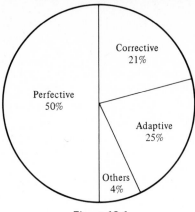

Figure 13.1

illustrated in Figure 13.1. The percentages shown in the figure are based on Lientz and Swanson's [4] study of 487 software development organizations. These data give the best information to date about the hidden proportions of the maintenance "iceberg."

13.2 MAINTENANCE CHARACTERISTICS

Software maintenance has until very recently been the neglected phase in the software life cycle. The literature on maintenance contains very few entries when compared to planning and development phases. Little research or production data have been gathered on the subject, and few technical approaches or "methods" have been proposed.

To understand the characteristics of software maintenance, we consider the topic from three different viewpoints:

1. The activities required to accomplish the maintenance phase and the impact of a software engineering approach (or lack thereof) on the efficacy of such activities
2. The costs associated with the maintenance phase
3. The problems that are frequently encountered when software maintenance is undertaken

In the sections that follow, the characteristics of maintenance are described from each of the perspectives listed above.

13.2.1 Structured versus Unstructured Maintenance

The flow of events that can occur as a result of a maintenance request is illustrated in Figure 13.2. If the only available element of a software configuration is source

Structured versus Unstructured Maintenance

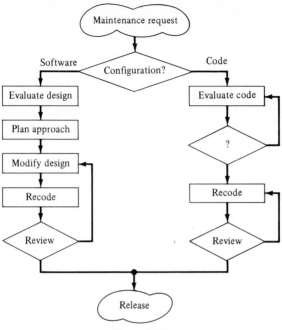

Figure 13.2

code, maintenance activity begins with a painstaking evaluation of the code, often complicated by poor internal documentation. Subtle characteristics such as software structure, global data structures, system interfaces, performance, and/or design constraints are difficult to ascertain and are frequently misinterpreted. The ramifications of changes that are ultimately made to the code are difficult to assess. Regression tests (repeating past tests to ensure that modifications have not introduced faults in previously operational software) are impossible to conduct because no record of testing exists. We are conducting *unstructured maintenance* and paying the price (in wasted effort and human frustration) that accompanies software that has not been developed by use of a well-defined methodology.

If a complete software configuration exists, the maintenance task begins with an evaluation of the design documentation. Important structural, performance, and interface characteristics of the software are determined. The impact of required modifications or corrections is assessed and an approach is planned. The design is modified (using techniques identical to those discussed in earlier chapters) and reviewed. New source code is developed; regression tests are conducted, using information contained in the *Test Specification;* and the software is released again.

The latter description of events comprises *structured maintenance* and occurs as a result of earlier application of a software engineering methodology. Although the existence of a software configuration does not guarantee problem-free maintenance, the amount of wasted effort is reduced and the overall quality of a change or correction is enhanced.

13.2.2 Maintenance Cost

The cost of software maintenance has increased steadily during the past 20 years. Figure 13.3 illustrates the past, current, and projected percentage of overall software budget expended on maintenance of existing software. Although industry averages are difficult to ascertain and are open to broad interpretation, the typical software development organization spends anywhere from 40 to 60 percent of all dollars conducting corrective, adaptive, perfective, and preventive maintenance.

The dollar cost of maintenance is the most obvious. However, other less tangible costs may ultimately be a cause for greater concern. To quote Daniel McCracken [5]:

> Backlogs of new applications and major changes that measure in years are getting longer. As an industry, we can't even keep up—let alone catch up—with what our users want us to do.

McCracken alludes to the maintenance-bound organization. One intangible cost of software maintenance is development opportunity that is postponed or lost because available resources must be channeled to maintenance tasks. Other intangible costs include:

- Customer dissatisfaction when seemingly legitimate requests for repair or modification cannot be addressed in a timely manner
- Reduction in overall software quality as a result of changes that introduce latent errors in the maintained software
- Upheaval caused during development efforts when staff must be "pulled" to work on a maintenance task

The final cost of software maintenance is a dramatic decrease in productivity [measured in lines of code (LOC)/person-month or $/LOC] that is encountered when maintenance of old programs is initiated. Productivity reductions of 40 to 1

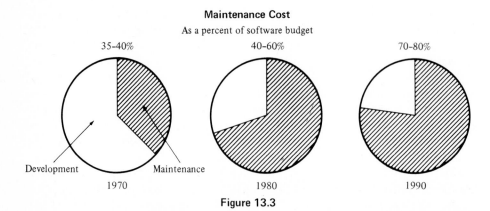

Maintenance Cost

As a percent of software budget

35–40% 40–60% 70–80%

Development Maintenance

1970 1980 1990

Figure 13.3

have been reported [6]. That is, a development effort that cost $25.00 per LOC to develop might cost $1000.00 for every LOC that is maintained!

Effort expended on maintenance may be divided in productive activities (e.g., analysis and evaluation, design modification, and coding) and "wheel-spinning" activities (e.g., trying to understand what the code does; trying to interpret data structure, interface characteristics, and performance bounds). The following expression [7] provides a model of maintenance effort:

$$M = p + K \exp(c - d)$$

where M = total effort expended on maintenance
   p = productive effort (as described above)
   K = an empirical constant
   c = a measure of complexity that can be attributed to a lack of structured design and documentation
   d = a measure of the degree of familiarity with the software

The model described above indicates that effort (and cost) can increase exponentially if a poor software development approach (i.e., a lack of software engineering) was used, and the person or group that used the approach is not available to perform maintenance.

13.2.3 Problems

Most problems associated with software maintenance can be traced to deficiencies in the way software was planned and developed. The classic "pay me now or pay me later" syndrome applies. A lack of control and discipline in the first two phases of the software life cycle nearly always translates into problems in the last phase.

Among the many classic problems that can be associated with software maintenance are the following:

- It is often exceptionally difficult to understand "someone else's" program. Difficulty increases as the number of elements in a software configuration decrease. If only undocumented code exists, severe problems should be expected.
- "Someone else" is often not around to explain. Mobility among software personnel is currently at epidemic levels. We cannot rely on a personal explanation of the software by the developer when maintenance is required.
- Proper documentation doesn't exist or is grossly inadequate. Recognition that software must be documented is a first step, but documentation must be understandable and consistent with source code to be of any value.
- Most software is not designed for change. Unless a design methodology is used that stresses the concept of modularity and module independence (Chapter 7), modifications to software will be difficult and error-prone.
- Maintenance has not been viewed as very glamorous work. Much of this perception comes from the high frustration level associated with maintenance work.

All the problems described above can, in part, be attributed to the large number of programs currently in existence that have been developed with no thought of software engineering. A disciplined methodology should not be viewed as a panacea. However, software engineering does provide at least partial solutions to each problem associated with maintenance.

A number of technical and management issues arise as a consequence of the problems associated with software maintenance. Is it possible to develop software that is well-designed and maintainable? Can we maintain the integrity of software when it has to be modified? Are there technical and management approaches that can be successfully applied to software maintenance? These and other issues are discussed in the sections that follow.

13.3 MAINTAINABILITY

The characteristics described in the preceding section are all affected by the *maintainability* of software. Maintainability may be defined qualitatively as the ease with which software can be understood, corrected, adapted, and/or enhanced. As we have stressed throughout this book, maintainability is a key goal that guides the steps of a software engineering methodology.

13.3.1 Controlling Factors

The ultimate maintainability of software is affected by many factors. Inadvertent carelessness in design, coding, and testing have an obvious negative impact on our ability to maintain the resultant software. A poor software configuration can have a similar negative impact, even when the aforementioned technical steps have been conducted with care.

In addition to factors that can be associated with a development methodology, Kopetz [8] defines a number of factors that are related to the development environment:

- Availability of qualified software staff
- Understandable system structure
- Ease of system handling
- Use of standardized programming languages
- Use of standardized operating systems
- Standardized structure of documentation
- Availability of test cases
- Built-in debugging facilities
- Availability of a proper computer to conduct maintenance

In addition to these factors, we might add (half facetiously): the availability of the person or group that originally developed the software.

Many of the factors stated above reflect characteristics of hardware and software resources that are used during development. For example, there is no question that the absence of high-level language compilers (necessitating the use of assembler language) has a detrimental affect on maintainability. Other factors indicate a need for standardization of methods, resources, and approach.

Possibly, the most important factor that affects maintainability is planning for maintainability. If software is viewed as a system element that will inevitably undergo change, the chances that maintainable software will be produced are likely to increase substantially.

13.3.2 Quantitative Measures

Software maintainability, like quality or reliability, is a difficult term to quantify. However, we can assess maintainability indirectly by considering attributes of the maintenance activity that can be measured. Gilb [9] provides a number of *maintainability measures* that relate to the effort expended during maintenance:

1. Problem recognition time
2. Administrative delay time
3. Maintenance tools collection time
4. Problem analysis time
5. Change specification time
6. Active correction (or modification) time
7. Local testing time
8. Global testing time
9. Maintenance review time
10. Total recovery time

Each of these measures can, in fact, be recorded without great difficulty. Such data can provide a manager with an indication of the efficacy of new techniques and tools.

13.3.3 Reviews

Because maintainability should be an essential characteristic of all software, we must assure that the factors noted in Section 13.3.1 are built in during the development phase. At each level of the software engineering review process, maintainability has been considered. During requirements review (Chapter 5), areas of future enhancement and potential revision are noted; software portability issues are discussed, and system interfaces that might impact software maintenance are considered. During both formal and informal design review (Chapter 6), structure and procedure are evaluated for ease of modification, modularity, and functional independence. Code reviews (Chapter 11) stress style and internal documentation, two factors that influence maintainability. Finally, each test step (Chapter 12) can provide hints about portions of the program that may require preventive maintenance before the software is formally released.

Maintainability reviews are conducted repeatedly as each step in the software engineering process is completed. The most formal maintenance review occurs at the conclusion of testing and is called the *configuration review*. Discussed in Chapter 12, the configuration review assures that all elements of the software configuration are complete, understandable, and filed for modification control.

The software maintenance task itself should be reviewed at the completion of each effort. Methods for evaluation are discussed in the next section.

13.4 MAINTENANCE TASKS

Tasks associated with software maintenance begin long before a request for maintenance is made. Initially, a maintenance organization (*de facto* or formal) must be established; reporting and evaluation procedures must be described, and a standardized sequence of events must be defined for each maintenance request. In addition, a record-keeping procedure for maintenance activities should be established and review-evaluation criteria defined.

13.4.1 A Maintenance Organization

As we have noted elsewhere in this book, there are almost as many organizational structures as there are software development organizations. For this reason, "recommended organization structures" have been avoided. In the case of maintenance, however, formal organizations rarely exist (notable exceptions are very large software developers), and maintenance is often performed on a catch-as-catch-can basis.

Although a formal maintenance organization need not be established, an informal delegation of responsibility is absolutely essential for even small software developers. One such schema is illustrated in Figure 13.4. Maintenance requests are channeled through a *maintenance controller* who forwards each request for evaluation to a *system supervisor*. The system supervisor is a member of the technical staff who has been assigned the responsibility to become familiar with a small subset of production programs. Once an evaluation is made, a *change control authority* must determine the action to be taken.

Each of the above job descriptors serves to establish an area of responsibility for maintenance. The controller and change control authority may be a single person or (for large program products) a group of managers and senior technical staff. The system supervisor may have other duties, but provides a "contact" with a specific software package.

When responsibilities are assigned prior to the start of maintenance activity, confusion is greatly reduced. More importantly, an early definition of responsibilities can temper any hard feelings that develop when a person is preemptively "pulled off" a development effort to conduct maintenance.

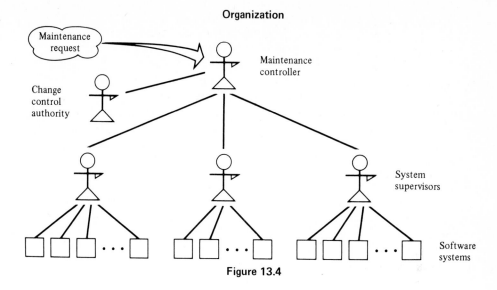

Figure 13.4

13.4.2 Reporting

All requests for software maintenance should be presented in a standardized manner. The software developer normally provides a *maintenance request form* (MRF), sometimes called a *software problem report,* that is completed by the user who desires a maintenance activity. If an error is encountered, a complete description of the circumstances leading to the error (including input data, listings, and other supporting material) must be included. For adaptive or perfective maintenance requests, a brief *requirements specification* is submitted. The maintenance request form is evaluated by the maintenance controller and system supervisor as described in the preceding section.

The MRF is an externally generated document that is used as a basis for planning the maintenance task. Internally, the software organization develops a *software change report* (SCR) that indicates (1) the magnitude of effort required to satisfy an MRF, (2) the nature of modifications required, (3) the priority of the request, and (4) after-the-fact data about the modification. The SCR is submitted to the change control authority for approval before further maintenance planning is initiated.

13.4.3 Flow of Events

The sequence of events that occurs as a result of a maintenance request are shown in Figure 13.5. The first requirement is to determine the type of maintenance that is to be conducted. In many cases a user may view a request as an indication of software error (corrective maintenance) while a developer may view the same

Flow of Events

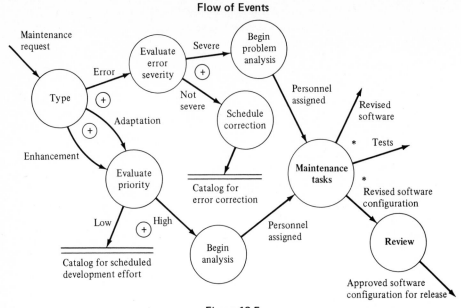

Figure 13.5

request as adaptation or enhancement. If a difference of opinion exists, a settlement must be negotiated.

Referring to the flow shown in Figure 13.5, a request for corrective maintenance (*"error"* path) begins with an evaluation of error severity. If a severe error exists (e.g., a critical system cannot function), personnel are assigned under the direction of the system supervisor, and problem analysis begins immediately. For less severe errors, corrective maintenance is scheduled in conjunction with other tasks requiring software development resources.

Requests for adaptive and perfective maintenance follow the same flow path. The priority of each request is established and the required work is scheduled as if it were another development effort. (For all intents and purposes, it is.) If an extremely high priority is set, work may begin immediately.

Regardless of maintenance type, the same technical tasks are conducted. These maintenance tasks include modification to software design, review, requisite code modification, unit and integration testing (including regression tests that use previous test cases, validation tests, and review. Emphasis will shift with each maintenance type, but the overall approach remains the same. The final event in the maintenance flow is a review that revalidates all elements of the software configuration and assures that the MRF has, in fact, been fulfilled.

There are, of course, requests that do not fit neatly into the measured flow described above. Such requests, called "fire-fighting" maintenance, occur when dramatic software problems arise. For example, a process control system for a paper mill has a bug that causes paper (traveling at 200 feet/second) to spew across the building! In such cases resources are applied to the problem immediately. If fire fighting is standard operating procedure for an organization, management and/or technical competence must be suspect.

After the software maintenance task is complete, it is often a good idea to conduct a *situation review*. In general, the review attempts to answer the following questions:

- Given the current situation, what aspects of design, code, or test could have been done differently?
- What maintenance resources should have been available and weren't?
- What were the major (minor) stumbling blocks for this effort?
- Is preventive maintenance indicated by the types of request being reported?

The situation review can have an important influence on the conduct of future maintenance efforts and provides feedback that is important to effective management of a software organization.

13.4.4 Record Keeping

Historically, record keeping for all phases of the software life cycle has been inadequate. Record keeping for software maintenance has been nonexistent. For this reason, we are frequently unable to assess the effectiveness of maintenance techniques, incapable of determining the "goodness" of a production program, and unwilling to determine what maintenance really costs.

The first problem encountered in maintenance record keeping is to understand which data are worth recording. Swanson [3] provides a comprehensive list:

1. Program identification
2. Number of source statements
3. Number of machine code instructions
4. Programming language used
5. Program installation date
6. Number of program runs since installation
7. Number of processing failures associated with item 6
8. Program change level and identification
9. Number of source statements added by program change
10. Number of source statements deleted by program change
11. Number of person-hours spent per change
12. Program change date
13. Identification of software engineer
14. MRF identification
15. Maintenance type
16. Maintenance start and close dates
17. Cumulative number of person-hours spent on maintenance
18. Net benefits associated with maintenance performed

The above data are collected for each maintenance effort. Swanson proposes these items as the foundation of a maintenance database that can be evaluated as described in the following section.

13.4.5 Evaluation

An evaluation of software maintenance activities has been complicated by a lack of valid data. If record keeping is initiated, a number of "measures of maintenance performance" [3] may be developed. Again from Swanson [3], we present an abbreviated list of potential measures:

1. Average number of processing failures per program run
2. Total person hours spent in each maintenance category
3. Average number of program changes made per program, per language, per maintenance type
4. Average number of person hours spent per source statement added or deleted due to maintenance
5. Average person hours spent per language
6. Average turnaround time for an MRF
7. Percentage of maintenance requests by type

The seven measures described above can provide a quantitative framework from which decisions on development technique, language selection, maintenance effort projections, resource allocation, and many other issues can be made. Clearly, such data can be applied to evaluate the maintenance task. Although some data have been collected by large software firms, few meaningful analyses have been published to date. It is fair to conclude that most maintenance activities are still conducted by use of guesswork and intuition.

13.5 MAINTENANCE SIDE EFFECTS

Modification of software is dangerous. All of us have heard the following lament: "but all I did was change this one statement. . . ." Unfortunately, each time a change is introduced to a complex logical procedure, the potential for error grows. Design documentation and careful regression testing help to eliminate error, but maintenance *side effects* will be encountered.

When used in the context of software maintenance, the term side effects implies an error or other undesirable behavior that occurs as a result of modification. Freedman and Weinberg [10] define three major categories for side effects that are discussed in the following sections.

13.5.1 Coding Side Effects

A simple change to a single statement can sometimes have disastrous results. The inadvertent (and undetected) replacement of a "," with a "." had near-tragic consequences when flight control software for an Apollo space flight failed. Although not all side effects have such dramatic consequences, change invites error and error always leads to problems.

We communicate with a machine by use of programming language source code. The opportunities for side effects abound. Although every code modification has the potential for introducing error, the following set of changes [10] tends to be more error prone than others:

1. A subprogram is deleted or changed.
2. A statement label is deleted or modified.
3. An identifier is deleted or modified.
4. Changes are made to improve execution performance.
5. File open or close is modified.
6. Logical operators are modified.
7. Design changes are translated into major code changes.
8. Changes are made to boundary tests.

Coding side effects range from nuisance errors detected and remedied during regression testing to problems that cause software failure during operation. Again, we paraphrase Murphy's law: "if a change to a source statement can introduce error, it will. . . ."

13.5.2 Data Side Effects

The importance of data structure in software design was noted in Chapter 9. During maintenance, modifications are often made to individual elements of a data structure or to the structure itself. When data change, the software design may no longer "fit" the data, and errors can occur. Data side effects occur as a result modifications made to software information structure.

The following changes [10] in data frequently result in side effects: (1) redefinition of local and global constants; (2) redefinition of record or file formats; (3) increase or decrease in the size of an array or higher-order data structure; (4) modification to global data (e.g., Fortran COMMON); (5) reinitialization of control flags or pointers; and (6) rearrangement of arguments for I/O or subprograms. Data side effects can be limited by thorough design documentation that describes data structure and provides a cross-reference that associates data elements, records, files, and other structures with software modules.

13.5.3 Documentation Side Effects

Maintenance should focus on the entire software configuration, and not on source code modification alone. Documentation side effects occur when changes to source code are not reflected in design documentation or user-oriented manuals.

Whenever a change to data flow, software structure, module procedure, or any other related characteristic is made, supporting technical documentation must be updated. Design documentation that doesn't accurately reflect the current state of the software is probably worse than no documentation at all. Side effects occur in subsequent maintenance efforts when an innocent perusal of technical documents leads to an incorrect assessment of software characteristics.

To a user, software is only as good as the documentation (both written and interactive) that describes its use. If modifications to the executable software are not reflected in user documentation, side effects are guaranteed. For example, changes in the order or format of interactive input, if not properly documented, can cause significant problems. New undocumented error messages can cause confusion; outdated tables of contents, indexes, and text can cause user frustration and dissatisfaction.

Documentation side effects can be reduced substantially if the entire configuration is reviewed prior to further release of the software. In fact, some maintenance requests may require no change to software design or source code, but indicate a lack of clarity in user documentation. In such cases the maintenance effort focuses on documentation.

13.6 MAINTENANCE ISSUES

A number of important supplementary issues must be addressed during a discussion of maintenance. Frequently, we must maintain software that is poorly designed and documented. How do we proceed? Should preventive maintenance be conducted to improve the maintainability of working programs? Are there new philosophies to program development that may impact the maintenance phase? We discuss these issues in the sections that follow.

13.6.1 Maintaining "Alien Code"

Nearly every mature software development organization must maintain programs that were developed 10 or more years ago. Such programs are sometimes called *alien code* because (1) no current member of the technical staff worked on development of the program, (2) no development methodology was applied, and thus poor design and documentation (by today's standards) exist, and (3) modularity was not a design criterion, and the concepts of structured design were not applied.

Earlier in this chapter we discussed the necessity for a *system supervisor*—a person who becomes familiar with a subset of production programs that may require maintenance. Familiarization with programs developed with the use of a software engineering approach is facilitated by a complete software configuration and a good design. What can be done with alien code? Yourdon [11] provides a number of useful suggestions to the system supervisor who must maintain alien code:

1. Study the program before you get into "emergency mode." Try to obtain as much background information as possible . . .

2. Try to become familiar with the overall flow of control of the program; ignore coding details at first. It may be very useful to draw your own (structure diagram) and high-level flow chart, if one doesn't already exist.

3. Evaluate the reasonableness of existing documentation; insert your own comments in the (source) listing if you think they will help.

4. Make good use of cross-reference listings, symbol tables, and other aids generally provided by the compiler and/or assembler.

5. Make changes to the program with the greatest caution. Respect the style and formatting of the program if at all possible. Indicate on the listing itself which instructions you have changed.

6. Don't eliminate code unless you are sure it isn't used.

7. Don't try to share the use of temporary variables and working storage that already exist in the program. Insert you own variables to avoid trouble.

8. Keep detailed records (of maintenance activities and results).

9. Avoid the irrational urge to throw the program away and rewrite it.[1]

10. Do insert error checking.

Each of the above guidelines will help in the maintenance of old programs. However, there is a class of programs with control flow that is the graphic equivalent to a bowl of spaghetti, with "modules" that are 2000 statements long, with three meaningful comment lines in 9000 source statements, and with no other elements of a software configuration. Incredibly, such programs may work for years, but when maintenance is requested, the task may be untenable. In the next section we examine what can be done.

13.6.2 Preventive Maintenance

In maintenance situations for programs like the one described above, three options exist:

1. We can struggle through modification after modification, "fighting" the design and source code to implement the necessary changes.

2. We can redesign, recode, and test those portions of the software that require modification, applying a software engineering approach to all revised segments.

3. We can completely redesign, recode, and test the program.

There is no single "correct" option. Circumstances may frequently dictate the first option even if the second or third is more desirable.

Preventive maintenance of computer software is a relatively new and controversial issue. Rather than waiting until a maintenance request is received, the development or maintenance organization selects a program that (1) will remain in

---

[1] Author's note: This "urge" is sometimes both rational and practical!

use for a preselected number of years, (2) is currently being used successfully, and (3) is likely to undergo major modification or enhancement in the near future. Then, option 2 or 3 above is applied.

The preventive maintenance approach was pioneered by Miller [12] under the title "structured retrofit." He defined this concept as "the application of today's methodologies to yesterday's systems to support tommorrow's requirements."

At first glance, the suggestion that we redevelop a large program when a working version already exists may seem quite extravagant. Before passing judgment, we should consider the following points:

1. The cost to maintain one line of source code may be up to 40 times the cost of initial development of that line.
2. Redesign of the software structure, with the use of modern design concepts, can greatly facilitate future maintenance.
3. Because a prototype of the software already exists, development productivity should be much higher than average.
4. The user now has experience with the software. Therefore, new requirements and the direction of change can be ascertained with greater ease.
5. A software configuration will exist on completion of preventive maintenance.

When a software development organization sells software as a product, preventive maintenance is seen in "new releases" of a program. Many large in-house software developers (e.g., a business systems software development group for a large consumer products company) may have 500 to 2000 production programs within its domain of responsibility. These programs can be prioritized by importance and then reviewed as candidates for preventive maintenance.

13.6.3 A "Spare Parts" Strategy

A classic characterisitic of hardware maintenance is removal of a defective part and replacement with a spare part. A concept called *software prototyping* may lead to the development of *spare parts* for programs. The prototyping concept is described by Spiegel [13]:

> Software prototyping is a process (the act, study, or skill) of modelling user requirements in one or more levels of detail, including working models. Project resources are allocated to produce scaled down versions of the software described by requirements. The prototype version makes the software visible for review by users, designers and management. . . . This process continues as desired, with running versions ready for release after several iterations.

If various prototype levels were developed, it might be possible to have a set of software spare parts [14] that could be used when requests for corrective maintenance are received. For example, an analysis module might be designed and implemented in two different ways but with the same external interface. One version of the module is included in the working software. If that module failed, a spare part could be incorporated immediately.

Although the spare parts strategy for software does seem a bit unconventional, there is no evidence that it is any more expensive, when we consider all life cycle costs. However, further experience must be obtained before sweeping conclusions (pro or con) can be drawn.

13.7 SUMMARY

Maintenance, the last phase of the software life cycle, accounts for a majority of all dollars spent on computer software. As more programs are developed, a disturbing trend has emerged—the amount of effort and resources expended on software maintenance is growing. Ultimately, some software development organizations may become maintenance-bound, that is, unable to embark on new projects because all resources are dedicated to maintenance of old programs.

Four types of maintenance are performed on computer software: (1) corrective maintenance, which acts to correct errors that are uncovered after the software is in use; (2) adaptive maintenance, which is applied when changes in external environment precipitate modifications to software; (3) perfective maintenance, which incorporates enhancements that are requested by the user community; and (4) finally, preventive maintenance, which improves future maintainability and reliability and provides a basis for future enhancement.

Technical and management approaches to the maintenance phase can be implemented with little upheaval. However, tasks performed during earlier phases of the software life cycle define maintainability and have an important impact on the success of any maintenance approach.

Software engineering offers the key to improved maintenance productivity. With careful design, thorough documentation, and a complete series of reviews and testing methods, errors will be easier to diagnose and correct when they do occur, software will be amenable to change, and a configuration will guide individuals who are unfamiliar with the software. Fewer person-hours will be expended on each maintenance request. Resources will be freed to develop new software that will be required in the increasingly complex systems, services, and products demanded by the advance of technology.

REFERENCES

1. Canning, R., "The Maintenance 'Iceberg'," *EDP Analyzer,* vol. 10, no. 10, October 1972.
2. Rochkind, M., "The Source Code Control System," *IEEE Transactions on Software Engineering,* vol. 1, no. 4, December 1975, pp. 364–370.
3. Swanson, E. B., "The Dimensions of Maintenance," *Proceedings of the Second International Conference on Software Engineering, IEEE,* October 1976, pp. 492–497.

4. Lientz, B., and E. Swanson, *Software Maintenance Management,* Addison-Wesley, 1980.

5. McCracken, D., "Software in the 80s—Perils and Promises," *Computerworld* (special edition), vol. 14, no. 38, September 17, 1980, p. 5.

6. Boehm, B., "Software Engineering—R&D Trends and Defense Needs," in *Research Directions in Software Technology,* P. Wegner, (ed.), MIT Press, 1979, pp. 44–86.

7. Belady, L., and M. Lehman, "An Introduction to Growth Dynamics," in *Statistical Computer Performance Evaluation,* W. Freiberger, (ed.), Academic Press, 1972, pp. 503–511.

8. Kopetz, H., *Software Reliability,* Springer-Verlag, 1979, p. 93.

9. Gilb, T., "A Comment on the Definition of Reliability," *ACM Software Engineering Notes,* vol. 4, no. 3, July 1979.

10. Freedman, D., and G. Weinberg, in *Techniques of Program and System Maintenance,* G. Parikh, (ed.), Winthrop Publishers, 1981.

11. Yourdon, E., *Techniques of Program Structure and Design,* Prentice-Hall, 1975, p. 24.

12. Miller, J., in *Techniques of Program and System Maintenance,* G. Parikh, (ed.), Winthrop Publishers, 1981.

13. Spiegel, M., *Software Prototyping,* Colloquium Series, Wang Institute of Graduate Studies, March 2, 1981.

14. Gilb, T., in *Techniques of Program and System Maintenance,* G. Parikh, (ed.), Winthrop Publishers, 1981.

PROBLEMS AND POINTS TO PONDER

13-1 Your instructor will select one of the programs that everyone in the class has developed during this course. Exchange your program randomly with someone else in the class. *Do not* explain or walk through the program. Now, implement an enhancement (specified by your instructor) in the program you have received.

(*a*) Perform all software engineering tasks including a brief walkthrough (but not with the author of the program).

(*b*) Keep careful track of all errors encountered during testing.

(*c*) Discuss your experiences in class.

13-2 Attempt to develop a software rating system that could be applied to existing programs in an effort to select candidate programs for preventive maintenance.

13-3 Are corrective maintenance and debugging the same thing? Explain your answer.

13-4 Discuss the impact of high-level languages on adaptive maintenance. Is it always possible to adapt a program?

13-5 Should maintenance costs be incorporated in the software planning step? Are they?

13-6 Will the overall duration of the software life cycle expand or contract over the next decade? Discuss this issue in class.

13-7 This is intended as a team project. Develop an automated tool that will enable a manager to collect and analyze quantitative maintenance data. Use Sections 13.3.2 and 13.4.4 as a source for software requirements.

13-8 Discuss the viability of a spare parts strategy. Consider both technical and economic issues.

13-9 This is intended for the practitioner: relate a maintenance "horror story."

13-10 Research the literature in an attempt to find recently published papers, books, and (most important) quantitative data on software maintenance. Write a paper on your findings.

FURTHER READINGS

As we noted early in this chapter, the literature on software maintenance is only beginning to grow. Excellent sources of information include Lientz and Swanson's study [4] and Parikh's anthology (*Techniques of Program and System Maintenance*, Winthrop Publishers, 1981).

Books by Gunther (*Management Methodolgy for Software Product Engineering*, Wiley, 1978) and Bersoff, Henderson, and Siegel (*Software Configuration Management*, Prentice-Hall, 1980) contain useful guidelines for maintenance of program products and a general approach to management of existing software. Another text that stresses the importance of the maintenance step in *Managing Software Development and Maintenance* (C. McClure, Van Nostrand Reinhold, 1981).

Papers by Reutter ("Maintenance Is a Manager's Problem and a Programmer's Opportunity") and Chapin ("Productivity in Software Maintenance") may be found in the 1981 *Proceedings of the National Computer Conference* (AFIPS, vol. 50). The former is an interesting characterization of management concerns, and the latter provides a series of program characteristics that affect maintenance.

EPILOGUE

An engineering approach to the development of computer software is a philosophy whose time has come. Although debate continues on specific tools and techniques, software engineering is accepted as a viable remedy to the software crisis. Why then, are we only recently seeing its broad adoption? To quote Fred Gruenberger:

> The process of accepting new tools is so slow, it makes [data processing] people look like an irrational crew. The industry is producing new and powerful tools in profusion, but the acceptance rate is pitiful. . . .
>
> There are . . . explanations for this slow acceptance: inertia is just human nature; that is, people don't change very rapidly . . . the dramatic changes in consumer attitudes are due to massive advertising campaigns.[1]

Software engineering has not had the benefit of massive advertising, but as time passes, the concept sells itself. In a way, this book serves as an "advertisement" for that concept.

The software engineering process and the software life cycle have been described in a way that conjures visions of a vortex. The planning steps—system definition, software planning, and software requirements analysis—reside on "streamlines" that grow progressively closer to the central core that we call *development*. Design and coding move us into the core, and a series of testing steps

---

[1] Fred Gruenberger in *Datamation*, January 1981, p. 108.

pull us back out toward the boundaries. Finally, the maintenance phase starts the process over again. In this book we have come full circle.

Slowly, the art of software development is being replaced with a creative, yet systematic methodology. Although we may (in weaker moments) mourn the passing of an artform, software development professionals recognize that complex systems of the 1980s require a more controlled approach.

You may not agree with every approach described in this book. Some of the techniques and opinions are admittedly controversial; others must be tuned to work well in different software development environments. It is my sincere hope, however, that *Software Engineering: A Practitioner's Approach* has delineated the problems we face, demonstrated the strength of a software engineering concept, and provided a framework of techniques and tools.

The enormous potential of computing will have a profound impact on the world community during the last two decades of this century. Let us hope that the people who tap that potential—software engineers—will have the wisdom to develop systems that improve the human condition.

INDEX